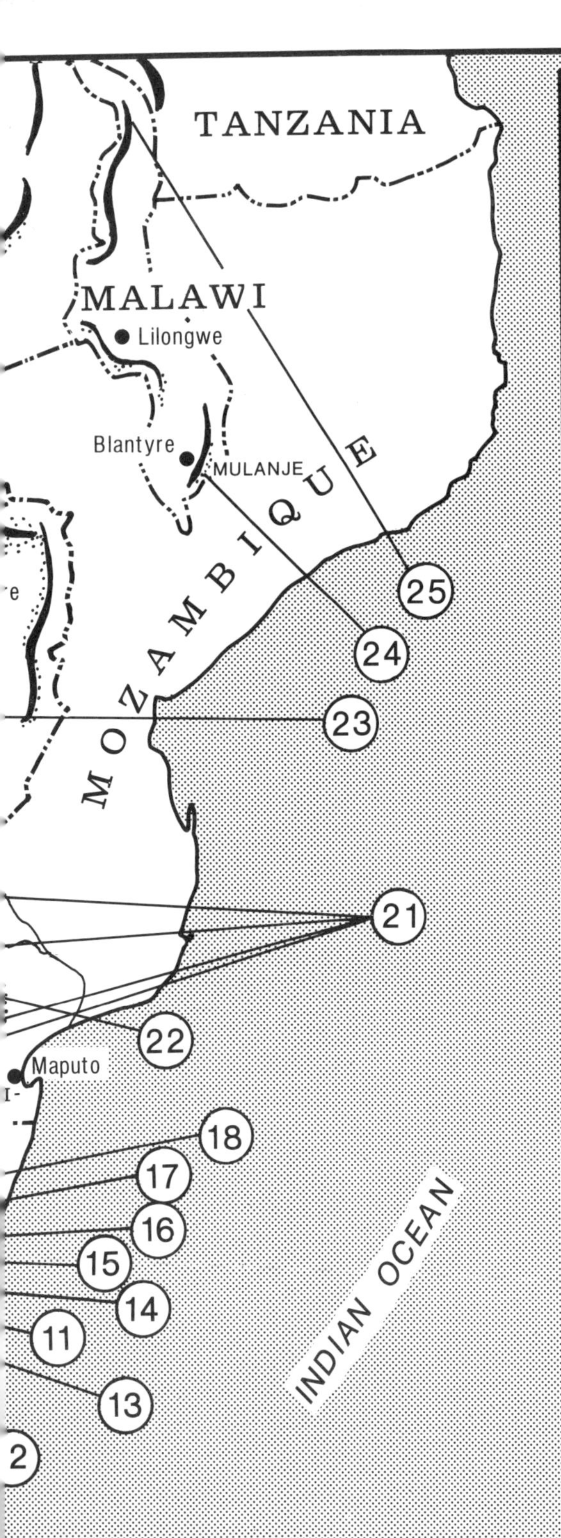

1. Wate
2. Ugab River Guided Wilderness Trail
3. Brandberg Backpacking Area
4. Fish River Canyon Backpacking Trail
5. Cederberg Backpacking Area
6. Groot - Winterhoek Backpacking Area
7. Boosmansbos Backpacking Area
8. Groendal Backpacking Area
9. Tsolwana Guided Trails
10. Sehlabathebe Backpacking Area
11. Lesotho Pony Trek
12. Southern Drakensberg – Mzimkulu Backpacking Area
13. Central Drakensberg – Mkhomazi Backpacking Area
14. Central Drakensberg – Giant's Castle Backpacking Area
15. Northern Drakensberg – Mdedelelo Backpacking Area
16. Northern Drakensberg – Cathedral Peak Backpacking Area
17. Northern Drakensberg – Royal Natal Backpacking Area
18. Ntendeka Backpacking Area
21. Kruger National Park Guided Wilderness Trails
22. Wolkberg Backpacking Area
23. Okavango Delta Mokoro Safari
24. Mulanje Mountain Backpacking Area
25. Nyika Guided Wilderness Trails

No. 19 — refer to p. 194 for location
No. 20 — refer to p. 205 for location

# THE GUIDE TO BACKPACKING AND WILDERNESS TRAILS

FOR HOWARD,
CHRISTMAS 1989.

FROM JOHN & GLORIA
WITH LOVE.

# THE GUIDE TO BACKPACKING AND WILDERNESS TRAILS

Willie and Sandra Olivier

ISBN 1 86812 069 4

First edition, first impression 1989

Published by
Southern Book Publishers (Pty) Ltd
PO Box 548, Bergvlei 2012
Johannesburg

Illustrations by Lesley Coombes
Maps by Wendy Job
Graphs by Ingrid Booysen
Set in 9½ on 11 pt Rockwell
by Industrial Graphics, Johannesburg
Printed and bound by National Book Printers, Cape

# *Foreword*

As we approach the end of the twentieth century AD, mankind is at last comprehending the unique and frightening situation in which we find ourselves. We are the first primate ever to dominate the planet, and our success is manifesting itself in a most dangerous way.

The seeds of our self-destruction lie in our own expansion, an increase of 84 million people every year. In 1930 there were about two thousand million people, and by 1988 this had grown to more than five thousand million. Like a fully-laden oil tanker under way in the ocean, we cannot grind to a halt and stabilise our numbers right away. It will take 50 to 70 years, by which time we will number around eleven thousand million human beings.

There is little doubt that mankind is heading for trouble, as we are placing intolerable demands on the soils that provide our food, the water without which we cannot live, and the diversity of life on earth that offers us a storeroom full of chemical products, a genetic library of vast potential to make our lives more healthy, interesting and productive.

How do we begin to change human attitudes, and see these translated into meaningful changes of human behaviour? Wisdom is not inherited, and each human generation has to go through a learning process to reach a plateau of understanding about how the planet earth functions, and about the constraints that evolution and genetics place upon all living creatures.

Where do we go on this crowded planet to find the stillness and aloneness that we need to reach that understanding? There are many quiet and beautiful places to go to, and Willie and Sandra Olivier will lead you to them.

I am impressed by the way they have shared their experiences on the backpacking and wilderness trails of Southern Africa, and thank them for putting it all together. I wish I could have read this book before I walked the Fish River Canyon Backpacking Trail recently. Then I would not have been so surprised to get drenched by a sudden thunderstorm, or so annoyed when some rodent chewed a hole in my plastic squeeze-tube to get at the peanut butter!

And my reflections under the starlit sky about the workings of the world would have been enhanced by knowing that 45 000 years before my visit, people living nearby had carved patterns on ostrich eggshells, still around for us to see. Is my reckless generation now going to be responsible for destroying the planet that has been a home to man for four million years? We certainly have the capacity to do so.

But we are also unique in having the potential not to do so. It is within our ability to slow and then halt the human population explosion, to remove the threat of a nuclear holocaust, and to manage the resources of the planet to sustain future human generations in adequate, if not lavish, circumstances that will maintain a reasonable quality of life for all of mankind.

This book will open the door for you to visit some of the world's most beautiful landscapes. When you do go to these wonderful places, think in stillness and aloneness about the meaning of being alive. Think about the Big Picture, the future of mankind, and what you can do about it. Then come back more aware, knowing and caring – a Planet Manager.

**John Ledger**
**Director, Endangered Wildlife Trust**

# Acknowledgements

When you are neither a botanist, zoologist, archaeologist, historian nor a geologist, writing a book of this nature is impossible without the assistance of experts in these fields. Many people have been called upon during the past nine years and we apologise for any person or body that may have been inadvertently omitted. We wish to thank the following:

Theuns van Rensburg, PRO of the National Hiking Way Board, who not only verified all State wilderness areas, but also made useful suggestions; the following foresters: Theo van der Merwe of Boosmansbos; Dave Osborne of Monk's Cowl; H Swanevelder of Groendal; W P Small of Cathedral Peak; K D Riggien of Garden Castle; R Bartholomew of Ngome; V M Nemaangani of Wolkberg. Officials of the Natal Parks Board once again assisted us with enthusiasm and efficiency from which other conservation bodies stand much to learn.

Our appreciation also goes to Trevor Dearlove for verifying information on the wilderness trails in the Kruger National Park, and the staff of the Wilderness Leadership School for verifying the chapter on trails conducted by the school. A special word of thanks to Ts'eliso Ramakhula of the Lesotho Tourist Board for ensuring the accuracy of information on pony trekking and Mrs M Mothepu of Lesotho's Ministry of Agriculture for checking our chapter on Sehlabathebe National Park.

Dr E Joubert of the Directorate of Nature Conservation and Recreation Resorts made useful suggestions to improve the information on SWA/Namibia and Mike Muller of the State Herbarium in Windhoek assisted not only with identification of trees but also with information. Roger Swart of the Geological Survey in Windhoek corrected our sections on the geology of SWA/Namibia, and Dr Tony Williams and Chris Brown, ornithologists of the Directorate of Nature Conservation and Recreation Resorts, were always ready to assist with information on the birds of SWA/Namibia. We are grateful also to Joe Walter, who willingly shared his intimate knowledge of the Brandberg with us, as well as John Kinahan of the State Museum in Windhoek, for his comments and suggestions on the archaeology of SWA/Namibian trails.

Our appreciation also to Jenny Hobbs for suggestions and changes to our first aid section, Johan Marais for his advice on snakebite and Leon Prinsloo for information on the Groendal Wilderness Area.

The appeal of this book was considerably enhanced with the attractive line drawings of Lesley Coombes and the accurate mapwork of Wendy Job. Thank you, it was a pleasure working with you.

The enthusiasm and efficiency of Sally Antrobus, the General Books Editor of Southern Book Publishers, was greatly appreciated, as was the meticulous editing of the manuscript by copy editor Catherine Murray. Thanks to Basil van Rooyen, Managing Director, who had the faith to publish this book. Our gratitude also to all other Southern staff involved with the book.

Finally, our appreciation to those who have dedicated their lives to the conservation of Southern Africa's natural heritage and made possible the wilderness experiences that we and many others continue to enjoy.

# Contents

## PART 7: BOTSWANA AND MALAWI



## PART 8: REFERENCES

# Introduction

Our first book, *Discovering Southern Africa on Foot — the Guide to Hiking Trails,* was initially intended to include most hiking, backpacking and guided wilderness trail opportunities in Southern Africa. Owing to sheer volume, however, it became impractical to include all the information in one book and it was decided to make *The Guide to Backpacking and Wilderness Trails* a separate volume.

Backpacking and guided wilderness trails differ markedly from *hiking trails.* On a backpacking trail you have to consult either a sketch map or a topographical map of the area before deciding on the route you want to follow. Unlike hiking trails, routes are not marked, and there is no comfortable hut at the end of each day's trailing. Instead you create your own experience and have to be completely self-sufficient. As a result backpacking trails are more demanding than hiking trails and it is suggested that only fairly experienced hikers should attempt them.

Guided wilderness trails, on the other hand, allow you to enjoy a 'wilderness' experience where most of your gear is usually supplied and because of the danger of wild animals, you are led by an expert guide who shares with you his knowledge of the surroundings. The guide will also plan walks to suit the physical condition and specific interests of the group. None of the guided wilderness trails is described in much detail in this book — by giving a broad outline of these areas we intend merely to whet your appetite.

The information we have provided is the result of many kilometres of backpacking during seven years of trailing and research. We hope that this book will take you, the reader, on many exciting and rewarding journeys of discovery and that the knowledge we share with you will lead you to a greater love and appreciation of the many beautiful unspoilt areas in Southern Africa.

Willie and Sandra Olivier
Windhoek

**AUTHORS' NOTE**

The authors have taken every care to ensure the correctness of all information, particularly in respect of trail descriptions. However, the authors do not accept any responsibility for injury, death or inconvenience arising from any backpacking or guided wilderness trail.

**CARTOGRAPHER'S NOTE**

Maps have been reproduced under authority of:
The R.S.A. Government Printer (Authority 8547 of 8 July 1986).
The Department of Surveys and Lands of Botswana.
The Office of the Surveyor-General of SWA/Namibia.

# How To Use This Book

If you are planning a backpacking or guided wilderness trail you very likely already have a particular area in mind. Before turning directly to the section of the book dealing with that area and making reservations, it is vitally important that you know more about what lies ahead of you.

Part 1: Backpacking Basics and More on pages 5-39 contains important information about equipment, food, planning a trail, safety and first aid. Seasoned backpackers will probably be acquainted with most of the information supplied and this section is therefore a commonsense guide aimed more specifically at the novice backpacker. These aspects are covered in greater detail than in *The Guide to Hiking Trails*, especially the section dealing with equipment, although comprehensive coverage would require a book on its own. A number of excellent books on these aspects have been written and you should refer to the bibliography on page 273 should you require more information.

The trails are arranged in a logical geographical sequence, starting in SWA/Namibia, continuing down through the Cape and in a semicircle along the eastern part of the country to the Transvaal and finally into Botswana and Malawi. A map indicating the positions of all the trails described can be found on the inside covers.

An alphabetical, tabulated summary of the backpacking areas and wilderness trails can be found on pages 261 to 263. Here you can see at a glance the particular attractions of each area and trail.

Each trail described covers the following aspects:

**Location**

A brief outline of where the trail area is situated and directions on how to get to the starting point are given. A detailed location map is also provided.

**Distance and Classification**

In most of the areas various backpacking options are available but where possible the total length of trails and the number of days required are given. On guided wilderness trails the trails usually last a specific number of days, but the distance covered varies from trail to trail.

The degree of difficulty of each trail is indicated by means of a grading. A indicates easy, B moderate and C indicates a more difficult trail. Where a '+' is used with a grading it indicates that the trail is more difficult than usual, but easier than the next grade. The grades were given on the basis of a person of average fitness, backpacking under ideal conditions, but it should be borne in mind that your level of fitness, mental preparedness and prevailing climatic conditions could place a trail in a different grade.

**Permits**

It is essential to obtain a permit and/or make a reservation well in advance. The name, address and telephone number of the relevant authority, as well as the maximum/minimum group size, are given. Remember that these details, particularly telephone numbers, may change.

**Maps**

Maps are not required for guided wilderness trails but you should not set off on a backpacking trail without a good map of the area. A sketch map is usually available but where this is inadequate the Government Printer's topographical map numbers are provided. The only high-quality trail maps available of backpacking areas are the maps in the Drakensberg Recreational Series and the Cederberg Wilderness Area map published by the Forestry Branch of the Directorate of Environment Affairs.

### Relevant Information

For each area there is specific relevant information which you should be aware of when planning a particular trail. This section is therefore *essential reading.* If, for example, ticks or malaria are prevalent in the area, consult the section on First Aid, where preventive measures are discussed.

### Facilities

Accommodation and other facilities provided at the start of the trail and on the trail are decribed here.

### Climate

Where reliable rainfall and temperature figures were available they are represented graphically, so that the expected conditions in any month can be seen at a glance. However, *average* figures were used in these graphs and often the weather stations are at lower altitudes than the trail area. As a result, actual conditions experienced could vary considerably and the data supplied should be used as a guide only. In a number of instances, however, reliable data were not available and a brief outline of the climate is given instead.

### Flora and Fauna

These are described in an attempt to make you more aware of your surroundings, and will assist you in choosing a trail according to your interests.

During their research the authors were often frustrated by the inconsistent usage of common names, especially plant, bird and animal names. To avoid confusion the standard reference numbers of all trees and birds are given wherever the species is listed for the first time on a particular trail. The only exceptions are in respect of trees mentioned in the chapters dealing with Mulanje Backpacking Area and Nyika Guided Wilderness Trails where numbers of the National List of Indigenous Trees are not given. For the sake of uniformity the following reference works have been used throughout:

*Flora* The **vegetation** types follow the classification of Acocks (1975) in South Africa and Giess (1971) in SWA/Namibia, and the **scientific plant names** follow that of Gibbs Russell (1984). The *National List of Indigenous Trees* (1986) was used for the common English names of **trees**, as well as the reference numbers in brackets.

*Fauna* In the case of **mammals** the common English names and statistical data come from *The Mammals of the Southern African Subregion* (Smithers, 1983) and the conservation status of mammals follows the *South African Red Data Book — Terrestrial Mammals* (Smithers, 1986). That of **reptiles** and **amphibians** follows McLachlan (1978). The common English **bird** names, as well as the reference numbers in brackets, are according to *Roberts' Birds of Southern Africa* (Maclean, 1985). The conservation status of birds is according to the *South African Red Data Book — Birds* (Brooke, 1984).

The *South African Red Data Book* series is an attempt to collate information on endangered, rare and threatened plant and animal species. To date several of these books have been published by the South African Council for Scientific and Industrial Research and information supplied includes status, present and former distribution, habitat, reasons for decline, numbers in captivity and protective measures in operation, as well as those proposed.

Part 8: References, contains lists of mammal, bird and tree species mentioned in the text. Birds and trees are listed in number order and the scientific and common English and Afrikaans names are given. Mammals are listed alphabetically according to the common English name, followed by the scientific and common Afrikaans names.

### History

In order to provide a better understanding of the area in former times, a brief history is outlined. In some cases a clear picture of the earlier inhabitants is still emerging and the information provided may become outdated. Some areas are especially interesting historically and it is hoped that this aspect will encourage interest in the earlier inhabitants of the area. The abbreviation BP (Before Present) is generally used in preference to BC and AD when reference is made to archaeological dates.

### Geology

Where geological formations are an obvious feature of the area and you are likely to be intrigued as to how they were formed, these are briefly discussed.

### Trail Synopsis

This section contains either a detailed description of the more popular routes or a brief summary of the backpacking opportunities in the area. It should be borne in mind that routes do change from time to time. In respect of guided wilderness trails only a general description is given as experiences usually vary considerably from group to group.

### DON'T MISS

This section is included only where there is an aspect of particular interest in the area that you should not miss.

This format is used in respect of all the backpacking trails, but aspects such as the flora and fauna are usually only briefly outlined in the trail synopsis of guided wilderness trails as a trails officer will be at hand to broaden your knowledge.

# Part 1
# BACKPACKING BASICS AND MORE

# Before you go

Backpacking trails require more outdoor knowledge and skills than hiking trails and it is therefore advisable that you do a few hiking trails before attempting a backpacking trail. Much less preparation is usually required for a guided wilderness trail as guidance, equipment, accommodation, and in some cases even food, are provided. This section is consequently more specifically aimed at backpackers.

### Gaining Information

One of the best ways of familiarising yourself with backpacking and other aspects of the outdoors is to join one of the numerous hiking or mountaineering clubs that have been established in most major Southern African centres in recent years. There you will inevitably meet up with fellow backpackers with years of experience and stand to learn much in this way. A list of these organisations can be found in Part 8: References – Useful Addresses, on page 269.

Another way of gaining information is to consult any of the number of books available that deal with equipment and backpacking written by experienced outdoor people, whose advice will make your life a lot easier on the trail (see Part 8: References – Bibliography, page 273).

### Obtaining the Necessary Equipment

Until a few years ago backpacking was reserved for that adventurous breed of outdoor enthusiasts known as mountaineers. Equipment was not only limited but also heavy and often impractical. With the onset of the backpacking revolution, all this has changed and backpackers today have a wide range of scientifically designed, lightweight equipment to choose from. By the time you are ready to graduate from hiking or guided wilderness trails to backpacking trails, you should consider investing in your own equipment. You will probably have had the opportunity to try out borrowed equipment, in which case you will have formulated a few personal preferences.

Following is a discussion of essential items of specialist equipment required for backpacking trails. The designs and features of equipment are changing continuously and only the general features and principles are discussed here.

### Golden rules when buying equipment

- Carefully consider your requirements. It would serve very little purpose, for instance, to buy a lightweight artificial-fibre sleeping-bag suitable for caravanning if you intend to hike often in the Drakensberg during winter.
- Before buying your equipment spend some time talking to fellow backpackers, browse through manufacturers' catalogues and consult some of the literature available on equipment. Shop assistants of specialist backpacking stores are another invaluable source of information.
- Unless you know your exact requirements, do not be tempted to buy equipment from supermarkets. It might be cheaper, but in most cases their staff simply do not have the expertise to advise you.
- Always buy equipment with a reputable brand name. Some manufacturers of backpacks, for instance, guarantee their products for life. This does not, however, mean that you have to buy the most expensive equipment in the store.
- Buy what is comfortable and practical, not what is fashionable. Over the last few years equipment has tended to change frequently. What you buy should ultimately be dictated by your requirements and personal taste.

- Finally, decide on the price you wish to pay. Be realistic but never compromise quality for price.

### Footwear

On any trail comfort starts at ground level — your feet. Few things can spoil a backpacking trip as much as blistered and aching feet. Footwear can be divided into four basic categories:

- lightweight footwear suitable for casual rambling over easy terrain
- mediumweight boots suitable for hiking and backpacking trails in rugged mountainous terrain and snow
- specialist rock climbing boots
- mountaineering boots suitable for hiking and backpacking

In recent years there has been a worldwide trend towards lightweight footwear and in South Africa the use of Alpine-type mountaineering boots — once the norm — has to a large extent become restricted to winter backpacking trips in the Drakensberg. This was brought about partly by the lower quality and poorer performance of leather boots as the cost of leather soared and partly because of environmental considerations.

Taking general trailside conditions in Southern Africa into consideration, mediumweight boots are probably the most suitable for backpacking.

When buying boots the most important considerations are size, comfort and protection. To ensure a good fit you should wear the socks you will use for backpacking when trying on a pair of boots. Before tying the laces, push your foot as far forward as possible, until your toes rub against the toecap. If you can still manage to squeeze a finger down the inside of your heel, you know that you have the right fit. This extra room is necessary to allow your feet to expand and to prevent your toes from rubbing against the front end of the boot on downhill stretches. Do up the laces firmly but not too tightly, and ensure that the boots do not constrict the broad part of your feet and that there is sufficient room for your toes to move freely. Walk up and down the shop and check to see that your heels are held firmly in the back of the boots. If they rise more than about 6 mm you should try a smaller size.

Always try boots on both feet. Most people have one foot slightly bigger than the other and although a boot might fit one foot perfectly, you could find that the other boot of the same size is either too big or too small!

Once you have found the right pair of boots it is important to give them a chance to adjust themselves to the shape of your feet before embarking on your first backpacking trip. The time taken to break in your boots will depend on the stiffness of the sole and the leather. Begin by wearing the boots around the house and on day hikes until you are satisfied that they are properly worn in.

Boots have become increasingly expensive and should, therefore, be properly cared for. One of the most common mistakes backpackers and hikers make is to dry wet boots in front of a fire. This causes shrinkage, which could cause the sole to separate from the uppers. Wet boots should be aired as much as possible and then walked with until they are dry.

In the course of your travels your boots will be subjected to a great deal of hard wear, rain and sunshine. To revitalise the unique qualities of leather boots — breathability, suppleness, strength and durability — you should occasionally treat your boots with boot polish or dubbin. This will at the same time waterproof your boots, without affecting their breathability. Contrary to popular belief, dubbin does not cause stitch-rot. However, be careful to remove all dirt, especially in seams, before applying boot polish or dubbin. After treating your boots, ensure they are dry, stuff them with newspaper and store them in a dry place.

### Backpack

After footwear, your backpack is the item of equipment most likely to spoil or add to your enjoyment of a backpacking trip. Comfort is once again of the utmost importance.

It is important to select the correct size of backpack, ie the correct length of backpack or frame. This is, however, not as simple as it sounds. For instance, just because you are tall it does not mean you should buy a long frame or pack — the size of the frame or pack must be related to your torso size.

Try on the pack or frame and fasten the hip belt so that the top edge is just above your hip bone. Adjust the shoulder straps until the pack or frame fits snugly against your back. The top harness point should not be more than 5 cm below your high prominent neck bone. Ask a shop assistant or friend to help you gauge this position correctly. Because the sizes of packs and frames vary, you might have to try several before finding the correct fit.

Another major consideration is the capacity of the pack, ie the cubic capacity measured in litres, and here the old backpacking adage applies: if it's a large pack — fill it up; if it's a small pack — it will not fit in. Considering general weather and other conditions in Southern Africa, packs with a capacity of 70 litres and 55-60 litres can be considered adequate for men and women respectively.

Whether you should buy an internal or external type of backpack is purely a matter of personal choice. Backpack designs are changing continuously and over the last few years there have been some revolutionary designs on the market.

A few seemingly minor aspects could have a considerable influence on your comfort. Ask yourself the following when deciding on a new backpack:

- are the hip belt and shoulder straps well padded?
- are the shoulder straps easily adjusted?
- does the hip belt have a quick-release buckle?
- how many side-pockets are there?
- is there a map flap?
- is there a sac extension?
- on external frame packs, is there a mesh backband to allow ventilation?
- is the zip covered with a flap to make it shower-proof?

### Sleeping-bag

When choosing a sleeping-bag your choice will be between a down bag or an artificial-fibre bag. Once again there are several factors you should consider — weight, packed size, design, warmth and, finally, price. Your final choice will be determined by how these factors relate to the circumstances under which you intend using the sleeping-bag.

Down sleeping-bags have the advantages of being light, compact and warm, but on the negative side, they lose their insulating properties when wet and are expensive.

As a result of extensive research, the quality of artificial-fibre sleeping-bags has improved tremendously in recent years and some artificial-fibre bags compare favourably with down bags in respect of warmth. Advantages of artificial-fibre bags include ability to retain their insulating properties when wet, and their price. On the negative side, they are generally heavier and bulkier than down bags.

Two basic styles of sleeping-bags are available: mummy-shaped and rectangular. If you are likely to spend much of your time in cold weather conditions a mummy sleeping-bag makes good sense, as its body-contoured shape provides the most satisfactory warmth-to-weight ratio. The bag should have a well-shaped hood or cowl which can be drawn over your head and a drawstring. In very cold weather the cowl can be drawn over your face so that just a breathing hole remains. In this way heat loss from the head, neck and shoulders — the body's major sources of heat loss — is prevented. Mummy bags do not usually have zips, but some long styles have a short zip. Another feature of a well-designed mummy bag is a circular, insulated footpiece which not only provides added warmth but also gives better foot space.

Rectangular bags are the most popular sleeping-bags in South Africa. They usually come with full zips, which gives you the advantage of being able to control the temperature in the bag. On a warm evening you can unzip the bag to reduce the temperature, and in cold weather you can zip two bags together for extra warmth. At home the bag can be used as a duvet. Ensure that the bag has a down-filled draught tube behind the zip to prevent heat loss.

Although waterproof (Goretex) sleeping-bags are available overseas, sleeping-bags in South Africa are at best shower resistant. However, never try to waterproof your sleeping-bag, as this will destroy its breathability and you will wake up in an uncomfortable pool of sweat.

A properly cared for down sleeping-bag will ensure many warm, comfortable nights.

### *How to care for your sleeping-bag*

- Keep your bag dry. If it does get wet, dry it out in the open as soon as possible. Gently squeeze out excess water, but do not wring it out. Handle the bag with care to prevent the baffles from being damaged.
- Never expose your bag to excessive heat such as direct sunlight, or even worse a fire, as this could lead to a hardening of the down.
- Store your bag loosely — preferably by hanging it up when not in use. By compressing the bag for extended periods the natural resilience of the filling is strained.
- Keep your sleeping-bag as clean as possible both inside and out. The use of an inner sheet and a sleeping-bag cover will not only keep your bag clean, but will also give added warmth, although they will add about one kilogram in weight.
- Down sleeping-bags should always be hand-washed. Fill a bathtub with enough lukewarm water to cover the bag and add special down soap. Gently wash the bag, avoiding harsh twisting or wringing. Drain the tub, and gently rinse the bag in fresh water. Repeat this process until all the soap is removed. Press down gently onto the bag to squeeze out as much water as possible before lifting it out by supporting it underneath. Dry the bag carefully in a warm place, away from direct heat. Gently massage down lumps into individual plumules. Alternatively, dry the bag in a tumble drier set on a low temperature. To prevent the down clumping, place a few tennis balls in the drier with the bag.

### Closed-cell Groundpad

To prevent cold creeping up from the ground when sleeping you will need some form of insulation. Before closed-cell groundpads were available backpackers used alternatives such as vegetation (eg renosterbos), newspaper or air beds for insulation.

At first you may find your groundpad a bit hard, but in terms of comfort, weight and size (rolled) it is superior to both open foam and air beds. Some high-quality closed-cell groundpads with a thickness of 9 mm are suitable for conditions down to −10 °C!

For backpackers who are prepared to forego lightness for the sake of comfort, a self-inflating mattress is the answer. These ingenious mattresses are ideal for backpacking — they are lighter than the conventional air beds, more compact and you do not need to waste time inflating them. Their disadvantages are that they are heavier than groundpads and more expensive.

### Emergency Blanket or Sportsman's Space Blanket

The emergency blanket is an extremely light (70 g) sheet of thin aluminium foil, one side of which is highly reflective. It takes up hardly any space, is relatively inexpensive and can be used for a variety of purposes, such as to provide extra insulation or as an emergency shelter against rain or sun. It does not stand up to rough handling, however, and should not be used as a groundsheet, except in emergencies. The sportsman's blanket is a more durable all-purpose 'blanket' which can be used as a groundsheet. It is heavier (310 g) and more expensive.

### Waterproof Garment

The selection of rain gear is bound to be problematic unless you are prepared to delve deep into your pocket to buy a garment made of Goretex.

Conventional rain garments are generally either showerproof or waterproof. Showerproof garments have the advantage of breathability and perform satisfactorily in light rain. However, on backpacking trails where adverse weather conditions can set in for prolonged periods these garments are totally inadequate.

Waterproof garments, on the other hand, provide a sealed shell which is unable to breathe. Large quantities of warm, humid air released by the body are unable to escape through the waterproof material, and water vapour is formed when the hot air comes into contact with the cold surface of the garment.

The most popular style of rain gear in Southern Africa is the cagoule, which is available as either a long rain jacket or an anorak. Other features are a full hood with drawstrings and a drawstring round the bottom of the garment. A major disadvantage is that it has only a short zip at the neck, which means that you have only two options — to have it on or off.

Rain jackets with a full zip are more versatile, as you can unzip the garment to improve ventilation without removing the jacket. At the same time a zip has the disadvantage of being vulnerable to leakage.

The answer to all these problems was provided a few years ago with the development of Goretex, a 100 per cent waterproof fabric which is breathable and yet virtually impenetrable by wind. The combination of these unique qualities was made possible by the development of an extraordinary skin-like membrane formed from expanded polytetra-fluroethylene (PTFE), which has some nine billion pores per square inch. The pores are 20 000 times smaller than a droplet of water, but 700 times larger than a water vapour molecule, allowing sweat vapour to escape while keeping rain out. The membrane is laminated onto an outer fabric and an inner lining material. Overseas the fabric is used for a wide range of equipment, including rain gear, sleeping-bags, tents and sports and leisure outerwear. The fabric is expensive, even overseas, and as a result is unfortunately not widely available in South Africa.

### Backpacking Stove

As fires are not permitted in most wilderness areas a backpacking stove is essential. There are three main types of backpacking stoves, which are classified according to the type of fuel they use: alcohol (methylated spirits); unleaded petrol (benzine); and liquid fuel (butane or propane). Various types of stoves are available, each with their own advantages and disadvantages, so your choice will be largely dictated by personal taste. The most important factors you should consider are efficiency, ease of operation, fuel economy, cooking capacity, size/mass and price.

**Benzine stoves** rate high on efficiency and fuel economy and, in addition, they burn clean. Their main disadvantages are that they have to be pre-heated and are difficult to refuel (both somewhat cumbersome operations).

**Methylated spirit stoves** (alcohol) are easy to erect and operate, and are efficient. They perform well in windy conditions, and their wide base makes them stable. A set of pots, a frying pan, potgrip and, with some models, a kettle, which pack into a compact unit are supplied with these stoves. On the negative side, they have a low fuel/heat ratio. On a short weekend outing this is not a problem, but on longer backpacking trips you will need a large supply of fuel, adding to your weight and taking up space. Another negative factor is that pots are blackened during cooking.

Compared with other makes, **liquid fuel (gas) stoves** are considerably cheaper and clean burning. When shielded from the wind they are reasonably efficient, but perform poorly in windy conditions and in cold weather. In some models the centre of gravity is high, making them unstable, while empty gas cartridges have become a major source of pollution.

### Tent

Unlike hiking trails where comfortable overnight accommodation is provided at the end of each day's hike, the backpacker has to be totally self-sufficient, and this includes accommodation. Never rely on finding a vacant cave — always carry a tent.

Until a few years ago most tents were single-skinned, which meant that if you accidentally touched the side of the tent when turning over in the night you were rudely awoken by a shower of water, caused by condensation. This problem was largely solved by the double-skinned tent, or tent with a fly-sheet, as it is more commonly known. The inner tent is made of either an absorbent cotton or a breathable nylon fabric, which is suspended from the tent poles in such a way that it does not come into contact with the outer tent. Vapour passes through the breathable fabric of the inner tent and condenses when it comes into contact with the cold outer sheet. At the same time the air trapped between the inner tent and the flysheet acts as an effective insulator.

Features of quality backpacking tents to look out for are a waterproof, sewn-in groundsheet with fairly high 'walls', mosquito netting and a bell on either side. The latter is useful for storing packs in the one end, while leaving the other side free for cooking in miserable weather.

The most common tent style is the A-frame, but in the last few years dome tents have become increasingly popular. The main advantages of these tents are that they are easy to erect, more spacious and can be pitched without guy-ropes. Because of their domed shape they can withstand high winds. They are, however, substantially more expensive than conventional styles.

In addition to the above-mentioned equipment you will also need to take along several other items on a backpacking trip.

### Clothing

Unless you intend doing regular winter backpacking trips into the Drakensberg, you are likely to have most items of clothing required for a backpacking trip.

Make sure to take a hat that will give you adequate protection against the sun. If you are trailing in an area where cold temperatures can be expected it is wise to pack a balaclava or a woollen cap that can be pulled over your ears, as about 30 per cent of the body's heat is lost through the head.

In summer short-sleeved shirts or blouses are more suitable than T-shirts, which provide little ventilation and tend to cling to one's body. Cotton shirts, on the other hand, are more airy and have the added advantage of a collar that can be turned up to protect your neck against the sun.

In winter it is advisable to pack a long-sleeved woollen shirt for extra warmth. You will also need a warm jersey or a thickly-knitted, fleecy-lined hooded tracksuit top. Avoid leisurewear tracksuits, as they generally do not keep the cold out. Wool is in all cases preferable to other fabrics on account of its excellent insulating qualities.

Even in wet, cold conditions training shorts are preferable to long trousers, which can cause discomfort and chafing once they are wet. Never wear jeans – they are heavy (and even heavier when wet) and take ages to dry.

Generally your normal underwear is sufficient, (cotton garments are most comfortable). For winter trailing, thermal underwear is recommended. Some backpackers prefer to hike with a string vest, whatever the time of the year, as it facilitates ventilation in warm weather, and during winter it is a surprisingly effective insulator. You do not need to take a change of underwear for every day's hike as it is usually possible to wash or rinse underwear on the trail.

A general rule to prevent loss of body heat is to cover the body with several layers of thin clothing, rather than a single, thick layer. This is because heat is prevented from escaping by the layers of dry air which are trapped between the different layers of clothing.

When it comes to socks there is no substitute for wool and although a wool/fibre mixture is acceptable you must ensure that the percentage of wool predominates. Avoid nylon socks as they will overheat your feet and cause blisters. Most hikers and backpackers prefer to wear two pairs of socks — a thin inner pair of either wool or cotton, and a thick woollen outer pair. This reduces the likelihood of blisters considerably as the socks absorb the chafing that would otherwise occur on your skin.

### Miscellaneous Items

- **Torch**. Although there are several torches available on the South African market, none is particularly suitable for backpacking. The well-organised backpacker will, however, have little need for a torch and the small hand-type torches are probably the best. They not only take up very little space, but are also very light, as are the spare batteries you should take along.

- **Water-bottle.** A 2-litre water-bottle or two 1-litre bottles are essential on any backpacking trip. Plastic water-bottles are the most commonly used, but have the disadvantage of giving water a plastic flavour when they are exposed to the sun for long periods. Some plastic water-bottles available in backpacking stores have a felt covering which helps to keep water cool when kept damp.
- **Cutlery.** A plastic, dish-shaped bowl or a plate with a raised rim is preferable to a flat plate. You will seldom need a fork on a trail; take a knife and a dessert-spoon from your kitchen drawer, rather than buying a 'special' cutlery set.

### Planning a Trail

Without careful planning, a backpacking trail can easily end up in a disaster, so do spend some time planning your trip. Keep the following in mind:

- Choose a trail to suit your level of fitness. Your first backpacking outing should ideally be a short, weekend trial. Always plan the outing with the weakest member of the party in mind and ensure that all party members are fit.
- Obtain the necessary permit from the authority in charge.
- Consider the climate. This factor is vitally important as it will determine what equipment, clothing and food you will take.
- Obtain the necessary maps. Unlike hiking trails, backpacking trail routes are not indicated with route markers and with the exception of the Cederberg Wilderness Area and the Drakensberg, special trail maps are not available. Moreover, make sure that you know how to use the maps and familiarise yourself with a compass.
- One of the golden rules of backpacking is *never set off alone*. Three people is the minimum, but four is a safe number.
- Check your equipment beforehand and ensure it is serviceable, especially boots.
- Obtain a weather forecast before setting off.
- Always inform someone of your intended route and expected time of return. Where a mountain register is provided it should be completed correctly and in detail.

### Nutrition

Until a few years ago compiling a menu was a major headache for anyone planning a trail as there simply wasn't much to choose from. Today, however, there is a wide variety of backpacking foods available and it is possible to enjoy a delicious meal after a hard day's trailing.

Most supermarkets stock a wide range of instant, dehydrated soya-protein meals, dehydrated vegetables, instant mashed potatoes, and instant soups and desserts. Soya-protein meals are considerably cheaper than freeze-dried foods, but have the disadvantage of tasting rather bland. With a little imagination and a few herbs and spices you will be surprised how much you can enhance the taste of soya-protein meals.

Backpacking stores usually carry a fairly wide range of backpacking foods, including freeze-dried meals. These are not only very palatable, but are also extremely light and in some instances require no cooking. The only disadvantage is that you may find the portions a bit small if you have a healthy appetite.

Although everyone's kilojoule intake varies, men on average burn up 17-21 000 kJ (4-5 000 cal) and women 13-17 000 kJ (3-4 000 cal) a day. About 4 185 kJ (1 000 cal) a day should be added for a trail averaging 15 km a day or when you're trailing in cold weather. Also remember that you will need about two and a half times as many kilojoules to gain 300 m in altitude as you will when walking on level terrain for an hour!

You do not need to be a dietician to ensure that you are well nourished on the trail. The following is a rough guide to the aver-

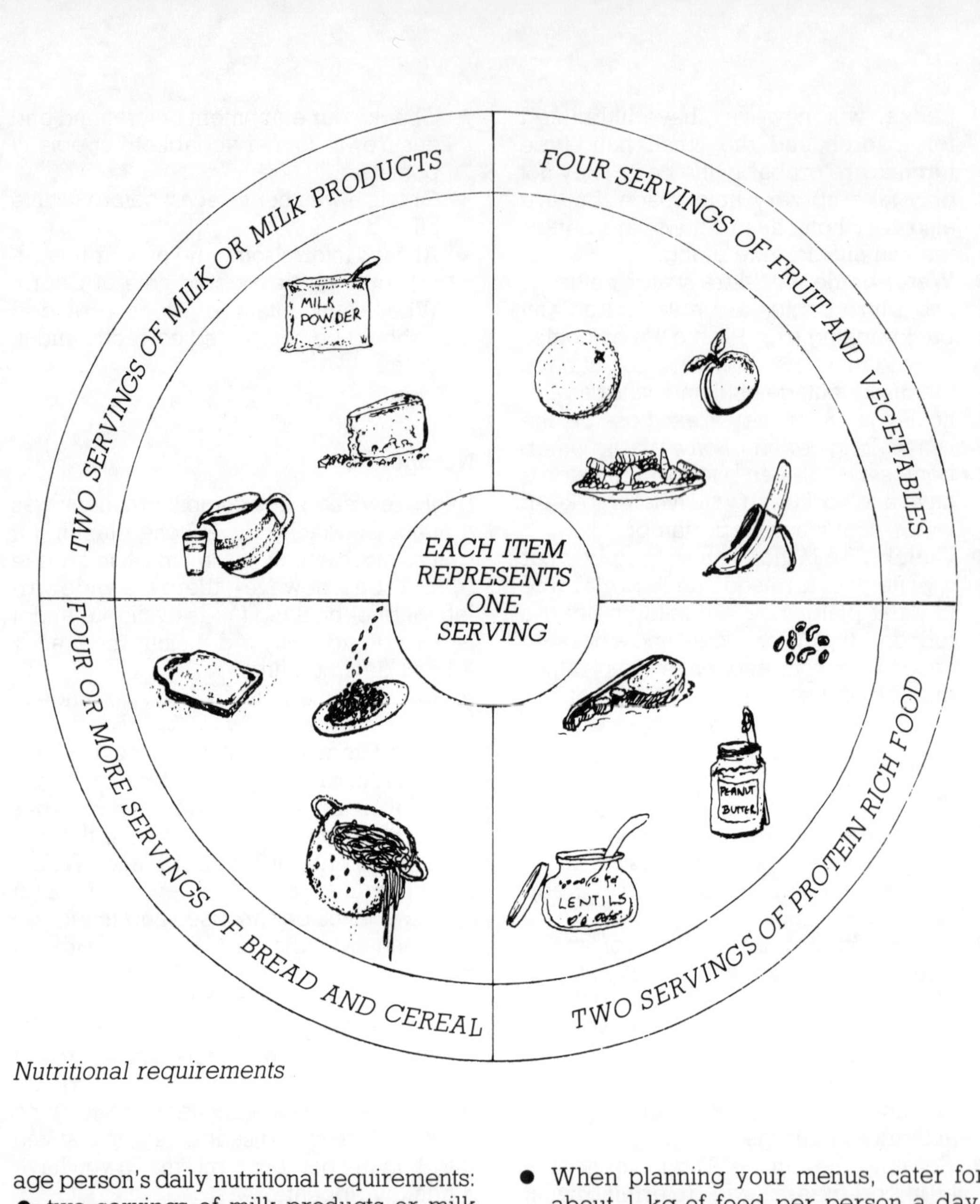


*Nutritional requirements*

age person's daily nutritional requirements:

- two servings of milk products or milk (one serving is 250 ml milk, 60 ml milk powder (dry), 45 g cheese),
- two servings of protein-rich food (one serving is 80-250 ml nuts, 60 ml peanut butter),
- four servings of fruit and vegetables (one serving is one piece of fruit, 125 ml cooked rehydrated vegetables),
- four or more servings of bread or cereal (one serving is one slice of bread, 125 ml cooked cereal, 125 ml cooked pasta or rice).

Also remember the following:

- When planning your menus, cater for about 1 kg of food per person a day, bearing in mind that in cold weather your appetite will be much bigger.
- Always carry an extra day's emergency rations of high-energy foods such as chocolate, nuts and raisins and glucose sweets. Don't be tempted to eat the rations before completing the trail!

The three-day sample menu following is designed to help you plan your own menu. The weights given are average and will vary according to the product brand. The menu is meant only as a guide and you can adjust it according to your requirements and personal taste.

## THREE-DAY MENU FOR THREE PEOPLE

| | Breakfast | | Lunch | | Supper | |
|---|---|---|---|---|---|---|
| **DAY 1** | muesli | 300 g | 6 slices rye bread | 375 g | 1 pkt soup | 35 g |
| | 3 rusks | 60 g | 6 cheese wedges | 100 g | instant mashed potato | 112 g |
| | 1 orange, quartered | 300 g | 1 mini salami | 200 g | 1 tin tuna | 200 g |
| | 3 sheets crispbread | 95 g | ½ pkt dried figs | 125 g | 1 small green pepper | 100 g |
| | coffee/tea | | peanuts & raisins | 150 g | dehydrated onion | 25 g |
| | | | 3 apples | 500 g | dehydrated peas | 50 g |
| | | | 1 litre isotonic drink | 80 g | tomato whirls | 15 g |
| | | | | | 1 pkt instant pudding | 100 g |
| | | | | | coffee/tea | |
| **DAY 2** | oats | 150 g | 6 sheets crispbread | 190 g | 1 pkt soup | 25 g |
| | 3 rusks | 60 g | 3 hard-boiled eggs | 190 g | macaroni | 200 g |
| | 1 grapefruit | 300 g | 1 tin sardines | 106 g | Bolognese soya mince | 120 g |
| | 3 slices rye bread | 190 g | 1 fruit roll | 80 g | Parmesan cheese | 50 g |
| | 6 cheese wedges | 100 g | 3 crunchie biscuits | 60 g | 1 chocolate bar | 200 g |
| | coffee/tea | | 1 litre isotonic drink | 80 g | coffee/tea | |
| **DAY 3** | muesli | 300 g | 6 sheets crispbread | 190 g | 1 pkt soup | 50 g |
| | 3 rusks | 60 g | 6 cheese wedges | 100 g | curry soya mince | 120 g |
| | stewed fruit | 200 g | 1 mini salami | 200 g | rice | 150 g |
| | coffee/tea | | ½ pkt dates | 125 g | chutney | 75 g |
| | | | peanuts & raisins | 150 g | 1 pkt instant pudding | 100 g |
| | | | 3 apples | 500 g | coffee/tea | |
| | | | 1 litre isotonic drink | 80 g | | |

| MISCELLANEOUS | | |
|---|---|---|
| peanut butter | 250 g | **Total mass:** 8,527 kg |
| jam | 300 g | ÷ 3 people |
| milk powder (4 litres) | 400 g | ÷ 3 days |
| 6 coffee bags | 75 g | = an average of 947,44 g |
| 18 tea bags | 54 g | per person per day to |
| salt, pepper, herbs | 25 g | carry |

### Packing for the Trail

The kitlist on page 16 is for a five-day backpacking trail. Do not follow it religiously, but use it as a guide and adapt it to suit the trail type, trail length and your personal needs. The kitlist is applicable to backpacking trails only. On guided wilderness trails much of your equipment is usually supplied. However, this varies from trail to trail so refer to the Relevant Information section of the particular trail, which gives details of what you need to take along.
Remember that the masses given are *approximate* and will vary from product to product.

Finally, here are some hints to assist you in packing your backpack.

- Limit the weight. Your pack should never exceed more than a third of your body weight. Ideal weights are 20 per cent of the body weight of females and children and 25 per cent of the body weight of males.
- Before packing, line your backpack with a large garbage bag or sac liner. This will ensure that the contents of your pack remain dry should you have to backpack in rain for an extended period. Although most good-quality backpacks stand up to their claim of being waterproof, water does sometimes seep through seams and zips. A sac liner has the advantage of durability and can, therefore, be used several times.
- Pack systematically to ensure that unnecessary items are not packed and that

nothing is left behind. Few things are as frustrating as discovering on the trail that you have forgotten to pack something!

- Items that you are likely to use often during the day and your rain gear should be packed in an easily accessible place, such as a side pocket.
- To conserve energy when walking the bulk of the weight in your pack should be in line with your centre of gravity. This is best achieved by packing heavier items in the top half of the pack, closest to your back, leaving the bottom half for lighter items.

## KITLIST

This is a kitlist for a five-day backpacking trail (without overnight facilities). You can adapt it to suit the trail length and your personal needs.

| **ITEM** | **APPROX. MASS (g)** | ● Essential<br>* Optional<br>x Refer to Relevant Information |
|---|---|---|
| Backpack | | |
| framed backpack with hipbelt | 1 800 | ● |
| spare clevis pins (external frame pack only) | 10 | ● |
| pack cover | 25 | * |
| **Sleeping gear** | | |
| sleeping-bag | 1 800 | ● |
| inner sheet | 500 | * |
| groundsheet | 720 | x |
| closed-cell groundpad | 400 | ● |
| tent | 3 000 | ● |
| emergency blanket | 70 | ● |
| sportsman's blanket | 310 | * |
| **Footwear** | | |
| mediumweight boots/walking shoes | 1 800 | ● |
| spare laces | 50 | ● |
| spare footwear | 750 | ● |
| woollen socks (2 pairs) | 400 | ● |
| cotton socks (2 pairs) | 200 | ● |
| gaiters | 150 | * |
| **Clothing** | | |
| woollen cap/balaclava | 125 | ● |
| sunhat | 75 | ● |
| 2 cotton shirts | 400 | ● |
| 1 woollen long-sleeved shirt | 250 | ● |
| anorak/warm jersey | 700 | ● |
| 2 pairs shorts | 300 | ● |
| 3 pairs underwear | 150 | ● |
| thermal underwear | 300 | * |
| tracksuit | 700 | ● |
| gloves | 100 | * |
| handkerchief | 10 | ● |
| waterproof rain gear | 600 | ● |
| swimming costume | 150 | * |

| ITEM | APPROX. MASS (g) | ● Essential<br>* Optional<br>x Refer to Relevant Information |
|---|---|---|
| **Cooking and food** | | |
| cutlery | 50 | ● |
| plate and mug | 110 | ● |
| can opener | 20 | * |
| backpacking stove<br>pots<br>pot-grip<br>fuel container(s)<br>(fuel mass depends on stove and fuel) | 1 700 | ● |
| matches | 15 | ● |
| pot-scraper | 20 | ● |
| dishcloth | 80 | ● |
| litter bag | 25 | ● |
| emergency rations | 500 | ● |
| trail snacks | 500 | * |
| trail food for 5 days | 5 000 | ● |
| 2-litre water-bottle (full) | 2 075 | ● |
| **Toiletries** | | |
| tissues | 10 | * |
| toilet paper and trowel | 100 | ● |
| small towel | 250 | ● |
| biodegradable soap | 25 | ● |
| toothbrush and toothpaste | 45 | ● |
| comb | 15 | ● |
| sun protection cream | 120 | ● |
| lip-ice | 20 | ● |
| moisturiser | 75 | ● |
| insect repellent | 50 | x |
| **Miscellaneous** | | |
| first aid kit | 300 | ● |
| malaria tablets | 10 | * |
| torch, spare batteries and bulb | 115 | ● |
| candle | 60 | * |
| camera and film | 1 000 | * |
| compact binoculars | 400 | * |
| map | 50 | ● |
| compass | 100 | * |
| permit | 7 | ● |
| passport/visa | 40 | x |
| waterproofing bags | 50 | ● |
| survival bag | 240 | * |
| cord (5 m, thin nylon) | 50 | ● |
| notebook and pencil | 50 | ● |
| whistle | 10 | ● |
| relevant literature | — | * |

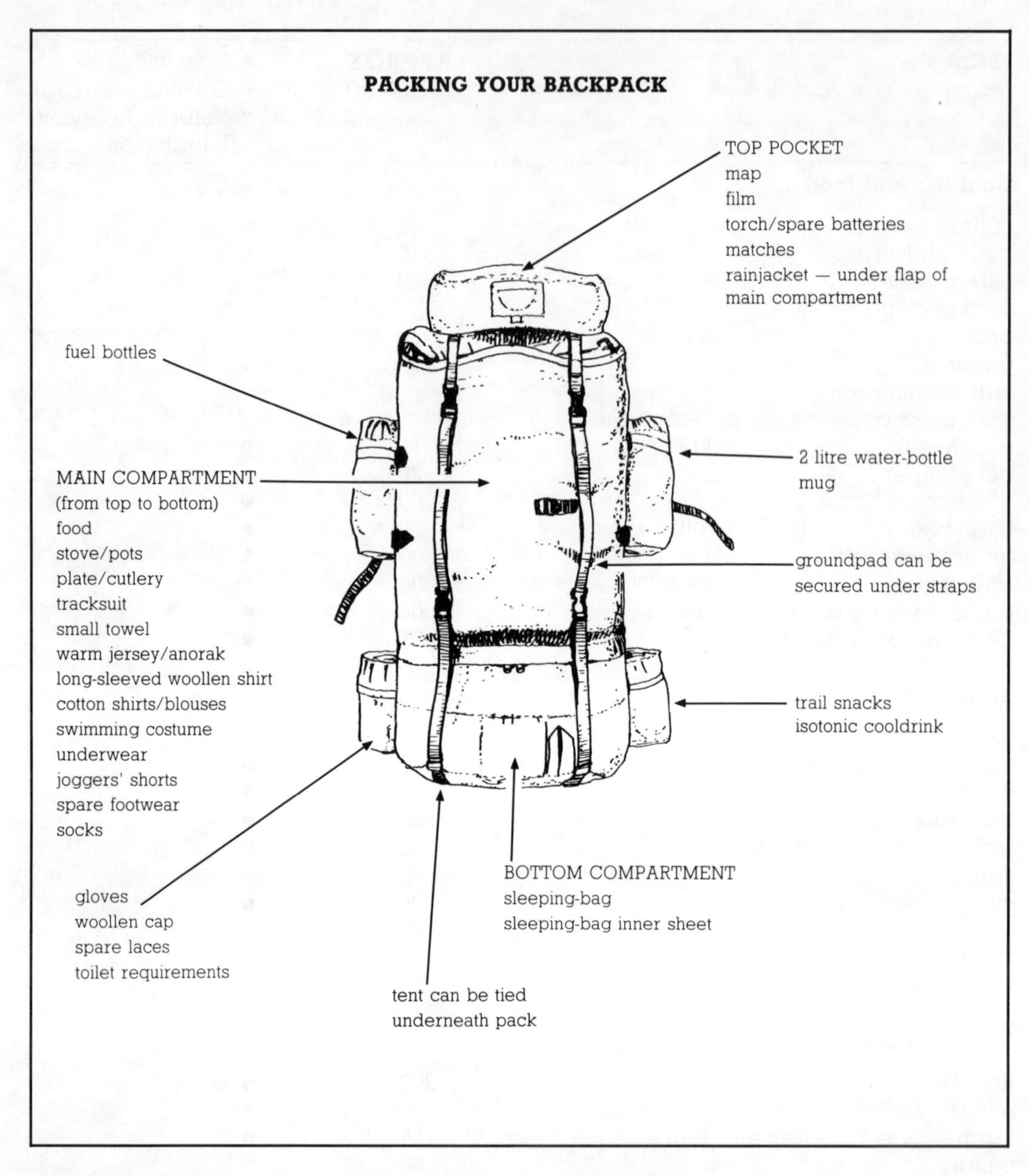


*Use this illustration as a guide to packing your backpack*

# *On the Trail*

The following points should always be borne in mind when on a trail. They will not only ensure pleasant backpacking but could also save lives.

- The party should always be led by the most experienced backpacker.
- Plan each day carefully. Start off as early as possible if you have a long day's backpacking ahead of you, if the terrain is difficult, unfamiliar, or in hot weather.
- Keep in mind that the days are considerably shorter in winter than in summer.
- Large parts of Southern Africa receive rain in the summer and thunderstorms are common in the afternoon. Try to reach your destination before the rains set in.
- Hike at a steady pace. Three kilometres an hour is a good average. For every 300 m you gain in altitude an hour can be added. On steeper sections it is advisable to shorten your stride slightly, while maintaining your rhythm. Avoid frequent long breaks — rather have short rest stops and take the opportunity to appreciate your surroundings.
- Keep the party together. A member lagging behind is almost always a sign of trouble, usually exhaustion or exposure. Establish the cause of the problem, assist the person by spreading the weight of his/her pack among the other members of the party and keep him/her company. In large groups it is advisable to appoint someone to bring up the rear. In this way you will always know who the last person is.
- Keep your energy level up by eating snacks — peanuts and raisins, glucose sweets, chocolate and dried fruit — between meals.
- If you encounter bad weather or if the route proves too physically demanding, do not hesitate to turn back.
- Mist occurs frequently at high altitudes. Seek a suitable shelter if it sets in and stay put until it has cleared.
- In the event of snow, seek shelter and move off the summit at the earliest opportunity to avoid being trapped if conditions deteriorate.
- Be aware of the dangers of flash floods. Never cross a flooding river. Either wait until the flood has subsided or make a detour. Fortunately most South African rivers soon return to their normal flow after flooding.
- Some routes necessitate frequent river crossings. At times it might be possible to boulder-hop across, but avoid long jumps with a heavy pack which could result in a slip, and not only a soaking, but also serious injury. If you are uncertain about a river's depth always probe it first without your pack. If the river is fordable, undo the hip-belt of your backpack and loosen the shoulder straps for quick off-loading.
- Avoid crossing rivers near the mouth unless there is a definite sandbar. These rivers are more likely to be shallow and slower where they are wide. Steer clear of bends, as the water is usually deeper here and the flow stronger.
- Avoid the dangers of lightning during summer thunderstorms by staying clear of prominent features such as trees, ridges, summits, shallow caves and large boulders. Find an open slope, sit on a groundpad or a backpack, preferably on a clean rock, with your knees drawn up, feet together and hands in your lap. If you are in your tent during an electric storm, sit in a crouching position and avoid touching the sides.
- Always carry a 2-litre water-bottle. Remember that smaller streams are often dry during winter months in summer rainfall areas and dry during the summer months in winter rainfall areas. Unless ample water is available along

the route, ensure that you always keep a reserve supply of water.

- Water-bottles should always be filled from safe, fast-running streams above human habitation. Water below human habitation, especially in rural areas, is unsafe and should not be drunk before it has been boiled.
- Water suspected of being infested by bilharzia, cholera or other waterborne diseases should be boiled for at least five minutes. This method is preferable to using commercially available chemicals. Strain water through a handkerchief to remove debris before boiling it.
- In the event of a veld fire, try to find shelter in a kloof or ravine rather than going up a slope. Avoid waterfalls and take care and time to minimise unnecessary risks.

### Useful Hints

Few things can be frustrating as arriving at the end of a hard day's backpacking in the rain to discover that your matches are soaking wet or that the batteries of your torch have run down. As you gain more experience of the outdoors you will learn how to avoid these annoying mishaps and turn a good trip into a memorable one. Here are a few basic, commonsense hints:

A good **waterproof raincoat** is essential on any outing, whether it is a day ramble of a week-long expedition. In the mountains and at the coast the weather can change rapidly from beautiful and sunny to violently stormy. The authors have even experienced a thunderstorm in the Fish River Canyon in mid-winter! Your raincoat will be of little use in a sudden downpour if it is safely packed away in the bottom of your pack, so do keep it in a handy place.

To avoid that feeling of despair when you switch on your **torch** and nothing happens, turn one of the batteries the wrong way round when not in use. Remember to take **spare batteries** and a **spare bulb** along.

**Waterproof matches** can be bought at specialist backpacking stores, but are unjustifiably expensive. Take a **cigarette lighter** along, as well as keeping some matches and a small piece of striker in an empty film container — it is 100 per cent waterproof when closed properly!

A **pot-grip** will allow you to move hot pots without getting your fingers burnt or even worse, watching your meal end up on the ground. Also useful is a **long-handled spoon.**

Avoid glass bottles — they are not only heavier than plastic or aluminium, but are also more than likely to break on the trip. Decant all liquids into screw-top **plastic bottles** or **aluminium containers.** Some aluminium containers are available in different colours to ensure that you do not confuse your water and fuel bottles.

A very handy container for substances like honey, jam, peanut butter and condensed milk is a **squeeze tube** which is filled from the one end and then sealed with a sliding clamp. It is re-usable, but remember not to turn the screw-top too tightly or it will crack.

A small but extremely important item is a **whistle,** which can be used to attract attention should you get lost. Remember the international SOS — three short, three long and three short whistles. Avoid noise pollution and never use it unnecessarily.

Where large, wide rivers, have to be crossed take along a **survival bag** — a large orange heavy-duty plastic bag — to float equipment across. As the name implies, it has numerous other uses as well and although somewhat sweaty, it can also be used as a bivvy bag.

Although each group should have a well-equipped first aid kit it is advisable that each person carries their own **plasters.**

Backpackers often complain about sore feet on the trail. An extra pair of **light shoes,** eg running shoes, sandals or towelling slippers will give your feet the much needed rest they deserve after a hard day's backpacking. Although towelling slippers are comfortable and warm, they serve little purpose in wet weather.

A 5 m length of thin **nylon rope** is useful for emergency repairs and as a washing line.

Always remember to take **precautions against the sun** — sunhat, sunscreen lotion, etc.

Remember to **pack all food away** before going to sleep or you might discover to your annoyance in the morning that mice or small predators have made off with your provisions. Nordenstam describes how on his third visit to the Brandberg in April 1964 rodents were '... gnawing at everything, including paper, cigarettes, clothes and plastic bottles. They even managed to slip inside a rucksack which we had hung on a wire from a wild pear tree.'[1] Be warned!

One of the most handy backpacking items is a **Swiss army knife.** It is light, compact and most models have all the gadgets you will need on a trail, including a tin-opener, knife, tweezers and scissors. Attach it to your pack with a piece of string, so that you do not lose it.

### Backpacking by the Rules of Low Impact

The following suggestions on how to help conserve the natural environment you're backpacking through have been divided into five headings.

#### *Land*

- Do not litter. Tissues tucked into sleeves or under watch straps inevitably fall out and are one of the most common forms of litter in the outdoors. Other common forms of litter are cigarette ends, plastic sweet papers and toilet paper. Even orange peels, commonly regarded as biodegradable, should not be discarded as they can take up to five months to decompose. The following are estimates of how long it can take for litter to decompose under ideal trailside conditions: plastic-coated paper: 1-5 years; plastic bags: 10-20 years; plastic film: 20-30 years; nylon fabrics: 30-40 years; aluminium cans; 80-100 years; glass: indefinitely.

  Carry a refuse bag and pick up litter along the way. In May 1987 officials of the Directorate of Nature Conservation and Recreation Resorts of SWA/Namibia removed 16 large bags of rubbish from the Fish River Canyon during a four-day clean-up campaign.

  Never bury litter. In most cases it will be uncovered by the elements or animals such as baboons. This is not only unsightly, but broken glass and tins with sharp edges can cause injuries to animals.

  *Remember: Carry out what you carry in.*
- Avoid short-cuts. By taking short-cuts the trail's gradient and consequently its erosion potential is increased. The steeper gradient also demands greater exertion.
- Step over erosion bars, not on them, and avoid kicking up stones.
- Avoid areas with little or no vegetation. They are extremely susceptible to erosion and can take up to 25 years to recover after human trampling.
- Avoid scree or talus slopes for the same reason. Backpacking on them can cause miniature rock falls which destroy vegetation that has become established under difficult conditions.
- Never roll rocks down slopes or over cliffs. This could not only injure other people but could also cause fires and erosion and destroy vegetation.
- Disturb the area as little as possible when setting up camp where there are no developed campsites. Pitch your camp on level ground, not only for your own comfort, but also because sloping ground erodes easily once the vegetation is compacted.
- Keep your backpack as light as possible. This will not only lighten your load and thereby increase your enjoyment of the trail, but will also reduce compaction and erosion.

#### *Water*

Many of the rivers and streams of Southern Africa are the habitat of rare and endangered aquatic life, which can easily be destroyed by carelessness. Keep the following in mind:

- Avoid camping closer than 60 m from any water body, wherever possible.

1 Nordenstam, B. 1974. The Flora of the Brandberg. *Dinteria* 11, 8.

- Do not use soap in streams or rivers — a good swim is normally sufficient to clean up — and don't brush your teeth in rivers or streams.

### *Air*

One of the main reasons people go trailing is to seek solitude. Noise pollution is as objectionable as littering.

- Avoid shouting, yelling and whistling; it decreases your chances of seeing wildlife.
- If you smoke, take care, especially in dry grasslands. Never smoke while you are trailing. Stop, sit down and relax. Use a flat rock as an ashtray and remember to put the filter in your litter bag afterwards.
- Smoke from campfires also causes air pollution. Where fires are permitted, keep them small.

### *Flora and fauna*

- Do not pick flowers.
- Avoid short-cuts, which could damage or destroy sensitive or endangered vegetation.
- Fires are generally not permitted in wilderness areas. Where they are permitted, remember the following:
  - — if an old fireplace is available, use it, rather than making a new one
  - — choose a level spot where the fire will be protected from the wind
  - — don't make fires near vegetation or on the roots of trees
  - — clear the area around the fireplace of all leaves and humus
  - — keep the fire small — it is more comfortable to cook over, more intimate, easier to control and you will also conserve wood
  - — use only dead wood and do not break seemingly dead branches off trees; it is not only unsightly but often the branches are still alive
  - — never leave your fire unattended and keep water handy to dowse it if necessary
  - — extinguish your fire properly before going to sleep or breaking up camp; dowse it with water, stir the coals and dowse again.
- Do not cut vegetation to sleep on — carry a groundpad.
- Disturb animals and birds as little as possible, particularly those with young or in nests, as well as seemingly lost or injured animals or birds.
- Do not feed animals and birds. Some animals, especially baboons, soon learn to associate humans with food if they are fed and later become aggressive scavengers. In addition you may pass on harmful bacteria to the animals.

### *General*

- In some wilderness areas toilets are provided. Where not, human waste can be disposed of by using the 'cat method'. Select a flat, screened spot at least 50 m from the footpath and/or open water. Dig a hole no deeper than 20-25 cm to keep within the biological disposal layer and after use fill the hole with loose soil and trample lightly over it. Alternatively loose stones can be used to cover human waste, but either burn toilet paper or ensure that it is properly concealed and weighed down well.
- Do not sleep in caves with rock paintings, except where this is expressly permitted, and never tamper with or spray water over the paintings.
- Leave all archaeological sites untouched. In terms of the National Monuments Act it is an offence to disturb such sites in any way.
- Your enjoyment and appreciation of trailing will be considerably enhanced by reading more about the area beforehand. There are numerous small, pocket-size field guides on flora and fauna that can be taken along on your outings.

# First Aid

### First Aid Kit

A well-equipped first aid kit should always accompany a backpacking party. The following principles should be kept in mind when assembling a kit:

- Limit equipment to first aid essentials that will enable you to handle the illness or injury until help is obtained.
- Know *when and how to use* all your equipment.
- Equipment should generally be *palliative* rather than *curative.*
- If you or any of your party members have a *chronic disease,* eg diabetes, asthma, heart complaints, weak ankles or knees, make sure that you have enough of the medicine or equipment the person usually uses.

### Emergency First Aid

Most emergency situations are related either to extremes of weather or to a physical injury or disability. It is therefore essen-

**The following basic but adequate list can be used when compiling a first aid kit.**

Antibiotic (for long trips far from help)
Antihistamine cream or tablets
Antiseptic cream/solution (eg Merthiolate)
Antiseptic, analgesic ear drops (eg Aurone)
Bandages: wide crêpe, small gauze, triangular
Clingwrap
Cotton wool
Embrocation (eg Ellimans Royal Embrocation; Deep Heat)
Eye ointment
Gauze squares
Healing ointment for cracked skin (eg Vandol)
Indigestion tablets
Isotonic drink
Lip salve
Malaria tablets
Mosquito repellent (eg Tabard)
Nail scissors
Needle
Painkiller (eg Disprin or Codis for adults, Panado syrup for children)
Plaster (zinc oxide) for blisters
Plaster dressing strip/sealed individual plasters (for cuts etc)
Safety pins
Sore throat lozenges
Space blanket
Sunscreen lotion
Tissues
Tweezers
Wound dressings

tial that every backpacker should understand the principles of preventive measures and the methods of first aid. It is strongly advisable to read some of the many authoritative publications available on this subject, or to enrol for a course in first aid. The knowledge you will gain in this way will always be useful in any emergency situation.

Unless you are medically trained you will only be able to give emergency first aid, ie prevent any deterioration in the condition of the patient until a rescue party arrives.

The three most serious physical injuries or disabilities are:
(a) cessation of breathing;
(b) bleeding; and
(c) shock.
All of these situations call for immediate action and the following general directions should be followed:

1. **Take control of the situation.** The leader of the party must take control of the situation immediately. If it is the leader who is injured, the most experienced member of the party must take control. Remain calm, assess the situation and direct the other members of the party to improvise equipment or construct a shelter.
2. **Approach the casualty safely,** where necessary. In the event of a serious fall in difficult terrain, care should be taken not to cause rockfalls or to endanger the lives of other members of the party. If the casualty cannot be reached safely or the necessary equipment is unavailable, help should be summoned without delay.
3. **Apply emergency first aid procedures.** If the casualty can be reached, assess his condition. Treat the following emergencies first. **If the injury appears to be related in any way to the spine or neck, avoid moving him.**

- Check his breathing. Lick your fingers and hold them above his mouth and nose; put your other hand on his chest or stomach. If you cannot feel any breath or movement apply artificial respiration, first removing any obstruction to his air passages.
- Check his pulse. If there is none, apply cardiopulmonary resuscitation.
- Check for serious bleeding. Internal bleeding may be indicated if the casualty is pale, clammy and restless. Try to stop fast or heavy bleeding by:
  - Applying direct pressure, using a pad of folded cloth (a triangular bandage or clothing), and if possible elevating the wound.
  - Using a tourniquet in addition to direct pressure for a fast-bleeding wound on a limb. Use a belt or a strip of material (*not* thin rope) twisted tight with a stick. Be sure to loosen it every half hour for a few minutes.

4. **Treat the casualty for shock,** which may set in after any major injury. Signs of shock are: paleness, clammy skin, fast weak heartbeat, quick breathing, dizziness, weakness.
   - Lie him down with his feet higher than his head.
   - Loosen any tight clothing.
   - Cover him, but don't let him get too hot.
   - Reassure him, and keep him comfortable.
   - If he can drink and it is available, give him small sips of warm sweet tea or sugar water.
5. **Check for other injuries** and give first aid treatment. Start with the head and work your way down, examining all areas of the body for bleeding, sensitivity, fractures, pain or swelling.
6. **Plan what to do.** Your plan of action will depend on whether the casualty can carry on under his own power, whether he can be evacuated by the party, or whether he needs outside assistance. Take the following into account: the patient's injuries, the time of day, weather conditions, the terrain, the availability of shelter, the size and physical condition of the group and the availability of outside help.
7. **Execute the plan of action.** If the situation requires evacuation with outside help, at least two members of the party should be sent. They should preferably be stronger members of the party and must follow a predetermined route from which they should not deviate. They

should have the following information to report on their arrival at the source of help:

(a) where, when and how the accident occurred;
(b) the number of casualties as well as the nature and seriousness of the injuries;
(c) what first aid was administered, what supplies are still available and the condition of the casualties;
(d) the distance of the casualties from the nearest roads and the nature of the terrain;
(e) the number of people at the evacuation scene;
(f) what type of equipment might be necessary.

While waiting for help to arrive the remaining members of the party can make shelters and prepare hot meals and drinks for the casualty and themselves.

## Prevention and Cure

About 90 per cent of all ailments on trails are related to foot and leg problems. The best first aid is prevention and avoidance. Make early decisions and treat any wounds or ailments medically or behaviourally as soon as they occur, before the condition worsens.

If you are not an experienced first aider, it would be a good idea to photocopy the pages in this section and the previous one on emergency first aid, and pack them with your first aid kit.

### *Blisters*

Blisters are the most common cause of discomfort and should be treated before they form. If certain spots on your feet are prone to blisters, cover these areas with a plaster before putting on your boots. A potential blister can usually be detected when a tender 'hot-spot' starts to develop. Cover the affected area immediately with a zinc oxide plaster. If a blister forms and you have not yet completed your trip, it is best to pierce the blister with a needle or a pair of scissors. Take care, however, to avoid infection. Gently press out the fluid, dab the blister with antiseptic and then cover it with a dressing and zinc oxide plaster. Check the affected spot regularly for infection. If you have completed your trip, preferably leave the blister unpricked and uncovered to heal by itself.

### *Bruises*

You can keep swelling from a bad bruise down by holding the affected part under cold running water, and keeping it elevated and still.

### *Burns*

After blisters, sunburn (classified as a first degree burn) is probably the most common ailment suffered on trails. Prevention is better than cure, so wear a sunhat and apply sunscreen lotion frequently, especially on the nose and face. Turn up the collar of your shirt (one of the reasons why a shirt is preferable to a T-shirt) to prevent sunburn on your neck.

Scalds and minor burns should be treated by holding the affected area in cold water until the pain subsides. Do not apply greasy ointments, and do not prick burn blisters. If available, cover the burn lightly with a gauze dressing held on with a plaster: burns heal better if left open to the air.

Burns of a more serious nature should not be immersed in water. Instead cover the area immediately with a sterile dressing or a clean cloth. Clingwrap is even better if you have it. If clothing sticks, leave it on.

Treat the patient for shock and give him plenty of water or Game to drink. Help should be summoned as soon as possible.

### *Cramps*

Muscular cramps are caused by either a shortage of salt or water or both, combined with physical exercise. Allow the casualty to rest and keep the affected area warm and gently massaged. Administer an isotonic drink. The casualty should avoid further strenuous exercise until he is fully recovered.

### *Diarrhoea and vomiting*

For both complaints the patient should rest and be given frequent doses of isotonic

Game mixed to half strength. Diarrhoea is a natural body mechanism to dispose of harmful bacteria and should preferably not be treated with commercially available anti-diarrhoea medications.

Belly pains and feeling of illness with no diarrhoea and vomiting might be serious if accompanied by a persisting fever. The patient should rest and keep warm, and fluid intake should be kept up. Evacuation might be necessary.

### *Dislocations*

The symptoms of dislocations are visible deformity and severe pain. It is important to get skilled help quickly, because the dislocated joint will soon begin to swell. Do not attempt to push it back into place unless you are medically trained, as this can damage blood vessels and nerves, or cause fractures. Wrap the joint in wet cloths, keep it still (use splints if necessary) and get the injured person to a doctor as soon as you can.

### *Ear Infections*

Earache can be treated with an oily, antiseptic, analgesic eardrop such as Aurone. Middle ear infections are far more serious and can affect your balance. If you are more than 12 hours away from help and the person has a fever, a wide-spectrum oral antibiotic should be taken.

Foreign bodies, such as insects, can usually be floated out with warm water or oil. Heat a little in a teaspoon (testing a drop on the back of your hand so it is not too hot), pour into the ear and leave for five minutes before letting it run out. Take care not to push an object deeper into the ear in an attempt to get it out, and do not try to get a smooth, hard object out as you are more than likely to push it further in.

### *Exhaustion*

Avoid exhaustion by not overexerting yourself, eating trail snacks between meals and keeping up your water intake. If the condition does set in, the patient should be allowed to rest at a comfortable temperature and given water and food with a high glucose content.

### *Eye Injuries or Infections*

Foreign bodies should only be removed if you are able to take them out easily. Do not attempt to remove any object that is partially embedded in the eyeball. In such cases cover the eye with a sterile pad held on with a plaster or a loose bandage, and evacuate the patient. Care should be taken to ensure that the pad does not press onto a protruding object.

In most cases, however, natural watering of the eye will dislodge and wash away small objects. Bring the upper eyelid down over the lower lid for a second or two — the tears caused may wash the object away. If this does not have the desired effect, try to flush the object out with cooled boiled water to which a teaspoon of salt per litre of water has been added. Lie the person down and gently pour water into the inner corner of the eye. Carefully lift the lid by the lashes and let the water run over the eyeball. Blinking during irrigation might help. As a last resort you might try lifting the object out with the corner of a piece of moist sterile gauze.

Eye infections should be treated with a sulphacetimide eye ointment and covered with a light bandage.

### *Fever*

Normal human oral temperature is 37 °C. A temperature which drops below 35 °C should be regarded as serious, up to 39 °C means a mild fever, and over 40 °C indicates a high fever. The patient will require rest and a large fluid intake. Cool him down by removing any hot clothes or bedding, wiping him with a wet cloth and fanning him; give him aspirin too. If there is no obvious cause and the fever persists, evacuation should seriously be considered. (See also Malaria, page 29.)

### *Heat Exhaustion*

Heat exhaustion is caused by either exposure to a hot environment or overheating as a result of physical exertion. Symptoms are nausea, dizziness, thirst, profuse sweating and headache. Lay the victim in a cool, shady place with his feet higher than his head, loosen his clothing and cover him lightly. Administer frequent doses of isotonic Game.

### Heat Stroke or Sunstroke

Heat stroke is more serious than heat exhaustion as it affects the nervous centre that controls your body temperature. This condition can set in very rapidly, and occurs as a result of failure of the sweating process and other body heat regulatory mechanisms.

Symptoms are an excessively high body temperature, dry red skin, headache, irrational behaviour, shivering, cramps, dilated pupils, and, finally, collapse and unconsciousness. Cool the patient down immediately by putting him in the shade, taking off tight clothing, pouring water over him or wiping him down with wet cloths, and fanning him. If he is conscious, give him fast-acting aspirin (eg Codis) and plenty to drink. Get medical help as quickly as you can.

### Hypothermia

Hypothermia is the lowering of the body's core temperature to the point where the heat lost exceeds the heat gained. It is usually a result of a combination of unfavourable weather, inadequate food intake and unsuitable clothing, as well as overexertion. One or more of the following symptoms may be present: weakness, slowing of pace, shivering, lack of coordination, irrationality, blue skin colour, decreased heart and respiratory rate, dilated pupils and unconsciousness.

It is most important to prevent further heat loss by keeping the patient warm. Find or erect the best possible shelter. Remove wet clothing and immediately replace with warm, dry clothes. The patient should then be zipped into a pre-warmed sleeping-bag, or warmed up between two people, well covered with sleeping-bags. If the patient is able to eat, warm food and drinks (sugar/glucose water, chocolate and soup) should be taken. No alcohol, coffee or any stimulants must be given. Do not rub the victim to restore circulation, or put him near a fire — direct heat is dangerous.

No further exertion should be encouraged as this uses up essential energy.

### Lung and Throat Infections

A sore throat without fever can be treated by gargling with salt water or an antiseptic solution, or sucking throat lozenges. A sore throat with fever may require the administration of antibiotics and the patient should be kept warm and given rest.

Bronchitis can be serious and the patient will need rest, warmth and a wide-spectrum antibiotic. If fever persists the patient should be evacuated.

### Nosebleeds

Changes in altitude, increased activity and cold temperatures are the main causes of nosebleeds. Fortunately, most nosebleeds are minor and bleeding can be stopped by applying direct pressure firmly against the nostril or pinching the nose for 5 or 10 minutes. If bleeding persists, pack the nostril with gauze or cotton wool, pinch for 10 more minutes, then leave the dressing in for two hours or so. Remove it carefully. Do not blow your nose after a nosebleed for at least four hours.

### Pain

Treat general pain with the pain killer in your first aid kit, taken with lots of fluid. If the pain persists and there is no obvious cause, seek medical attention.

### Snakebite

This is a subject which usually evokes much discussion, but fortunately the chances of being bitten by a snake are extremely small. Only about 16 of the 160-odd South African snake species are deadly and the number of deaths resulting from snakebite is minimal compared to other unnatural causes.

Once again, it is best to take preventive action:

- Keep your eyes open, especially where the path is overgrown. If you are carrying a stick, swish it in the grass in front of you.
- Wear stout walking shoes or boots and trousers when backpacking off the beaten track — about 75 per cent of all bites are inflicted on the leg, ankle, foot and toe.

- Do not turn over logs or rocks; step onto them, not over them. Look under and around a log or rock before you sit down on it.
- Look before you place your hand behind a rock — about 15 per cent of snakebites are inflicted on the hand and finger.

Except in unusual circumstances, the life of a snakebite victim will seldom be in immediate danger. The venom of the puff adder, which is responsible for most bites, is seldom life-threatening within 10 hours of the bite, while cobra bites take about two to four hours to display distressing symptoms. Although mamba bites can seriously affect breathing within one to two hours, there is no question of dying within five minutes as is popularly believed.

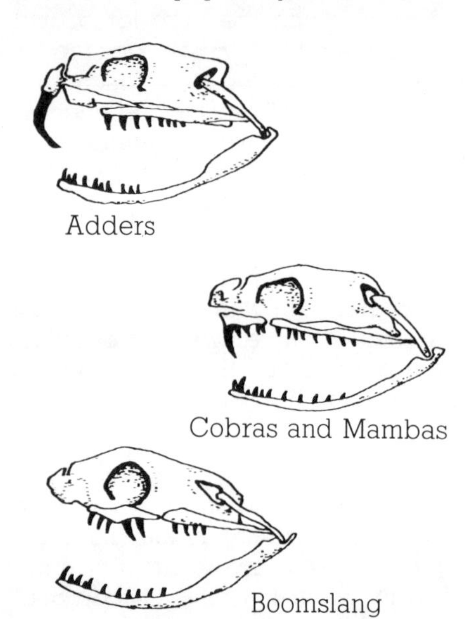


*Skulls of the three poisonous snake groups showing position of fangs*

In the event of a snakebite the following first aid treatment must be given:

- Immediately apply firm finger pressure above the bite. It is not advisable to try and kill the snake as a second person may be bitten.
- Immobilise the victim, as any unnecessary movement will increase the heart rate and consequently the spread of the venom. Keep the bite below heart level.
- If the bite is from a mamba or a cobra and on a limb, apply a crêpe bandage or torn strips of cloth firmly (but not too tightly) from just above the bite to the top of the limb. **Do not use a tourniquet.** Cold wet cloths (ice would be ideal) applied over the bite will further slow down the action of the poison.
- If the bite is from an adder, a viper or a boomslang, **do not bandage or use a tourniquet.** Immobilise the victim and apply cold water or cold wet cloths over the bite.
  — **Antivenin should not be used unless by a medically trained person.**
  — **Do not cut the skin, as blood vessels or nerves may be severed.**
  — **Do not try to suck the poison out.**
- Reassure the victim and administer a painkiller if necessary. Do not allow intake of alcohol.
- Two members of the party should be sent to summon help and to alert the nearest doctor or hospital.
- If the snake is not identified, clean the affected area and wait 10-15 minutes to see if symptoms develop. If no symptoms develop, keep the victim immobilised and under observation for two to three hours.
- If attacked by a spitting snake (cobra or rinkhals) wash the eyes out immediately with plenty of water, for at least 10 minutes. Lift the eyelids up so that water washes under them too. Further treatment should not be necessary, but if there is any irritation, see a doctor. Do *not* attempt to wash the eyes out with diluted antivenin.

### *Sprains and Strains*

Sprains are caused by either tearing or stretching ligaments or a separation of muscle tendon from the bone and are most common in the ankle, wrist, knee and shoulder. The symptoms are extreme pain and a rapid and severe swelling which is caused by fluid or blood accumulating in the tissues. Elevate the injured limb and lightly apply cold water or wet cloths. This will reduce swelling and also minimise deep bleeding. If you are skilled, bind the joint with a long crêpe bandage or clingwrap. Give a painkiller if the pain is severe. Keep the sprained joint as still as possible in a resting position. After 24 hours, change over to heat treatment: warm the sprained joint by the fire or in the sun, or soak it in hot water three or four times a day. It is often difficult to differentiate between a sprain and a fracture and if pain persists, splint the affected limb and seek medical help. Other signs of fractures are a floppy foot or hand, or trouble moving the fingers or toes.

Strains are caused by overextending or tearing muscular fibre and are usually less serious than sprains. Treat as for sprains.

### *Tickbites*

Do not pull ticks off your skin, as they may leave their heads behind. You can make them fall off by pouring on a little paraffin or covering them with Vaseline or holding a lighted cigarette near them.

## Three Hazards of Backpacking in Southern Africa

### *Malaria*

A bite by an infected *Anopheles* mosquito can transmit microscopic blood parasites, resulting in malaria.

By referring to the map below you will note that there are certain areas where there is always the risk of contracting malaria (endemic areas), and areas where there is usually only a risk during summer (epidemic areas). However, it is advisable to take anti-malaria precautions when visiting both these areas, even if you are only passing through.

Consult your doctor or chemist at least a week before entering the area as to which brand of preventive tablet should be taken. This is necessary as the medication changes from time to time as the mosquitoes become immune to certain medication.

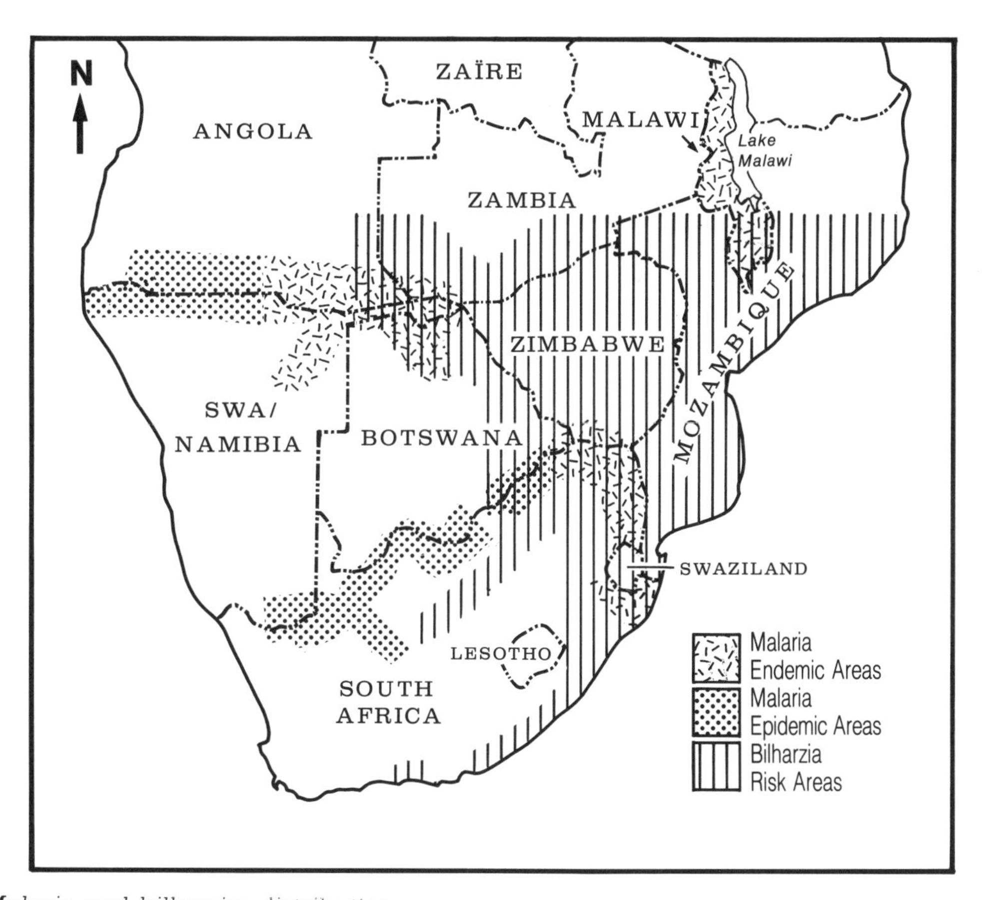


*Malaria and bilharzia: distribution*

Read the instructions carefully with regard to how long in advance, how often and how long after leaving the area the course should be continued.

In the early stages malaria is easily cured, so it is essential to consult a doctor immediately should you develop any symptoms. These are vomiting, general body ache and severe fever.

As mosquito bites are normally unpleasant, take a few simple measures to make walking in the bush more bearable. After sunset wear long trousers and long-sleeved shirts. Light cotton clothing serves this purpose well in summer, and is not too hot. Apply mosquito repellent to bare areas but remember to reapply every two to three hours as it does evaporate.

### *Bilharzia*

Bilharzia is a common disease in large parts of the Far East, South America and Africa and is caused by a parasite which attacks the intestines, bladder and other organs of its mammalian hosts, which are humans, stock and game.

During its life-span the bilharzia parasite or schistosome undergoes a complicated life cycle. The eggs are dispersed by either human or animal faeces, or are passed out in urine. When they come into contact with water they hatch, releasing miracidia. Soon after hatching, the miracidia penetrate the soft parts of their snail hosts, seeking them out by moving with the flow of the water or by self propulsion. However, only certain snail species act as hosts.

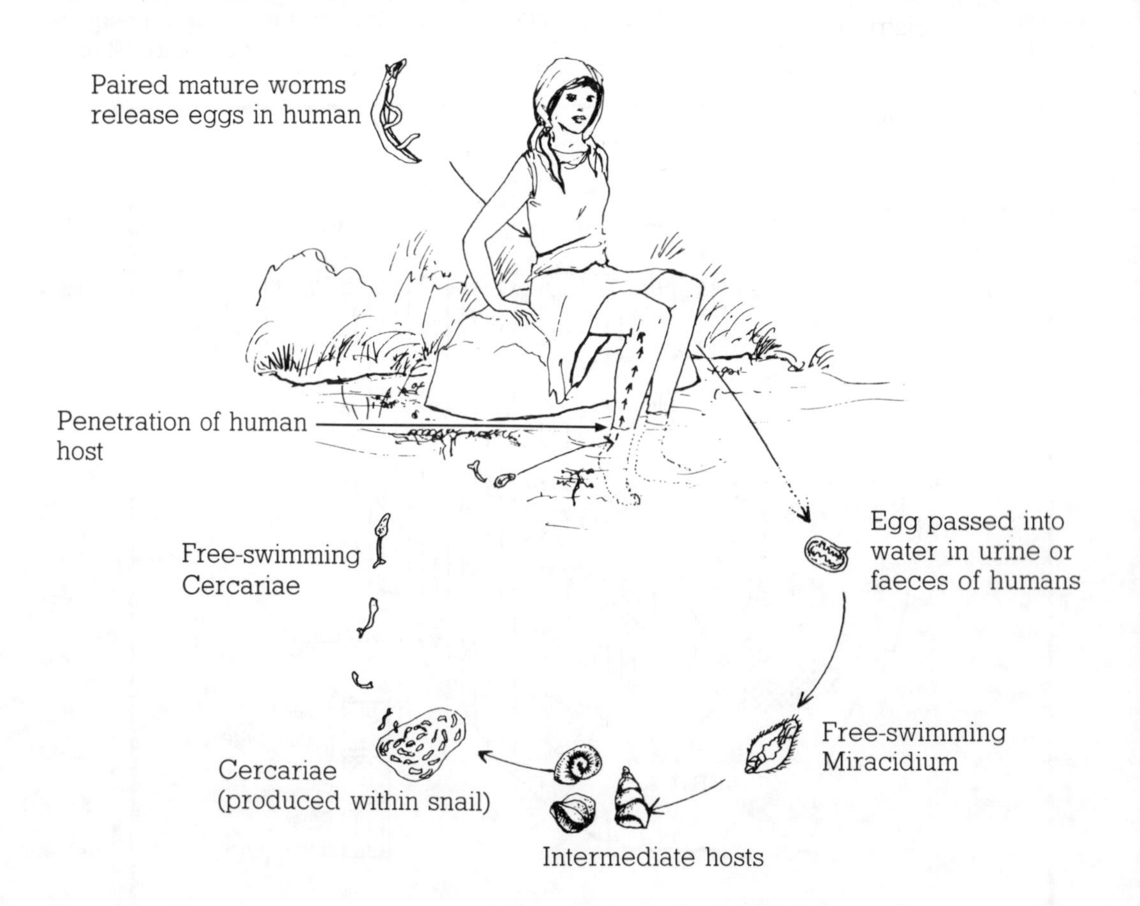


*Simplified life-cycle of the bilharzia parasite*

The development stage of the bilharzia parasite within the snail host takes about four to five weeks, and in summer thousands of cercariae are released daily between 10h00 and 14h00. This is the infective stage for man and animal and the mobile cercariae seek out their human and animal hosts when they enter the water. The skin of the mammalian host is penetrated and on reaching maturity the cercariae start a new cycle by laying eggs in the blood vessels of the bladder or the gut.

Any fresh water body, especially around the edges of quiet pools, dams, streams and irrigation canals, could contain snail hosts. They attach themselves to water-lilies and other vegetation, the undersurface of stones and dead wood. Snail hosts are more likely to occur in open pools which are exposed to the sun, and in water shallower than 1,5 m. Refer to the map on page 29 for the present distribution of bilharzia in Southern Africa.

Bilharzia does not occur in Lake Malawi and is almost non-existent in mountain streams and rivers above 1 200 m in altitude because of the unsuitability of fast-flowing water as a snail habitat. It is also less likely to be found in any water body mixed with sea water.

Human habitation is usually associated with bilharzia, so avoid drinking, swimming or washing in water downstream from any human settlement. If bilharzia is suspected, it is wise to be cautious and boil water for at least five minutes before drinking. This will also prevent infections such as cholera and typhoid. Water temperatures of 0 °C for three to four nights are also sufficient to kill snail hosts, while water temperatures of over 28 °C for several days are also poorly tolerated by snails.

The symptoms of bilharzia do not normally appear immediately. However, any sign of blood in urine or faeces should be reported to a doctor as soon as possible.

### *Sleeping Sickness or Trypanosomiasis*

Sleeping sickness is caused by a parasite transmitted to man by the bite of an infected tsetse fly. The fly is a little larger than the common house fly, grey with scissor-like wings and difficult to swat because of its hard, tough body. Livestock is also susceptible to the disease, known as *nagana,* but game is immune, although certain species such as warthog, buffalo, bushbuck and kudu are important host species.

The disease is limited to the Okavango Delta in Botswana, the Caprivi Strip in Namibia, south-east Angola, Zimbabwe and Central Africa. Eradication campaigns against tsetse fly have taken place, especially in the Okavango Delta, minimising your chances of being bitten. A sharp pain will indicate a bite, but this does not necessarily result in the disease being transmitted. If the bite becomes sore or inflamed, a doctor should be consulted as soon as possible and a blood sample taken. Other symptoms include swelling of the lymph glands and a severe headache.

Bites can be prevented by wearing long sleeves and trousers in dull colours. The flies are thought to be attracted to brightly coloured floral and check patterns and apparently dislike light blue clothing. Insect repellent can be applied to exposed skin.

# Trail Terminology

The proliferation of hiking, backpacking and guided wilderness trails since the opening of the Fanie Botha Hiking Trail in 1973 has unfortunately brought about a bewildering array of terms. The term 'wandelpad', for instance, conjures up visions of an easy ramble, and many hikers have had their illusions shattered when the trail has turned out to be far more strenuous than that. The term, meaning hiking trail, is variously used for overnight hiking trails, short day walks and guided wilderness trails. Add to this terms such as backpacking trail, nature trail, nature walk, walk and interpretative trail, and most hikers and backpackers are completely in the dark as to what is meant. This section is intended to clear up the confusion and define the terms commonly used in hiking and backpacking. Definitions are based on Volume 2 of the *National Outdoor Recreational Plan: Outdoor Recreation Glossary*, published by the Department of Environment Affairs (1979).

### Backpacking Trail (Veldstap(pad) or Pakstap)

Backpacking trails follow routes where no designated trails exist or where trails are not necessarily followed. Routes can be management paths, footpaths between villages and bridle paths (eg in Lesotho), or animal tracks. No overnight facilities are provided and backpackers sleep in caves or other natural shelters, in the open or in their own tents. All provisions, such as equipment and food, are carried by the backpacker.

In South Africa backpacking is primarily undertaken in proclaimed wilderness areas. Although some areas have overnight huts (eg Cederberg) and all have footpaths, they are generally not marked (as with hiking trails). In other words, distances are not indicated and there are no route markers or footprints indicating the route, swimming places and/or drinking water. Unlike most hiking trails, for which comprehensive trail maps are published, there are no such maps for backpacking trails, with the exception of the Cederberg and Drakensberg wilderness areas. It is essential, therefore, to use the standard 1:50 000 topographical maps published by the respective authorities in conjunction with the sketch map usually issued by the relevant authority.

### (Guided) Wilderness Trails (Begeleide Wildernisstaptoer)

Unlike hiking and backpacking trails which are self-guided and where you create your own experiences, these trails are conducted under the supervision of an armed ranger in natural and wild areas such as national parks and game reserves.

*Guided wilderness trails differ markedly from hiking and backpacking trails in respect of the following:*

- they are not confined to specific demarcated routes;
- an expert guide is in charge of the group and will share his knowledge of the area with you. The length of each day's walk depends on factors such as the physical condition of the group, age and climate;
- walks are undertaken from a central base camp to which trailists return each day.

At the same time guided wilderness trails should not be confused with game viewing tours. Often far less game is encountered on foot than you would see from the comfort of your car, as animals will tolerate a vehicle at much closer range than a person on foot. In addition, you cannot approach dangerous animals too closely on foot. Game viewing is therefore only one aspect of a guided wilderness trail and by no means the aim of the trail.

*See pages 34 to 39 (Who's in Charge) for the position of proclaimed wilderness areas as opposed to wilderness areas such as those set aside by the Natal Parks Board and in the Kruger National Park.*

**Hiking Trail (Voetslaanpad)**

A continuous, well-defined marked route through a natural or manmade environment, on which the user carries his essential overnight gear and food in a backpack. Overnight accommodation ranging from basic shelters to converted houses and train coaches is provided at the end of each day's hiking. Facilities at overnight stops usually include bunk-beds with mattresses, water, toilet facilities and in some instances fireplaces and firewood.

Ideally the huts are situated well away from built-up areas but this is not always possible.

**Interpretative Trail (Vertolkingspaadjie)**

A short circular trail (usually not more than 2 km) on which the emphasis is on education and interpretation of the environment. A comprehensive booklet is supplied to guide you along the route, and at intervals along the route numbered markers are used to draw your attention to interesting features which are explained in the booklet. Interpretative trails often link up with displays in visitors' centres.

**Mountaineering (Bergklim)**

Although the term is a comprehensive one, including rock climbing, backpacking, hiking and rambling, it is normally associated with the climbing of a mountain or mountain peak with the purpose of reaching the top, by means of ropes, pitons and other specialised equipment.

**Nature Walk (Wandelpad)/Nature Trail (Natuurpaadjie)**

A route planned to link natural features of interest, along which some form of interpretation is provided to explain basic natural history, conservation and management principles of these features. It is sometimes also referred to simply as a Trail (eg Bushman's River Trail [Boesmansrivier*trek*]) or Walk (eg Elephant Walk). Usually a circular route varying in length, but not exceeding one day.

# Who's in charge

Backpackers and trailists are often confused as to where to make reservations and enquiries, as there is no centralised body responsible for the control and management of areas where backpacking and guided wilderness trails are undertaken. These areas are under the control of various conservation bodies and these will be discussed in this section. Although hiking trails fall outside the scope of this book, they are also dealt with in this chapter to give a better perspective of trailing opportunities in Southern Africa.

**The Provincial Administrations**

Although the various provincial administrations have been responsible for nature conservation in their respective provinces for some time, certain non-commercial activities were also undertaken by the Forestry Branch of the Department of Environment Affairs. Following a Cabinet decision taken in 1985 to transfer certain executive functions to second tier governments, the conservation functions of the Forestry Branch were transferred to the various provincial administrations on 1 December 1986. In Natal these functions were not transferred to the Natal Parks Board, which fulfils the conservation functions in that province, because of administrative technicalities which arose from the board's non-government status, but to the provincial administration.

The functions transferred include control and management of mountain catchment areas, nature reserves, proclaimed wilderness areas and driftsand reclamation areas. In the Cape Province, for example, the amalgamation of the conservation functions of the Forestry Branch and the Marine Development Branch of the Department of Environment Affairs with the existing functions of the Department of Nature and Environmental Conservation of the Cape Provincial Administration resulted in the creation of the largest conservation body in South Africa. Some 784 000 ha of state forests, nature reserves and proclaimed wilderness areas, as well as 590 000 ha of mountain catchment areas, were transferred to the Department of Nature and Environmental Conservation of the Cape as a result of this policy.

*At the time of writing (1988) administrative procedures have not yet been completed and information such as the names of wilderness areas/nature reserves, the title of the person to whom enquiries should be addressed (eg officer-in-charge, forester) and the addresses for reservations of areas affected could change.*

**Wilderness Areas**

A wilderness area has been defined as '... an area where the earth and its community of life are untrammelled by man, where man himself is a visitor who does not remain ... land retaining its primeval character and influence, without permanent improvements or human habitation ... and which generally appears to have been effected, primarily by the forces of nature, with the imprints of man's work substantially unnoticeable: has outstanding opportunities for solitude or a primitive and unconfined type of recreation; ... is of sufficient size as to make practicable its preservation and use in an unimpaired condition and may also contain ecological, geological, or other features of scientific, educational, scenic or historical value.'[1]

Not all areas referred to as wilderness areas in South Africa enjoy legal status.

1 Van Zyl, P.H.S. 1972. The United States Forest Service: A Public Agency Involved in Administering Wildernesses. Unpublished report, Yale University.

Although the wilderness principles and ideals are essentially the same for all wilderness areas, note should be taken of this state of affairs to understand the concept of wilderness areas in the South African context. Firstly there are those wilderness areas which have been established in terms of an Act of Parliament and therefore enjoy a legal status. These areas were managed by the Forestry Branch until 1 December 1986, when control was transferred to the various provincial administrations. Provision for the establishment of proclaimed wilderness areas was made when the State President signed the Forest Amendment Act, No 37 of 1971, which empowered the Minister of Forestry to set aside any state forest or portion thereof as a wilderness area for the preservation of forests and natural scenery. These areas are protected against encroachment in terms of a provision which requires the sanction of Parliament for any developments, eg the construction of roads and the erection of powerlines. Furthermore, before proclaiming a wilderness area it is necessary to obtain the recommendation of the National Monuments Council and to consult the council in the management of the area. Proclaimed wilderness areas are set aside for three reasons:

- their *scientific* value as natural ecosystems unchanged by civilisation;
- their *aesthetic* value as areas unspoilt by roads, railways and powerlines; and
- their *recreational* and *spiritual* value.

Three criteria are considered before proclaiming a wilderness area:

- It must be an intrinsically wild area uninhabited by man. Although there are few areas which have not been adversely affected by man, it must be possible to rehabilitate the area.
- It must be at least 1 000 ha in size to give visitors a feeling of isolation and to be representative of an ecosystem.
- It must give the general impression that the area has resulted from the combined effects of natural forces.

The following proclaimed wilderness areas are currently controlled and managed by the conservation division of the various provincial administrations:

*Cape:* Boosmansbos, Cederberg, Groendal, Groot-Winterhoek.
*Natal:* Mdedelelo, Mkhomazi, Mzimkulu and Ntendeka.
*Transvaal:* Wolkberg.

### *General Conditions Applicable to Proclaimed Wilderness Areas*

The following general conditions applied to wilderness areas previously managed by the Forestry Branch. Under the management of the provincial conservation divisions certain changes could be effected.

- The total number of visitors is restricted in proportion to the size of the area.
- The maximum group size is either 10 or 12 people, depending on the area.
- Depending on the maximum group size, at least one adult must accompany each group of 9 to 11 persons under the age of 18.
- No fires are permitted and backpackers should carry backpacking stoves.
- No firearms are allowed.
- No pets are allowed in a proclaimed wilderness area or at a camp or picnic area.
- No motor vehicles, power bikes or other mechanical vehicles are permitted.
- Littering is a serious offence. All litter (including cigarette butts) must be carried out.
- Swimming in streams is permitted, but the use of soap in streams is strictly prohibited.
- Plants, trees, animals and rocks may not be damaged or disturbed in any way. The picking of flowers is strictly prohibited.
- No pack or riding animals are permitted.

Apart from these general conditions, most proclaimed wilderness areas also have specific conditions such as entry points, points where vehicles must be left, etc.

The term 'wilderness area' is also used to refer to several other unspoilt, primitive areas which do not enjoy the legal status of those areas proclaimed in terms of the Forest Act. In South Africa the first wilderness area was created as early as 1958 when the Natal Parks Board set aside

12 500 ha as a wilderness in the Umfolozi Game Reserve in Zululand. The Board also pioneered the concept of guided wilderness trails and conducted the first such trail in March 1959 in the reserve. The concept of wilderness areas was subsequently expanded to other Natal reserves and adopted by other conservation bodies such as the National Parks Board. These areas are in every respect as unspoilt and scenic as those areas proclaimed under the Forest Act.

**Hiking Trails**

In the Cape Province a number of hiking trails which were previously managed by the Forestry Branch were transferred to the Department of Nature and Environmental Conservation of the CPA. These trails are:

- Alexandria -- eastern Cape
- Boland: Section Hottentots-Holland -- western Cape
- Boland: Section Limietberg -- western Cape
- Swellendam -- western Cape

Several hiking trails have been established in provincial nature reserves in the Transvaal by the Department of Nature Conservation in that province.

In Natal, the Drakensberg Hiking Trail: Section Giant's Cup was transferred from the Forestry Branch to the Natal Provincial Administration.

Hiking trails in Southern Africa are listed on pages 264 to 268. A brief outline of each trail and where to make reservations are given.

**Natal Parks Board**

Natal is the only province where the nature conservation function is carried out by a board. The Natal Parks Board (Natal Parks, Game and Fish Preservation Board) was established in 1947 in terms of Section 4(1) of the Natal Parks, Game and Fish Preservation Ordinance, No 35 of 1947 as a statutory body.

Prior to the establishment of the Board, the responsibility for nature conservation in Natal was shared by the Natal Fisheries Board (1916), the Inland Fisheries Board (1935) and the Zululand Game Reserves and Parks Board (1939). However, owing to the farsightedness of a former Administrator of Natal (1945/46), Douglas Mitchell, the Board came into being on 1 December 1947 and assumed control of all aspects of conservation and public resorts in the province.

The Board's aim in conservation is to promote the wise use of natural resources in perpetuity, and to prevent degradation of the environment. To achieve its stated aim, the Board is guided by five important activities:

- the acquisition and safeguarding of land for nature reserves;
- the proper management of such land;
- provision of facilities to enable people to use and appreciate reserves;
- encouragement of the wise use of wild flora and fauna outside reserves;
- the promotion of public awareness of the need for conservation in its broadest sense.

The Board consists of up to 12 people appointed by the Administrator. Funds are obtained by way of an annual subsidy from the Natal Provincial Administration as well as from revenue generated by its own activities.

When the Board was established there were 10 reserves in the province, including Hluhluwe, Umfolozi and St Lucia, which were proclaimed in 1897 and are, therefore, among the oldest existing game conservation areas in Africa. At present the Board manages some 55 areas in Natal, covering more than 393 979 ha.

The Board pioneered the concept of setting aside wilderness areas and established the first guided wilderness trails in South Africa. At present the Board manages guided wilderness trails on foot in the Umfolozi, St Lucia and Mkuzi game reserves and the Itala Nature Reserve, as well as trails on horseback in the Giant's Castle Game Reserve. In addition to the large number of short walks and nature trails in areas under its control, the Board also administers two hiking trails, the Mziki Hiking Trail in the Eastern Shores Nature Reserve and the Dugandlovu Hiking Trail in False Bay Park.

Among the Board's most notable achievements is the successful conservation of the white (square-lipped) rhinoceros. However, it has also received international recognition for its marine turtle and crocodile research and breeding programmes.

During 1984/85, 1 763 686 day visitors and 97 648 overnight visitors visited the Board's parks, game and nature reserves and public resorts. The Board has a total staff of 3 042, including 1 724 conservation and research staff. The annual budget exceeds R40 million.

### The National Parks Board

South Africa's first National Park, the Kruger National Park, came into being when the Minister of Lands, P G W Grobler, tabled the Act on National Parks in Parliament on 31 May 1926. The bill was enthusiastically passed by both houses of Parliament and the first board meeting was held in Pretoria on 16 September 1926. Mr Grobler attended this historic occasion which was held under the chairmanship of W J C (Jack) Brebner. Although the Act made provisions for the proclamation of other national parks, its main objective was to proclaim the consolidated Sabie and Shingwedzi reserves a national park, namely the Kruger National Park.

In 1983 the National Parks Act was amended to make provisions for 'contractual parks'. Whereas national parks before the Act were inviolate, the amendment made it possible to include suitable, privately owned or state-owned land adjacent to a national park into a larger area. The amendment allows for the multi-functional utilisation of 'contractual parks' and provides, for example, for the retention of mineral rights and the continuation of farming in these 'buffer areas'. The first contractual park came into being in August 1987 when the Oude Post Nature Reserve became part of the Langebaan National Park.

In another development in 1983 responsibility for the administration of the Lake Areas Development Act was transferred to the National Parks Board and management of the Wilderness Lakes Area passed into the hands of the Board. The name was changed to the Wilderness National Lake Area in 1986 and in November the following year the status of the area was raised to that of a national park.

At present the Board consists of 12 members, comprising seven members appointed by the State President and five *ex officio* members – the administrators of the four provinces and one member nominated by the Wildlife Society of Southern Africa.

To date (June 1988) 15 more national parks and one national lake area have been proclaimed and at present the Board administers the national parks and national lake area listed on page 39.

| Park | Region | Ha | Year Proclaimed |
|---|---|---|---|
| Kruger National Park | Eastern Transvaal | 1 948 528 | 1926 |
| Kalahari Gemsbok National Park | North-western Cape | 959 103 | 1931 |
| Addo Elephant National Park | Eastern Cape | 8 596 | 1931 |
| Bontebok National Park | South-western Cape | 2 786 | 1931 |
| Mountain Zebra National Park | Cape midlands | 6 536 | 1937 |
| Golden Gate Highlands National Park | North-eastern Free State | 6 241 | 1963 |
| Tsitsikamma Coastal National Park[2] | Southern Cape | 2 840 | 1964 |
| Tsitsikamma Forest National Park | Southern Cape | 478 | 1964 |
| Augrabies Falls National Park | North-western Cape | 9 415 | 1966 |
| Groenkloof National Park[3] | Central Transvaal | 6,76 | 1968 |

2 In addition to a land area of 2 840 ha, the Tsitsikamma Coastal National Park also extends 5 km offshore. In December 1987 the 2 533 ha De Vasselot Nature Reserve was proclaimed part of the Tsitsikamma Forest and Coastal National Park.

3 In 1965 the Pretoria City Council donated part of the Bronberg to the National Parks Board to erect its head office there.

| Park | Region | Ha | Year Proclaimed |
|---|---|---|---|
| Karoo National Park | Karoo | 27 011 | 1979 |
| Zuurberg National Park | Eastern Cape | 20 777 | 1985 |
| Langebaan National Park | Cape west coast | 6 000 | 1985 |
| Knysna National Lake Area | Southern Cape | ± 15 000 | 1985 |
| Vaalbos National Park | North-western Cape | 22 696 | 1986 |
| Tankwa Karoo National Park | North-western Cape | 27 063 | 1986 |
| Wilderness National Park | Southern Cape | 10 000 | 1987 |

Four guided wilderness trails are conducted in the Kruger National Park, while five hiking trails have been established in other national parks, namely the Klipspringer (Augrabies Falls Park), Springbok (Karoo Park), Rhebok (Golden Gate Highlands Park), Mountain Zebra (Mountain Zebra Park) and the Otter (Tsitsikamma Coastal Park). The Otter Hiking Trail was the first official hiking trail in South Africa. In addition, there are several short walks and nature trails in national parks.

### The Forestry Branch of the Department of Environment Affairs

As pointed out earlier, the conservation functions of the Forestry Branch in areas other than those with extensive indigenous forests and plantations, ie water catchment areas, wilderness areas and driftsand reclamation areas, have been transferred to the various provincial conservation authorities. Consequently, several hiking trails which were established in such areas by the Department of Forestry, now known as the Forestry Branch, have been taken over by the provincial conservation authorities. However, the Forestry Branch still administers a number of hiking trails in areas under its jurisdiction. At present (March 1988) the following hiking trails are still managed by the various regional offices of the Forestry Branch (listed alphabetically):

Blyderivierspoort Eastern Transvaal
Fanie Botha Eastern Transvaal
Kaapsche Hoop Southern Transvaal
Kologha Eastern Cape
Magoebaskloof: Section Dokolewa
  Northern Transvaal
Magoebaskloof: Section Grootbosch
  Northern Transvaal
Ngele Southern Natal
Outeniqua Southern Cape
Prospector's Eastern Transvaal
Soutpansberg: Section Hanglip
  Northern Transvaal
Soutpansberg: Section Entabeni
  Northern Transvaal
Tsitsikamma Southern Cape

The possibility of establishing a network of hiking trails stretching from the Soutpansberg in the north to the Cederberg in the western Cape was first mooted by a former Minister of Forestry, Mr S P Botha, in 1973 after the opening of the first section of the Eastern Transvaal Trail (renamed the Fanie Botha Trail) near Sabie.

Two years earlier the first positive step had been taken towards establishing something similar to the American Appalachian trail system in South Africa. Following a world conference on forestry in America in 1971, the former Chief of Silvicultural Services of the then Department of Forestry, Danie Ackerman, instructed an official of the Department studying for his Master's degree at Yale Forestry School, Paul van Zyl, to examine the Appalachian trail system with a view to establishing a similar system in South African state forests.

In 1975 the Forest Act was amended to make provision for, amongst others, a National Hiking Way Board, a National Hiking Way System and a National Hiking Way Fund. The Board was charged with the management of the National Hiking Way System and the maintenance of those trails. The opening of a new section is recommended by the Board on the grounds of priorities determined by recreational needs and the natural characteristics of the environment. Eight regional advisory committees have been established to date to assist the Board with the planning, construction, management and maintenance of the system on a local basis.

The Board consists of representatives of state departments, the various provincial conservation authorities, the National Parks Board, the South African Agricultural Union, and the Mountain Club of South Africa, as well as representatives of major recreational and youth organisations. It functions under the auspices of the Forestry Branch of the Department of Environment Affairs.

### Guided Wilderness and Hiking Trails Managed by Private Enterprise and Town Councils

In addition to the authorities discussed earlier, guided wilderness trails are also conducted by the **Wilderness Leadership School,** a non-profit environmental education body. Some town councils (eg Fouriesburg and Waterval Boven) as well as private landowners have also established hiking trails (eg Holkrans and Korannaberg hiking trails).

### Backpacking and Guided Wilderness and Hiking Trails in other Southern and Central African Countries

#### *SWA/Namibia*

The **Department of Agriculture and Nature Conservation of SWA/Namibia** has established two guided wilderness trails, a backpacking trail in the Fish River Canyon and a hiking trail in the Naukluft Mountains.

#### *Malawi*

The Mulanje Mountain in Malawi lends itself to numerous backpacking excursions. The mountain is managed by the **Department of Forestry of Malawi's Ministry of Forestry and Natural Resources.** Backpacking and guided wilderness trails in Malawi's national parks are controlled by Malawi's **Department of National Parks and Wildlife.**

#### *Botswana*

Botswana's Okavango Delta does not lend itself to backpacking, but one can either join a guided wilderness trail arranged by a safari company or explore the waterways of the Delta in a mokoro (dugout canoe). The Moremi Wildlife Reserve, a 1 800 km$^2$ conservation area in the Delta, is administered by the **Department of Wildlife and National Parks of Botswana.**

#### *Ciskei*

The Ciskei offers several hiking options ranging from the coast to the mountains, as well as a guided trail. These trails are managed by either the **Ciskei Department of Wildlife Resources and Parks** or the **Ciskei Department of Forestry.**

#### *Transkei*

Hiking trails have been laid out along the entire length of the Transkei Wild Coast by the **Nature Conservation Section of the Transkei Department of Agriculture and Forestry.**

#### *Lesotho*

No formal hiking or backpacking trails have been established in Lesotho. It is, however, possible to backpack in the Sehlabathebe National Park in south-east Lesotho. The park falls under the **National Parks Division of Lesotho's Ministry of Agriculture.** In addition, several guided pony trekking expeditions are arranged by the **Lesotho Tourist Board** and **Basotho Pony Trekking.**

# Part 2
# South West Africa/Namibia

# 1 Waterberg Guided Wilderness Trail

SWA/Namibia is generally thought of as an arid country, and yet the Waterberg Guided Wilderness Trail is conducted in well-watered and relatively lushly vegetated surroundings, which are the habitat of several uncommon game and bird species. Fascinating sandstone formations, sheer cliffs and numerous springs at the base of the cliffs are other attractions of this unique area.

### Location

The Waterberg Guided Wilderness Trail is conducted in the Waterberg Plateau Park east of Otjiwarongo. The park is reached by turning off the B1 main road, 29 km south of Otjiwarongo, onto route 101 (C37) to Okakarara. You continue along this road for about 44 km before turning left onto the D2512. The park gate is reached 27 km on.

### Distance and Classification

Distances covered depend on the fitness of the group, but do not exceed 15 km a day. A+ grade

### Permits

Groups must consist of a minimum of six and a maximum of eight people. Written reservations can be made 18 months in advance and are held on file and confirmed 11 months before the trail date. Applications must be addressed to The Director, Direc-

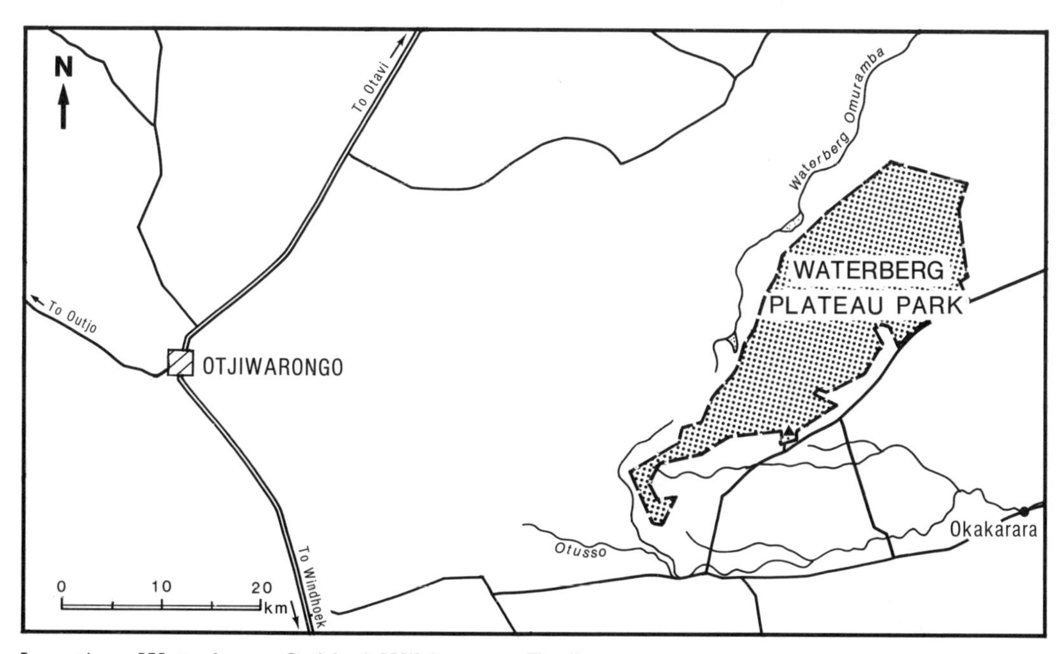


*Location: Waterberg Guided Wilderness Trail*

torate of Nature Conservation and Recreation Resorts, Private Bag 13267, Windhoek 9000, SWA/Namibia, Telephone (061) 36975. Should you cancel, the trail fee is not refundable.

### Maps

As no set trails are followed, a topographical trail map is of little value other than for orientation. The area is covered by 1:50 000 topographical map numbers 2017AC, 2017AD and 2017CA, obtainable from the Surveyor-General, Department of Justice, Private Bag 13182, Windhoek 9000, SWA/Namibia.

### Climate

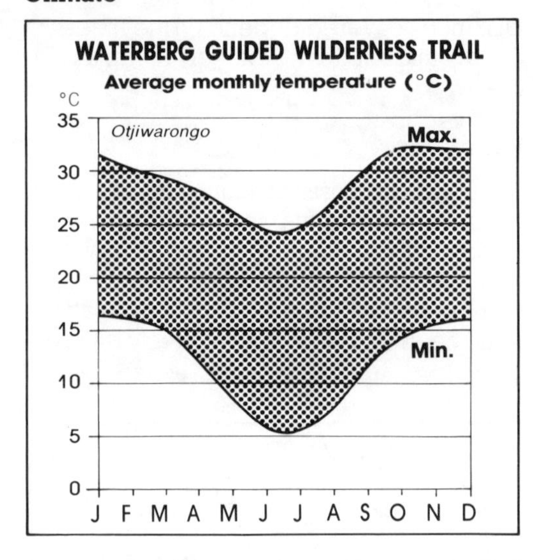


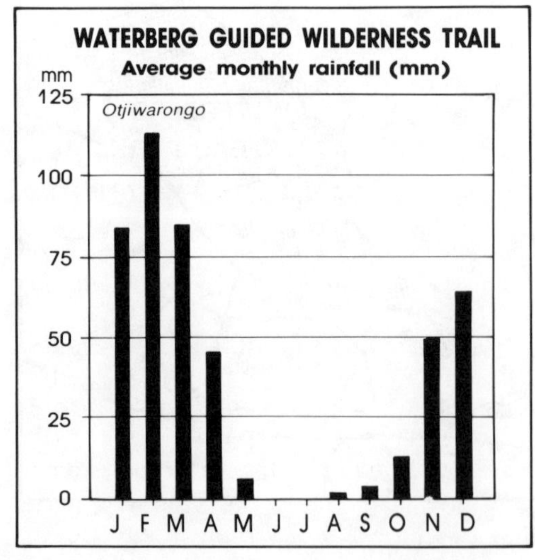


### Relevant Information

- Trails are conducted on the second, third and fourth weekends of every month between April and November. The trails commence at 16h00 on Thursdays, ending early on Sunday afternoon. You must enter the park before 15h00.
- You must provide your own food and sleeping-bags.
- Backpacks, water-bottles, all cooking and eating utensils and basic first aid equipment are supplied.

### Facilities

Accommodation on the trail is at either the Huilboom or Anthephora trail camps on the plateau. Facilities include huts with groundsheets, campbeds with mattresses, water, washing facilities (cold water only), a toilet and firewood.

A modern rest camp is scheduled for completion in 1989. Amenities will include chalets, campsites, a shop where meat, groceries and liquor can be purchased, a restaurant and a swimming pool.

### Flora

The vegetation of the area has been classified by Giess as Tree Savanna and Woodland (Northern Kalahari) (Vegetation Type 11), which is the dominant vegetation type over the north-eastern region of SWA/Namibia. Grassland with trees and bigger shrubs in dense or open clumps of varying sizes is the characteristic feature of this vegetation type. In the park it can be subdivided into two main types: rock-seam vegetation and sand-bound vegetation.

The rock-seam type comprises the vegetation on the slopes of the Waterberg and that of the Karakuwisa Mountain on the northern boundary of the park. It has a characteristic 'large bush' appearance and includes species such as *Combretum*, the mountain thorn (171), three-hook thorn (185.1), cork bush (226) and the wild plum (361).

The sand-bound vegetation type can be subdivided into two main sub-types, namely the tree savanna and the shrub/bushwillow community. The tree savanna grows in a belt of several hundred metres wide

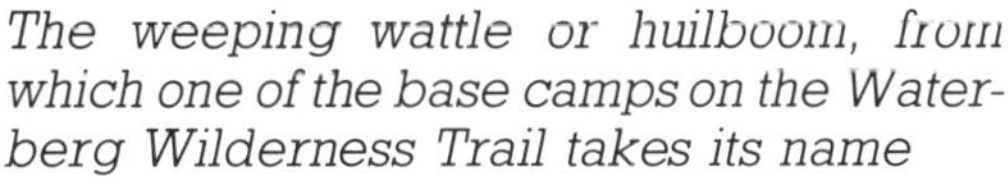

*The weeping wattle or huilboom, from which one of the base camps on the Waterberg Wilderness Trail takes its name*

*Leaves and flowers*

*Fruit*

along the south-eastern side of the plateau. The grasses are dominated by finger grass (*Digitaria* spp.) and stick grass (*Aristida* spp.), while important tree species include *Combretum* spp., wild seringa (197), Kalahari apple-leaf (239), wild plum (361) and weeping wattle (215).

One of the trail camps takes its name from the Afrikaans common name for the weeping wattle, huilboom. In SWA/Namibia this species occurs in wooded grassland north of Otjiwarongo. It grows as a small to medium-sized tree of 5 to 10 m high and is particularly attractive between September and February when the tree is covered in showy sprays of bright yellow flowers. The tree is one of the 'rain trees' of Africa and derives its name from an unusual feature. The 'rain' is produced by the larvae of spittle bugs which frequent the trees in summer and occurs just prior to the start of the summer rains. After piercing the bark with their sucking mouth parts, the larvae produce a frothy substance by bubbling air through the juices which they extract from the tree. This foam protects the insects against the sun and predators. At times the larvae produce such large quantities of the frothy substance that the excess drips from the tree, sometimes forming pools of 'water' on the ground.

The shrub/bushwillow sub-type occurs centrally on the plateau and westwards towards the Karakuwisa Mountain. The grasses mainly comprise unpalatable species such as stick grass (*Aristida* spp.), finger grass (*Digitaria* spp.) and wool grass (*Anthephora pubescens*) after which one of the camps is named. The hairy red bushwillow (532.1) is the dominant tree species, while the shrubs are dominated by wild seringa and gemsbok bean (*Tylosema esculentum*).

The Omuverume Plateau to the west is more densely covered in large trees than the remainder of the park. This is largely due to the fact that the area was not affected to the same extent by fires and grazing by domestic animals prior to the proclamation of the park. Common grass species here include stick grass (*Aristida* spp.), finger grass (*Digitaria* spp.) and blackfooted brachiaria (*Brachiaria nigropedata*).

SWA/Namibia is not generally associated with ferns, but in localities where water is available all year round ferns can usually be found. In the Waterberg the luxuriant growth of ferns in the vicinity of springs and below the cliffs is particularly impressive.

**Fauna**

The Waterberg lies in the centre of the home range of SWA/Namibia's eland population and it was originally recommended that a reserve should be established to protect this species. Before the reintroduction of animals commenced the writings of Sir Francis Galton and Charles Andersson were thoroughly researched to ensure that only animals that occurred historically in the area were reintroduced. Blue wildebeest were transferred from the Daan Viljoen Game Park near Windhoek, white (square-lipped) rhinoceros were obtained from Natal, common duiker from Tsumeb and red hartebeest from a farm in the vicinity. Roan were translocated from Kavango and sable from west Caprivi after being kept in quarantine in the Etosha National Park. Eland and giraffe were obtained from Mangetti in the north of the country.

The Waterberg is an important breeding nucleus for both roan and sable, which at present (1987) respectively number some 270 and 90. The roan is one of only three South African mammals classified as endangered in the *South African Red Data Book — Terrestrial Mammals*. Today in

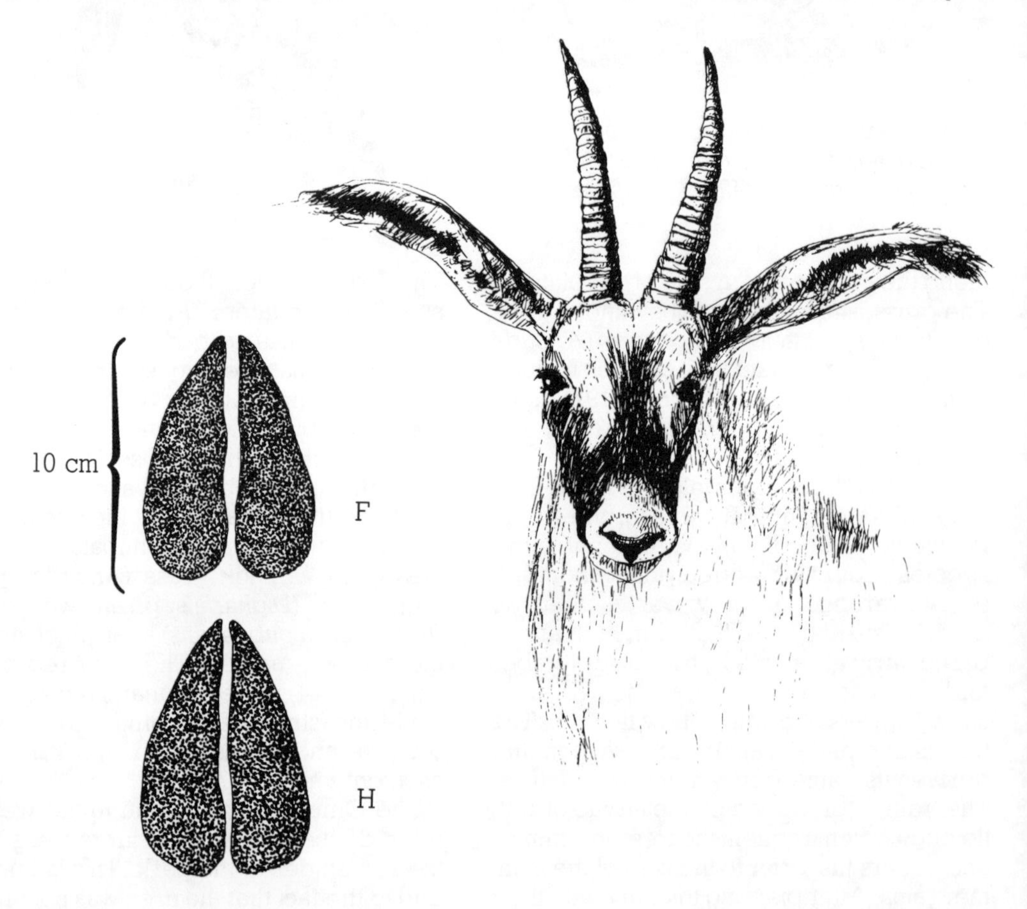


*The roan of the Waterberg Plateau Park form an important breeding nucleus for the translocation of this species to other areas*

South Africa free-ranging herds are found only in the Kruger National Park (1 700) and on private properties in the Waterberg (Transvaal) district (150). Elsewhere in SWA/Namibia they occur naturally in east and west Caprivi, and Kavango, and including Waterberg, their numbers are estimated at fewer than 700.

Smaller animals that inhabit the park include steenbok, klipspringer, rock dassie, wild dog, side-striped jackal, black-backed jackal, caracal and chacma baboon. Lesser bushbaby also occur and can frequently be seen in the palm trees near the Plantage.

Plans are afoot to re-introduce reedbuck, waterbuck and black (hook-lipped) rhinoceros in the near future.

The park is also the habitat of a large number of bird species, including the only breeding colony of the Cape vulture (122) in SWA/Namibia. Their numbers in the park have decreased from more than 500 in the late 1930s to less than 20 in 1980. One of the most important factors that has contributed to their decline is the bush encroachment on the farmlands surrounding the Waterberg. The Cape vulture is adapted to open savanna habitats, but as a result of the encroachment of black thorn (176) and sickle bush (190) the birds' ability to see carcasses has been seriously reduced and access to carcasses is impossible in many areas. In addition, vultures have to run to take off after feeding, which requires ample open ground, and as a result of the bush encroachment the birds do not have sufficient 'take-off areas'.

The most important cause of their decrease has been the indiscriminate use of poisons. The Waterberg is surrounded by farmlands and some farmers unfortunately still use poison against predators such as cheetah, caracal and black-backed jackal. Understandably, one poisoned carcass could wipe out the entire Cape vulture population here.

To save the vultures the Directorate of Nature Conservation has initiated various strategies, including controlled burning and an extensive educational programme aimed particularly at farmers.

Considerable success has been achieved in reverting bush-encroached land under control of the Directorate to grassland by means of controlled burning. This is, however, a long-term programme and in addition it represents only a small percentage of the home range of the vultures of the Waterberg. A vulture 'restaurant' where carcasses are provided to supplement their diet has also been established. Food is supplied throughout the year on a weekly basis in an open area near the breeding cliffs. However, the vultures are still largely dependent on carcasses they find on the surrounding farmlands and this measure is only temporary until such time as the bush encroachment has been checked and eradicated.

Other bird species occurring in the park include whitebacked (123) and lappetfaced (124) vultures, booted eagle (136), African hawk eagle (137), the bateleur (146) with its characteristic flight pattern and gabar goshawk (161).

The Waterberg is the habitat of several species which have 75 per cent of their population restricted to SWA/Namibia. Some of these, such as Hartlaub's francolin (197), Rüppell's parrot (365), Bradfield's hornbill (461), Monteiro's hornbill (462) and rockrunner (662) have a limited distribution in SWA/Namibia, while others like the rosyfaced lovebird (367) and the shorttoed rock thrush (583) are more widely distributed.

Species on the plateau include Coqui francolin (188), purple roller (449), lilacbreasted roller (447) (less frequently seen), fawncoloured lark (497), shorttoed rock thrush (583) and white helmetshrike (753). The latter species occurs in small flocks and can be easily identified by its conspicuous black-and-white flight pattern, which has been likened to that of a butterfly.

The cliffs of the Waterberg are an ideal breeding site for black eagle (131), rock kestrel (181), rosyfaced lovebird (367) and palewinged starling (770). Three swift species which probably breed in the park have also been recorded. The whiterumped swift (415) is an intra-African migrant, while Bradfield's (413) and Alpine (418) swifts are nomads.

On the scree slopes you might see crested (189) and redbilled (194) francolins, swallowtailed bee-eater (445), scimitarbilled

*Monteiro's hornbill – one of the Waterberg 'specials' to keep an eye out for*

woodhoopoe (454), pied barbet (465), cardinal woodpecker (486) and brubru (741).

Among the species you are most likely to observe in the *Acacia* woodlands at the base of the cliffs are the Kalahari robin (615) and the Marico flycatcher (695). With patience you might also spot redbilled woodhoopoe (452), groundscraper thrush (580), barred warbler (658) and tawnyflanked prinia (683).

**History**

Millions of years ago the Waterberg was inhabited by dinosaurs such as Melanorosaurus, Tritylodon, Massospondylus and Pachygeneles — all herbivores — and Gryponyx, the only carnivore. Although these animals disappeared from the face of the earth more than 100 million years ago, there is still evidence of their existence in the form of fossils and tracks.

In more recent times the Waterberg was inhabited by Stone Age peoples, who left their mark in their engravings of animal tracks on the rocks surrounding a large water-hole in the wilderness area.

The first whites to visit the Waterberg were Francis Galton and Charles Andersson, who passed through the area in 1851 while on an expedition. Of the Otjozondjupa fountain, where the two explorers spent a couple of days, Andersson wrote: 'In the course of the day, we arrived at a magnificent fountain, called Otjironjuba — the Calabash — on the side of Omuvereoom. Its source was situated fully two hundred feet above the base of the mountain, and took its rise from different spots; but, soon uniting, the stream danced merrily down the cliffs. These cascades, falling to the plain below, flowed over a bed of red gravel.'[1] Andersson also relates their discovery of the remains of a large 'Hill-Damara' kraal and their contact with a few San. While encamped at the fountain he ascended the Waterberg from where he '... had a very extensive view of the country to the eastward; but, excepting for a few periodical water-courses which originated in the sides of the mountain, nothing but an immense unbroken bush was to be seen'.[2]

In 1871 the Waterberg was visited by the Rhenish missionary Carl Hugo Hahn, who had instructions to establish a series of mission stations in the north of the country. At the time of Hahn's visit, the area was inhabited by the Herero under their well-known chief, Kambazembi. The first missionary, Heinrich Beiderbecke, arrived in the Waterberg on 15 November 1873 and established a mission station at Otjozondjupa, where Galton and Andersson had rested for a few days 20 years earlier. The mission station was destroyed during the Khoikhoi/Herero war of 1880 and rebuilt 11

1 Andersson, C.J. 1974. *Lake Ngami* (Facsimile reprint). Cape Town: C. Struik, 153.
2 *Ibid.*, 154.

years later when the missionary Wilhelm Eich arrived at Otjozondjupa.

Like so many other areas of SWA/Namibia, the Waterberg contains numerous reminders of the conflicts that took place during the latter part of the nineteenth century and the first decade of this century. It was here that the famous last battle between the Herero and the Germans took place in 1904. The fear of losing their land when large areas were allocated to white farmers and the German policy of the gradual impoverishment of the blacks incited the Herero to rise against German rule in 1904 while the Germans were engaged in quelling an uprising by a Nama tribe, the Bondelswarts, in the south.

German forces were rushed from abroad and although the first shots between the Germans and the Herero were fired in January 1904, it was not until August of that year that the Herero were finally defeated at Waterberg and south of Okakarara. The Germans were divided into five forces which consisted of 96 officers, 1 488 men, 30 cannons and 12 machine guns. Communications between the five groups were severely hampered by dense vegetation and a heliograph station was put into action on the plateau above Otjozondjupa. This station is visited by groups taking part in the guided wilderness trail. On 2 October 1904 the commander of the German forces in German SWA, General Lothar von Trotha, issued his notorious extermination order: 'The Herero nation must now leave the country ... Within the German frontier every Herero, with or without a rifle, with or without cattle will be shot. I will not take over any more women and children, but I will either drive them back to your people or have them fired on. These are my words to the nation of the Hereros.'[3] Large numbers of Herero, including their chief Samuel Maharero, fled eastwards to Serowe in present-day Botswana, while smaller groups fled to Owambo and Kaokoland.

Following the uprising a strong presence of Schutztruppe was maintained at Waterberg. In 1907 the country was divided into police districts and the following year the mission station was leased to the Landespolizei, who temporarily used it as a depot until the police station and Rasthaus was completed in 1910. Farms were subsequently laid out and the eastern part of the plateau was used for grazing. In 1955 the Rasthaus was converted into a guest house for tourists. On account of the mountain's unique character and fine Etjo Sandstone formations, the Waterberg was proclaimed a monument area in 1956.

The Waterberg Plateau Park was created in June 1972 for the breeding and subsequent translocation of Namibia's uncommon game species to other suitable areas. The Waterberg is also the heartland of Namibia's eland population, which, at the time of proclamation, roamed the plateau in fairly large numbers. Several other antelope also occurred in the Waterberg, making the mountain ideal as a game reserve. A wilderness area covering some 18 600 ha was set aside on the plateau in 1984.

### Geology and Geomorphology

Covering some 40 549 ha, the Waterberg complex can be subdivided into three distinct areas, namely the Small Waterberg in the south, the Omuverume Plateau, which forms part of the Waterberg Plateau and the Waterberg Plateau proper, which is widest in the north-east, tapering to a sharp point in the south-west. The plateau is about 48 km long and varies from 8 to 16 km in width. The highest point of the Waterberg (1 885 m) is at Omuverume in the south-west, while the Karakuwisa Mountain (1 878 m) is the highest point on the plateau.

The Waterberg is renowned for its fascinating column-like rock formations which have been sculpted by countless aeons of extremes of temperatures, wind and rain, and these are best seen in the surrounding cliff-faces of the Karakuwisa Mountain. With the exception of the northern side, the Waterberg is capped by perpendicular cliffs, 70-75 m high. Towards the north, the

---

3 Parsons, N. 1982. *A New History of Southern Africa*. London: Macmillan Education, 205.

plateau becomes more broken and lower and is approximately the same height at the north-eastern side as the surrounding plain.

The Waterberg is an erosional relic of a sandstone casing which millions of years ago covered a large area of this region of SWA/Namibia. It consists of sedimentary rock from the Karoo Sequence and from the base upwards can be divided into two sections. The lower Omingonde Formation consists of reddish-brown mud-, silt-, sand- and gritstone and conglomerate and was probably deposited by rivers in a shallow lake. This formation is about 350 m deep and is

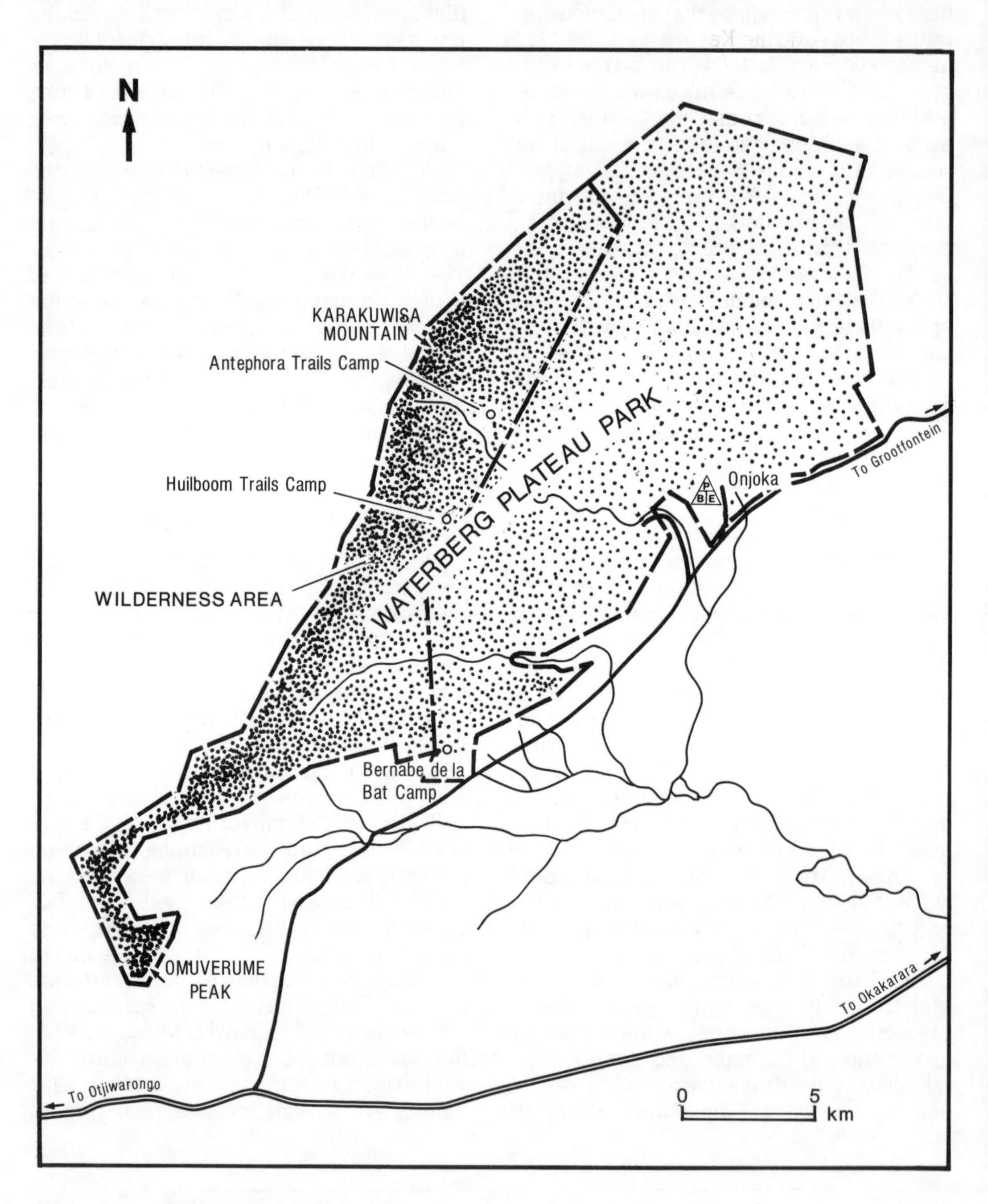


*Waterberg Guided Wilderness Trail*

mostly concealed on the slopes by rock rubble. The upper Etjo Formation is composed of brown sandstone, which forms the perpendicular cliffs below the crest. This formation was shaped by windblown sand which gradually settled in the lake.

Two factors are mainly responsible for the elevated position of the mountain. Millions of years ago the Karoo layers south of the line that joins Grootfontein and Omaruru were lifted in a north-west/south-east direction as a result of pressure in the earth's crust. In addition, the resistance of the Etjo Formation to weathering prevented the erosion of the mountain. The flexing of the earth's crust resulted in pillar-like seams developing in the Etjo Formation. Rainwater on the plateau flows into the seams and seeps down the mountain until it is blocked by the impermeable Omingonde Formation where it is forced to the surface, giving rise to numerous springs at the base of the Waterberg.

**Trail Synopsis**

Experiences on any wilderness trail vary considerably and consequently a detailed trail description is not given here.

You will be met at the Onjoka park headquarters by the trail ranger, who will transport you with all your personal gear in a four-wheel-drive vehicle to one of the two base camps on the plateau, about 18 km from Onjoka. The daily programme is flexible, but you will hike along dry water courses and game tracks and through canyons. As with other wilderness trails, there will be the excitement of stalking game on foot, perhaps coming face to face with a white (square-lipped) rhinoceros or admiring the aristocratic sable at close range. However, the trail is primarily intended to give you a better understanding of this fascinating area — its history, geology, game species and numbers and the park management goals and techniques. Your trail experience will not only focus on your immediate environment, but also on the constellations and stars, which are a highlight of the trail on clear evenings. Each trail is conducted by a nature conservation trails officer who is thoroughly acquainted with all aspects of the park.

You will be transported back to Onjoka on the final day of the trail.

# 2 Ugab River Guided Wilderness Trail

To many people a trail in the desert may sound uninspiring, but the Ugab River Guided Wilderness Trail allows you to explore one of the most fascinating deserts in the world. Features such as the vegetated Ugab River, the seemingly barren gravel plains, the impressive canyon slopes and granite outcrops and the notoriously formidable Skeleton Coast are some of the interesting aspects of this area.

### Location

The trail is situated in the Skeleton Coast Park on the northern coast of SWA/Namibia. The trail starts at the entrance gate to the park at the Ugab River, which marks the southern boundary of the park. The Ugab River is situated about 200 km north of Swakopmund and is reached by following the Henties Bay/Cape Cross road from Swakopmund.

### Distance and Classification

50 km (approximately)
3 days
B+ grade

### Permits

Groups must consist of a minimum of six people and a maximum of eight. Written reservations are accepted 18 months in advance and held on file, but are only confirmed 11 months prior to the trail date. Telephone and personal applications are accepted 11 months in advance. Reservations should be made with The Director, Directorate of Nature Conservation and Recreation Resorts, Private Bag 13267, Windhoek 9000, SWA/Namibia, Telephone (061) 36975. The trail fee is not refundable, should you cancel.

### Maps

As the trails are led by an experienced trails officer and no set routes are followed, a map is unnecessary.

### Relevant Information

- Trails are conducted every second and fourth Tuesday of every month throughout the year. On your day of departure you are advised to report at the office at Ugab Mouth by about 08h00 to facilitate an early start. Trails end on Thursdays at a time arranged to suit your requirements.
- On confirmation of your reservation a medical certificate will be forwarded to you and this must be completed by a doctor not earlier than 40 days prior to the trail. The certificate must be handed to the trails officer on commencement of the trail.
- Unlike most other guided wilderness trails, no equipment is supplied and trailists must provide their own backpacks, sleeping bags and other equipment, as well as food.
- Access to the Skeleton Coast Park is restricted to overnight visitors. Should you plan to travel in the Skeleton Coast Park before or after the trail, you must be in possession of reservation advices issued by the reservation office in Windhoek. Only camping facilities are available at Torra Bay, while accommodation at Terrace Bay includes three meals a day and bedding is supplied. There is also a shop and a filling station.

### Facilities

No facilities are provided on the trail as sleeping is in the open.

The night before the trail begins (Monday night) can be spent at the Mile 108 campsite about 40 km south of the Ugab River gate.

Facilities include fireplaces and ablutions. Water is carted to the campsite and a small fee is payable for showers and drinking water. A filling station and a shop/kiosk are open during the December/January school holidays only.

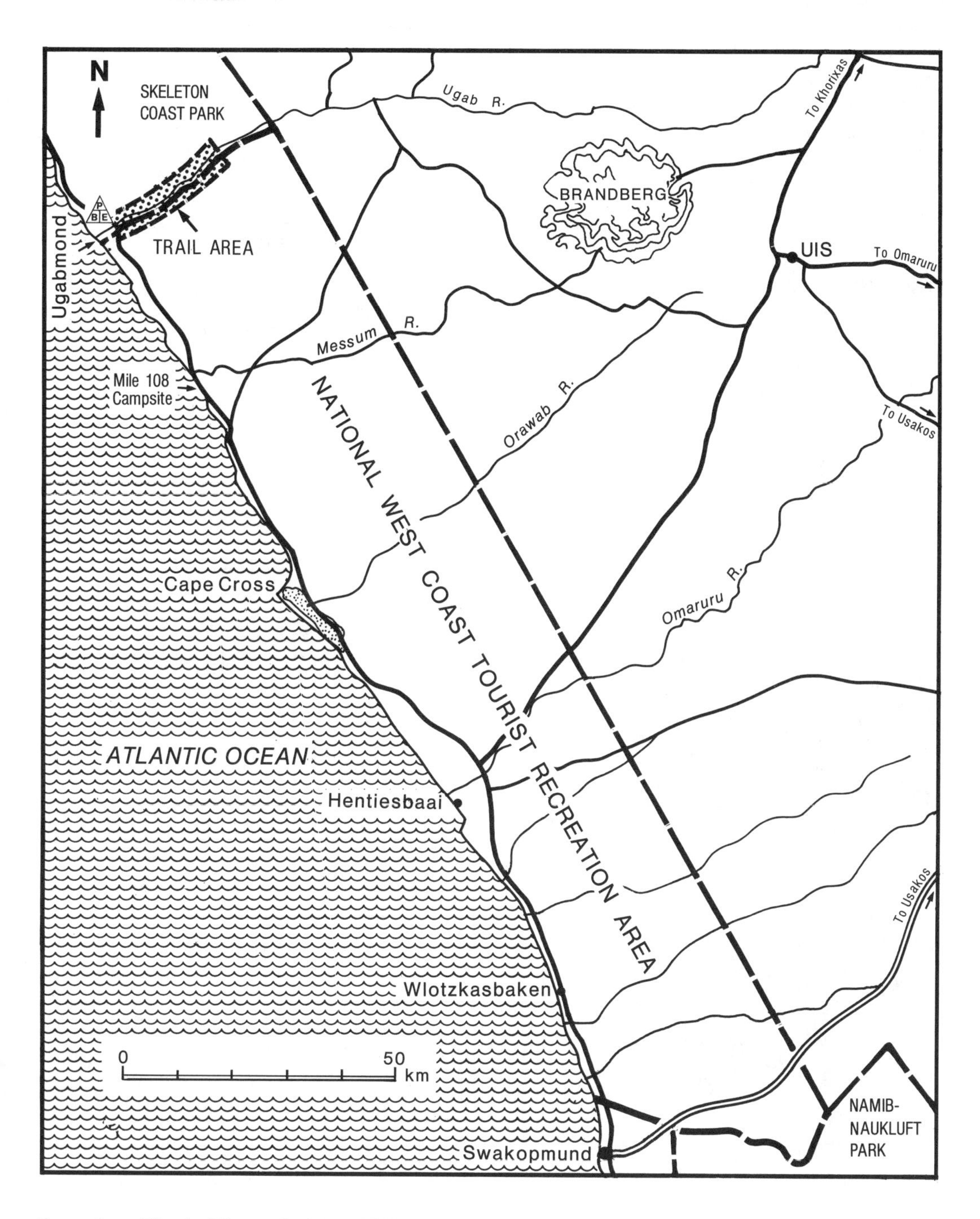


*Location: Ugab River Guided Wilderness Trail.*

## Climate

With the moderating influence of the sea, average minimum and maximum temperatures along the coast are fairly cool and do not fluctuate as much as those further inland. The average annual minimum temperature is just below 14 °C and the maximum is about 18 °C. Temperatures increase, however, as you progress further inland and 30 km from the coast the average annual temperature increases from 16 °C at the coast to about 19 °C.

Thick fog is common along the coast (the average annual number of days with fog at Swakopmund is 113), especially between April and August.

The average annual rainfall of the area is a mere 16 mm. It is most likely to rain in January, February and March.

During late autumn and early winter warm, dry and dusty easterly winds sometimes cause unpleasant conditions.

## Flora

The vegetation of the Ugab River is included in Riverine Woodland (Giess Vegetation Type 15), which forms part of the Woodlands group, but falls in the Central Namib Vegetation Type (Giess Vegetation Type 2). The latter type occurs between the Huab and the Kuiseb rivers, stretching inland for between 50 and 100 km.

Large trees and shrubs are limited to the Ugab River and among the species you will encounter are ana tree (159), camel thorn (168), wild tamarisk (487) real mustard tree (622) and inkbos (*Suaeda plumosa*). Temporary pools in the river are fringed with *Phragmites* reed-beds.

After the summer rains, white desert grasses dominated by *Stipagrostis* species are especially plentiful on the gravel plains, which are also the habitat of numerous welwitschias (21.1). These extraordinary plants look like stranded octopuses on the gravel

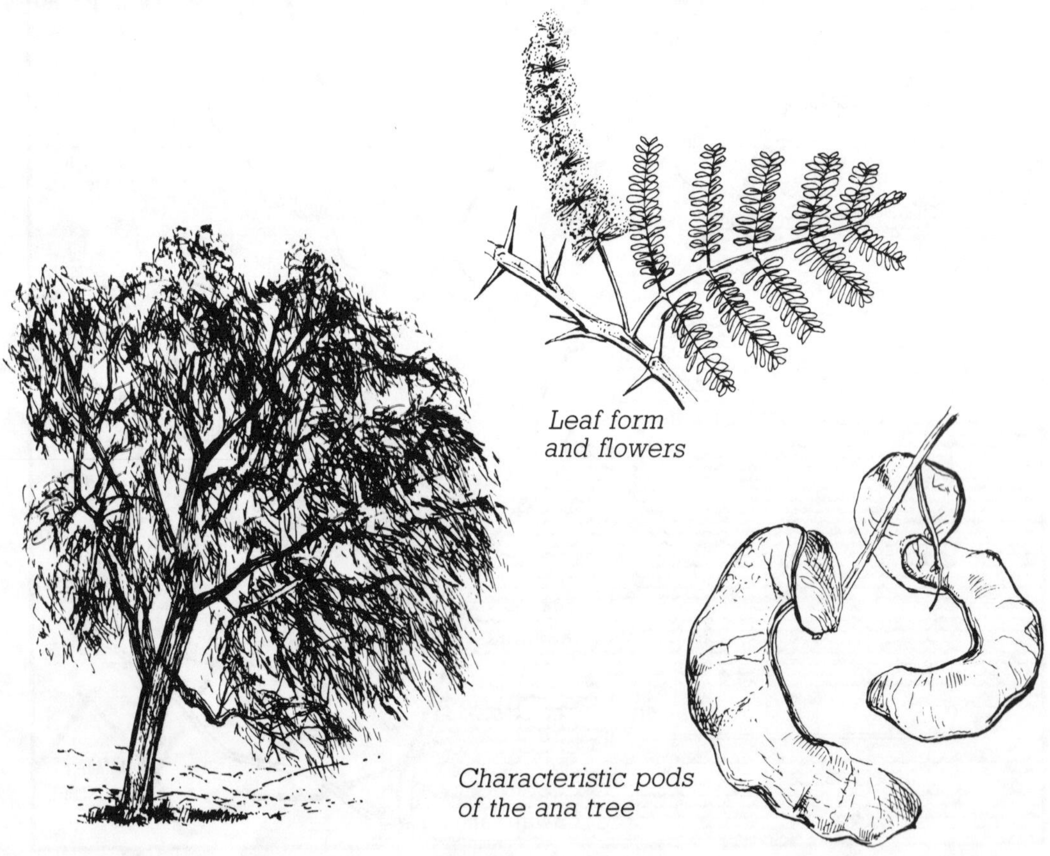

*Leaf form and flowers*

*Characteristic pods of the ana tree*

*Ana trees are characteristic of the river courses in the Central and Northern Namib*

plains (see flora of the Brandberg Backpacking Area for a detailed description of the *Welwitschia*). *Zygophyllum stapffii* (dollarbush) and *Arthraerua leubnitziae* occur in the shallow river-beds and depressions on the gravel plains.

Another form of plant life which will fascinate you is the lichen. The lichen fields between Swakopmund and Terrace Bay are amongst the largest of their kind in the world. Some lichens are dependent on moisture for their survival and their distribution is determined by the penetration of fog into the Namib.

Lichens consist of two primitive plants growing together, namely fungi and algae. At night the thread-like fungi absorb moisture from the fog and before the fog evaporates in the morning, the unicellular algae, which contain chlorophyll, react to the water and sunlight to produce sugar and starch. This type of interdependence is known as symbiosis.

The lichens cling to rocks and rock banks and are mainly limited to the stable gravel plains along the coast. More than 60 species have been identified and it is thought that there could be as many as 120 species along the coast. They vary in colour from green to brown and orange-yellow. During the day they are soon dehydrated by the harsh temperatures, giving them the appearance of dead plant material. However, in the early morning sunlight they transform the gravel plains of the Namib into beautiful pastel shades.

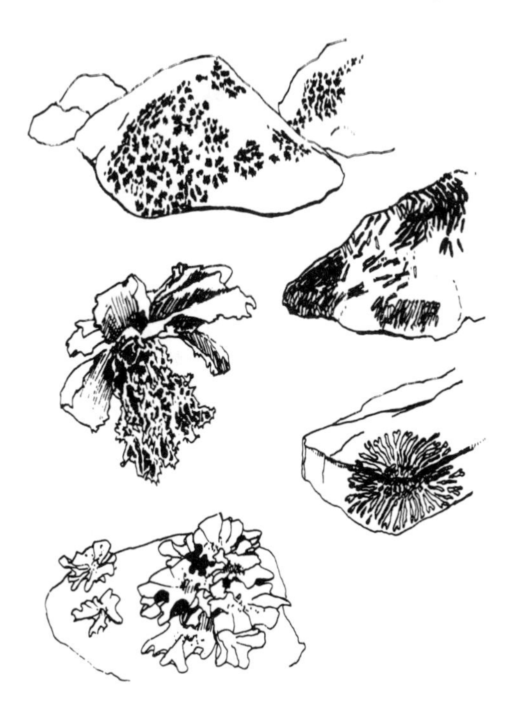

*Over 100 species of lichens occur in the Namib Desert*

Lichens grow at an incredibly slow rate — only half a millimetre a year — irrespective of the amount of precipitation they receive. During times of drought they are an important source of food to numerous desert animals, including gemsbok and springbok.

**Fauna**

Unlike other areas of Southern Africa that support large numbers of game, the Namib Desert is the habitat of only a few species of larger mammals. However, as a result of the harsh environment several beetles, reptiles and smaller animals have evolved and adapted themselves to survive in this arid region, which receives less than 30 mm of rain a year.

Without much rainfall or many permanent water bodies the fog, which blankets the coast for up to 100 days a year, is crucial to the survival of both animals and plants. Along the coast the fog is formed by changes in the atmospheric pressure as a result of the high daytime temperatures and the low temperatures at night. Moist sea air is consequently drawn inland over the cold Benguela Current and cold water forced upwards by upwelling. The moist sea air is cooled and by way of condensation small drops of vapour are formed as fog.

Among the larger mammal species occurring in the area are black (hook-lipped) rhinoceros, lion, gemsbok, Hartmann's mountain zebra and springbok.

In the 1970s the black rhino population of the Kaokoveld (Damaraland and Kaokoland further north) was subjected to large-scale poaching and their numbers were severely reduced. As a result of action by the Directorate of Nature Conservation and conservation bodies such as the Namibia Wildlife Trust and the Endangered Wildlife Trust, the illegal hunting of rhino and elephant was brought under control by mid-1983 and their numbers are again increasing. A survey was conducted in 1986 by the renowned conservationist Garth Owen-Smith, who estimated the number of black rhino north of the veterinary cordon fence at between 61 and 68. Three black rhino were recorded south of the veterinary fence during a survey carried out in July/August 1986 by the Directorate of Nature Conservation, but this number could be slightly higher.

Unlike the other black rhino populations of Africa, the Kaokoveld rhino are adapted to survive in a practically waterless and vegetationless environment. Their habitat is characterised by barren plains, varying from sandy valleys to stone-littered plains. Surrounding these plains are high, rugged mountains dissected by a few rivers which have carved their way to the sea over countless ages. The animals cover large distances — sometimes as much as 30 km — to reach the few water holes and well-trodden paths criss-crossing the stony terrain testify to the animals' presence in the area for many generations.

Although the Ugab River comes down in flood only during the summer months, game is naturally attracted to the vegetation in the river-bed and the temporary pools. This in turn attracts predators such as lion, which have also been observed feeding on beached whales and seals along the coast. Other predators occurring in the river valleys and along the coast include brown hyaena and black-backed jackal, as well as leopard.

A number of smaller mammal species such as steenbok and common duiker as well as several smaller predators also occur.

To date some 203 bird species have been recorded in the Skeleton Coast Park with a further 23 species off-shore and 10 extralimital. Less than 20 per cent of the species occur away from water bodies. As a result of the availability of nutritive food, the sea off the Skeleton Coast Park attracts large numbers of sea and sea shore birds, and

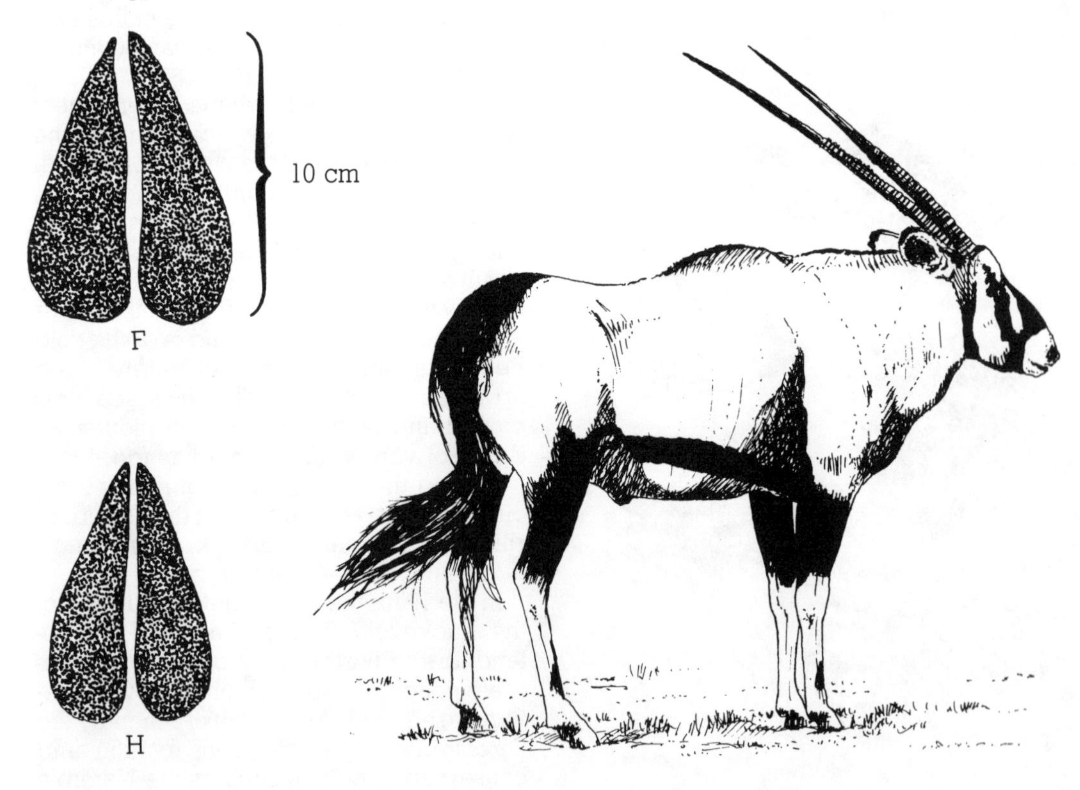


*Gemsbok – a typical species of arid areas such as the Namib Desert*

some 47 species (23 per cent) have been recorded in these habitat types. At least 17 of these are Palaearctic migrants.

Among the species that are attracted to the pools in the Ugab River are dabchick (8), which breed upstream, Egyptian goose (102) and water dikkop (298). Dove species along the watercourse of the Ugab include the laughing (355) and Namaqua (356) doves.

The rocky areas of the Ugab River are the habitat of species such as rock martin (529), mountain chat (586), which are widely distributed in rocky areas of the park, and the less common familiar chat (589), which has been recorded in the Ugab River Valley in autumn.

The gravel plains attract ostrich (1), Rüppell's korhaan (236) and Gray's lark (514), a species endemic to the Namib Desert.

Raptors are scarce as there is not much prey about to attract them and the three species you are most likely to see are the augur buzzard (153), rock kestrel (181) and the black eagle (131), which have been recorded from the upper Ugab River Valley. With some luck you might also see the lappetfaced vulture (124), which is widespread in the eastern part of the park, or a pair of peregrine falcons (171) which is sometimes seen in the Ugab River Valley.

A bird that deserves special mention is the Damara tern (334), of which there are less than 2 000 breeding pairs in the world. About 90 per cent of the total world population breeds along the SWA/Namibian coast, while 70 per cent of this number breeds along the coastal strip between the sea and the main road between Swakopmund and Terrace Bay. The Damara tern is listed as rare in the *African Red Data Book — Birds.* In South Africa the numbers of this species are estimated at less than 250 breeding pairs, while less than 1800 pairs breed along the coast of SWA/Namibia.

**History**

The inhospitable coastline of the Skeleton Coast was inhabited for thousands of years by bands of Stone Age hunter-gatherers. These people possessed an intimate knowledge of their harsh environment and supplemented their diet by exploiting the marine environment. They collected mussels and other sea food and also lived off beached seals, penguins and whales. Knives and other domestic implements were fashioned from bone, and their shelters were sometimes constructed from whale ribs.

Archaeological research indicates that Stone Age sites along the Ugab River were occupied between AD 400 and 100 years ago.

The first white person to set foot on the coast of SWA/Namibia was the Portuguese navigator Diogo Cão, who in 1486 erected his second and last *padrão* (cross) at Cape Cross, some 75 km south of the Ugab River. He perished soon afterwards and became the first recorded victim of the Skeleton Coast.

The cross was removed in January 1893 by a certain Captain Becker and can be seen in a museum in East Berlin in almost perfect condition. Cão planted his first cross on the southern headland of the Congo River.

The barren, treacherous coastline is often blanketed in fog and was a source of abject fear for early mariners. Running aground meant certain death and the numerous shipwrecks, some of which are partly buried by sand, anchors, pieces of machinery and harpoons bear testimony to the Skeleton Coast's claim of being the biggest ship graveyard in the world.

One of the first whites to explore the coast was Captain W Messum, who in the 1840s searched for guano deposits and other commercially useful products. Messum also surveyed the coast and Charles Andersson later used his map of the coast between Walvis Bay and 20° South (Terrace Bay) for a map in his book *Lake Ngami.* Andersson used the remainder of Messum's map as a basis for his own map.

The Skeleton Coast Park was proclaimed in 1971 and is divided into two zones. The southern section stretches between the Ugab and the Hoanib rivers, while the northern section lies between the Hoanib and Kunene rivers. The latter is considered a wilderness area and the only access for tourists is by way of exclusive fly-in safaris conducted from Windhoek.

## Trail Synopsis

The Ugab River, with its vegetation, has made it possible to undertake a guided wilderness trail into the Namib Desert, territory which is usually considered unsuitable for backpacking.

The trail is not confined to specific routes, which means that it can be adapted to climatic conditions and the requirements of the group. The terrain varies from the gravel plains just south of the Ugab River to the soft river sand and rocky slopes of the Ugab River.

Unlike other guided wilderness trails, no facilities are provided, which requires you to be totally self-sufficient. You have to carry your own water during the day, but water and firewood are transported to the overnight campsites. Evenings are spent around the campfire with the clear desert sky above you, an experience never to be forgotten.

Your trails officer will gladly share with you his intimate knowledge of this fascinating area, which the San believe was created by the Devil in one of his foul moods.

On the final day of the trail you will be transported to the coast, where you will be shown the remains of a whalebone hut settlement at the Ugab River mouth. The age of this site has been estimated at about 200-600 years.

The trail will give you a new appreciation of one of the most fascinating and beautiful deserts in the world.

## DON'T MISS

- the attractive early German architecture in Swakopmund, including the railway station, Woermann House and the gaol. You will probably pass through Swakopmund *en route* and it is worth spending time visiting some of these old buildings.
- the Welwitschia Nature Drive. If you are exploring the area before starting the trail, obtain a permit and guide pamphlet from the Nature Conservation office in Swakopmund. The drive takes at least three hours and will take you 40 km into the Namib Desert. Several fascinating natural and historic features are marked and these are explained in the pamphlet.
- the large breeding colony of Cape fur seals at Cape Cross, 115 km north of Swakopmund. Stop here *en route* to the start of the trail, but note the visiting times: 16 December to end February — 08h00 to 17h00; 1 March to 30 June — open only on Saturdays, Sundays, public holidays and April school holidays from 08h00 to 17h00; and 1 July to 15 December — open only on Wednesdays from 12h00 to 16h00. Entry permits and an information leaflet are obtainable at Cape Cross. Also to be seen here is the replica of Diogo Cão's cross, erected by the National Monuments Council on 11 October 1980 on the exact site of the original.

# 3 Brandberg Backpacking Area

Covering some 750 km², the Brandberg rises abruptly from the surrounding plains. It is a harsh and inhospitable area of deep ravines choked by massive boulders, which in the early morning and late afternoon take on a deep, warm glow.

For over 70 years Königstein — the highest point in SWA/Namibia (2 573 m) — has presented a formidable challenge to backpackers. However, on account of the rugged terrain, extremes of temperature and lack of water, the Brandberg should be attempted only by fit and experienced backpackers after careful preparation.

Although there are several routes along which Königstein can be reached, only the easiest ascent, the route via the Hungorob Ravine, is described here.

### Location

The Brandberg is situated about 40 km west of Uis in central Damaraland.

The starting point of the trail described up the Hungorob Ravine is reached by turning off the R64 (C36) onto the road signposted Brandberg West, about 10 km south of Uis on the Hentiesbaai road. Continue along this road for just more than 40 km until you reach the Messum River. On account of a few sandy patches it is not advisable to continue up the river unless you have a

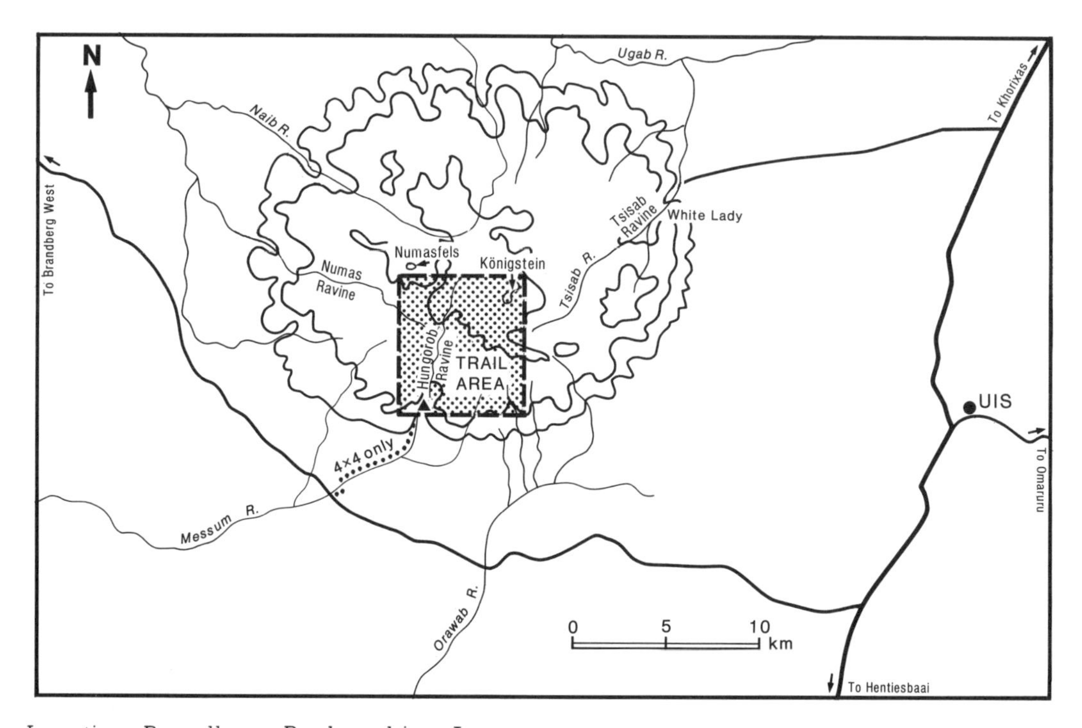


*Location: Brandberg Backpacking Area*

four-wheel-drive. Here you leave the road and turn right onto a track which is not always obvious. The track crosses the river and you continue along its left-hand side for about 7 km to reach a large *heitsi eibib* (stone cairn). The track forks here but you continue straight ahead to a triple fork a short distance further. Here you take the middle track, which is followed for a few hundred metres to where it ends at a shady camel thorn (168).

### Distance and Classification

There are a number of routes to Königstein, which at 2 573 m is the highest point both in the Brandberg and SWA/Namibia. The easiest ascent is along the Hungorob Ravine on the southern side of the mountain, but even this route is not recommended for inexperienced hikers.
3 days or longer
C+ grade

### Permits

At the time of writing (1988) no permits are required to backpack in the area. As control over the area is likely to change in future it is advisable to make enquiries with The Director, Directorate of Trade and Tourism, Private Bag 13297, Windhoek 9000, SWA/Namibia, Telephone (061) 22-6571.

### Maps

The area is covered by 1:50 000 topographical map numbers 2114BA and 2114AB, which are essential for excursions into the Brandberg. The maps are obtainable from the Surveyor-General, Department of Justice, Private Bag 13182, Windhoek 9000, SWA/Namibia.

### Relevant Information

- The terrain of the Brandberg is extremely rugged and an excursion into the area should *only be undertaken by experienced and fit backpackers* and after thorough preparation.
- A good sense of direction and map reading skills are essential. As a result of local magnetism a compass is of little use.
- Excursions should be limited to the months between April and June when temperatures are more bearable. You are also more likely to obtain water during these months, provided the mountain has had good summer rains. Do not count on finding water at all the springs marked on the topographical maps as some of them have dried up since the maps were compiled. Where water is available, remember that it is a scarce commodity. Take only as much as you need and never waste it. Remember that fellow backpackers, animals and birds are also reliant on the limited water supply.
- Carry a small backpacking stove. Although firewood is available in the ravines there is little available on the plateau. Should you make a fire, keep it small.
- One of the secrets of enjoying the Brandberg is to limit the weight of your backpack to the *absolute minimum*. Leave all unnecessary equipment and luxuries in your vehicle — you will appreciate them more on your return than after lugging them up the mountain.
- Mosquito repellent and sunscreen lotion are essential.
- Trousers are useful to protect your legs against thick scrub on the plateau.

### Facilities

At present (1988) there are no camping facilities at the Brandberg. Plans are under way to build a rest camp near the entrance to the Tsisab Ravine on the north-eastern side of the mountain.

Petrol can be obtained at Uis between 07h00 and 19h00 Mondays to Saturdays and between 10h30 and 16h30 on Sundays. There is also a small supermarket where fresh bread and groceries can be obtained between 08h00 and 14h00 and between 16h00 and 20h00 Mondays to Saturdays and from 11h00 to 14h00 and 16h00 to 20h00 on Sundays.

## Climate

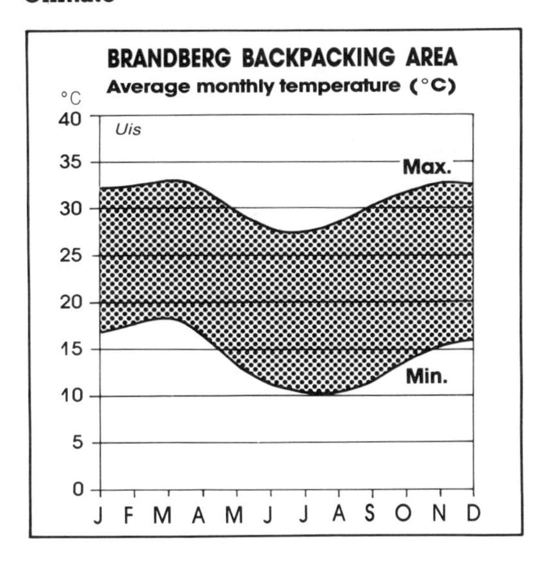


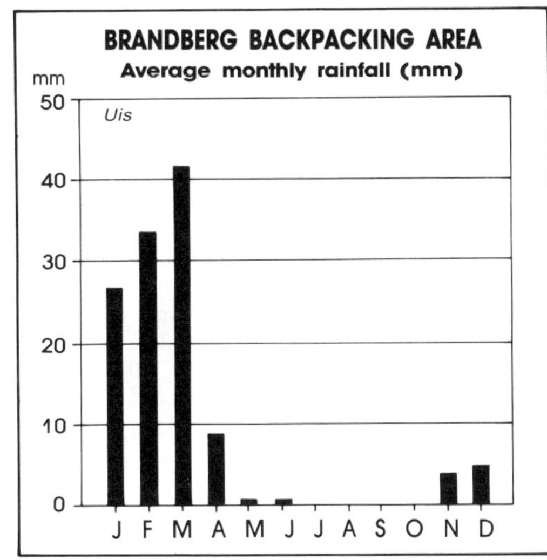


## Flora

The vegetation of the area has been classified by Giess as Semi-desert and Savanna Transition of the Escarpment Zone (Vegetation Type 4). However, the composition of the flora of the Brandberg differs markedly from that of the surrounding gravel plains because of the higher rainfall on the mountain.

According to Nordenstam, the mountain lies at the north-western corner of the Karoo-Namib floristic region and consequently the vegetation of the Brandberg is largely composed of species typical of this region. In addition to a number of species endemic to the Brandberg, the area is also the habitat of several species endemic to southern Angola and north-western SWA/Namibia (Kaokoveld, Outjo, Omaruru, Swakopmund and Karibib districts). The best-known member of this latter group is the fascinating welwitschia (21.1), which occurs on the western and southern sides of the mountain. Large numbers of this primitive plant are seen on the barren, rocky plains to the west of the Messum River and in the shimmering heat of the day they add to the weirdness of the almost lunar landscape of Damaraland.

The welwitschia was brought to the attention of the world following its almost simultaneous discovery by Friedrich Welwitsch and the explorer and traveller Thomas Baines. Welwitsch 'discovered' these strange plants '... which looked for all the world like octopuses stranded in the sea of sand' near Mocamedes Bay in southern Angola in September 1859 while he was conducting a survey of the flora and fauna of Angola. In August of the following year he described his unusual find in a letter to Sir William Hooker, but did not send any material. In May 1861 Thomas Baines 'discovered' the plant in the Swakop River and sent a sketch of the plant and specimen cones to Sir William Hooker. Although Baines's sketch and specimen were the first ever seen of this botanical curiosity, the plant was named after Dr Welwitsch who provided the first description.

Welwitsch and Baines were, however, not the first white people to encounter the welwitschia. Several plants were collected in 1857 by the explorer Charles Andersson and a director of the Walvisch Bay Mining Company who accompanied him, while the traveller, hunter and trader James Chapman took the first known photograph of a welwitschia in the Swakop River around 1859.

Although the plant appears to have several leaves, only a single pair of olive green, leathery leaves, which can reach up to more than 8 m in length, are produced. The leaves grow at a rate of between 100 and 200 mm a year and are shredded by the extremes of temperature, wind-blown sand and the scorching winds to give it the ap-

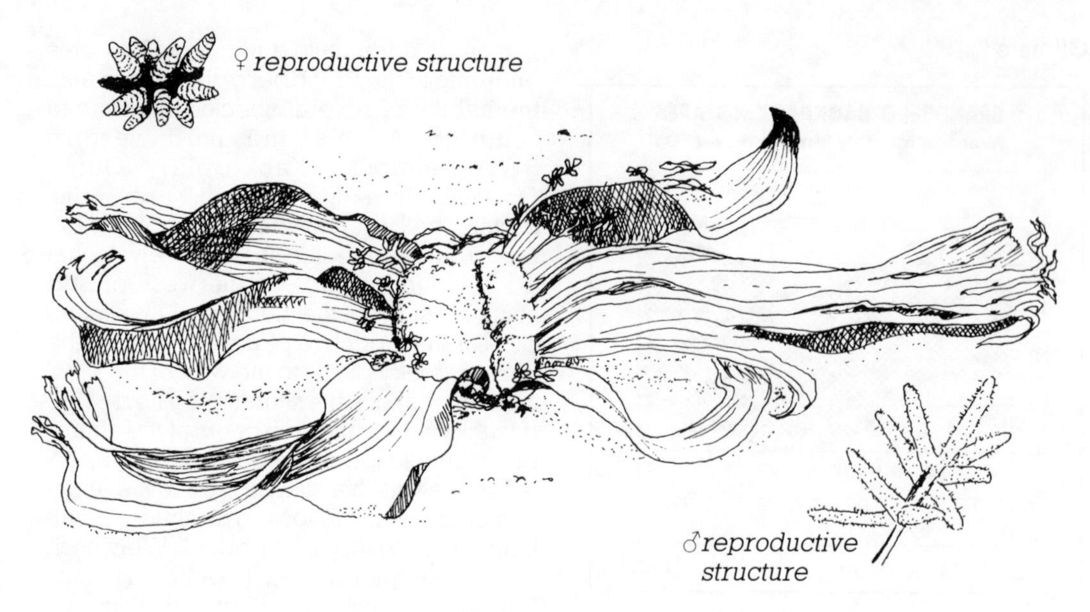


*Welwitschia mirabilis – a unique species which fascinates both scientists and visitors to the Namib*

pearance of a plant with several leaves. It has been calculated that a plant of 2 000 years could '... in its lifetime, provide sufficient green carpeting, 3 m wide, to cover a 400-metre athletic track.'[1]

The lifespan of these plants has been estimated to be upwards of 2 000 years. The age of the well-known Husab welwitschia of the Welwitschia Plains, north of the Swakop River in the Namib Park, has been estimated at between 1 500 and 2 000 years.

The 'flowers' of the welwitschia are borne separately by male and female plants. The male flowers are responsible for the production of pollen grains, while the female reproductive structures resemble the cones of pine trees. Large female plants bear between 100 and 200 cones, each containing about 100 seeds. Despite the potential yield of between 10 000 and 20 000 seeds, a large percentage of the seeds are sterile or infested with fungus, leaving between 20 and 200 seeds that are germinable. Pollination is by wind and not via the pyrrhocorid bug (*Probergrothius sexpunctatis*) — an orange bug with six identifying black marks on the body — as is often assumed.[2]

One of the most conspicuous trees in the valleys of the Brandberg is the Brandberg thorn (177), which derives its name from the mountain, although it also occurs in Kaokoland further north. This species reaches up to 8 m in height and is often multi-stemmed from the base, giving it a broom-like appearance. The bark is shiny red in young trees with a brown, papery cortex, while older trees have a dark grey bark. The tree has hook-thorns, which are paired, and cream to yellow flowering spikes are produced in November and December.

The common cluster fig (66) is found at some of the larger water-holes in the Brandberg, either in small groups or as an occasional large specimen.

Several *Commiphora* species have been identified and you will recognise some of them by their papery bark, which is often flaked.

Another species that is unlikely to escape your attention is the phantom tree (137),

---

1 Bornman, C.H. 1978. *Welwitschia: Paradox of a Parched Paradise.* Cape Town: C Struik, 27.
2 *Ibid.*, 35, 37.

which grows on the rocky slopes of the valleys. This unusual tree has a thick, succulent, swollen stem. The light green leaves grow in clusters near the ends of the branches.

Several *Aloe* species have been identified, including the quiver tree (29), mopane aloe (29.4), *Aloe hereroensis* and *A. viridiflora* with its typical green flowers.

**Fauna**

The plains surrounding the Brandberg are the habitat of mammal species such as Hartmann's mountain zebra and springbok. Numerous burrows testify to the presence of antbear and aardwolf, which are nocturnal and predominantly nocturnal respectively.

The aardwolf has an average shoulder height of about 50 cm and a mean mass of 8,8 kg. The colour of the coat varies from pale buff to yellowish-white with four or five black stripes on the back and flanks, and it has a dorsal mane of long hair and a bushy, black-tipped tail. It is widely but sparsely distributed throughout South Africa, SWA/Namibia and Zimbabwe, except in forested areas, the arid Richtersveld in the north-western Cape and the desert areas of SWA/Namibia. Unlike its close relations, the spotted hyaena and the brown hyaena, which are carnivorous, the aardwolf is primarily insectivorous. Termites are their principal source of food and their distribution is largely determined by the availability of sufficient food.

Several smaller mammal species such as hares, ground squirrels, springhares and smaller predators also inhabit the plains.

By contrast the mountain supports very little mammal life on account of the rugged terrain. You could well see klipspringer and rock dassie, while several rodents also occur. You may come across leopard spoor but are highly unlikely to catch sight of this elusive, nocturnal species.

Bird species to look out for on the plains surrounding the Brandberg include ostrich (1), lappetfaced vulture (124), Rüppell's korhaan (236), Ludwig's bustard (232), long-billed lark (500) and tractrac chat (590).

You are unlikely to miss the shrill, metalli shriek of the rosyfaced lovebird (367), which is found in small flocks in the lower, more vegetated parts of the ravines. Other

*(Actual size)*

*The timid aardwolf occurs singly or in pairs*

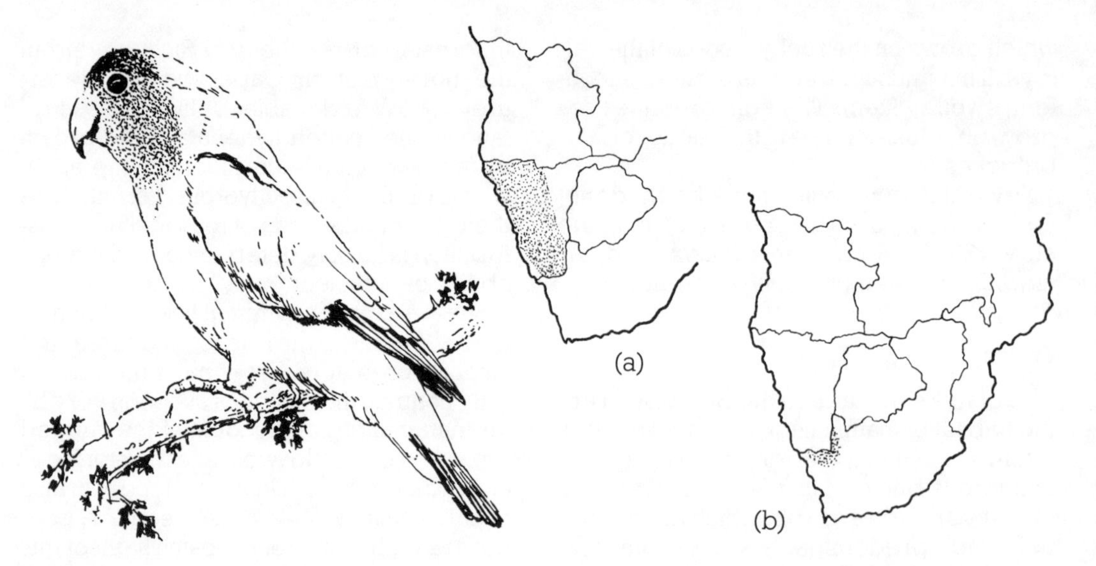


*Rosyfaced lovebirds have a characteristic shrill metallic shreek call*

*Distribution of rosyfaced lovebird in* (a) *SWA/Namibia and* (b) *South Africa*

species that are prevalent here include scimitarbilled woodhoopoe (454), redeyed bulbul (567) and mountain chat (586).

At higher elevations you are likely to hear the deep coos of the rock pigeon (349). Keep an eye open here for the Herero chat (618), which is restricted to a narrow belt stretching from the Naukluft Mountains to south-western Angola, rock martin (529) and palewinged starling (770).

### History

Archaeological finds from the plains surrounding the Brandberg provide evidence of inhabitation of the area by people of the Early and Middle Stone Ages.

The Brandberg itself is perhaps best known for its painting of the famous White Lady in the Tsisab Ravine on the north-eastern side of the mountain. Several hundred other rock painting sites have been located in the massif. Many of these sites were recorded by Harald Pager, who spent some eight years (1977 to 1985) in the Brandberg recording and tracing the paintings. These paintings were executed by the last of the Later Stone Age people, the San.

Archaeological excavations at a site in the upper Hungorob Ravine have revealed three phases of occupation. The initial phase was dated at about 4380 BP and yielded numerous Later Stone Age tools. Dung thought to have been that of domestic stock was associated with the second phase of occupation, which has been dated at about 2100 BP. More recent occupation of the cave has been dated at about 730 BP. Artefacts related to pastoral people include an iron-tipped adze, a string of copper and iron beads attached to a string of cowry shells and pottery fragments.

One of the densest concentrations of stone-walled sites associated with pastoral people in the central Namib is to be found at the entrance of the Hungorob Ravine, where some 150 sites have been located. A large *heitsi eibib* or cairn can be seen near the entrance to the ravine. According to legend these cairns were built to mark the repeated burial of a mythical trickster of that name and it is customary to add to the cairn when passing by. Numerous huts, which were intermittently occupied over the last 700 years, are to be found in the area. Other features include hearths, windbreaks, seed pestles, cairns and keeps where the young of small stock were presumably kept.

Higher up in the ravine is the Mid-Hungorob site, which is situated between the 1 100 m and 1 200 m contour lines. This site is thought to have been used as a halfway station by pastoralists migrating to the upper Hungorob. In order to facilitate the herding of animals to the upper Hungorob an artificial pathway was constructed on the eastern side of the ravine between the 1 100 m and 1 200 m contours. The route of the pathway is marked by small cairns of cleared rubble and rubble-filled ground and is still visible below the 'half-way' station.

The pastoralists occupied the gravel plains during the early part of the summer, retreating to the upper ravine with the failing of the pastures on the plains. Not only are the water resources better distributed and reliable in the upper ravine, but the carrying capacity reaches its optimum at an elevation of about 2 000 m. It has been estimated that while a herd of 100 sheep would need to cover 500 ha to survive for six months at the foot of the mountain, the same herd could in principle be maintained on 10 ha of the grassy plain at the 2 000 m contour for the equivalent period.[3]

The first white people to set eyes on the Brandberg were probably Diogo Cão and his men, who planted a *padrão* (cross) at Cape Cross roughly 100 km south-west of the mountain in 1486. The mountain was mentioned in about 1846/48 by Captain W Messum, but it is not known whether he personally visited it. The fiery, burnt appearance of the mountain, which Messum estimated to be 3 200 feet (975 m) high, deprived him of the honour of having it named after him, and by 1889 the name Brandberg was already commonly used. A range of low hills which form the rim of a crater south-west of the Brandberg and one of the major rivers draining the mountain have, however, been named after this intrepid explorer.

Apart from the travel report of the missionary Dr Carl Hugo Hahn written in 1871 and the impressions of Dr George Gürich, published in 1889, there are few references to the Brandberg in early records.

The first account of rock paintings was provided by *Oberleutnant* Hugo Jochmann, who explored the Tsisab Ravine on the eastern side of the mountain in 1909. One of the painting sites in the lower Tsisab now bears Jochmann's name and the date of the discovery is inscribed on a rock close by. It was only five years later that the first authenticated ascent of the Brandberg was recorded when two members of the survey division of the Schutztruppe reached what they thought was the highest point of the mountain. During an expedition in 1955 the iron beacon which they had erected was discovered on the Horn (2 519 m), a peak 7 km north-west of Königstein. On 2 January 1918 Reinhard Maack, a surveyor, Professor A Gries, a high school principal from Windhoek, and Lieutenant George Schultze of Keetmanshoop became the first whites to set foot on the Königstein. On their descent, Maack discovered the world-famous painting which was later to become known as The White Lady of the Brandberg.

**Trail Synopsis**

There are various backpacking possibilities in the Brandberg but the easiest, although not the shortest, route to Königstein has been described here. If your time is limited, backpack as far as possible and turn back. A day-to-day description is not given as it is difficult to predict the rate at which you will progress over the rugged terrain.

From the end of the track you follow the river course for a short while before crossing over a flat, sandy plain where you must be on the lookout for an indistinct footpath leading to the left-hand bank of the river. Here you join a fairly well-defined track which is followed for about 2 km before you cross over to the right of the ravine.

There are several streams here, but be sure that you are in the stream-bed on the extreme right. The trail gets more demanding as you progress higher and large boulders will frequently block your way. Do not become despondent, though. Take time to enjoy the incredible scenery that unfolds around you and work your way patiently around the boulders.

---

3 Kinahan, J. 1986. The Archaeological Structure of Pastoral Production in the Central Namib Desert. *South African Archaeological Society Goodwin Series* 5: 69-82.

If you are observant you will notice some cairns close to where a side branch joins the river from the right — about an hour's steady walking from the start. Follow the cairned route, but if you miss it, just work your way up systematically.

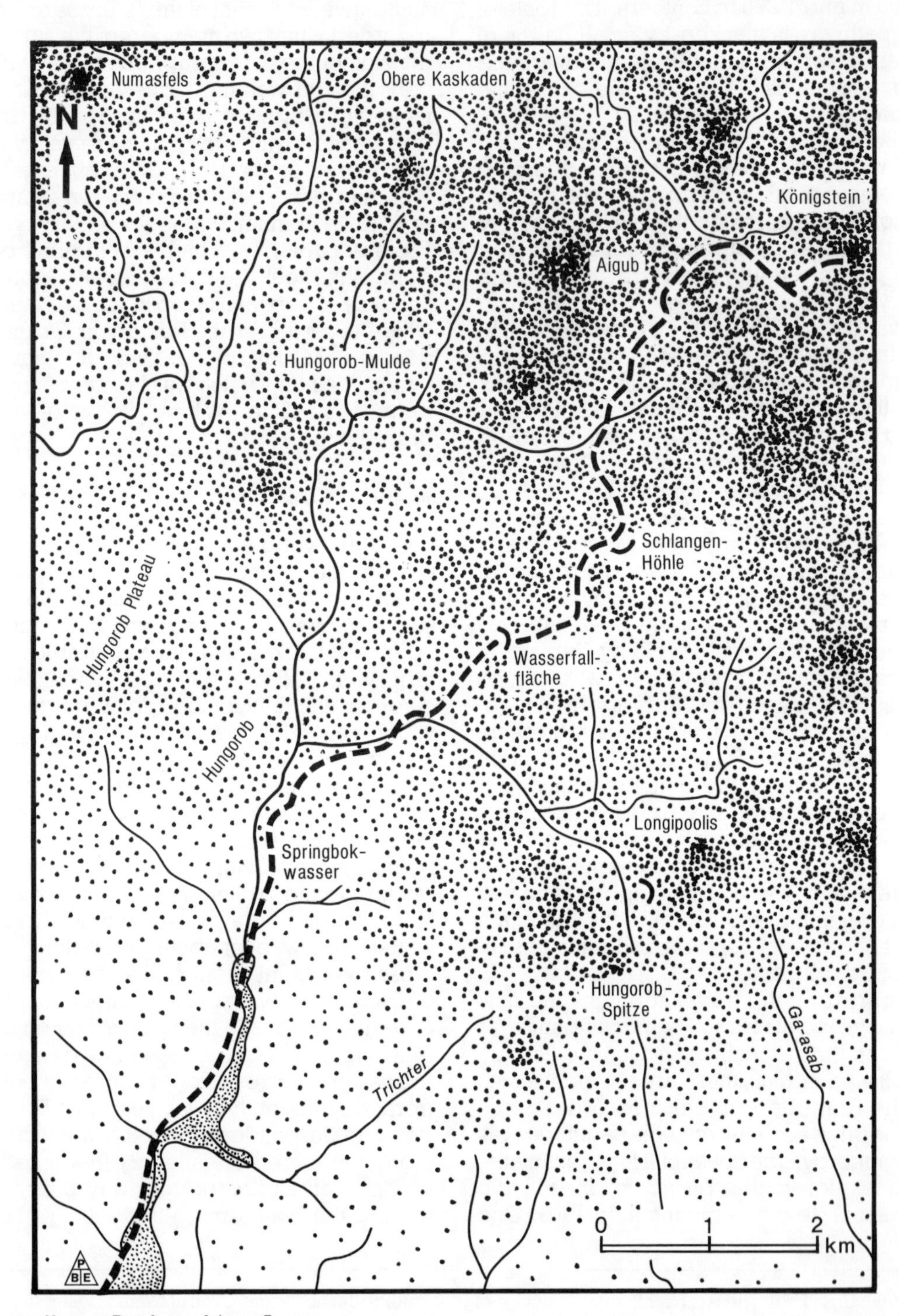


*Brandberg Backpacking Area*

The route winds back towards the main course of the river and you will soon find yourself scrambling over large boulders once more. Keep an eye open for a large African star-chestnut (474) which grows from a crack in a large, flat rock shelf. You should have little difficulty in identifying this species, which grows among rocks in the vicinity of water. It has smooth, white to light brown bark which peels and flakes to reveal its eye-catching pastel-coloured and marbled underbark. Greenish-yellow flowers with red veins can be seen from September to November before the new leaves sprout. The seed pods consist of one to five boat-shaped segments which split down one side to reveal blue-grey seeds that look like ticks — hence the less frequently used common name, tick tree.

If you are in need of water you might be lucky enough to find some in the vicinity of the tree. Make your way down into the river-bed, passing another African star-chestnut, and peep under rocks, into crevices and caves and your efforts may well be rewarded. Although they are not marked on the map, the pools here are known as Springbokwasser. Do not count on finding water here, however, and if you do, remember to take only as much as you need. There are a number of suitable camping spots in the vicinity, but mosquitoes can be a nuisance if there is water around.

From here you must start to make your way up to Damaradorf. Leave the river-bed and head for the nek between the low koppie ahead of you and the spur to the right. This ascent is quicker than you might expect and is easy enough if you manage to find the path used by early pastoralists to herd their sheep and goats up into the Brandberg. Once you reach the nek you will immediately recognise Damaradorf by the stone circles packed by the early inhabitants. There are also rock paintings in the vicinity.

From here the route is marked with cairns leading in a north-easterly direction. Look around for the first stone cairn and follow them up the slope to your right. After about half an hour the path levels out and you now continue high above a side ravine of the Hungorob. You will notice a high waterfall below you in the ravine and shortly after this the cairns lead down into the river-bed. You can look for water amongst the boulders above the waterfall but, once again, don't count on finding any.

Extraordinary large boulders block the ravine where the path leads down to it but they also create a cool resting place. Depending on when you set off and your progress, this is a good overnight camping site, especially with the possibility of finding water a little lower down. It takes between one and a half and two hours to reach this spot from Damaradorf.

It is necessary to cross over to the left side of the ravine where cairns will initially guide you. Here the trail becomes more difficult and after a while a side stream enters the ravine from the left. Large boulders obstruct your progress, but with some patience you will get around them. There is a steep ascent of some 300 m in elevation ahead of you. As you climb up be on the lookout for two quiver trees (29) at the top of the ridge and head for them.

On completing the ascent, the terrain levels out and you continue in a north-easterly direction before reaching a west-facing cave. This section leads through dense, thorny scrub and if you have long trousers in your pack, put them on to protect your legs. Water can usually be found in a gully a short distance above the cave.

From here you head in an easterly direction, crossing a plain marked Wasserfallfläche on the topographical map. After about half a kilometre you turn north and continue for roughly 1 km, after which you turn east, passing Schlangen Höhle. The cave, which faces north, is a popular base camp from which to explore the area and contains some fine rock paintings.

To ascend Köningstein from here you continue northwards for about 1 km before rejoining the Hungorob River, which you follow upstream, ignoring a tributary which enters the river from the left. Keep to the right-hand side. About 1 km further on the stream splits, but you remain with the right fork, aiming for a nek. On reaching 2 326 m (marked on the topographical map) you continue to the Numas River where there is also the possibility of finding water. After a short stretch along the Numas you leave it, heading in a south-easterly direction over a level section. Aim for an obvious, massive boulder from where you gain some 100 m in altitude. You then turn left (north-east) and after a short, level walk ascend the final 100 m to the highest point in SWA/Namibia!

Unless you are familiar with the mountain it is best to return along the same route. Depending on your water supply and time, you may decide to spend a few rewarding days exploring the area from the base camp. You will find that you make much better time on the return route.

**DON'T MISS**

- the famous rock painting of the White Lady in the Tsisab Ravine. To reach the ravine take the Kamanjab turnoff (R76[C35]) on leaving Uis and after 14 km turn left onto the road signposted to the Witvrou (Afrikaans for White Lady). Continue along this road for about 28 km, after which the road ends at a car park. From here it is about an hour and a half's walk up the Tsisab Ravine to the overhang with the White Lady and other rock paintings. The route is well marked.
- 10 major sites and seven minor sites with rock paintings, including Jochmann Shelter, which are within a kilometre and a half further upstream from the White Lady. This is where the first rock paintings were recorded in the Brandberg, and it is worth spending some time here to look around.

# 4 Fish River Canyon Backpacking Trail

This trail offers you the opportunity of backpacking through total wilderness, following the course of the second largest canyon in the world. The canyon — over 600 m deep in places and stretching for more than 160 km — is one of Africa's greatest natural wonders, formed over aeons by titanic forces from below and the erosive action of water. You will be enraptured by the beauty surrounding you on the trail, the scenery gradually changing as the canyon slowly broadens towards Ai-Ais.

## Location

Approaching from Cape Town, the turnoff to Ai-Ais is reached 37 km north of Noordoewer on the B1. From here you follow a gravel road for approximately 82 km. The usual route from Johannesburg is via Karasburg and Grünau with the route to Ai-Ais branching off to the right approximately 30 km south of Grünau. From here it is a further 74 km on a gravel road. The main viewpoint, where the trail starts, is roughly 80 km north of Ai-Ais.

## Distance and Classification

100 km along the entire river course; 86 km approximately taking short-cuts into account.
4 or 5 days
C grade
Even during the winter months daytime temperatures can soar to over 40 °C, which can make the trail exhausting. When the river is high frequent river crossings can be trying.

## Permits

Written reservations are accepted up to 18 months in advance and held on file, but are only confirmed 11 months prior to the trail date. Telephone and personal applications are accepted 11 months in advance. Applications must be addressed to The Director, Directorate of Nature Conservation and Recreation Resorts, Private Bag 13267, Windhoek 9000, SWA/Namibia, Telephone (061) 36975. The trail fee is not refundable should you cancel. Groups must consist of a minimum of three people and a maximum of 40 people are allowed to set off each day. Owing to excessive summer temperatures and the danger of flash floods, backpacking is only permitted from 1 May to 31 August.

## Maps

A free map of the trail which also contains interesting information is forwarded to you with the permit. The area is covered by 1: 50 000 topographical maps 2717DA, 2717DC and 2717CD, which are available from the Surveyor-General, Department of Justice, Private Bag 13182, Windhoek 9000, SWA/Namibia.

## Relevant Information

- Even during the cooler winter months temperatures can soar to over 40 °C, so be sure to take adequate sun protection measures.
- During periods of excessive heat, walking should be restricted to between first light and 11h00 and then after 15h00. When planning the distance to be covered each day remember that camp must be established before 18h00 as it gets dark very quickly in the canyon.
- The first section of the trail to Palm Springs is the most spectacular but the large boulders and stretches of sand

can be trying. It is therefore important to plan your trail in such a way as to ensure sufficient time to enjoy this section.

- Sleeping is in the open and a tent is unnecessary.
- Remember to take a light raincoat as unexpected thunderstorms have been experienced in mid-winter.
- This is one of the few backpacking areas where you are allowed to make a fire. However, as trees are scarce in the canyon, do not make your fire under a tree or on tree roots. Make it in a shallow hole in the sand and extinguish it properly before breaking up camp. Use only drift wood, and never break off seemingly dead branches from trees. Keep other backpackers in mind and use wood sparingly.
- On making a reservation a medical form will be forwarded to you which must be completed by a doctor not earlier than 40 days prior to the trail. The certificate must be produced at Hobas, or the control point near the northern viewpoint.
- An information centre at Hobas, a few kilometres east of the main viewpoint, is scheduled for completion in the first half of 1989. Backpackers will be briefed here before they set off on the trail.

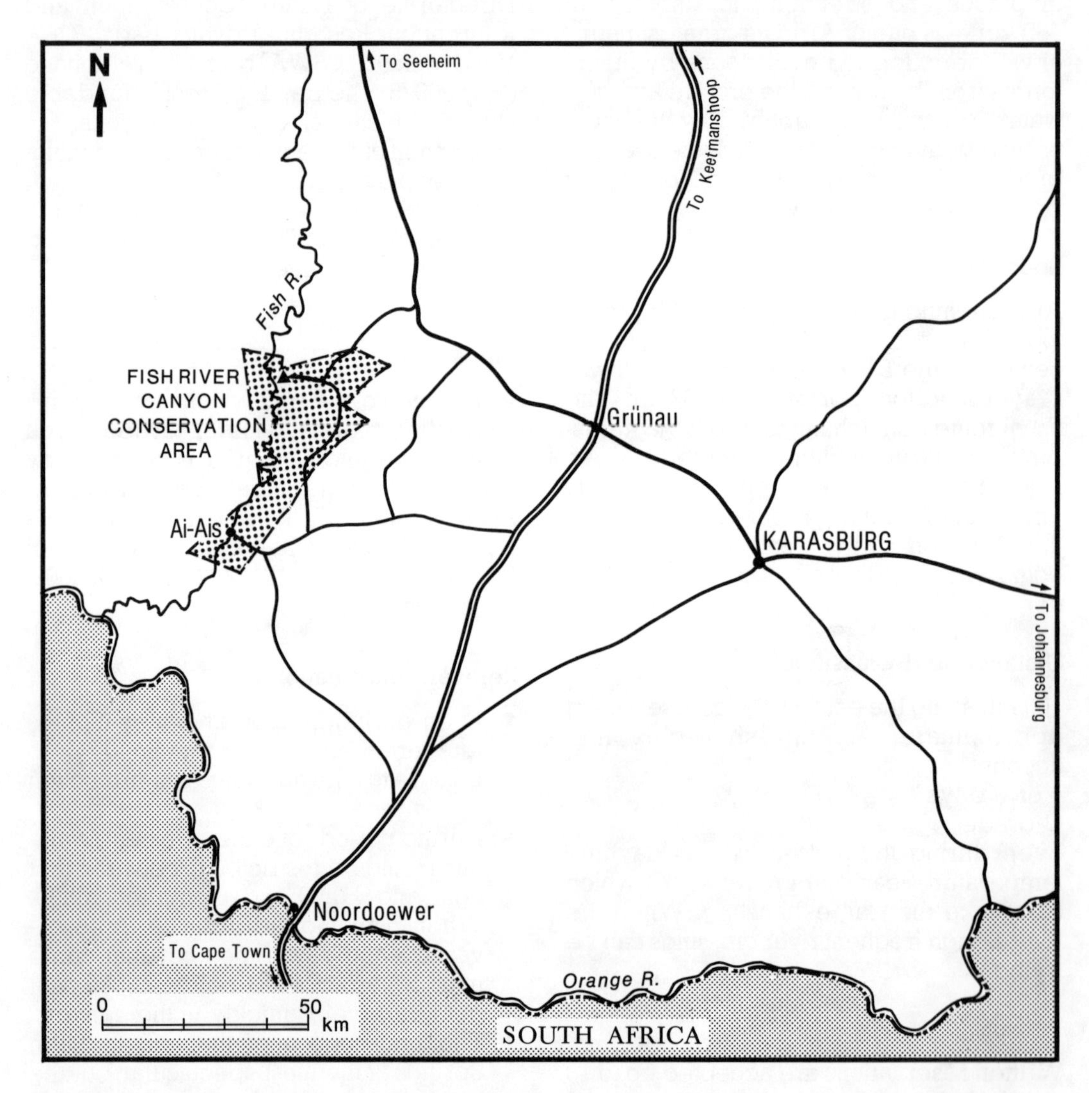


*Location: Fish River Canyon Nature Reserve*

## Facilities

Accommodation at Ai-Ais varies from camping and caravan sites to caravan accommodation, flats and tents with beds and bedding. Reservations must be made when booking the trail as they can only be made through Windhoek. Most commodities, including bread, frozen meat and liquor, are available from the shop at Ai-Ais, where there is also a licensed restaurant.

A campsite for backpackers at Hobas, a few kilometres east of the main viewpoint, is due for completion in the first half of 1989. The usual camping facilities (including water) will be provided. Backpackers will not be permitted to sleep at the northern viewpoint once these facilities have been completed.

## Climate

The average annual daily maximum temperature at Ai-Ais is in the region of 30 °C, with day temperatures fluctuating between 20 °C and 25 °C from May to August. However, midday temperatures of up to 40 °C are not uncommon in the canyon between these months. The evenings from May to August are generally pleasant, but temperatures can drop to 5 °C or lower.

The average annual rainfall varies between 50 and 100 mm, but the rainfall is erratic. Although 60 to 70 per cent of the rain occurs in the form of thunderstorms from October to March, unexpected showers occur during the winter months, so be prepared.

## Flora

The vegetation has been classified by Giess as Dwarf Shrub Savanna (Vegetation Type 9), which occurs in the arid regions of southern SWA/Namibia, reaching its northernmost limit near Rehoboth.

With the exception of reeds (*Phragmites australis*) and rushes (*Juncus arabicus*) which grow in the river-bed, the vegetation in the canyon is mainly restricted to the river-banks. The most common tree species are sweet thorn (172), camel thorn (168), which is appreciated for its shade, buffalo-thorn (447), ebony tree (598), which grows either as a shrub or medium-sized tree with drooping branches, karree (386) and the Namaqua fig (51). The Namaqua fig was first described by Le Vaillant in 1773 from a specimen he found at the Heerenlogement Cave near Clanwilliam. It is a medium-sized tree which grows to about 10 m high and is characteristically associated with rocks where its roots flatten against the rock faces.

The sweet thorn is the most widely distributed *Acacia* species of Southern Africa, occurring throughout most of South Africa and Zimbabwe as well as Lesotho, Swaziland, Mozambique, Malawi, eastern Botswana, southern Angola and large parts of SWA/Namibia.

With a characteristic dark to black trunk, trees usually grow to a height of about 3 to 5 m, but sometimes reach up to 15 m. They occur over a wide range of habitats and are often found along dry watercourses where they form dense stands. The leaves are darkish lime-green, while the sickle-shaped seed pods vary from yellow or reddish-brown to brown.

Shrubs include wild green-hair tree (214), shepherd's tree (122) and the velvet raisin (459.1). A species you are likely to identify easily is the wild tamarisk (487) with its small yellowish grey-green scale-like leaves. The wild tamarisk grows as a small to medium-sized tree and favours dry river-beds and river-banks in and on the fringes of desert areas in the west of South Africa and SWA/Namibia.

During May and June the white, trumpet-like flowers of *Datura innoxia*, a poisonous member of the potato family, can be seen in bloom. It is an alien from South America which was introduced into the country in contaminated fodder and has invaded many of SWA/Namibia's rivers.

Scattered on the barren slopes are ring-wood tree (136), quiver tree (29), *Euphorbia mauritanica*, *E. virosa* and *Aloe gariepensis*. The latter species was named after the Orange River, which was initially known as the Gariep. The flowers vary from yellow to red-green and are usually seen between July and September.

## Fauna

The pools in the canyon are usually well populated with fish. Five species have been recorded: small-mouthed yellow fish (*Barbus holubi*), large-mouthed yellow fish (*B. kimberleyensis*), catfish (barbel) (*Clarias gariepinus*), carp (*Cyprinus carpio*) and blue kurper (*Oreochromis mossambicus*), which is possibly the best eating fish of the five species. You must, however, obtain a permit from Ai-Ais if you intend fishing.

Yellow fish prefer fast-moving water and are usually found below a rapid or in an eddy. They are renowned as sporting fish, but are unfortunately too bony to serve as a good table fish. They are best prepared by soaking them overnight in vinegar to dissolve the small bones.

Barbel are common in the pools and are easily caught because they take any live or meat bait. Owing to their rather hideous appearance, however, they are not popular table fish. They are extremely hardy fish and during a drought will bury themselves in mud, where they can survive for considerable periods. During 1983 when the canyon was extremely dry chacma baboon were observed digging barbel from the mud to supplement their diet.

A very effective bait for carp is soft-boiled maize pips. However, carp are not good table fish and it is quite an art to prepare them tastefully.

The pools are also the habitat of water monitor (leguan) (*Varanus niloticus*), which sometimes betray their presence by taking to the water with a splash as you approach. Fossil records of the family Varanidae show that the water monitor differs very little from its ancestors of 60 million years ago. When threatened its first reaction is to escape, and it will use its tail to defend itself against small predators. Contrary to popular belief, however, the tail is not strong enough to break your leg should you get too close! The leguan is covered with small, smooth scales and can reach up to 2 m in length. Freshwater mussels, crabs, frogs, snails, water birds, eggs and insects are its main sources of food.

Three mammals you are likely to see on the rocky slopes are klipspringer, rock dassie and chacma baboon. Klipspringer are

*Hartmann's mountain zebra – a species restricted to mountainous areas in the west of SWA/Namibia*

usually seen in pairs and they will often startle you with their high-pitched alarm call before making off with great agility over the rocks. Their characteristic spoor, two small oval prints, is frequently seen in the damp sand on the edge of the river. There are a number of chacma baboon troops in the canyon, and at the start of the backpacking season when they are still fairly shy, you are more likely to hear the warning bark of the sentinel than actually see them. However, as they become used to more backpackers passing through, they become less concerned about people and, later in the backpacking season, are often seen at close range.

The canyon is also the habitat of kudu, leopard and several smaller mammals such as the ground squirrel and the dassie rat.

Hartmann's mountain zebra (*Equus zebra hartmannae*) are seldom seen and often the only indications of their presence are droppings, spoor or rolling places. They are very wary animals and normally only come down from the plateau above the canyon at night to quench their thirst.

Their distribution in SWA/Namibia is restricted to the mountainous transitional zone between the Namib and the inland plateau. In the south they occur in the Fish River Canyon and the Huns Mountains and after a break in their distribution of about 400 km, they re-occur in the Naukluft Mountains and the Khomas Hochland further north. A small, isolated population inhabits the Erongo Mountains south-west of Omaruru. They also occur in a narrow strip from the Ugab River northwards to Kaokoland and south-western Angola and eastwards to farms in the Outjo district. About 1 700 mountain zebra inhabit the Naukluft Complex, while their total numbers in conservation areas are estimated at 3 500. About half of this number inhabit the rugged Kuiseb Canyon north-west of Naukluft.

At first glance the Hartmann's mountain zebra appears similar to the southern subspecies, the Cape mountain zebra (*Equus zebra zebra*), but it differs in a number of respects:

- it is slightly larger than the Cape mountain zebra, with a shoulder height of 1,5 m as opposed to 1,3 m, and bears a closer resemblance to a horse in build;
- the stripes are more widely spaced, with the result that the pale stripes are either equal or slightly wider than the black stripes;
- the legs are almost equally banded black and buff, and the mane is well developed.

Hartmann's mountain zebra occur either in family groups, consisting of a stallion, mares and foals, or in bachelor groups. Solitary stallions are occasionally encountered. Although most births occur between November and April, foals can be born at any time of the year, after a gestation period of about 12 months.

They feed mainly after first light and between 15h00 and sunset, resting in the shade of trees during the hottest part of the day in summer. During the summer months they must drink water at least once a day. This species is more nomadic than the Cape mountain zebra and covers distances of up to 100 km in search of grazing.

With the exception of a few individuals that might occasionally cross the Orange River at low water from SWA/Namibia, wild populations of Hartmann's mountain zebra no longer occur in South Africa. Small numbers have, however, been reintroduced into the Hester Malan Nature Reserve near Springbok and extralimitally in the Cape of Good Hope Nature Reserve at Cape Point. Their distribution in the Cape was originally centred around the Kamiesberg and the Richtersveld south of the Orange River.

Although the Fish River does not flow throughout the year, it has several large permanent pools in the middle reaches which make it an important transit route for birds moving further north to Hardap Dam and the Naukluft Mountains. Bird species you are most likely to see are those attracted to the open water. The Egyptian goose (102) can be identified by its honk-haah-haah cry, which is often heard early in the morning or late afternoon. When disturbed it will fly a little ahead of you, escorting you away from its territory. You should easily identify the hamerkop (81) with its distinctive hammer-shaped head. It is a uniform dark brown and is usually seen hunting in shallow water, where it feeds on frogs and other aquatic animals. The grey heron (62) and the threebanded plover (249) are two more bird species occurring in the canyon.

Among the birds of prey are the African fish eagle (148), which perches in trees near the river, the black eagle (131), which is sometimes observed soaring on the thermals, and the small rock kestrel (181).

The smaller birds are represented by species such as the Cape wagtail (713), pied kingfisher (428), palewinged starling (770) and the familiar (589), sicklewinged (591) and mountain (586) chats. The mountain chat enjoys looking for crumbs and scraps left by backpackers. Although the sicklewinged chat is paler than the familiar chat, the two species are difficult to tell apart. You are also likely to hear the cheerful call of the redeyed bulbul (567), which has a fairly obvious pale yellow undertail. Fiscal shrike (732) and rock martin (529) have also been recorded in the canyon.

Should you do any bird-watching in the reed-beds near Ai-Ais, you might spot moorhen (226), African black duck (105), purple gallinule (223), and Cape white-eye (796). The Cape (601) and the Karoo (614) robins have also been recorded in the riverine bush, with the Karoo robin preferring the more open areas.

Although you are unlikely to encounter any snakes, the Egyptian cobra (*Naja haje haje*), horned adder (*Bitis caudalis*), manyhorned adder (*B. cornuta*) and the puff adder (*B. arietans arietans*) have been recorded in the canyon.

### History

Among the earliest evidence of early man in SWA/Namibia is an Early Stone Age site which dates back some 400 000 years a few kilometres south of the Kuiseb River in the central Namib Desert. Other sites in this region testify to inhabitation of this area by Middle and Later Stone Age people.

Further south, occupation of the Apollo 11 Cave in the Hunsberge, near the confluence of the Orange and Fish rivers, has been dated at about 50 000 BP. The main interest in this cave was the discovery of engraved ostrich egg shells which date back at least 45 000 years. Also discovered here were painted rock slabs, dated at between 25 500 and 27 500 BP, which are among the earliest rock paintings recorded in Africa. Other layers in Apollo 11 Cave yielded evidence of occupation by Middle and Later Stone Age people. The most recent layer indicates occupation some 300 to 500 years ago and material includes pottery.

The vegetated Fish River Canyon, with its relatively abundant resources of water, fish and game was an oasis to the early inhabitants of this otherwise arid region. A survey of the archaeological sites in the trail vicinity was conducted in June 1981 and 27 sites were located.[1] From these sites it was apparent that the size of the settlements increased as the canyon widens towards Ai-Ais.

Early (pre 125 000 BP) and Middle Stone Age artefacts were recorded from nine sites, while more recent settlements were evident at the other 18 sites. These more recent settlements were located mainly on the insides of bends in the river.

To its early inhabitants, the Fish River Canyon must have had some supernatural significance. According to a San legend, the canyon owes its meandering course to the serpent, Kouteign Kooru, which made the place its lair in the distant past. He was relentlessly pursued by hunters and to escape from them he retreated into the desert where he carved deep scars into the earth.

The southern and central parts of SWA/Namibia were also inhabited by the Nama, a nomadic Khoikhoi race of cattle and sheep farmers. They never practised agriculture but husbanded cattle, fat-tailed sheep and goats and supplemented their diet by hunting and gathering. At the beginning of the nineteenth century the Nama tribes were waging a relentless war against the Herero, who lived further north and competed for the same grazing areas. The area remained turbulent and only in 1898 did the Germans succeed in bringing shortlived peace to the southern area. In 1903 one of the Nama tribes rebelled but was subjected four years later. It was during this

1 Kinahan, J. 1987. Archaeological sites in the Fish River Canyon, southern SWA/Namibia. *Madoqua*, Vol. 15, No. 1, 17-19.

period that Ai-Ais was used as a base camp by the German forces. Grim reminders of this almost forgotten war are seen at Gochas Drift in the lower reaches of the canyon, where you will pass the grave of a German soldier, Lieutenant Von Trotha.

Unlike the other large rivers in SWA/Namibia, the Fish River does not flow westwards but from north to south, more or less parallel to the coast. Early maps of Africa indicate the flow westwards, entering the sea near Lüderitz. These maps were drawn from a description given by the French traveller, François le Vaillant, in his book *Second Journey from the Cape of Good Hope into the Interior of Africa in the years 1783, 1784 and 1785,* in which he described his journey from east to west along the river which he named Fleuve de Poissons — the Fish River. The South West African German historian, Dr Heinrich Vedder, refers to Le Vaillant's discovery as '...the creation of a fertile imagination', as it is certain that Le Vaillant returned to France in June 1784 and that he made no further journeys into Africa after that date.

## Geology

One of the most interesting aspects of the canyon is its geology. Backpacking under the endless succession of towering cliffs one cannot help but wonder what titanic forces played a role in shaping the canyon.

Looking across the canyon from the main viewpoint you will see the various geological layers which have been exposed by centuries of erosive action. Once in the canyon look upwards and you will see some of the various geological formations. The steep slopes leading from the riverbed originally comprised sediments and lavas which were deposited 1 800 to 1 000 million years ago.

Some 1 300 to 1 000 million years ago the Namaqua Metamorphic Complex developed when these deposits were subjected to phases of folding, metamorphism, and the intrusion of granite. Later dolerite intrusions can be clearly seen in the form of dark wall-like dykes which run to the top of the Namaqua Metamorphic Complex but not beyond into the overlying rocks of the Nama Group. This indicates that the intrusions must have taken place post-Namaqua but pre-Nama, and are thought to have occurred about 880 million years ago. These dykes were indicated on earlier maps issued by the Directorate of Nature Conservation as 'basalt reefs' and are useful for orientation in surroundings without too many prominent landmarks. The name is, however, a misnomer as they are not 'basalt reefs' but intrusions of dolerite. Dolerite is genetically related to basalt but differs in that magma (molten matter) has been forced into its position in the surrounding rocks without reaching the surface.

About 750 to 650 million years ago the southern part of SWA/Namibia was inundated by a shallow sea and sediments from higher lying areas washed into this basin. These sediments now form the flat-lying Nama Group. The contact of the Nama Group and the Namaqua Metamorphic Complex is called in geology an unconformity and represents a break in the geological record, during which time the deformed strata were eroded to a plane surface before resumption of sedimentation on the erosion plane. The Nama Group is composed of several layers. The small pebble conglomerate at the base of the Group is only a few metres deep and is referred to as the Kanies Member. This is followed by a 150 to 200 m thick layer of carbonates, grits, sandstone and quartzite known as the Kuibis Subgroup. Overlying these two groups is a 10 m band of dark limestone, shale and sandstone of the Schwarzrand Subgroup.

About 300 million years ago the early valley, which had developed about 200 million years previously as a result of a system of north-south running fractures which facilitated erosion, was deepened by southward-moving glaciers during the Gondwana Ice Age. This was followed by another period of fracturing which produced faults, which allowed water, heated deep in the earth, to flow to the surface as springs, the best known being those at Palm (Sulphur) Springs and Ai-Ais. At a later stage incision by the Fish River gave the canyon its present morphology, the most striking features having developed mainly during the past 50 million years.

The Fish River is the longest river in

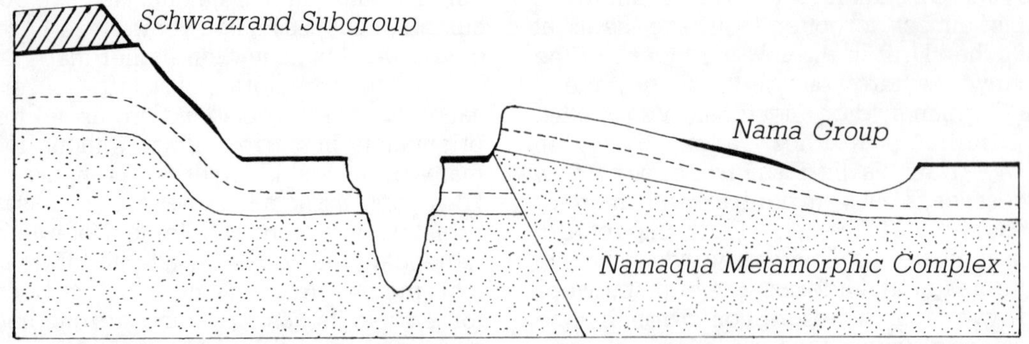


*Geomorphology of the Fish River Canyon*

SWA/Namibia and from its source in the Nauchas Mountains in western Rehoboth, it follows a course of more than 800 km to its confluence with the Orange River, 110 km east of the Atlantic Ocean. For the first few hundred kilometres the river runs with barely any incision past Mariental, Gibeon and Tses, but south of Seeheim it starts descending and at the junction of the Gaab River the incision reaches a depth of approximately 50 m. A few kilometres south of the Gaab River it drops in quick succession over two waterfalls and enters the canyon proper.

With the exception of SWA/Namibia's boundary rivers, the Fish River is the only river in the country that usually has permanent pools in its lower and middle reaches outside of the rainy season. The flow of the river varies with the rainfall, which occurs from mid-November to the end of March, but since the construction of the Hardap Dam near Mariental in 1963 flooding of the river depends on its tributaries south of the dam. When in flood the Fish River becomes a raging torrent, moving at a speed of between 12 and 14 knots and flowing more than 100 m wide in places.

**Trail Synopsis**

From the starting point, at the northernmost viewpoint, to Ai-Ais you will cover approximately 86 km, and this is usually completed in four to five days. There are no set overnight spots, allowing you to backpack at your own pace.

The first section of the descent into the canyon is rather steep, but fortunately there are chains to hold onto. The descent takes anything between 45 minutes and one and a half hours and you are well advised to take it easy. Once the canyon floor is reached, you should not miss the opportunity to swim in the enormous pool awaiting you.

Palm Springs is one of the most popular overnight spots. Unfortunately, it is a fairly long slog of at least 15 km to the spring. The terrain, consisting predominantly of large boulders interspersed with stretches of sand, can be very tiring. The path mainly follows the left bank of the river, but closer to Palm Springs it is best to cross over to the right-hand bank. Approximately 2 km before Palm Springs the alternative route starting at the Palm Springs Lookout is seen on the left bank of the river.

Before you spot the palm trees at Palm Springs, faint wafts of sulphur will indicate that you are close to your destination. The trees at Palm Springs are not indigenous to either South Africa or SWA/Namibia, and their presence has given rise to several stories, the most popular being that they grew from date stones discarded by two German prisoners of war who escaped from the internment camp at Aus during World War I. One of them is said to have suffered from skin cancer and the other from asthma, but after bathing in the sulphur spring for two months both were miraculously cured. (This story is very often confused with that of the two Germans who fled into the Kuiseb Canyon during World War II to escape internment, and whose story has been immor-

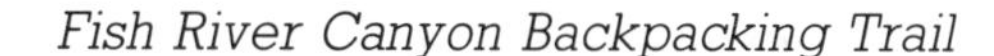


talised in the book *The Sheltering Desert.*)

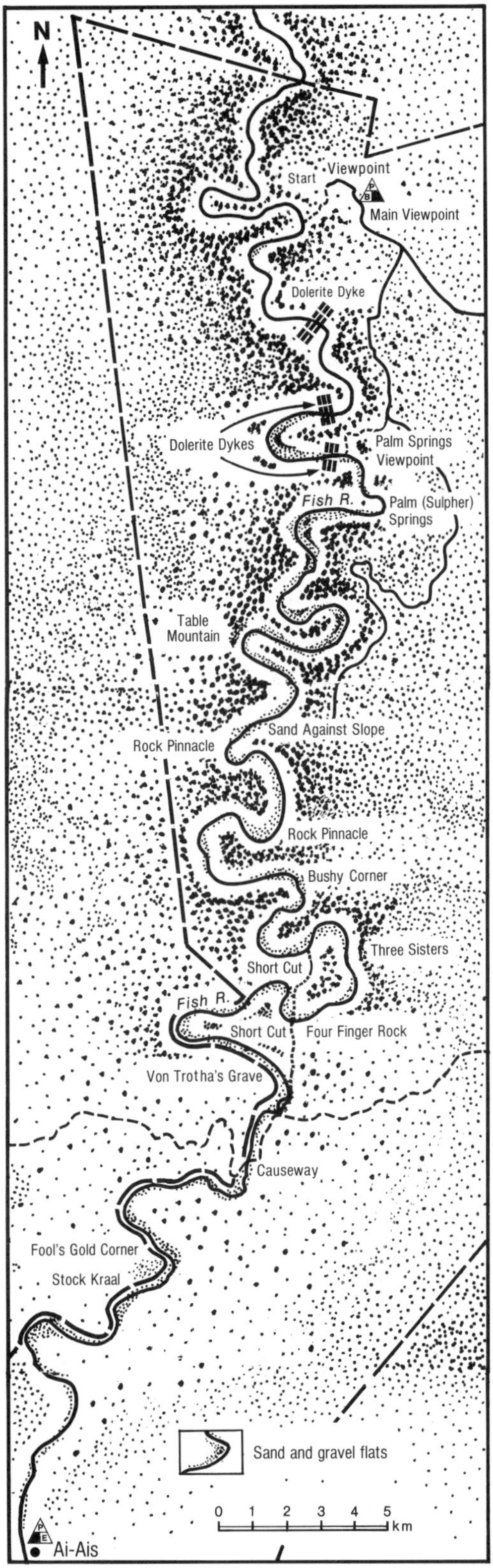

The hot spring is caused by surface water filtering down cracks and fissures in the rocks to depths of about 1 000 m before it is forced back to the surface at a flow estimated at about 30 litres per second and a temperature of 57 °C. It is rich in fluorides, chlorides and sulphates, the latter being responsible for the pungent odour. Here the weary backpacker can soothe his aching muscles.

Palm Springs is unfortunately the most polluted place in the canyon, mainly owing to inconsiderate day visitors who leave their litter behind without concern for the pristine beauty of the canyon.

From Palm Springs the boulders give way to stretches of sand, round river stones and later gravel plains, which make progress considerably easier. Table Mountain, a huge flat-topped mountain, is a familiar landmark and useful for orientation.

There are several short-cuts, the longest being just before the formation known as the Three Sisters. This short-cut is situated on the right bank of the river, with a clump of wild tamarisk trees (487) almost blocking the entrance. From the river you ascend up Kooigoedhoogte and once the summit is reached, Four Finger Rock comes into view. The route then meanders across a gravel plain and after about 2,5 km rejoins the river. Shortly after passing a 'seep' with its large white salt deposits, the river comes into view on the right, but the correct route lies straight ahead towards Four Finger Rock. After joining the river again you follow a jeep track, ascending the slopes of the canyon to the west of Four Finger Rock. This well-known feature marks the end of the deepest part of the canyon and further south the Nama sediments give way to deeply dissected mountainous terrain of basement rock.

The canyon now widens considerably and it is here, in the lower reaches of the river, that fierce fighting took place between the Nama and Germans between 1903 and 1907. About 2 km south of Four Finger Rock you will reach the grave of Lieutenant von Trotha, a German officer who was shot in the back during a skirmish with the Nama in 1905 and buried near the site where he fell. He was the nephew of General Lothar von Trotha, who was rushed from Germany to suppress the Herero uprising of 1904. The grave has been packed with stones and a metal plaque placed on it, but it blends in so well with the surroundings that it is easily missed. It is situated on the western edge of the valley leading from Four Finger Rock, so keep to the right of the valley rather than following the dry river course.

Ai-Ais is a good day's walk further south from here. The spring at Ai-Ais — said to mean 'scalding hot' — is said to have been discovered in 1850 by a Nama shepherd searching for stray stock, although it is likely that the spring was known thousands of years earlier. The swimming pool is fed by the spring and the water temperature is about 60 °C. When General Louis Botha invaded South West Africa in 1915 with the South African Forces, wounded German soldiers found a safe refuge here in the mountains and many were able to recover from their wounds.

After World War I the spring was leased to a businessman from Karasburg, who provided basic facilities for visitors. In 1962 it was proclaimed a national monument and six years later a game reserve. The modern rest camp was officially opened on 16 March 1971. Almost exactly a year later the Fish River came down in flood with a magnitude which happens only once in 10 000 years, and almost everything except the main building, which is on higher ground, was washed away. In February 1988 the camp was forced to close for three months after again being flooded.

**DON'T MISS**

- the ramble to the top of the highest peak opposite the rest camp. This takes about 45 minutes and affords you a bird's eye view of the rest camp complex, the rugged terrain towards the west and north as far as Four Finger Rock.

# Part 3
# Cape and Ciskei

# 5 Cederberg Backpacking Area

Few mountain regions in Southern Africa can boast the magnificent mountain scenery of the Cederberg.[1] Centuries of wind and rain have carved extraordinary rock formations out of the soft sandstone, gnarled cedar trees seemingly grow from the rocks on the highest peaks, while several plant species such as the snow protea and the rocket pincushion are unique to the Cederberg range. The Cederberg is criss-crossed by an extensive network of well-maintained footpaths and today it is one of the most popular backpacking and climbing areas in South Africa.

## Location

The Cederberg Wilderness Area lies to the east of the N7 between Citrusdal and Clanwilliam in the western Cape and stretches from Pakhuis Pass in the north to Grootberg in the south.

The main entry point is along the provincial road which branches off the N7, 26 km north of Citrusdal. You follow the road for about 17 km before you reach Algeria Forest Station. From Algeria the road continues over the Cederberg Pass to Welbedacht, Eikeboom, Dwarsrivier and finally Ceres.

## Distance and Classification

A large number of routes are available to backpackers. Options range from day excursions from a base camp to weekend and week-long trips.
B and C Grade, depending on the route taken.

## Permits

Permits must be obtained before entering the Cederberg wilderness area by writing to the Officer-in-Charge, Cederberg Wilderness Area, P O Citrusdal 7340, Telephone (02682) 3440. This also applies to backpackers intending to use private farms in the area as a base camp. Addresses for the privately owned areas are supplied under Facilities on page 83.

The wilderness area has been divided into three areas: the northern part, which includes Pakhuis; the central part; and the western and southern part. A maximum of 50 people per day are permitted into each area and the maximum group size is 10. When applying for a permit you must state which part of the wilderness area you intend visiting, as well as your alternative option. If the maximum capacity for a particular area has been reached for the dates required, a permit will be issued for your alternative choice.

If you are camping and backpacking on private property the restrictions on the number of visitors still apply.

## Maps

The 1:50 000 topographical map of the Cederberg published by the Forestry Branch is the most detailed and up-to-date map of the range. The area from Pakhuis Pass to Cederberg Pass is printed on the one side and Cederberg Pass to Grootberg on the reverse. Paths, huts and rock formations are clearly indicated, as well as interesting features such as the sites of an old

1 Cederberg is the spelling form which has been accepted by the National Place Names Committee. In some early publications the form Cedarberg is commonly used.

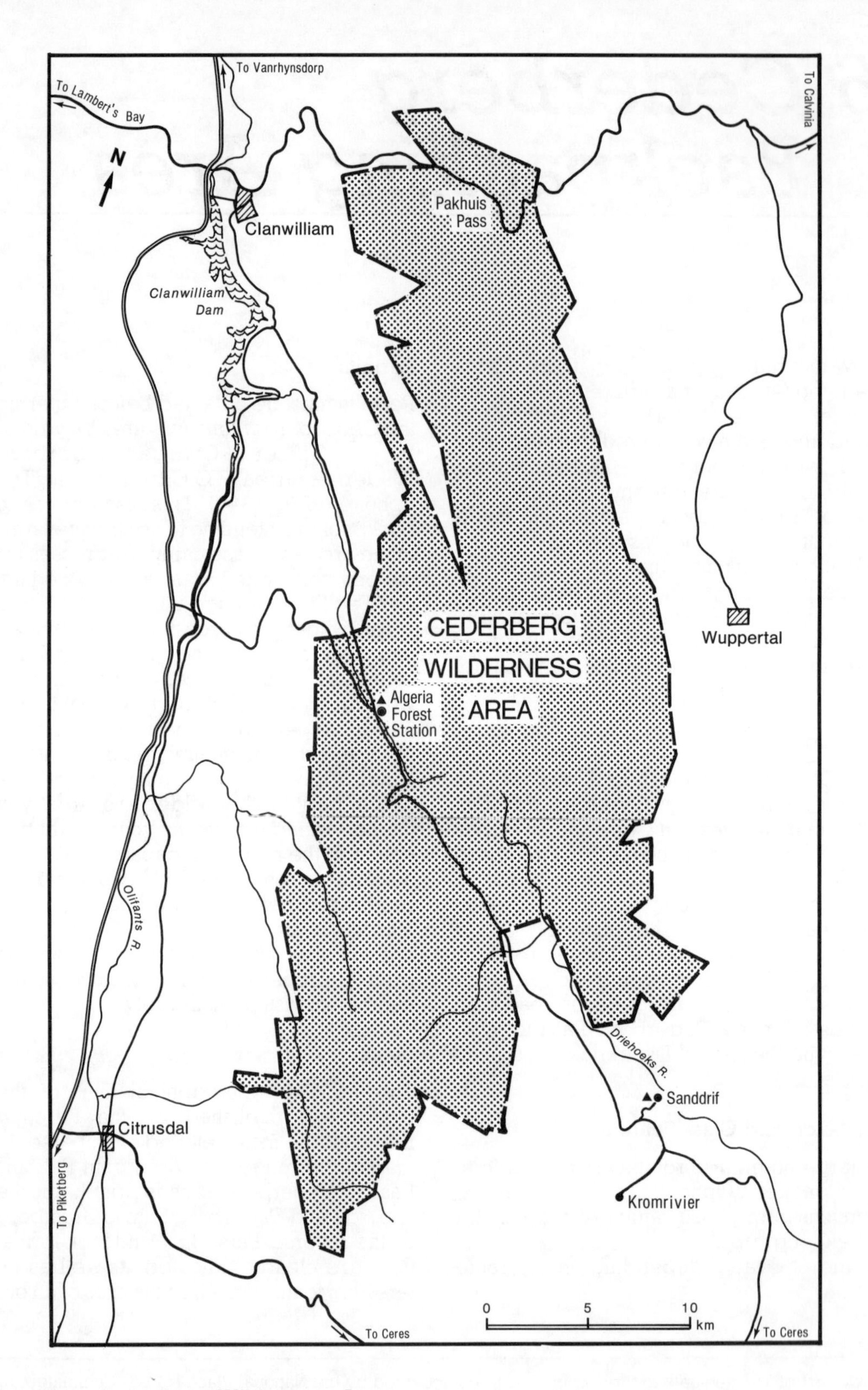


*Location: Cederberg Wilderness Area*

leopard trap, an old cedarwood station and two blockhouses.

The area is also covered by a 1:50 000 map published by *Camp and Climb.* Although it is not as detailed, it is useful for orientation.

### Relevant Information

- Fires are strictly forbidden in the wilderness area and it is essential to carry a backpacking stove.
- A number of rough stone huts originally built for use by forestry rangers are nowadays frequented by backpackers. No facilities are provided and they are occupied on a first come, first served basis. From time to time, however, the huts are still used by forestry personnel. It is therefore advisable to carry a tent, especially during winter when snow may occur.

### Facilities

The camp/caravan site on the banks of the Rondegat River at Algeria Forest Station is most picturesquely situated. There are 36 tent/caravan sites and modern ablutions with hot and cold water. Firewood is available and some of the sites have their own fireplace, picnic table and benches. A beautiful natural swimming pool is situated above a causeway.

An old forestry house and an outbuilding at Uitkyk, 5 km south of Algeria, is available to groups and can accommodate 16 people. It is equipped with bunk-beds with mattresses, a shower, toilet and fireplace. You must supply your own firewood, cooking utensils, eating utensils and bedding.

Reservations for Algeria and Uitkyk should be made when obtaining your permit from the same address.

Another popular campsite is at Sanddrif on the farm Dwarsrivier, 30 km south of Algeria. The campsite is on the banks of the Driehoek River and only veld toilets and cold water taps are provided. Fires are permitted. Cottages equipped with beds, a stove and fridge, hot and cold water and flush toilets are also available here for hire. Sanddrif is conveniently situated should you wish to explore the Wolfberg Cracks and Arch and the Maltese Cross. Reservations should be directed to Messrs Nieuwoudt, Dwarsrivier, P O Cederberg 7341, Telephone (0682) 1521.

The Cederberg Tourist Park on the farm Kromrivier, about 6 km further on, also offers campsites and bungalow accommodation. Reservations can be addressed to the Cederberg Tourist Park, Private Bag Kromrivier, P O Citrusdal 7340, Telephone (0682) 1502.

### Climate

The average daily summer temperatures in the Cederberg vary between 25°C and 30°C, while in winter temperatures often drop to below freezing point at night. Frost often occurs in the low-lying areas during winter, while snowfalls occur on mountain peaks and higher-lying areas.

Algeria Forest Station, with an average of 59 rainy days a year, has an annual rainfall of 647 mm, but, on account of the rugged topography the rainfall varies considerably locally. Although Middelberg is only 3 km from Algeria, the area receives an average rainfall of 938 mm a year, 291 mm more than Algeria. Clanwilliam at the north-western end of the range has an average rainfall of 248 mm and Wuppertal, east of the range, 216 mm. The highest rainfall is recorded between May and August and rainy conditions and mist often last for several days.

### Flora

The vegetation has been classified by Acocks as Mountain Fynbos (Veld Type 69, formerly Macchia). It can be roughly divided into three categories: waboom veld, which is dominated by the wagon tree (86); vegetation of the shale band; and vegetation of the uppermost elevations.

As a result of exploitation by early woodcutters and uncontrolled fires, the Clanwilliam cedar (19) is confined to scattered populations on rocky outcrops and mountain tops at altitudes between 1 000 and 1 650 m. It belongs to the cypress family (Cupressaceae) and is therefore not related to the cedar trees of the Middle East and North Africa, which are classified as members of the Pinaceae family. The Clanwil-

*Bleached skeletons of cedar trees are a familiar sight in the Cederberg*

liam cedar normally grows between 5 and 7 m high but trees in protected places can reach up to 20 m in height with a trunk diameter of up to 2 m. The massive, gnarled old trees are a characteristic sight, as are the bleached skeletons of trees devasted by fires in previous centuries. The leaves of the young trees are needle-like in contrast to the scale-like leaves of the adults, which grow up to 4 mm long.

The wagon tree is another conspicuous species and is common on talus slopes. It grows as a gnarled tree usually reaching up to 5 m, although old specimens reach up to 7 m and 1 m in diameter. Some fine specimens can be seen in Sederhoutkloof. The common name was given to the tree because it provided wood for wagon making and brake blocks. The botanist Pappe wrote that crushed wagon tree leaves mixed with a saturated solution of iron in water produced a tolerably good ink. The reddish-brown wood was also used for making household furniture such as *botterbakke* (butter-dishes) and *potterakke* (pot stands), while the bark has been used for tanning hides.

Of particular interest is the snow protea *(P. cryophila),* which is endemic to the Cederberg. The species name means 'fond of the cold', a fitting description, for these plants are often completely covered in snow during the severe winter months. They are limited to the highest mountain summits between altitudes of 1 750 m and 1 900 m, stretching for about 25 km from Sneeukop to Sneeuberg. The immature flowers are pure white and have the appearance of a fluffy snowball. The flowers open during February, revealing their striking red inner surfaces.

Another Proteaceae species limited to the Cederberg is the rocket pincushion *(Leucospermum reflexum),* which grows naturally only in the northern Cederberg. In recent years it has become a familiar species in urban gardens and the name is derived from the crimson-red flowers which curl outwards to resemble a pointed rocket-head. During the six-month flowering period between July and December, a single mature plant may produce more than 1 000 blooms. *L. reflexum* var. *luteum* with its exceptionally beautiful pale yellow flowers also occurs, but is less frequently found.

Several other Proteaceae species are also endemic to the Cederberg, including three species listed as critically rare in the *South African Red Data Book: Plants — Fynbos and Karoo Biomes.* They are *Paranomus tomentosus, Serruria flava* and *S. leipoldtii,* which was named after the well-known Afrikaans poet C Louis Leipoldt, who was a keen botanist. *Leucadendron dubium* and *L. nitidum* are also endemic to the area, while *L. concavum* is limited to the Pakhuis Pass area and listed as vulnerable.

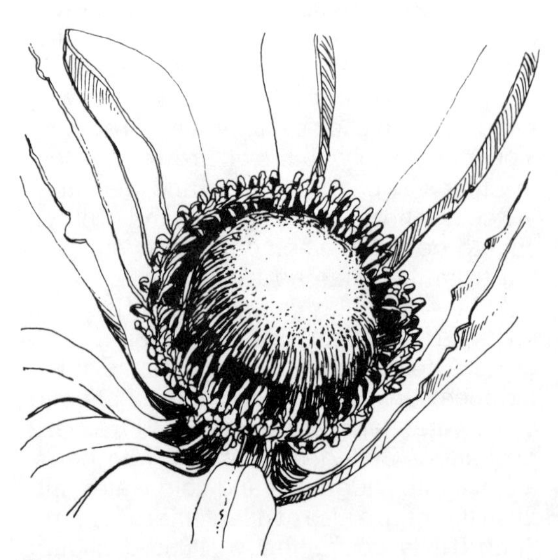

*The snow protea – a species endemic to the Cederberg*

*The crimson-red flowers of the rocket pincushion create a spectacular display between July and December*

Among the several *Erica* species that grow on the slopes and among the rocky outcrops are the pink flowered species such as *Erica eugenia*, *E. inflata* and *E. junonia*, while the large white flowered *E. monsoniana* and the red and yellow Malay heath *(E. thunbergii)* can also be seen.

The shale band which is locally known as Die Trap stretches from Sanddrif past Tafelberg to Sneeukop and further. Here typical *Protea* species include *Protea punctata*, the Cedarberg protea *(P. acuminata)*, *P. laevis* and the dwarf green protea *(P. acaulos)*. Also characteristic of the shale band is the renosterbos *(Elytropappus rhinocerotis)*.

An orchid endemic to the Cederberg between 730 and 990 m in dry fynbos, is *Disperis macrocorys*. It can grow up to 17 cm tall and the slender plant bears only one pale yellow flower at a time. A more common and widespread orchid to be on the lookout for on dry mountain slopes at between 300 and 1 000 m is *Disa filicornis*. Flowers varying from white to deep pink can be seen between October and December. This species usually grows in full sunshine and its distribution ranges from the Cederberg to Humansdorp.

Two plants of considerable economic importance also occur in the Cederberg. Rooibos tea bushes *(Aspalathus linearis)* grow as multibranched, erect shrubs of up to 2 m high. The leaves are simple, narrow and reach up to 3 cm in length. Small, yellow flowers occur singly or in small groups at the ends of branches. The leaves and stems of the plant are harvested and dried and are then ready to be used for brewing tea. This species occurs naturally in the Gifberg near Van Rhynsdorp and the Calvinia and Clanwilliam areas, where it is cultivated commercially. The last harvest of Rooibos tea in the wilderness area took place in 1969, before which some 4 000 kg were harvested annually.

The harvest of buchu *(Agathosma betulina)* provided an important source of income during the last two decades of last century and the beginning of this century. More than 45 000 kg were harvested annually in the Western Cape and the sale of buchu was an important source of income of the Woods and Forests division of the Cape Colonial Government. It grows as a compact shrub, about half a metre high, although it may reach up to 1,5 m. The plant's tiny leaves have a distinct aroma, and are still used for making buchu brandy, vinegar and buchu oil. The flowers vary from white to pink and mauve to bluish-purple.

## Fauna

The mammals of the Cederberg are mainly those species occurring in the other mountains of the south-western Cape, but because it borders on the Karoo, certain Karoo species that do not occur in all south-western Cape mountains are also found here.

Among the animals of the mountain areas that have disappeared are the Cape mountain zebra and eland, while black (hook-lipped) rhinoceros, springbok, gemsbok and red hartebeest roamed the plains surrounding the Cederberg.

Of the 36 mammal species recorded in the range, half are classified as carnivores. Leopard occur in reasonable numbers but are seldom seen owing to their nocturnal and shy behaviour. You may see the small grey mongoose, a diurnal species, as well as rock dassie, chacma baboon, klipspringer, which inhabit the higher mountainous areas, and grey rhebok, which favour mountain plateaux.

The Cederberg is also the habitat of the aardwolf, a species listed in the *South African Red Data Book — Terrestrial Mammals* as rare. They are widely but sparsely distributed throughout Southern Africa, except in the forested areas of the southern Cape, the north-western corner of the Cape Province and the coastal desert of SWA/Namibia.

Another interesting *Red Data Book* species is the charming spectacled dormouse, which, unfortunately, is seldom seen on account of its nocturnal habits (see also page 99).

Some 200 bird species have been recorded in the Clanwilliam district, while at least 81 species have been identified in the Cederberg. The cliffs and gorges are the habitat of species such as rock pigeon (349), black swift (412), rock martin (529) and redwinged starling (769). Birds you are most likely to see are those associated with rocky slopes and outcrops. These include the ground woodpecker (480), Cape rock thrush (581), sentinel rock thrush (582), mountain chat (586), familiar chat (589) and the Cape rockjumper (611).

Among the birds of prey, the black eagle (131) and the rock kestrel (181) are the most common. Other raptors include the black-shouldered kite (127), steppe buzzard (149) and the African marsh harrier (165).

The greywing francolin (190) and the Cape francolin (195) inhabit the fynbos scrub and sometimes you are only aware of their presence when they scurry out from the fynbos alongside the path as you walk by. The Cape sugarbird (773) with its long tail, the orangebreasted sunbird (777) and the lesser doublecollared sunbird (783) are commonly found in *Protea* veld. Other species to look out for are the European bee-eater (438), Cape penduline tit (557), Karoo chat (592), Cape robin (601) and the pintailed whydah (860).

## History

The area between Citrusdal and Clanwilliam is rich in rock paintings dating back to the Later Stone Age, with a large concentration in the Pakhuis Pass area in the northern Cederberg. From the various sites it appears that the San (Bushmen) preferred the open plains to the more mountainous areas. An analysis of 46 painting sites covering 104 km$^2$ east of Clanwilliam has shown that human figures greatly predominated over animals as subject matter. Of a total of 1 901 figures, 430 (23 per cent) depicted animals while 1 471 (77 per cent) depicted humans. This appears to be due mainly to the fact that humans were painted in sizeable groups, while animals were represented singly or in groups of two or three.

Antelope account for about half of the total number of animal paintings, with eland constituting about 37 per cent of these. Other recognisable animals include elephant (40), zebra (8), possible zebra (17), chacma baboon (8), rhinoceros (3) and birds (5).[2]

The surrounding plains of the Cederberg were also inhabited by groups of Khoikhoi (Hottentots) who preferred the more grassy areas. An excavation at De Hangen in the vicinity of Clanwilliam yielded sheep and domestic ox bones dated at about 1465 AD. An analysis of other bones found at the site showed that 90 per cent of the animals were either rock dassie or tortoise.

The first recorded contact between whites and the San was in 1655, when an expedition led by Jan Wintervogel encoun-

2 Willcox, A.R. 1984. *The Rock Art of Africa*. Johannesburg: Macmillan, 181.

tered a San party and described them as '... of very small stature, subsisting meagrely, quite wild, without huts or anything in the world, clad in skins like the Hottentots and speaking almost as they do.[3]

Five years later Jan Danckaert reached the upper reaches of the Olifants River and was helped by a '... poverty stricken band of tiny people'[4] to cross the mountains.

The first trekboers settled along the banks of the Olifants River at the beginning of the 1700s and trouble soon arose when the farmers intruded upon the traditional hunting domains of the San. In retaliation the San raided the farms, making no distrinction between game and domestic stock. Initially the raids were carried out at night but later they became more aggressive and were undertaken even in broad daylight. To counter the raids, a commando system was initiated in 1715 and during the last commando raid in 1772, over 500 San were killed and 293 captured between Piketberg and the Sneeuberg north of Graaff-Reinet. It is, therefore, unlikely that the San inhabited the area after the turn of the eighteenth century.

Early explorers who journeyed northwards avoided the rugged Cederberg, following a route either along the Olifants River Valley or to the west of the coastal mountain range. The earliest recorded mention of cedarwood was made in a report to the Here XVII in 1700 by Governor Simon van der Stel, who described the wood as suitable for use by farmers wanting to settle in the area. The missionary-traveller Charles Barrow listed it as one of the usable trees of the Cape in his work of 1796 and the German naturalist Henry Lichtenstein described it as good timber wood.

In October 1805 the Livestock and Agricultural Commission, consisting of Messrs van Ryneveld, Truter and Huizer, visited the 'Cedar houte Bergen'. They reported that coloureds living in the Cederberg made their living by cutting the timber in the forests, which they calculated to be about 'four hours long and half an hour wide'. They predicted that the forests would soon be destroyed if the felling continued and extracted a promise from the woodcutters that they would sow seeds in the kloofs during April each year. This was the first attempt to regenerate the forests by human agency.

In 1836 the British geographer Sir James Alexander visited the cedar forests. Since the first commisson's visit to the area 31 years earlier no steps had been taken to put an end to the felling and Sir James complained bitterly about the wanton destruction and uncontrolled burning. Eight years later the German traveller W von Meyer visited the area and voiced similar complaints.

A forest ranger was finally appointed in 1876 to exercise control over the Cederberg, but being stationed at Clanwilliam made it impossible for him to exercise effective control and the destruction continued unabated. From 1879 only dead trees were allowed to be exploited, but in the annual report of that year the Superintendent of Woods and Forests wrote that about 1 000 poles were ready for use as telegraph posts. In a report five years later it was stated that cedarwood had been used as telegraph posts between Piketberg and Calvinia. Assuming one pole was used every 40 m, 7 250 poles would have been required over the distance of 290 km.

The French forester who was appointed Superintendent of Woods and Forests of the Cape Colony in 1880, Count M de Vasselot de Régné, visited the Cederberg in 1882. Earlier in his career he had worked in the French colony of Algeria, and the Cederberg, with its cedars and rugged scenery, apparently reminded him so much of the Atlas Mountains that he suggested the name Algeria for the forest station. George Bath was appointed the first forest ranger in 1905 and gave the station the name as suggested by De Régné.

During the Anglo-Boer War (1899-1902) Groenberg, an excellent vantage point

3 Willcox, A.R. 1976. *Southern Land: The Prehistory and History of Southern Africa*. Cape Town: Purnell, 158, 160.

4 *Ibid.*, 160.

overlooking Clanwilliam a few kilometres north of Heuningvlei, was occupied by Boer commandos. The headquarters of the Boer forces were situated at Van Rhynsdorp some 100 km further north, and several skirmishes between the Boers and the British took place in the Cederberg. To limit the movement of the Boer forces across the Cederberg the British built blockhouses to guard narrow passages, the remains of which can still be seen at Krakadouwpoort in the northern Cederberg and at Boskloof near Citrusdal. The grave of Lieutenant G V W Clowes on Pakhuis Pass, also known as the Englishman's Grave, is a telling reminder of the war. Clowes, a member of the 1st Gordon Highlanders, was riding well ahead of his scouting party when he ran into a Boer commando. He was gunned down when he charged the Boers with his sword drawn and was buried near the spot where he fell on 30 January 1901. Several metal crosses in the graveyard of the Anglican Church in Clanwilliam also testify to the battles fought in the area between Boer and Briton.

The Cederberg Wilderness Area — 71 000 ha of state forest land — was proclaimed on 27 July 1973 and was the third such area to receive this status in South Africa.

**Trail Synopsis**

The Cederberg lends itself to creating a large variety of routes, ranging from short weekend outings to more extensive backpacking expeditions lasting several days. Only a number of the more popular weekend routes are described here and these can be combined to create a variety of longer trails.

**Algeria to Crystal Pool and Back via Uitkyk**

This is a popular weekend excursion which offers a number of options, depending on the fitness of the group.

**Day 1: Algeria Forest Station to Crystal Pool**

The start of this route is at the top end of the campsite at Algeria Forest Station. After passing through a gate you cross a tributary of the Rondegat River and follow the path leading up the right-hand side of Helsekloof. Fortunately, the ascent is not as formidable as the name (Hell's Ravine), suggests, with the path following a zigzag pattern.

About halfway up the kloof a eucalyptus belt is reached. A detour to the left leads to a beautiful waterfall, which is particularly impressive after rain, and during February red disas *(Disa uniflora)* can be seen clinging precariously to the damp rocks. You then pass through a cedar plantation and you should reach the plateau about two hours after setting out. Middelberg huts are still about half an hour further. The huts were built in 1903 as forestry patrol huts and cedarwood was used for all the woodwork, including the beds. The nearby river with its small pools is a welcome resting spot on a hot day.

Immediately south of the huts you join the route to Crystal Pool, and this can be followed without any difficulty. You will follow a gradual zigzag up to the Geelvlei Plateau and further along a well-known landmark, Cathedral Rock, with its fluted towers and crenellated spires, is seen on your right. The path winds east over Grootlandsvlakte and you will pass several turnoffs to the right which should be ignored. The first two turnoffs lead to Uilsgat Needles, while the third leads to Sleepad hut, which can be seen on a small shelf to the east.

After continuing along the main route for about a kilometre, the path swings north and follows the Wildehoutdrift for about another kilometre before reaching Groot Hartseer, where you will gain about 150 m in altitude over a short distance. Once the plateau is reached it is about half an hour's easy walking to Crystal Pool. Several splendid burnt-out cedar trees are passed and the route snakes vigorously to avoid numerous large boulders.

Crystal Pool is idyllically situated in an amphitheatre surrounded by mountains, and in good weather you can normally camp among some huge boulders along the stream at the head of the valley. Red disas are prolific along the stream during midsummer and the large pool close to the

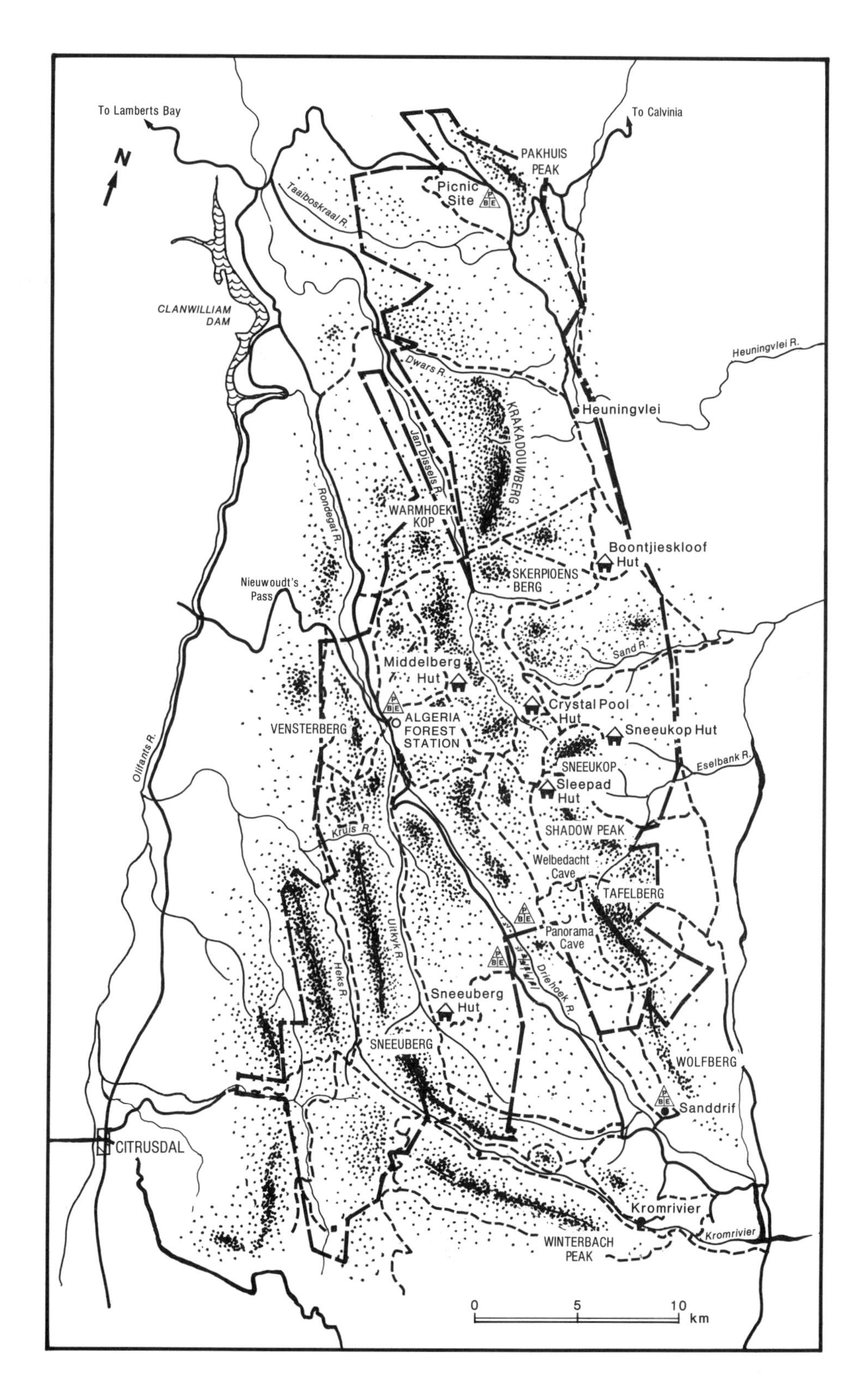


*Cederberg Backpacking Area*

campsite is an excellent place for a refreshing dip during summer.

Should bad weather force you to seek shelter, you first have to cross Klein Hartseer before reaching the hut. However, there is no water at the hut and during the dry summer months it is advisable to fill your water-bottles before ascending Klein Hartseer as the closest water to the hut is about 10 minutes' walk away.

### Day 2: Crystal Pool to Algeria via Uitkyk

From Crystal Pool you have the option of either retracing your steps and descending to Uitkyk or you can climb to Sleepad hut before descending to the Grootlandsvlakte and then to Uitkyk. The extra effort required on the latter alternative is well worth while, but is not recommended for the unfit!

### Crystal Pool to Algeria via Sleepad Hut and Uitkyk

From Crystal Pool the path continues in a north-easterly direction (ignore the turnoff to your left) for about 10 minutes before reaching Engelsmanskloof, where you turn south-east. Over the next 1,5 km you gain about 200 m in altitude, passing spectacular scenery — massive red cliff faces, rock formations towering like baroque castles, lichen-clad overhanging rocks and a single rock balancing precariously on the edge of the precipice.

A jeep track is joined at the shale band (locally known as Die Trap — The Step) below Sneeukop and you follow this in a southerly direction for roughly 45 minutes before you arrive at the two-roomed Sleepad hut. During November the mountain slopes are covered with masses of *Watsonia* spp. and in February large clumps of red disas *(Disa uniflora)* can be seen flowering along the streams.

The view from the hut is magnificent, with wide panoramas of the greater part of the Cederberg range. Late afternoon is particularly spectacular, when the harsh grey rocks slowly change colour — first to a golden yellow, then orange, blue and mauve and finally melting away with the darkness of the night.

Water can be obtained from a stream close to the hut, but unfortunately none of the pools is large enough for swimming. However, look for the small cascade a short way below the hut where it is possible to have a refreshing shower.

Sleepad hut was named after the route taken by ox-drawn sledges that were used to drag the equipment of the British astronomer Thomas Mann up to the shale band. Mann set up his station on Sneeukop in 1843 to measure the arch of the meridian for his colleague Thomas Maclear.

From Sleepad you descend steeply to Grootlandsvlakte, losing about 200 m in height, and you then follow the path to Algeria for a short while before branching off to the left. After about 1,5 km you turn right onto the path which winds down Die Gat to the old Uitkyk Forest Station. The route provides stunning views, but it is advisable to make an early start as the afternoons in Die Gat can be very hot. From Uitkyk it is about a one-and-a-half-hour walk along Van Der Merwe's Trail to Algeria Forest Station.

### Welbedacht to Sleepad Hut and Back

This easy circular weekend route is ideal for a one-car party. By using Welbedacht Cave as a base camp the trip can be extended to three days.

### Day 1: Welbedacht to Sleepad Hut

Welbedacht is reached by taking the left turnoff to Driehoek farm about 14 km south of Algeria. After following the road for a short distance, you turn left onto the road to the old Welbedacht forest post. A short distance along this road a notice board informs you that vehicles are not permitted into the wilderness area and you must leave your car at the car park. From here you walk along a forestry road through a pine plantation and after crossing the Driehoek River continue to the site of the old Welbedacht homestead.

Behind the site of the old homestead the path zigzags steadily up the kloof and you will see some fine specimens of the Clanwilliam cedar (19). Shortly before reaching the top of the kloof (about two to two and half hours after setting off) a track leads off to the right to Welbedacht Cave, which is also known to the locals as Die Klipgat. The cave can accommodate about 15 people, but is unsuitable in winter as the north-westerly wind drives rain straight into the cave.

Should you wish to ascend Cederberg Tafelberg, about 2 km south, the cave is an ideal base camp. Water can usually be obtained from the stream in Welbedacht Kloof. Unfortunately the rock paintings on the cave walls have been obliterated by the soot of fires of early woodcutters and early mountaineers.

From the cave it is a short climb to the jeep track, which is followed for about 6 km to Sleepad hut. After about 2,5 km you will reach another well-known campsite, Sederhoutkop. The spot is marked by a huge sandstone boulder with several stone shelters nestling against its base. The nearest source of water is in Donderkloof, about 100 m north of Sederhoutkop.

The jeep track continues to climb, alternating with level stretches. To your right the scenery is dominated by Langberg and to your left you will see the highest peak in the Cederberg, Sneeuberg, towering above the range. Sleepad hut is reached about an hour after passing Sederhoutkop.

### Day 2: Sleepad Hut to Welbedacht

On the second day you follow an easy route which is either downhill or level for most of the day and should take three to three and a half hours.

First thing in the morning you descend to Grootlandsvlakte, where you join the Middelberg/Crystal Pool route. Turn left and follow the path for a few hundred metres until you reach the Welbedacht route turning off to the left. Take this turning and after about 1,5 km you will pass the path to Uitkyk on the right, with the route to Welbedacht continuing to the left. You continue over fairly level terrain and further on you will pass the well-known landmark, Uilsgat Needles, named after the tapering rock spires on your left. Middelberg South dominates the scenery to your right.

The path descends steeply into the delightful Uilsgatkloof and you continue along a jeep track for the remainder of the way to Welbedacht.

## Eikeboom to Sneeuberg Huts and Cederberg Pass via Duiwelsgat

This is another enjoyable weekend trip but unfortunately it requires either a two-car party or arrangements with 'fetchers' as there is a distance of about 11 km between the starting and finishing points.

### Day 1: Eikeboom to Sneeuberg Huts

The start of this route is about 17 km south-east of Algeria on the main provincial road to Ceres and can easily be recognised by the clump of oak trees on the right-hand side of the road.

The route follows the jeep track up Sederhoutkloof and after about 1,5 km passes a well-preserved stone leopard trap. About half a kilometre further you pass through one of the finest stands of waboomveld in the western Cape. The route ascends steeply along the southern slopes of the valley, passing the deserted farm Hoogvertoon on the plateau.

Looking north-west, some of the best-preserved specimens of Clanwilliam cedars (19) can be seen among the crags and outcrops of the Koerasie Mountain. On the plateau the road covers fairly level terrain and after about 2 km a fairly indistinct short-cut leads off to the right. After ascending a small ridge the terrain once again levels out, with Sneeuberg dominating the scenery straight ahead.

About 2 km further on the track ends at Sneeuberg huts (roughly three to three and a half hours after setting off), which are situated at the foot of the mountain from which they take their name. One of the huts is an ingenious shelter built among the boulders directly behind the first hut. The huts make an ideal base camp for exploring the Maltese Cross and Sneeuberg itself.

The Maltese Cross is situated about 5 km south-east of the huts and is reached in about one to one and a half hours. You join the path immediately behind the huts and after about 10 minutes you ascend to the shale band at the base of Sneeuberg. You gain about 100 m in altitude before the route levels out, continuing in a south-easterly direction until you reach the Cross.

*The Cederberg is renowned for its fascinating rock formations – (left) the Wolfberg Arch, (right) the Maltese Cross*

The 20 m high formation is a rock pillar broadened at the upper end to form a cross, and is also known as the Cross of the Cedars. The cedars have along since disappeared and the Maltese Cross now keeps a lone watch over other strangely shaped rocks.

In rock-climbing terms the Maltese Cross is graded as F3 and has been described as a serious pitch with bad protection. The first ascent was made in 1949 by two climbers, Goodwin and Blacquiere. In their account they reported, 'It was then that we found traces which we decided could only be made by baboons . . . Evidently, then, baboons are more than a match for man in the most delicate rock-climbing . . .'[5]. Without underestimating the rock-climbing abilities of chacma baboon, a more reasonable explanation is that the droppings were those of eagles, possibly the black eagle (131).

More adventurous and fitter backpackers will find ascending Sneeuberg a worthwhile excursion. The ascent not only reveals spectacular views, but Sneeuberg is also one of the best localities to see the magnificent snow protea *(Protea cryophila)*, which flowers during late January and February.

Setting off from the Maltese Cross you retrace your steps towards the Sneeuberg huts for about 1,5 km. Midway along Sneeuberg a turnoff to your left is marked with a cairn close to where the path makes a short descent in a northerly direction. Turn left and continue up the gully, which is well marked with cairns. It should not take more than two hours to reach the nek and by that time you will have gained some 400 m in altitude.

The final ascent to the summit is also well marked along the south-eastern side of the peak and involves two fairly easy rock scrambles of C grade. You gain 200 m in height and about 45 minutes should be allowed for the ascent and 30 minutes for the descent. From the highest peak in the Cederberg you are rewarded with indescribably beautiful views of the Cederberg range and on a clear day you can even seen Table Mountain, some 150 km away. Across the valley is Cederberg Tafelberg, which is only 60 m lower than Sneeuberg, the Wolfberg and the wide, fertile valley of the Dwarsrivier. Looking south-east you can see Citrusdal, the Olifants River Valley and Boskloof Valley, which used to be a popular access point to the

5 Goodwin, R.F. 1949. So the Maltese Cross IS Climbable. *Mountain Club of South Africa Journal*, Vol. 52 , 54.

southern Cederberg in years gone by. To the north-east the landscape is dominated by the majestic Krakadouw peaks.

You return to Sneeuberg huts via the same route, turning left once you reach the main footpath at the bottom of the gully.

### Day 2: Sneeuberg Huts to Cederberg Pass via Duiwelsgat

From the huts the path leads north-west, covering easy level terrain for about 3 km before descending towards Duiwelsgat along Noordepoort. The path clings to the western slope of Koerasieberg and takes you past some of the most spectacular scenery in the Cederberg. The path mostly adheres to the 1 100 m contour, with magnificent views of the rugged Duiwelsgatkloof on your left, before ascending at the head of the kloof. You pass some fine cedars on the ascent and later on you will pass an old cedarwood station on your left, where logs were stored before being taken down the mountain.

The path levels out before dropping down to Klein Duiwelsgat, where a steep descent awaits you. You initially follow the course of the Uitkyksrivier and the path then drops down the kloof formed by Smalberg on your left and Uitkyk se Piek to the right.

Roughly three to four hours after setting off, the path ends at the hairpin bend on Cederberg Pass, about 6 km from Algeria. If a vehicle has been left at Algeria you can either follow the road back to Algeria or hike up Cederberg Pass and descend along Uitkyk Pass, following Van der Merwe's Trail back to Algeria (approximately 2,5 km). Although the latter route is longer, it is a worthwhile deviation if time allows. The descent along the old Uitkyk Pass starts at the summit of the Cederberg Pass, about 3 km from the hairpin bend.

Before the construction of the Cederberg Pass in 1969 the old pass had the distinction of being one of the steepest passes in South Africa. The pass, with a gradient of 1:10, was built by the Divisional Council of Clanwilliam at a cost of R50 000 and climbs some 300 m in just over 3 km. Many older mountaineers have colourful memories of the ingenuity they had to apply to reach the top of the pass in the motor carts of earlier days!

From the old Uitkyk Forest Station you can continue to Algeria either along the gravel road or along Van der Merwe's Trail, which winds along the Rondegat River.

### Dwarsrivier to the Wolfberg Arch and Cracks, and the Maltese Cross

Sanddrif, 27 km beyond Algeria on the farm Dwarsrivier, is ideally situated as a base camp for day excursions to some of the most spectacular rock formations in the Cederberg. The Wolfberg Cracks are on the property of Messrs Nieuwoudt and it is necessary to obtain a permit from them before doing the walk.

### Day 1: Circular Route from Dwarsrivier to the Wolfberg Arch and Cracks

The circular route past the arch and through the cracks covers about 18 km and eight to nine hours are required. The route to the Wolfberg Arch begins at Sanddrif and follows the road past the holiday cottages. Shortly after passing some labourers' cottages you turn left and about 1 km further on you will come to the route leading directly to the cracks on the right. This route is fairly steep and is only recommended if you intend visiting the cracks only and not the Wolfberg Arch as well. If you intend seeing both the arch and the cracks rather take the road to the left, which is the jeep track that follows the shale band for about 20 km to Sneeukop huts.

The jeep track covers easy terrain and after about two hours you reach the old De Rif farm. During the hot summer months the cool shade of the oak trees around the old homestead provides a most welcome rest stop. The small cedar forest at the foot of Gabriel's Pass is one of only five places in the Cederberg where the Clanwilliam cedar — which normally occurs on the Peninsula Formation — occurs on the Nardouw Formation above the shale band.

The path zigzags to the top of Gabriel's Pass, from where you have a magnificent view of Sneeuberg to the south-west and the

Tanqua Karoo to the east. After a short descent, the path leads off to the right and you ascend to the plateau along a well-cairned route. The section between De Rif and the arch is normally covered in one to one and a half hours.

The impressive Wolfberg Arch is most imposing when approached from this angle and the formation stands in isolation like a portal of a ruined cathedral. Centuries of wind, rain and extremes of temperature have carved a near-perfect symmetrical archway of about 15 m into the soft sandstone. Looking through the arch you gaze down over the Tanqua Karoo and the Bokkeveld Mountains in the hazy distance.

From the arch you follow a well-marked route in a south-easterly direction. The Wolfberg Cracks are about one to one and a half hours further on and the path winds past fascinating rock formations which at times create a lunar landscape in which human figures, faces and animals seem to leer out at you.

You should take care when approaching the Wolfberg Cracks as there are two far less spectacular cracks lower down to the right and you must be sure to follow the cairns.

The cracks consist of a vertical cleft 30 m deep which has been forged through the sandstone of the Wolfberg. In several places the cracks are so narrow that you have to squeeze feet first through tiny passages blocked by huge chockstones, and in one place it is necessary to hang onto a ledge in order to drop 2 m down to a lower level. This might sound a bit hair-raising, but it is not nearly as bad as it appears.

Once you have overcome these obstacles, the cracks widen considerably and you will see one of the most spectacular formations in the Cederberg — two enormous natural rock arches in the cracks. The entire bridge covers about 90 m in length. The larger arch has a span of 29 m, and the smaller arch 20 m.

A fascinating feature of the cracks is the spectacular colours that glow on the vertical stone walls in various shades of orange, ochre, yellow, rust brown and deep red, depending on the time of day.

The final stretch once again requires you to crawl along a narrow passage and finally, about an hour after entering the cracks, you reach the end of the passage. Straight ahead the tapering Cederberg range is framed by an enormous archway, while to your right there is a breathtaking view of Dwarsrivier, framed by 30 m high cliffs. After passing through the arch the path descends to the right, traverses a narrow ledge and then seemingly comes to a dead end. At this point you have two options. You can either descend via a chimney at the far end of the ledge or you can scramble down at the far end of the ledge where there are a number of good footholds. On your right is the wider, second crack which is normally used as a return route by backpackers exploring the cracks only.

From here the descent is steep and it is necessary to take care especially after rain. You will lose about 350 m in altitude during the descent, which takes about 45 minutes to an hour. The final section is once again along a gravel road.

### Day 2: Circular Route from Sanddrif to the Maltese Cross

From Sanddrif you reach the start of the route by driving along the road towards Algeria Forest Station. Shortly after passing the Dwarsrivier homestead, you will cross a small river and a little further on you turn left onto a fairly indistinct road. Continue along this road for about 6 km until it ends at the Dwarsrivier, where vehicles are left. However, before setting off enquire about the condition of the road, which is sandy in patches.

After crossing the Dwarsrivier, the path leads eastwards, following the course of a gully. The scenery becomes more dramatic the higher you get and looking across the broad valley behind you it is possible to see the Wolfberg Arch. Several Proteaceae species occur along this path, including the Cedarberg protea *(Protea acuminata)*, which also occurs on the Nieuwoudtville escarpment and in the mountains near Villiersdorp. They usually grow as small, erect shrubs of about one to one and a half metres and are a cold-resistant species which occur right up to the snowline, but at lower elevations than the snow protea *(P. cryophila).* The beautiful, deep red flowers are usually seen between June and September.

You should also be on the lookout for two *Paranomus* species. The tallest *Paranomus, P. tomentosus,* is found only in the Cederberg at altitudes between 1 200 m and 1 500 m. You will be able to identify it by its spiky leaves which are permanently covered by silvery-grey hairs. The pink, woolly flowers are produced only after the last snow has fallen and it is warmer. *P. bracteolaris* has a wider distribution than *P. tomentosus* and grows at altitudes between 280 m and 1 250 m. Shrubs can reach up to 2 m and flowers can be seen throughout the year, although a flowering peak is reached in spring.

The ascent takes about one and a half hours along a well-cairned route. The Maltese Cross has already been described on page 92 and the description is not repeated here.

You can return along the same route and the descent should take about an hour. Going downhill you will have splendid views of The Pup, a well-known landmark in the Cederberg, and it is often possible to see black eagle (131) soaring above the cliffs in search of rock dassies, their favourite prey.

Lower down in the valley, to the right, the site of the old Bokveldskloof farm is marked by a clump of exotic trees, while further along the patchwork of vineyards and orchards of Dwarsrivier farm can be seen.

Once the descent has been completed you can cool down in the pool in the Dwarsrivier, situated a short distance downstream from where the path crosses the river.

An alternative descent from the Maltese Cross is the route via Sneeuberg huts and Sederhoutkloof to Eikeboom, but as this route ends about 10 km from Dwarsrivier it is only feasible if you can make the necessary arrangements to be collected at Eikeboom. This alternative route covers approximately 12 km and requires about four hours.

**DON'T MISS**

- the Stadsaal Caves and rock paintings on the farm Matjiesrivier. Permits are required and can be obtained from the Matjiesrivier farmhouse about 10 km from Sanddrif on the road to Ceres. The turn-off to the caves and paintings is to the right, roughly 3 km before the farmhouse.

After passing through the gate you follow the road for about 1 km before you come to the track leading to the paintings turning off to the right. The paintings are in a shallow overhang in a rocky outcrop to the right. Five elephants are depicted as well as several hook-headed figures, some of which are dressed in long clothes, possibly karosses.

Return to the main track and continue for about 1 km to the Stadsaal Caves, which are a conglomeration of caverns, passages and pillars reminiscent of an ancient city in ruins. Several early travellers inscribed their names on the walls and unfortunately modern graffiti have also made their appearance. The formation is also known as the Elephant's Cave and from a certain spot inside the cave it is easy to imagine that you are standing under the belly of an elephant, looking outwards through the enormous hind legs.

Among the caves and pillars you are likely to see *Aloe mitriformis,* a sprawling species which normally grows with its stem lying horizontally on the ground. This is because the stems are too slender to support the heavy rosettes of leaves. This species does not transplant well, so do not be tempted to collect a plant for your garden!

If you have sufficient time on hand it is rewarding to explore the surroundings. A cairned path behind the cave leads to a shelf at a lower level where you will see paintings of human figures and eland.

# 6 Groot-Winterhoek Backpacking Area

With its wild countryside, profusion of spring flowers and magnificent mountain scenery, Groot-Winterhoek has become one of the most popular backpacking areas in the western Cape. The route to Die Hel leads alongside the Groot-Kliphuis River which has a number of excellent swimming pools, making it possible to backpack this trail even during the hot summer months. Groot-Winterhoek also offers numerous opportunities to the more adventurous backpacker who wishes to explore areas off the beaten track.

### Location

The Groot-Winterhoek Wilderness Area is near Porterville in the western Cape. The forest station is reached by taking the Porterville turnoff on the N7 at Piketberg. After 26 km turn left at the T-junction and follow the R44 for about 5 km before turning right onto a gravel road signposted Cardouws Pass. After a short distance you will reach the turnoff to Dasklip Pass, where you turn right. The remainder of the route is well signposted.

### Distance and Classification

26 km; 2 days — Groot-Winterhoek office to De Tronk via Groot-Kliphuis River and back
Shorter/longer options are also possible
A+ grade

### Permits

Permits must be obtained in advance from The Officer-in-Charge, Groot-Winterhoek Wilderness Area, P O Box 26, Porterville 6810, Telephone (02623) 1621. Groups are limited to a maximum of 10 people.

### Maps

The only maps of the area available to backpackers are the standard 1:50 000 topographical maps, sections 3219CB and 3219CC.

### Relevant Information

- Although there are several old fireplaces in the caves at Die Hel, fires are strictly forbidden and it is therefore essential to carry a backpacking stove.
- During the winter months it may be difficult to cross the Groot Kliphuis River near Weltevreden.
- It is advisable to carry a backpacking tent.

### Facilities

The closest campsite to the wilderness area is in Piketberg. There are no facilities at the start of the trail, but for backpackers arriving late in the afternoon there is an excellent camping spot about 15 minutes' walk from the forest station. The spot is marked by a number of large boulders to your left soon after crossing a stream.

Basic shelter is provided at Weltevreden, De Tronk, Groot-Winterhoek farmstead, Groot Kliphuis and Paarden Vallei, while a cave at Die Hel also provides shelter.

### Climate

Summer days in the Groot-Winterhoek Wilderness Area are usually hot and dry and the evenings warm. The average daily maximum temperature at Porterville is about 30 °C between November and March, and temperatures in Groot-Winterhoek seldom exceed this.

During winter, however, temperatures can drop to freezing point or below at night and frost can occur from April to as late as November.

It usually rains between April and September and once it sets in the rainy weather, accompanied by thick mist, can last for several days. Rainfall varies from 400 mm in the lower-lying areas to 900 and 1 500 mm in the higher-lying regions.

Snowfalls on the high mountain peaks generally occur in winter, but backpackers should be prepared for snow, rain and mist throughout the year.

**Flora**

The vegetation of the area has been classified by Acocks as Mountain Fynbos (Veld Type 69, previously Macchia Veld Type 69 and False Macchia Veld Type 70).

As a result of the higher rainfall the flora of Groot-Winterhoek is more diverse than that of the Cederberg further north. It has been said that there is a fresh flower in bloom in the mountain for every day of the year — a claim Groot-Winterhoek certainly lives up to. Among the more notable species you may find are *Anemone tenuifolia, Ixia viridiflora,* and a yellow variety of *Disa uniflora.* If you are observant you are also likely to spot the sundew *(Drosera* spp.*),* a low-growing herb which derives its name from the sticky glands that cover the leaves and in the glistening sun resemble drops of

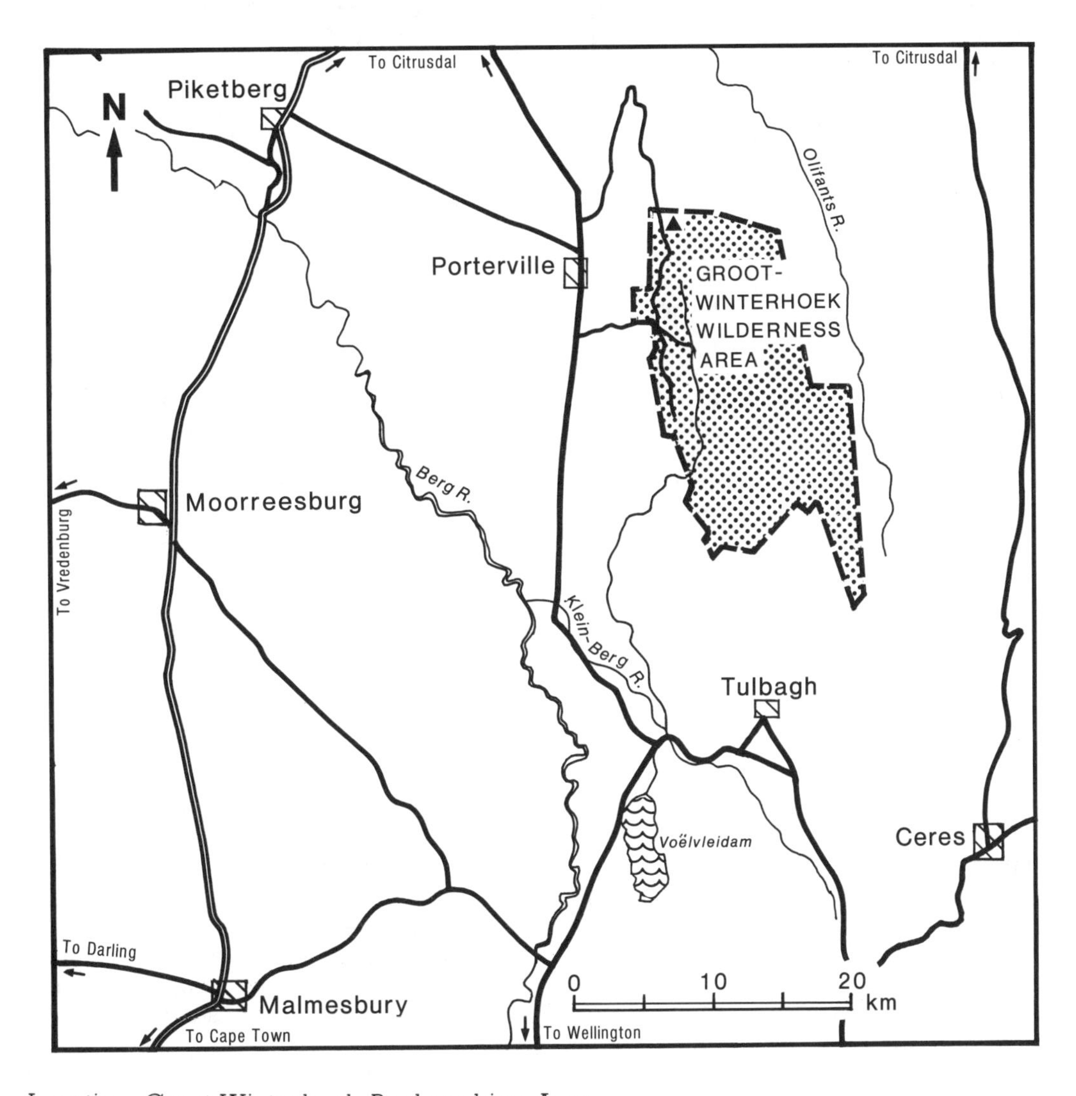


*Location: Groot-Winterhoek Backpacking Area*

*Groot-Winterhoek is well known for its floral splendour*

dew. *Drosera* are insectivorous plants which capture small insects with their sticky hairs and digest them by means of enzymes.

Among the *Erica* species you may see is *E. mammosa*, which grows up to 1 m tall. This species flowers between December and April and the tubular flowers vary from dark red to pink, scarlet, reddish-orange and pale green. Other species include *E. inflata* and *E. leucosiphon*, a species listed as critically rare in the *South African Red Data Book: Plants — Fynbos and Karoo Biomes*.

Several proteas also occur, including the wagon tree (86), bearded sugarbush (86.1) and *Protea recondita*. Other members of the family Proteaceae found in the area are *Leucadendron salignum* and the attractive *Leucospermum tottum*, which grows as a multi-branched shrub of medium height. This species has attractive buff-salmon flowers, which can be seen between September and January. It is distributed from the Cederberg southwards through the Kouebokkeveld to the mountains around Ceres, Tulbagh, Worcester, Paarl and Villiersdorp.

Two Proteaceae species listed in the *South African Red Data Book: Plants — Fynbos and Karoo Biomes* also occur in the wilderness area. *Spatalla tulbaghensis* is known to occur only in Groot-Winterhoek and the Agter Witzenberg Vlakte near Tulbagh and has been listed as endangered. *Sorocephalus scabridus*, listed as vulnerable, is restricted to the mountains near Porterville and Tulbagh. It grows as a sparsely branched shrub about 75 cm tall, favouring sandy areas at altitudes of 1 000 to 2 000 m. The pink flowers which grow in clusters appear in October and last until November.

Patches of indigenous forest of 15 m and higher are restricted to sheltered kloofs and along river banks. Species occurring include the red alder (140), white alder (141), Cape holly (397), Cape beech (578) and the Breede River yellowwood (15). The latter is the smallest of the four South African yellowwood species and is confined to the western Cape. It grows as a spreading shrub to a small rounded tree 3 to 6 m high and although it often grows on exposed mountainsides, it favours sandy soil along rivers and streams.

Smaller tree species include rockwood (368), spoonwood (418), false red pear (499), lance-leaved myrtle (559) and tree fuchsia (670).

## Fauna

Animals you are most likely to see are grey rhebok, especially near the plains around the forest station on the Voorberg and at Kliphuis, chacma baboon and rock dassie. Klipspringer occur on the upper elevations, but these alert little antelope will often retreat with great agility. Grysbok favour the scrub-covered flats close to the base of hills, but as they are mainly nocturnal they are seldom encountered. About nine leopard are known to inhabit the area and although their tracks are frequently seen, these solitary, noctural predators are extremely elusive. Other dominant species include porcupine and caracal.

Among the large number of smaller mammaks which occur but are not normally seen is the spectacled dormouse, a species which is widely but discontinuously distributed in rocky areas in the Cape. It does not occur, however, in the coastal regions of the south-western Cape and in the northern and north-western Cape. This species is listed in the *South African Red Data Book — Terrestrial Mammals* as rare and although primarily terrestrial, it is to some extent also arboreal.

Another species which has a limited distribution but is not uncommon within its area of distribution is Verreaux's mouse. It occurs mainly in fynbos from Clanwilliam to Knysna, but is also found on grassy hillsides, forest margins and in riverine forests.

The Olifants River, the largest river system in the Cape Province, rises in the Groot-Winterhoek and is of particular interest because eight of the system's 10 fish species are endemic. Two of these species, both listed as rare in the *South African Red Data Book — Fishes,* occur in the Groot-Winterhoek Catchment Area. The Clanwilliam redfin minnow (*Barbus calidus*) grows up to 9,5 cm long (measured from the nose to the fork of the tail) and is found in the Ratel, Thee, Noordhoek and Kunjes rivers. The Clanwilliam yellowfish (*Barbus capensis*) grows up to 91,4 cm long and reaches a mass of up to 10 kg. It is a well-known fish and is said to be, size for size, as powerful a sporting fish as the tiger-fish.

One of the main reasons for the threatened status of endemic fishes in the Olifants River System has been the introduction of exotic species such as large-mouth bass (*Micropterus salmoides*), bluegill sunfish

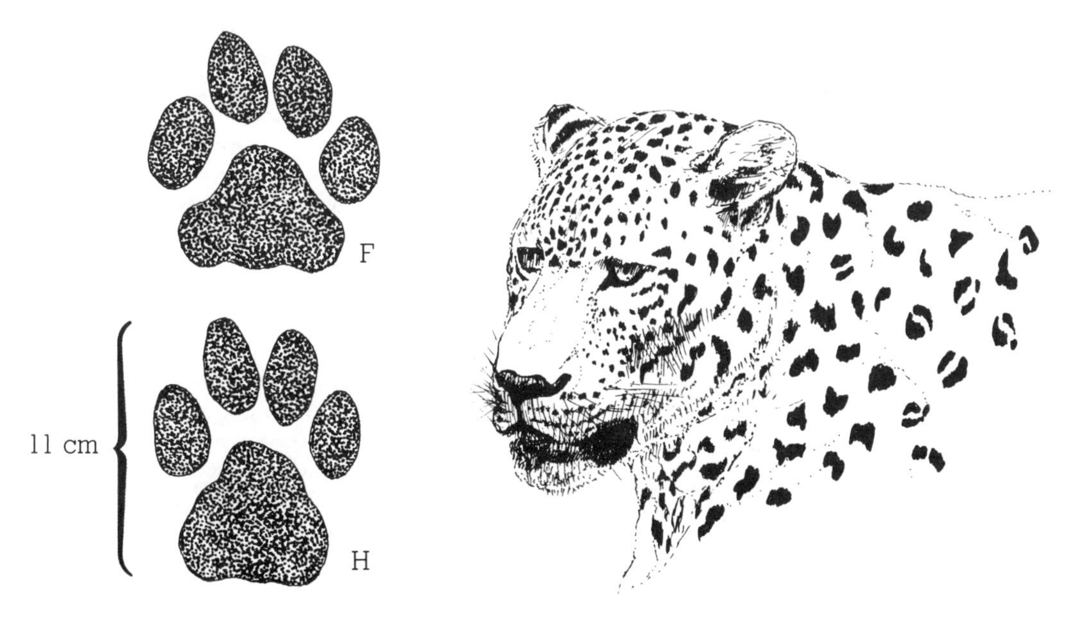


*Leopard – classified as rare – occur in the Groot-Winterhoek Wilderness Area, but are rarely seen owing to their secretive nature*

*The Cape rock thrush favours boulders, cliffs and rocky gorges*

(*Lepomis macrochirus*) and smallmouth bass (*Micropterus dolomieu*). However, other factors such as siltation and the building of dams and irrigation canals have also affected the endemic species adversely. A hatchery for the artificial propagation of yellowfish was built outside Clanwilliam in 1979 and the first experimental restocking of Clanwilliam yellowfish took place in 1982.

Birdlife in the Groot-Winterhoek includes several raptors, including the peregrine falcon (171), a species listed as rare in the *South African Red Data Book — Birds*. Other birds of prey you may see are the rock kestrel (181) and the jackal buzzard (152), while the forest buzzard (150) can sometimes be seen along the edges of forest patches.

Most of the species occurring in the area are associated with the fynbos vegetation. Among those you might observe are Victorin's warbler (641), protea canary (880), Cape sugarbird (773), which breeds in the mountains between February and August, and orangebreasted sunbird (777). Other dominant species include ground woodpecker (480), Cape rock thrush (581), mountain chat (586), Cape rockjumper (611) and the shy and unobtrusive Cape siskin (874).

**History**

Rock paintings in the wilderness area (as well as Ceres to the south and the Clanwilliam-Citrusdal area further north) attest to the presence of the last of the Later Stone Age people, the San (Bushmen). An interesting feature of these paintings is the large number that portray the activities of the early white settlers. The most accessible paintings in the wilderness area are in a fairly large cave at Die Hel, where a group of San figures are depicted.

Prior to 1720 the main areas settled by the expanding trekboers included the country east of the Hottentots-Holland Mountains and the Piketberg area north of the Berg River. Their need for permanent surface water and pastures inevitably brought them into conflict with the Cochoqua Khoikhoi, who were divided into two groups. One of these groups, under Gonnema, had their headquarters near Riebeeck Kasteel. These early pastoralists migrated seasonally in a near elliptical pattern in search of fresh pastures. During summer they grazed their cattle inland before migrating to the coast, reaching the vicinity of Vredenburg in about April. From here they headed south-east, passing just north of Darling in October before returning to their summer grazing area west of Gouda.

As the number of white settlers west of the mountains began to increase during the 1700s, conflict arose between them and the Khoisan. Large numbers of San and Little Nama Khoikhoi harassed the white settlers in the Piketberg area and the Bokkeveld region to the south-east of the wilderness area. So ferocious were their attacks that many farmers were forced to abandon their properties. This led to the introduction in 1715 of the commando system, the first purely civilian commando, and three punitive commando expeditions were carried out in which large numbers of livestock were recovered and many Khoisan killed.

The inhospitable mountains of Groot-Winterhoek served as a deterrent to early travellers. Besides, most of them believed that the fabulous treasures of Monomotapa lay to the north and wasted little time in trying to reach their destination.

Among the early references to the Vieren-Twintig Riviere is that of Governor Hendrik Swellengrebel, who travelled through the Porterville area in January 1777. He wrote, 'Although there are not twenty four rivers there are nevertheless so many streams and rivers, amongst them some which flow very strong and which should carry a large quantity of water after rains, that the district has been named the 24 Riviere.'[1]

The traveller Mentzel wrote 'The Vier-en-Twintig-Rivieren are nothing but a single river, consisting of many brooks flowing alongside each other and since these are deeper than the main bed, are very dangerous to cross in the rainy season ... The number of streamlets ... is not the same everywhere, but in one spot no less than twenty-four of them actually lie so close together that if you were to cross them with a wagon and a team of ten oxen, the front pair would enter the second stream while the hind wheels of the wagon would just be leaving the first one. In some places several brooks flow in one channel in such a way that one can count only 15, 16 or 18 of them.'[2]

### Trail Synopsis

You are not restricted to designated routes but may backpack where you wish. There are a number of options, the most popular being the route from the forest station to De Tronk via the Groot Kliphuis River, which is described.

### Day 1: Groot-Winterhoek Office to Die Hel

The path starts from the car-park below the office and turns left immediately after passing through the gate. It then leads through weathered sandstone formations, the route being either level or downhill. Although the scenery is similar to that of the Cederberg further north, the area is generally more vegetated on account of the higher rainfall.

After about an hour the path meets up with the Groot-Kliphuis River, which is followed for most of the remainder of the day. There are several delightful swimming places along the route, which add to the enjoyment of the trail during the hot summer months. Dominating the scenery is the impressive Groot-Winterhoek Peak (2 078 m), which is often covered with snow during winter.

About one and a half hours after joining the river (depending on how frequently you are tempted to cool off in the inviting pools), you cross the Groot Kliphuis River by means of a low-level causeway. From here you follow the jeep track to Groot-Winterhoek farm, ignoring the turnoff to Perdevlei. After a gentle descent you reach the Klein Kliphuis River, which is crossed by means of a bridge. Once again you will be tempted to cool off in the deep, crystal-clear pool below the bridge. A short ascent follows and shortly before reaching the old farmstead you will pass through an avenue of tall pine trees. Surrounding the old farmhouse are a number of buildings and almond and pecan tree orchards.

A ranger living in the farmhouse is likely to check your permit and will be able to advise you on the route to De Tronk or alternatively Die Hel, which is about an hour's walk south.

From the farm the path descends steadily to Die Hel, passing through patches of disused cultivated land. The final section to Die Hel descends steeply along a small gully and you are advised to take care, especially after rain.

Be on the lookout for a small cairn to your left approximately halfway down the gully. The cairn marks the turnoff to a cave, which is otherwise easily missed. From the cave you have a magnificent view over the Vier-en-Twintig Riviere, which has carved its way through the sandstone to form a deep gorge and a waterfall plunging into a large, deep pool. On the wall of the cave are a few rock paintings which have unfortunately been spoilt by human tampering.

Sleeping is not permitted in the cave and you can either return to the old farmhouse or De Tronk or find a suitable campsite in the area.

---

1 Raper, P.E. 1972. *Streekname in Suid-Afrika en Suidwes.* Cape Town: Tafelberg, 37.
2 *Ibid.*

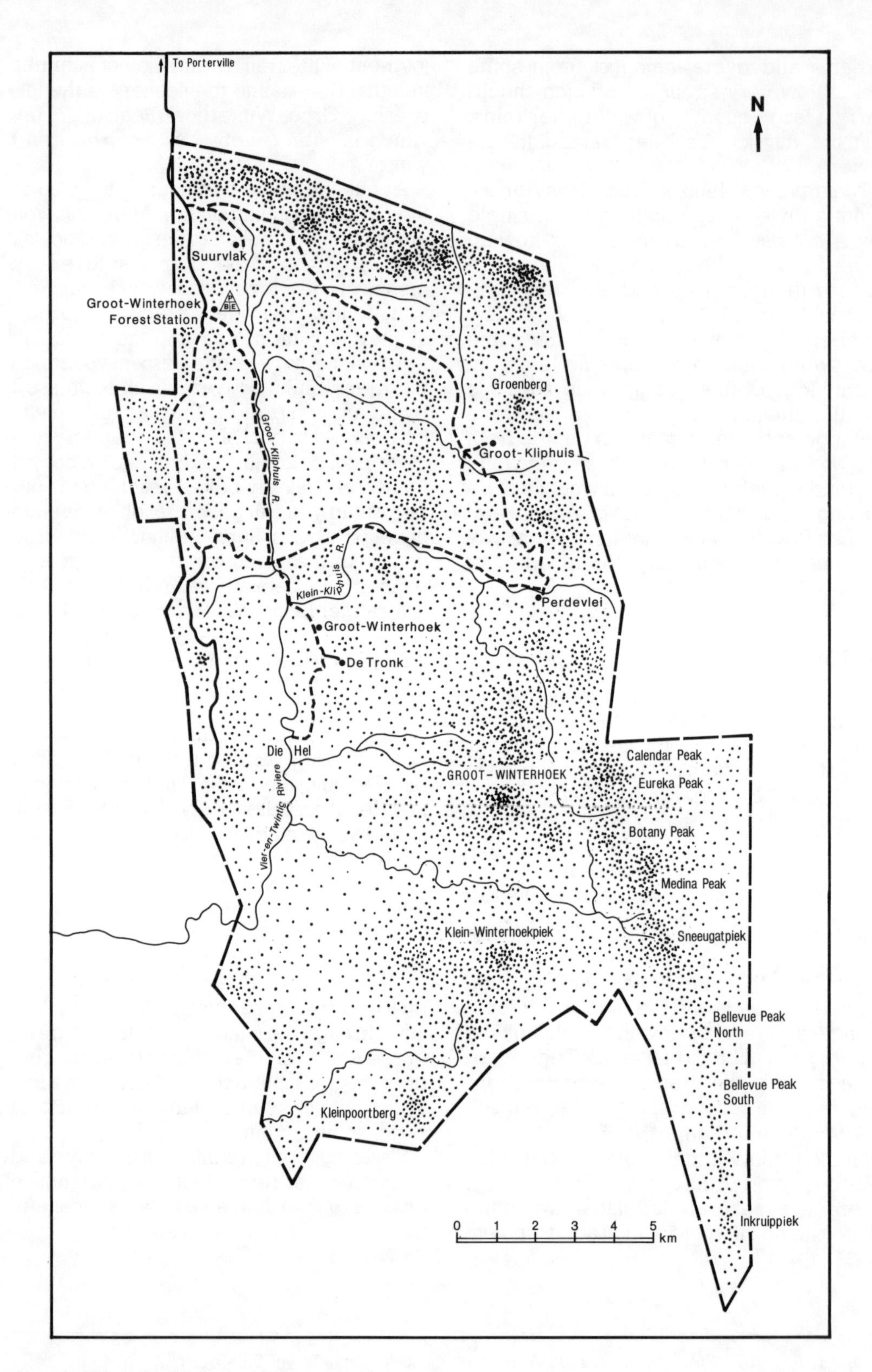


*Groot-Winterhoek Backpacking Area*

### Day 2: Return to Groot-Winterhoek Office

The day's hike ascends gradually along the same route. However, you should allow about half an hour longer for the return journey.

Alternatively you can return to the office via the jeep track. This route passes through beautiful fynbos vegetation, but is not recommended for the unfit because of the many long, steep uphill stretches.

### Alternative Routes

In addition to the route described, there are a number of other options open to backpackers.

The route to Groot Kliphuis via the jeep track covers easy terrain and takes you through interesting rock formations reminiscent of the Cederberg. During spring and early summer the area is particularly attractive when masses of flowering ericas present an unforgettable display. In addition the area near Kliphuis is the habitat of two *Red Data Book* plant species, *Sorocephalus scabridus* and *Spatalla tulbaghensis.* Water is available from three streams along the route.

From the Groot Kliphuis it is possible to continue along the jeep track to Perdevlei. However, it is essential to fill your waterbottle here before setting off for Perdevlei as there is no water available along the route. This route provides spectacular views of the western and northern sections of Groot-Winterhoek as well as the Swartland with its patchwork of wheatfields to the west. From Groot Kliphuis the jeep track ascends some 200 m before descending about 250 m to Perdevlei, another small abandoned farm where early farmers eked out an existence.

Shortly before reaching Perdevlei you will notice a path turning off to the right. This route skirts a spur of the Groot-Winterhoek Mountains and provides a convenient shortcut to the western part of the wilderness area. The path joins the jeep track between the Groot-Winterhoek office and De Tronk which enables you to plan an extended visit to the area.

# 7 Boosmansbos Backpacking Area

Boosmansbos is only 300 km from Cape Town, making it possible for Capetonians to enjoy this small, unspoilt wilderness over a weekend. In spring the southern slopes are blanketed in magnificent pink ericas and the northern slopes become a yellow sea of leucadendrons. Several footpaths in the area afford splendid views of deep ravines, imposing peaks and high krantzes.

## Location

The wilderness area is situated in the Grootvadersbos State Forest to the east of Swellendam in the Langeberg Mountain

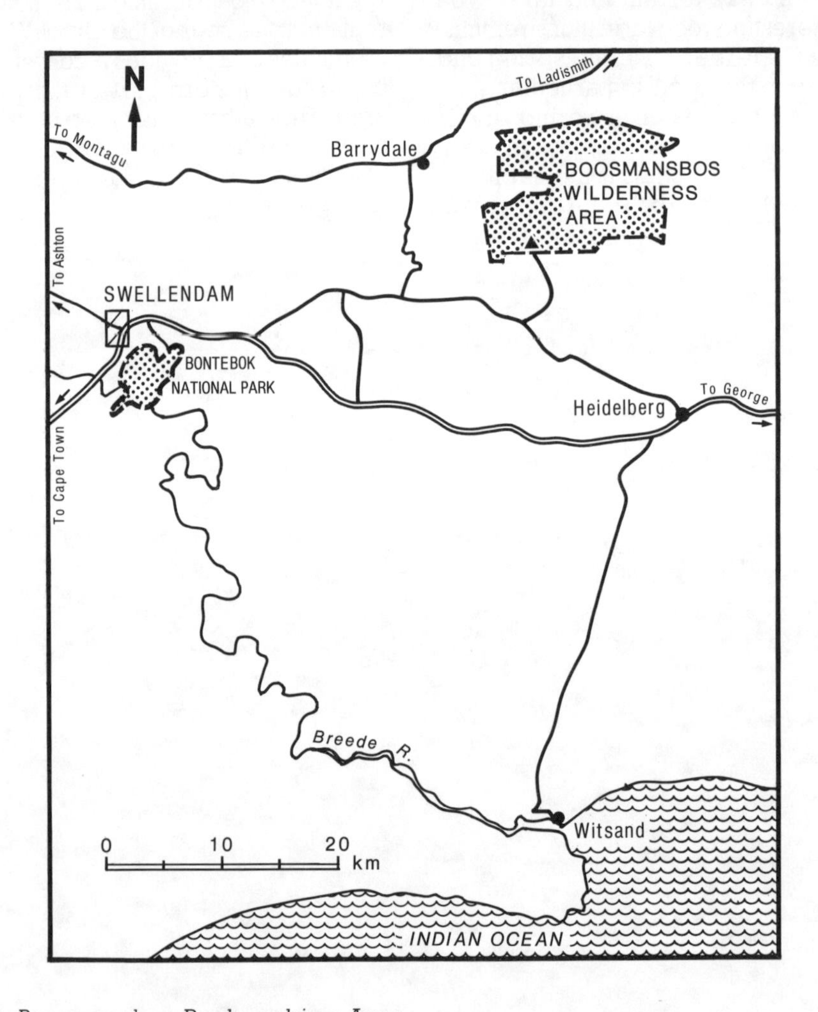


*Location: Boosmansbos Backpacking Area*

range. Take the Barrydale/Suurbraak turnoff (R322) approximately 2 km east of the small settlement of Buffeljagsrivier on the N2. Follow the road through Suurbraak and continue past the Barrydale/Tradouw Pass turnoff. Approximately 11 km beyond the Tradouw Pass turnoff there is a triple fork, the middle road being the route to Boosmansbos. From here the route is well signposted. From Heidelberg the forestry station can be reached by following the R322 to Barrydale until reaching the signposted turnoff to the wilderness area.

### Distance and Classification

27 to 74 km
2 days or longer
B+ grade

### Permits

The number of visitors is restricted and individual groups are limited to a maximum of 10 backpackers. Applications for entry should be addressed to the Officer-in-Charge, Grootvadersbos Wilderness Area, P O Box 109, Heidelberg 6760, Telephone (02962) 1812.

### Maps

A photocopy map and an information sheet are available on making a reservation. The main trail routes are marked clearly on the map but for backpackers wanting more detailed information, the area is covered by the 1:50 000 topographical map section 3320DD.

### Relevant Information

- Fires are not permitted in the wilderness area and it is essential to carry a backpacking stove.
- During dry periods it is advisable to set off with a full water-bottle and to use water sparingly as some of the streams may be dry.

### Facilities

No camping or overnight facilities are available at Grootvadersbos office, but the municipal caravan parks in Swellendam and Heidelberg are conveniently situated should you arrive in the late afternoon. Fully equipped bungalows are available at the Swellendam Municipal Caravan Park but advance booking is advisable. A toilet and hand basin are available at Grootvadersbos Forest Station, at the side of the office block.

Primitive mountain huts at Helderfontein and Klein Witbooisrivier, formerly used by foresters patrolling the area, are used by backpackers but as they are occupied on a first come, first served basis, it is advisable to carry a tent. Veld toilets are provided.

### Climate

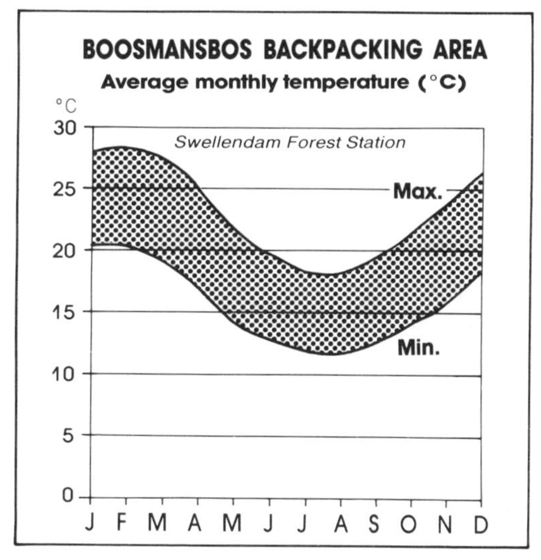


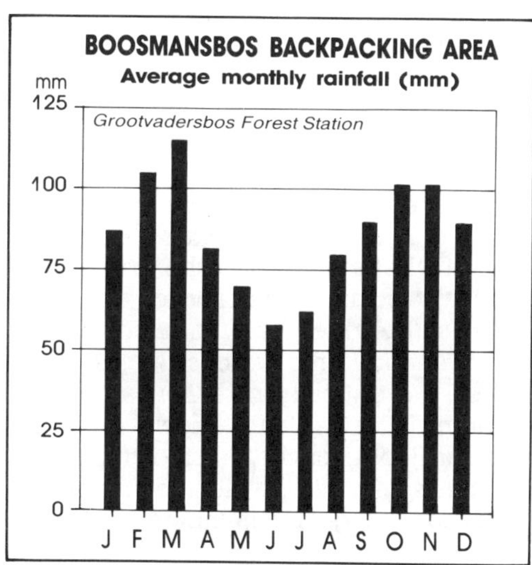

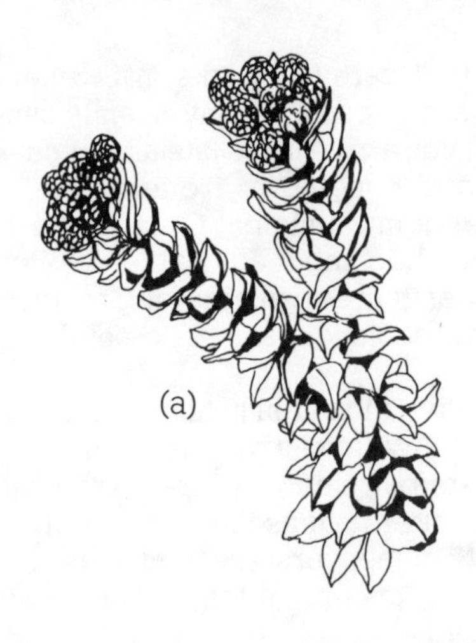


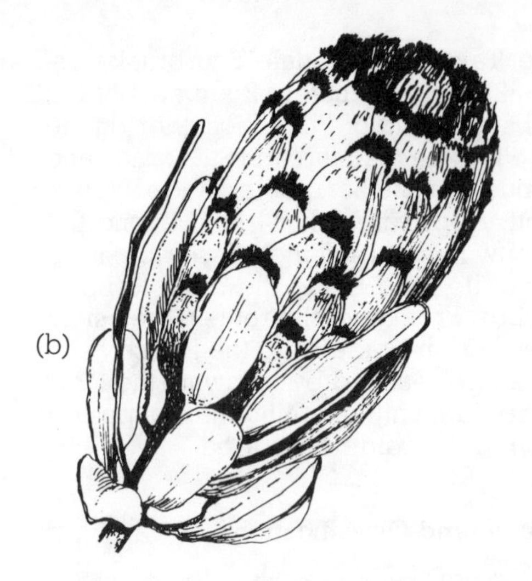


*(a) Strawberry everlasting and (b) brown-bearded sugarbush are commonly seen in the Boosmansbos Wilderness Area*

**Flora**

The vegetation of the area comprises an interesting association of Mountain Fynbos (Veld Type 69, previously False Macchia, Acocks Veld Type 70), and Knysna Forest (Acocks Veld Type 4). As a result of the higher rainfall on the southern slopes the vegetation is more lush and differs markedly from the drier northern slopes. Dense populations of tall yellowbush (81) on the northern slopes form a sea of yellow and from September to October the southern slopes are covered in various shades of pink-flowering ericas. The orange, bell-shaped *Erica blenna*, which grows on a long stem, is almost certain to catch your attention.

The Proteaceae family is well represented and includes the brown-bearded protea (*Protea speciosa*), which bears deep pink flowers with a brown beard between June and December, the giant protea (*P. cynaroides*) and *Leucadendron salignum.* Several other members of the Proteaceae family also occur, some of which are listed in the *South African Red Data Book: Plants — Fynbos and Karoo Biomes.* Such species include the critically rare *Leucadendron radiatum,* which is only known from two places in Boosmansbos, and the vulnerable *Mimetes splendidus,* which occurs over a 300 km long range, but numbers fewer than 500 mature plants.

Another critically rare species that is limited to Boosmansbos is *Spatalla nubicola,* which occurs in two small populations on Grootberg. They grow at altitudes of more than 1 500 m where they are often shrouded in cloud, hence the species name which is translated as 'living in the cloud'.

Several everlasting species (*Helichrysum* spp.) occur, including the silvery-white *H. vestitum,* which grows up to 80 cm high. A species which is often incorrectly assumed to be an everlasting is the spectacular strawberry everlasting (*Helipterum eximium*), after which one of the farms bordering the wilderness area, Strawberry Hills, is named. Between December and March the deep rosy-red buds, with their bright orange stamens, create an impressive display. Plants sometimes reach a height of up to 1,5 m and can easily be identified by their thick leaves which are felted with a silvery sheen.

You are also likely to notice the showy sprays of the creamy-white powder puffs (*Brunia nodiflora*) on the slopes and flats from April to December. The closely related *Berzelia lanuginosa,* which also occurs here, resembles *Brunia* but has smaller flower-heads. They occur on moist slopes and are commonly found on marshy flats and near streams.

One of the few trees of the open fynbos is the mountain cypress (20). It is the most widely distributed of the three South African members of the Cypress family and grows as a short (3-5 m) tree with a bushy crown. The closely related Clanwilliam cedar (19) is restricted to the Cederberg, while the Willowmore cedar (21) is limited to the Baviaanskloof and Kouga mountains.

Grootvadersbos is the largest indigenous forest west of Mossel Bay. A number of tree species reach, or almost reach, their westernmost limit of distribution here, namely the Cape chestnut (256), white silky bark (413), dogwood (452) and the Cape gardenia (693).

A list of 35 of the more common tree species of the forest can be obtained from the Officer-in-Charge. Typical species include the Outeniqua (16) and the real (18) yellowwood, stinkwood (118), Cape holly (397), candlewood (409), wild peach (494), assegai (570) and wild pomegranate (688). The blossom tree (221) occurs on the forest edges, while white alder (141), iron martin (366) and dogwood can be seen along the river banks.

About 1,5 km east of the footpath from the office are a number of redwood trees (*Sequoia sempervirens*), which were planted in 1910. The tallest redwood (46 m high) in South Africa can be seen in this forest and one of the trees has a diameter at breast height of 1,2 m.

**Fauna**

Like most mountainous regions in the western Cape, the Langeberg Mountains do not support a wide variety of wildlife, although you might spot klipspringer, grey rhebok and chacma baboon. Leopard, caracal and grysbok are also present but are unlikely to reveal themselves to the backpacker.

Grysbok are restricted to the southern and south-western Cape but as they are nocturnal your chances of seeing any would be best in the early morning or late afternoon. They occur in pairs, alone or a female with her offspring and you will be able to tell them apart as only the male has horns. During the day they lie up in dense cover and prefer the areas at the base of hills or mountain slopes and kloofs. Although they are predominantly grazers, they will also browse on leaves and wild fruits.

The grysbok has an average shoulder height of 54 cm and a mass of 10 kg which makes it larger and heavier than Sharpe's grysbok, which is restricted to the north-east of the country. The russet coat is speckled with white hairs, resulting in a grizzly-grey appearance, and the short tail is the same colour. The underparts are buff and

*(Actual size)*

*Grysbok – a species restricted to the southern and south-western Cape*

the face, neck, legs and flanks are yellowish-brown.

The birdlife of Boosmansbos can be divided into birds of the fynbos, including the rocky, mountainous habitats, and birds occurring in the forest or in forest margins.

Typical fynbos species you should see are greywing francolin (190), Cape francolin (195), black crow (547), whitenecked raven (550), Cape bulbul (566), grassbird (661), neddicky (681) and spotted prinia (686). Be on the lookout for the Cape sugarbird (773) and the malachite (775) and orange-breasted (777) sunbird near stands of proteas.

Montane raptors occurring in the area include black eagle (131), jackal buzzard (152) and rock kestrel (181). Other montane birds include the rock pigeon (349), black swift (412), whiterumped swift (415), Alpine swift (418), mountain chat (586) and redwinged starling (769).

The extensive Grootvadersbos and Boosmansbos are the habitat of several forest species, some of which reach or almost reach the western limit of their distribution here. These include the rednecked francolin (198), grey cuckooshrike (540), yellowthroated warbler (644), bluemantled flycatcher (708), olive bush shrike (750) and the forest canary (873). Knysna lourie (370) and Narina trogon (427) have also been recorded in Grootvadersbos.

Other species to look out for in the forest are Knysna woodpecker (484), blackheaded oriole (545), sombre bulbul (572) and olive thrush (577). In the forest edge you may catch sight of greater honeyguide (474), Victorin's warbler (641), dusky flycatcher (690) and swee waxbill (850). Birds of prey inhabiting the forest include crowned eagle (141), black sparrowhawk (158) and gymnogene (169).

### History

The area east of Swellendam was inhabited by the Hessequa Khoikhoi (Hottentots), who reportedly still had large herds of cattle and sheep in 1685, unlike those living closer to Cape Town. By the early 1700s farmers had crossed the Breede River and in 1723 the farm Melkhoutboom — later renamed Grootvadersbos — was granted to Roelof Oelofse.

In 1734 the Dutch East India Company (VOC) established its furthermost outpost at Rietvallei on the Buffeljags River to serve as a trading post with the Hessequa and to protect the farmers against marauding San (Bushmen). The outpost was manned by a corporal and seven soldiers and was built after the visit of Governor Johan de la Fontaine to the area in 1734. The site of the Oude Post is marked with a cairn 6 km after leaving the N2 and turning onto the Barrydale/Suurbraak road.

Other reminders of the Khoikhoi who inhabited the area are the mission village at Suurbraak and, further east, Tradouw Pass. The Suurbraak Mission Station, through which you pass a few kilometres west of Tradouw Pass, was established in 1811 by the London Mission Society to minister to the detribalised Hessequa Khoikhoi in this valley and resettled Attaqua Khoikhoi from further east. In 1857 control was transferred to the Dutch Reform Church.

Tradouw Pass (you will pass the turnoff to it on the way to Boosmansbos) was originally an established Hessequa route across the Langeberg between Barrydale Valley and Swellendam. The Hessequa who lived under chief Kees at Hottentotskraal used two routes to cross the range. The men followed a shorter but more difficult route via Zandfontein, while the women followed an easier but longer route known as the Tradouw (a Khoikhoi word derived from the words 'tra', meaning 'women', and 'douw', meaning 'path' or 'pass'). When Thomas Bain built the pass in 1873 he largely followed the early Khoisan footpaths.

After the journey of Baron Gustaf Willem van Imhoff to the area in 1743 it was decided to send Abraham Schietekat as a teacher to the area and a school was established at Grootvadersbos.

It did not take long for the exploitation of the Swellendam forests to extend to Grootvadersbos, 15 km north-west of Heidelberg. In 1772 Carl Thunberg, the famous Swedish botanist, visited the forest where he discovered the Cape chestnut (256). Thunberg also discovered the Cape gardenia (693) in Doktersbos above Swellendam and named the genus *Rothmannia* in honour of a Swellendam farmer, Rothmann, who acted as host and helper to Thunberg when he visited the area. When Thunberg revisited the forest a year later he reported that soldiers were being used to fell trees and that as much as a wagonload was being sent to the Cape every three months.[1]

Another Swedish scientist, Anders Sparrman, visited the forest in 1775 and wrote that 'Beam planks for flooring and timber for construction of waggons are fetched from hence both by farmers and Government.'[2]

The first journey in 1777 of the British botanist and traveller William Patterson took him eastwards over Houwhoek and past Swellendam to the Oude Post. He wrote that during his stay at the Oude Post he amused himself by '... joining in the chase of the Bonta Bocks which are found in this place in great numbers.'[3] His journey continued eastwards and he made mention of Grootvadersbos and of crossing the Duiwenhoks River, which he translated as the Dove Cote River.

Within 20 years of Sparrman's visit, John Barrow remarked in 1797 that the forest was '... now outstripped of most of the wood that was valuable.'[4] Grootvadersbos was proclaimed a forestry reserve in 1896. The Boosmansbos Wilderness Area, covering about 14 200 ha of the Grootvadersbos State Forest, was proclaimed on 20 January 1978.

### Trail Synopsis

A total of 74 km of footpaths are available for backpacking. Of these, 20 km pass over private property and the consent of the individual owners is required. Therefore, only routes falling inside the wilderness area are described and should you wish to hike to Helderfontein via Kopberg, please discuss the route with the Officer-in-Charge.

### Grootvadersbos Office to Helderfontein Huts and Back

This is an interesting weekend outing covering approximately 27 km, with a choice of two routes to the Helderfontein huts. The trail is less strenuous if followed in a clockwise direction via Loerklip and if you have more time available you can extend the weekend by two days with a detour to Klein Witbooisrivier. The alternative route is via Saagkuilkloof, which means that you will be hiking in an anti-clockwise direction.

### Day 1: Grootvadersbos Office to Helderfontein Huts via Loerklip

From the office the route follows a forestry track through the tall trees of Grootvadersbos Forest. After approximately 15 minutes a deviation is reached with the route via Loerklip continuing straight ahead. The path leading off to the right is the alternative route via Saagkuilkloof and consequently the return route if you are hiking in a clockwise direction.

The Loerklip route winds through pine plantations and after about 20 to 30 minutes you reach a fire break. Here you leave the plantation and as the rest of the trail is in the open you may as well enjoy a short rest in the cool shade of the trees before continuing. About 200-300 m after leaving the forest you pass the prominent rocky outcrop from which this section takes its name — Loerklip. The origin of the name is obscure, but it is thought to have been given on account of the excellent vantage it afforded early inhabitants of the area when they were searching for stray stock. (*Loer* can be translated as "watch".) From here the trail gains height steadily along the eastern slopes of Dwarsberg. The ascent takes much longer than expected because the route winds in and out of several kloofs. Towards the east you look down into the

---

1 Skead, C.J. 1982. *Historical Mammal Incidence in the Cape Province*, Volume 1. Cape Town: Department of Nature and Environmental Conservation of the Provincial Administration of the Cape of Good Hope, 792.

2 *Ibid.*

3 *Ibid.*, 549.

4 *Ibid.*, 793.

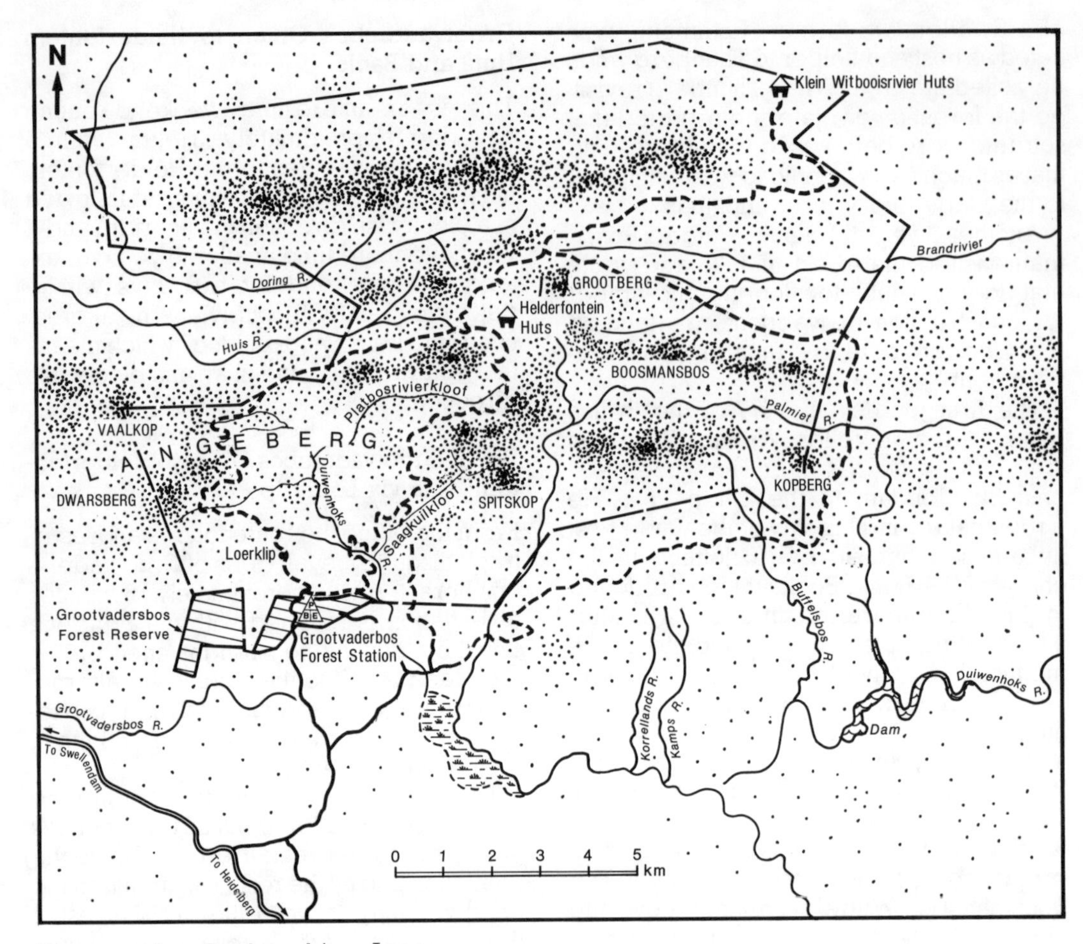


*Boosmansbos Backpacking Area.*

Duiwenhoks River, with the return route clearly visible. After about three and a half hours you reach a nek and from here the remainder of the trail mainly follows the 1 200 m contour in an easterly direction. Along this section you will notice that the vegetation is considerably drier, but you are rewarded with spectacular views of the Doring and Huis rivers far below in the valley. Looking west, the small village of Barrydale can be seen nestling against the northern slopes of the Langeberg.

About an hour and a half after leaving the nek you pass the turnoff to Klein Witbooisrivier and the zigzag route is clearly visible on the slopes of Grootberg. A short distance further the trail joins the jeep track leading to the huts, which are not much further.

The huts were originally built for forestry rangers patrolling the mountains but are today used by backpackers. They have no facilities and a lean-to has been erected to provide additional shelter. Water is available from the small stream flowing past the huts and there are pools big enough for you to enjoy a reviving dip. There is a particularly inviting pool with a waterfall should you venture a little way downstream.

**Day 2: Helderfontein Huts to Grootvadersbos Office via Saagkuilkloof**

Before returning to the office you should visit the Boosmansbos Forest, one of the highlights of this wilderness area. Follow the jeep track past the huts and across the stream. After about 15 minutes the jeep track ends and from here it is a steep descent into the forest. Common tree species of the forest include the Outeniqua (16) and real (18) yellowwood, stinkwood (118), red alder (140), Cape holly (397), candlewood (409) and the Cape beech (578).

The forest apparently took its name from a hermit who lived in a nearby cave about 100 years ago. He made a living by robbing bees' nests and collecting firewood and buchu (*Agathosma capensis*) and his bad temper and reclusive lifestyle gave rise to the nickname 'bose man' — wicked man — hence the name Boosmansbos.

From Helderfontein you follow a rough jeep track known as Barend Koen Pad. Barend Koen started the road in 1942 to reach the inaccessible kloofs of Tradouwsberg for afforestation, but the scheme was abandoned and nowadays the road is used only for patrolling, firefighting and backpacking. On leaving the huts the path climbs out of the valley. Once it levels out there is an impressive view to the left of the valley, forest and Grootberg Mountain, and it is definitely worth pausing here to absorb the panorama.

You continue along the jeep track for approximately 7 to 8 km before reaching a deviation to the right. To the left is the appropriately named Saagkuilkloof, which takes its name from the numerous sawpits used by early woodcutters. You turn right and follow the path, which leads to the Duiwenhoks River. Along this section there is a profusion of the Riversdale erica (*Erica blenna*) which flowers in early spring. After crossing a small plateau the path descends to the Duiwenhoks River, with the route out of the valley clearly visible on the opposite side of the valley. The shady trees and the river make this an ideal lunch stop, especially as the distance remaining to Grootvadersbos is not too far.

After crossing the Duiwenhoks River the trail climbs steeply for about 15 minutes before joining a forestry road. You turn left onto the road which skirts a pine plantation and after about half an hour you reach the turnoff to Helderfontein via Loerklip. At this point you turn left, following the road through Grootvadersbos, to the office which is close by.

### Extra Day Excursion from Helderfontein Huts to Grootberg

Over a long weekend it is worth doing a day hike to Grootberg, using Helderfontein as a base camp. From the huts you retrace the last few hundred metres of the previous day's hike (the Loerklip route), turning to the right onto the path leading to the Klein Witbooisrivier. After a short distance you start ascending the south-western slopes of Grootberg, reaching a fork after about an hour. The route to the left continues for approximately 10 km to the huts at Klein Witbooisrivier, while the path to the right is the Kopberg route.

After following the Kopberg route for about 45 minutes the path winds round the main Grootberg Peak (1 638 m). A short ascent brings you to the top of the highest peak in the area, from which there is one of the most impressive views in the country, with 360° of uninterrupted viewing. Looking eastwards, Cradock Peak above George is clearly visible 150 km away, while to the west the Langeberg melts into the Riviersonderend Mountains. Southwards you look over the rich patchwork wheatfields of Heidelberg and Riversdale, and to the north Toorkop, above Ladismith, is clearly visible in the Swartberg Range.

You follow the same route to return to the huts.

### DON'T MISS

- the Drostdy Museum complex in Swellendam. This includes the Drostdy, which was used as a courthouse and residence of the magistrate from 1747 to 1846, the old Gaol, which incorporates a crafts green where a replica of an undershot water-mill can be seen, and the Mayville homestead. Swellendam is known for its beautifully preserved historical buildings and a visit to the town will prove rewarding.
- the Bontebok National Park, 7 km south of Swellendam. It is the home of the bontebok, which nearly became extinct during the nineteenth century. You might also see grey rhebok, springbok, common duiker, steenbok and grysbok, and for bird-watchers, some 180 species have been recorded. The camping site is well positioned on the banks of the Breede River. Visitors may fish and swim in specific areas in the river.

# 8 Groendal Backpacking Area

Groendal was the first eastern Cape area considered pristine enough to be proclaimed a state wilderness area. It is characterised by the spectacular scenery of the Groot-Winterhoek Mountains, deep forested ravines, impenetrable valley bushveld and indigenous forests of yellowwood, red alder and Cape beech. If you are adventurous enough to explore the more inaccessible kloofs, you are likely to be rewarded by finding some of the numerous rock paintings of the San (Bushmen), who made this their last stronghold in the eastern Cape in the second half of the nineteenth century.

### Location

The wilderness area is situated near Uitenhage in the eastern Cape. The turnoff to the wilderness area is clearly marked in Uitenhage and after leaving the town the road follows the course of the Swartkops River for about 8 km.

### Distance and Classification

3 backpacking trails of either 18, 10 or 8 km
2 days or more
B grade

### Permits

The maximum group size is 10 people and the total number of visitors (groups) is also limited. It is therefore essential to obtain a permit in advance from the Officer-in-Charge, Groendal Wilderness Area, P O Box 445, Uitenhage 6230, Telephone (0422) 25418.

### Maps

A sketch map of the area is included in a pamphlet issued free of charge to backpackers. Should you require more detailed maps you will find the 1:50 000 topographical maps 3325CB and 3325CA useful.

### Climate

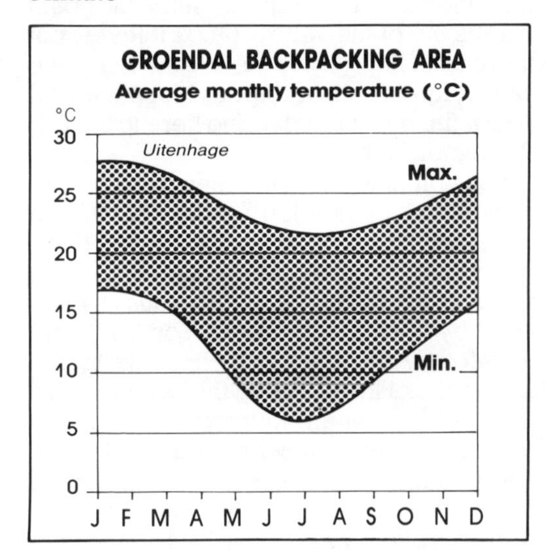


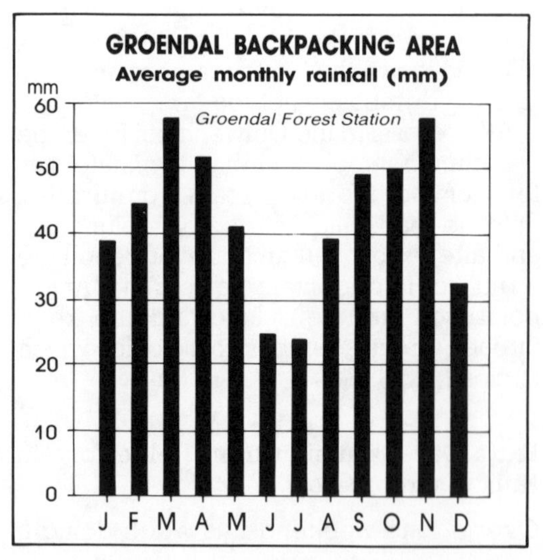

## Relevant Information

- Fires are not permitted in the wilderness area, making it essential to carry a backpacking stove.
- Although there are several caves in the area, it is advisable to carry a tent as the caves may either be occupied or if you are unfamiliar with the area you may not be able to find them.
- Several footpaths are indicated on the sketch map issued to you but these are not open to the public and prior arrangements must be made with the Officer-in-Charge.

## Facilities

A limited number of campsites with ablution facilities are situated behind the office block at Groendal. Fires are permitted here.

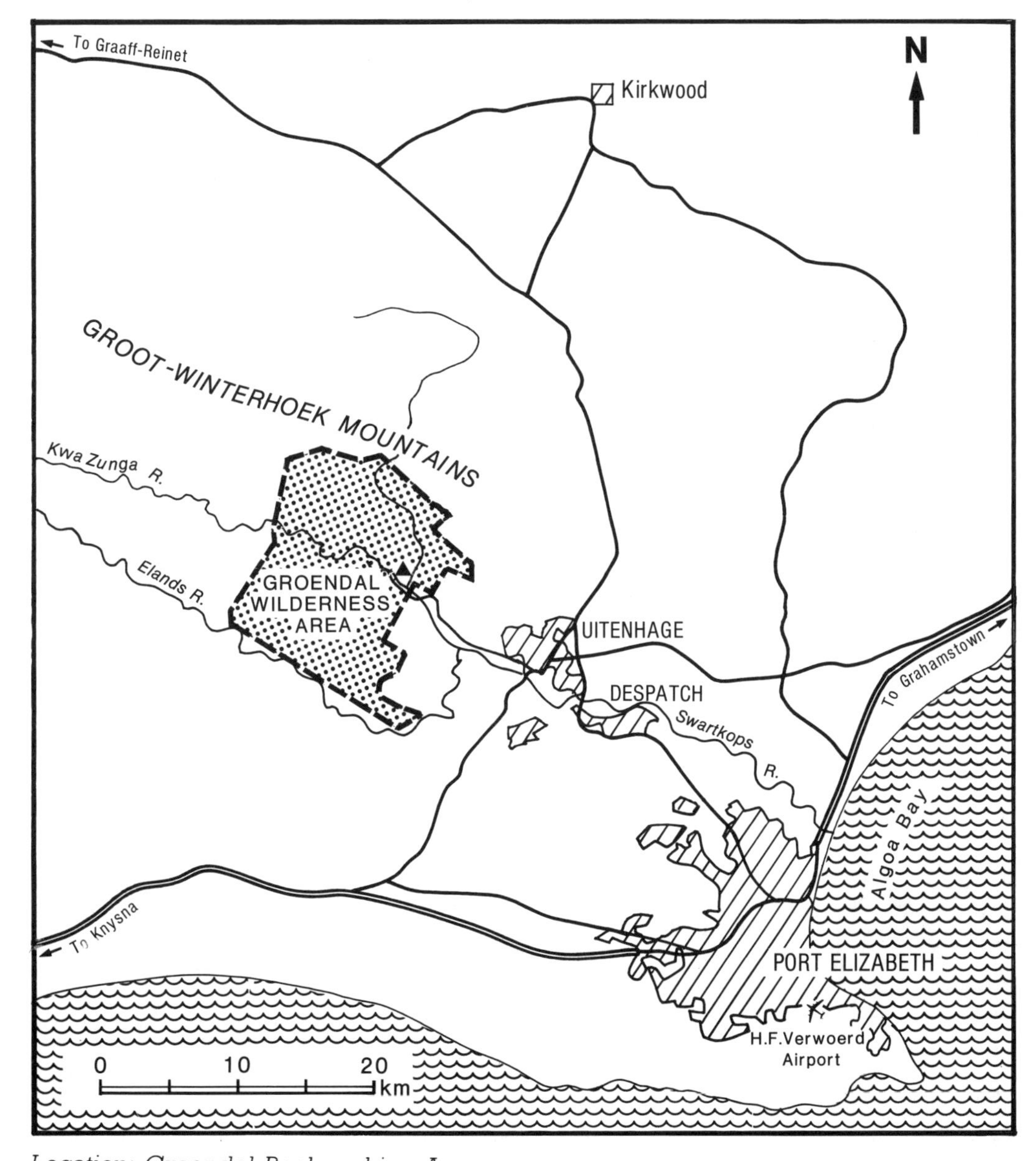


*Location: Groendal Backpacking Area*

**Flora**

The vegetation has been classified by Acocks as Valley Bushveld (Veld Type 23) and Mountain Fynbos (Veld Type 69) (previously False Macchia, Acocks Veld Type 70) with patches of indigenous forest occurring in the kloofs and ravines. In South Africa, Valley Bushveld is found in the valleys of the Gouritz, Kabeljouws, Great Kei and Sundays rivers. These rivers all drain into the Indian Ocean and the valleys are hot and receive less rain than the intervening ridges. In Groendal this vegetation type is limited to the lower lying area, occurring at altitudes varying from 300 to 630 m. *Euphorbia coerulescens* is dominant and among the other species occurring are porkbush (104), wild caper-bush (130), sneezewood (292), cat-thorn (451) and honey-thorn (669.1).

*Aloe gracilis* has been recorded in Groendal and this species appears to be restricted to the Port Elizabeth/Uitenhage area. Several upright stems branch out from the base of the shrub, which can reach up to 2 m in height. The grey-green leaves are relatively narrow and long with a serrated edge. Its brilliant red flowers which are yellowish at the mouth are unmistakable.

The deep intersecting ravines are the ideal habitat of indigenous forest species such as Outeniqua yellowwood (16), real yellowwood (18) and red alder (140). The Cape star-chestnut (473), a species with a

*Male and female cones of the tall yellowbush*

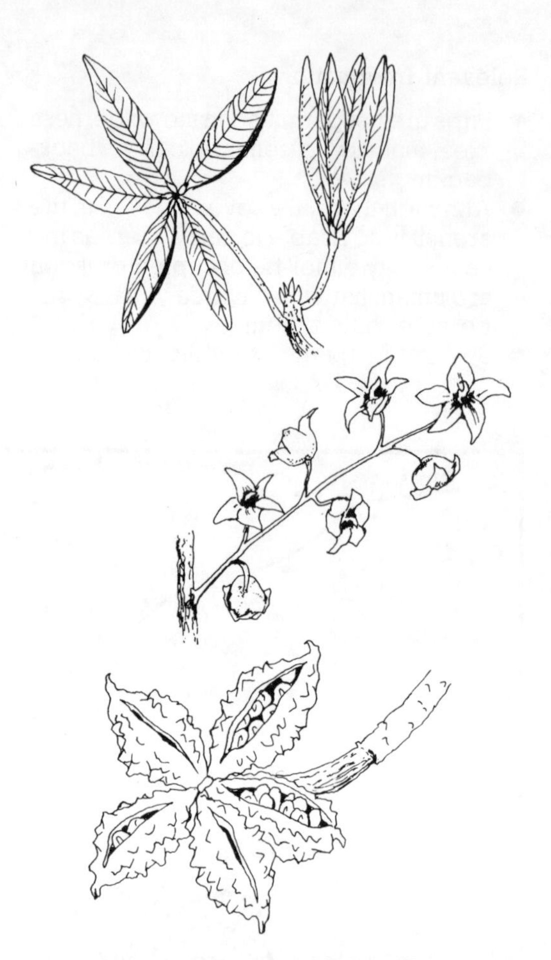

*Leaf, flower and fruit of the Cape star-chestnut – a species restricted to the Port Elizabeth/Uitenhage districts*

limited distribution, is restricted to the Port Elizabeth/Uitenhage districts. It grows as a small tree up to 5 m high with a pale bark, mottled with small raised dots. The flowers, varying from yellow to pale greenish cream with a reddish-purple throat, are borne in delicate sprays between May and September. The sprays are about 8 cm long and they appear before the new leaves. Towards the end of winter you should find the fairly obvious five-segmented fruit covered with yellow-brown hairs.

The mountain slopes consist mainly of Mountain Fynbos, which can be divided into three categories. The high moist fynbos occurs mainly on the higher southern slopes of the Groot-Winterhoek Mountains where the tall yellowbush (81) is the most conspicuous species.

The high fynbos occurs adjacent to the high moist fynbos, as well as on the steep slopes adjacent to the Valley Bushveld, the most abundant species being the blue sugarbush (93.1).

The most common type of fynbos in the wilderness area is the short fynbos. Typical species you will see are the common pincushion (84.2), the tall yellowbush (81), and the large-leaved sugarbush (*Protea foliosa*), which are interspersed with grasses dominated by redgrass (*Themeda triandra*). The large-leaved sugarbush is limited to the eastern Cape mountains in the vicinity of and north of Port Elizabeth. It grows up to 1 m high and the small yellow flowers are produced from May to June.

Trees in the wilderness area have been marked according to the *National List of Indigenous Trees* and can be identified by referring to the list on the pamphlet issued to backpackers, so remember to take it along.

**Fauna**

Among the mammals of the mountains and fynbos areas are chacma baboon, grysbok, grey rhebok and mountain reedbuck. The forested kloofs are the habitat of species such as bushpig, bushbuck, samango monkey, blue duiker and common duiker. Leopard also occur and spoor is frequently sighted in Lower Chases Kloof.

The birds of Groendal can be classified according to their preferred habitat into those of the fynbos, valley bushveld, indigenous forests and the rivers and dams.

The orangebreasted sunbird (777) is attracted to ericas and proteas and reaches the eastern limit of its distribution in the Port Elizabeth area. Other fynbos species to look out for include Cape francolin (195), rednecked francolin (198), grassbird (661), Cape sugarbird (773), which is easily identified by its long tail, especially in males, and the Cape siskin (874). The more rocky areas are the habitat of Cape rock thrush (581), familiar chat (589), mocking chat (593) and greybacked cisticola (669).

*Yellowbilled duck*

*Pied kingfisher*

In the valley bushveld be on the lookout for Knysna woodpecker (484), whitebrowed robin (613), dusky flycatcher (690), Cape batis (700) and southern tchagra (742).

The forests and kloofs are the habitat of species such as the Knysna lourie (370), Narina trogon (427), olive woodpecker (488) and the puffback (740), which obtained its common name from the characteristic way in which the male will raise and fluff his white rump feathers during courtship. Also favouring the forest are the lesser doublecollared sunbird (783) and the forest weaver (808). This is the south-eastern distribution limit of the forest weaver and you will immediately recognise this medium to largish bird by its bright yellow underparts contrasting sharply with its black upperparts.

The numerous rivers and Groendal Dam attract waterbirds such as the yellowbilled duck (104), African black duck (105), South African shelduck (103) and the Egyptian goose (102). Among the kingfishers you may see are the pied (428), giant (429), halfcollared (430) and malachite (431) kingfishers.

## History

By 1770 the frontier of the Cape had reached the Gamtoos River, which was proclaimed the eastern boundary in 1771. In an attempt to enforce the boundary, offenders were threatened with having their wagons, trading goods and bartered stock confiscated, corporal punishment and in some cases even death.

At the beginning of the nineteenth century the area was sparsely populated but much troubled by Xhosa raids. In 1804 Commissioner-General Jacob Abraham de Vries Uitenhage de Mist visited the eastern Cape and decided to establish a town — Uitenhage — as a stronghold and seat of authority in an attempt to promote central government control.

San (Bushmen) presence is verified by several rock painting sites in the wilderness area. One of these is in Skelm Kloof, which is a branch of Blindekloof and is fairly inaccessible.

The San were trapped between the north-eastern thrust of the whites and the southward migration of the Xhosa, forcing them to take refuge in the inaccessible kloofs on the Groot-Winterhoek Mountains. Between 1843 and 1880 they established their last stronghold in the mountain range between the Gamtoos and Kei rivers and used this rugged, inhospitable terrain to their advantage during raids on farms and transport wagons. Many cattle were driven into the inaccessible kloofs of the Groot-Winterhoek and the farmers retaliated by organising commandos against the San to retrieve their stolen cattle. The graves of San shot during one of the last commandos can still be seen on the farm Hill Place on the eastern edge of the wilderness area.

In 1896 five farms were consolidated and a total of 25 047 ha were placed under the management of the then Department of Forestry of the Cape colonial government. The state forest was originally known as the Elands River Forest Reserve. At the beginning of this century the land was divided into grazing areas which were leased to farmers by means of informal tenders. In an attempt to prevent overgrazing, cattle were limited to 200 per 1 000 morgen.

The forests also provided another source of revenue in the form of firewood and in 1926 more than 20 wagon loads of firewood were sold.

The wilderness area was opened on 14 February 1976 and extends over 21 793 ha.

## Trail Synopsis

As in other wilderness areas, there are various options and you are able to plan a route of your own choice. The three-day route is usually followed and this is described here.

### Day 1: Groendal Office to Emerald Pool

From the office a jeep track is followed for about 2-2,5 km before the route to Emerald Pool branches off to the left. Continue along this path and you will soon pass the plaque commemorating the official opening of the wilderness area in 1976. From here the footpath leads into Blindekloof and after about 1 km you reach a fork. The route to the right leads higher up into Blindekloof but you must turn left.

You now have a steep uphill section ahead of you along the western side of a ridge and you will gain some 250 m in altitude before joining the jeep track after about 3 km on the top of Ten Stop Hill (perhaps so named because 10 stops were required before reaching the top of the hill!). From here you continue in a westerly direction, crossing a plateau until the jeep track ends near an unnamed peak (682 m). The path then descends towards Chase's Kloof and the magnificent Emerald Pool.

Above Emerald Pool there are two caves, Eel and Percy's caves, which are suitable to overnight in. Eel cave is the lower of the two shelters and is the more popular. The route to Emerald Pool starts to the left of Eel Cave and drops steeply into Chase's Kloof, from where you pass through a forest. Keep to the right until the river is reached. A walk of not more than 10 minutes upstream brings you to Emerald Pool.

The pool is situated below a series of small rapids which cascade into the huge pool and a group of smaller pools. A 10 m high waterfall cascades into the main pool, which is surrounded by steep cliffs to the left and right, making it inaccessible from the top. Further upstream you will find Eel Pool, which is reached by taking the right-hand path from Eel Cave.

### Day 2: Optional Excursion to Strydomsbergpiek from Emerald Pool

The Emerald Pool area can be used as a base camp for exploring Strydomsbergpiek, which at 1 180 m is the highest peak in the wilderness area. To get to the peak you follow the path to the right down to the stream and continue along the stream before traversing the steep western slope of the kloof. Eventually you come out on a ridge which is followed in a westerly direction to Strydomsbergpiek.

The peak is only about 6 km north-west of Emerald Pool but this excursion should not be attempted by the unfit as the difference in altitude between Emerald Pool and the peak is over 800 m. The path is very overgrown and it is advisable to wear gaiters or long trousers to protect your legs.

### Day 3: Emerald Pool to Groendal Office

The inward route is usually retraced in returning to the office.

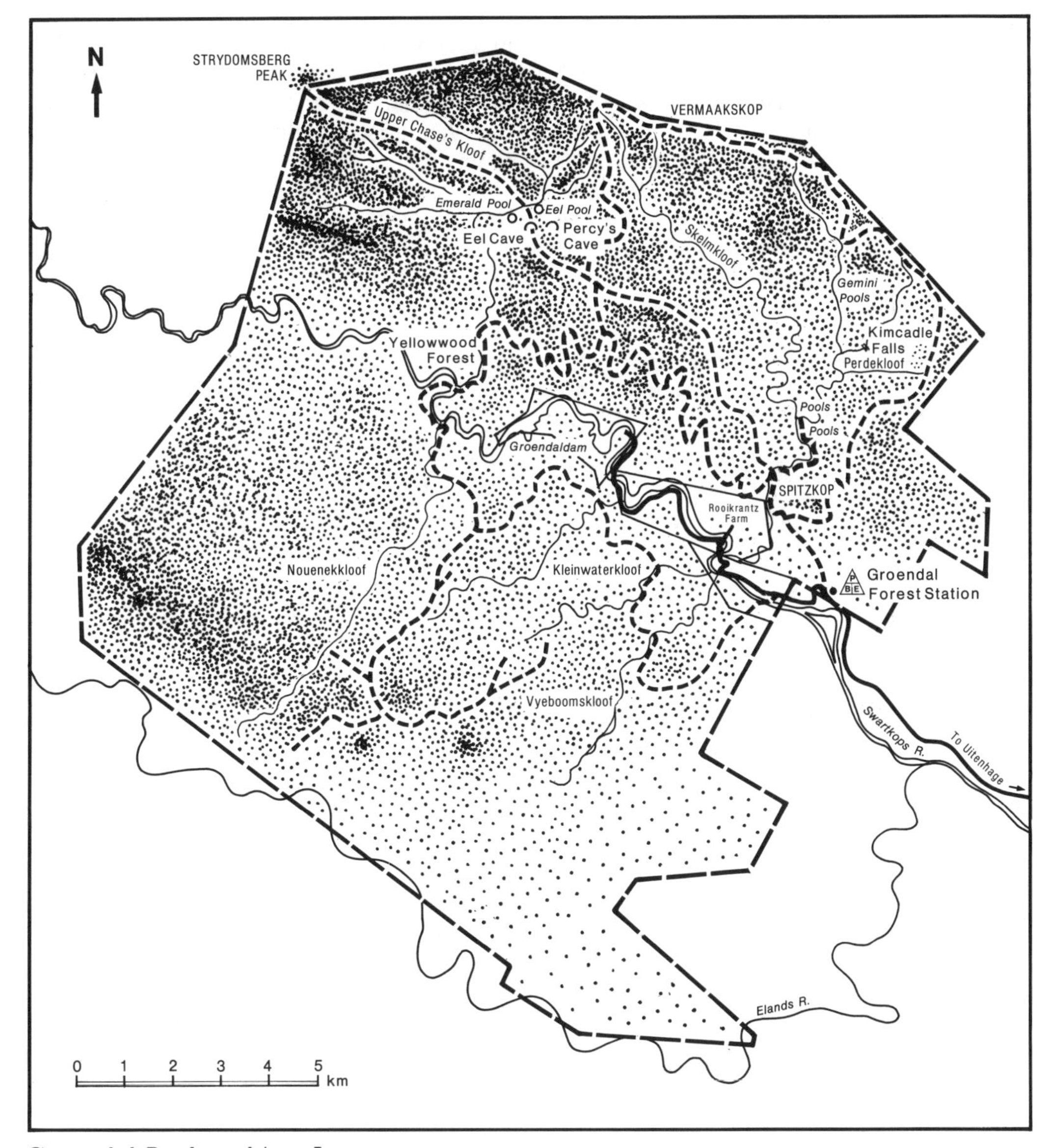


*Groendal Backpacking Area*

# 9 Tsolwana Guided Trails

Tsolwana means 'sharp little one' in Xhosa and takes its name from the prominent cone-shaped hill in the park. The area is characterised by rolling grasslands, drought-resistant karoo vegetation and scrub-covered slopes. Here it is possible to undertake a trail tailor-made to suit your needs. Not only can you determine the number of days you wish to spend trailing, but it is also possible to combine your trail with day and night vehicle drives, view rock paintings and experience traditional Xhosa dancing.

**Location**

The trails are conducted in the Tsolwana Game Park to the north-west of Whittlesea in the northern Hewu district of Ciskei. The park is about 40 minutes drive south-west of Queenstown and is reached by taking the Whittlesea road (R67) from Queenstown. At the Poplar Grove sign you turn right and continue to the second intersection (signposted Ruitjies, Upper Swart Kei and Donniebrook) where you turn left. The entrance to the park is signposted about 15 km on.

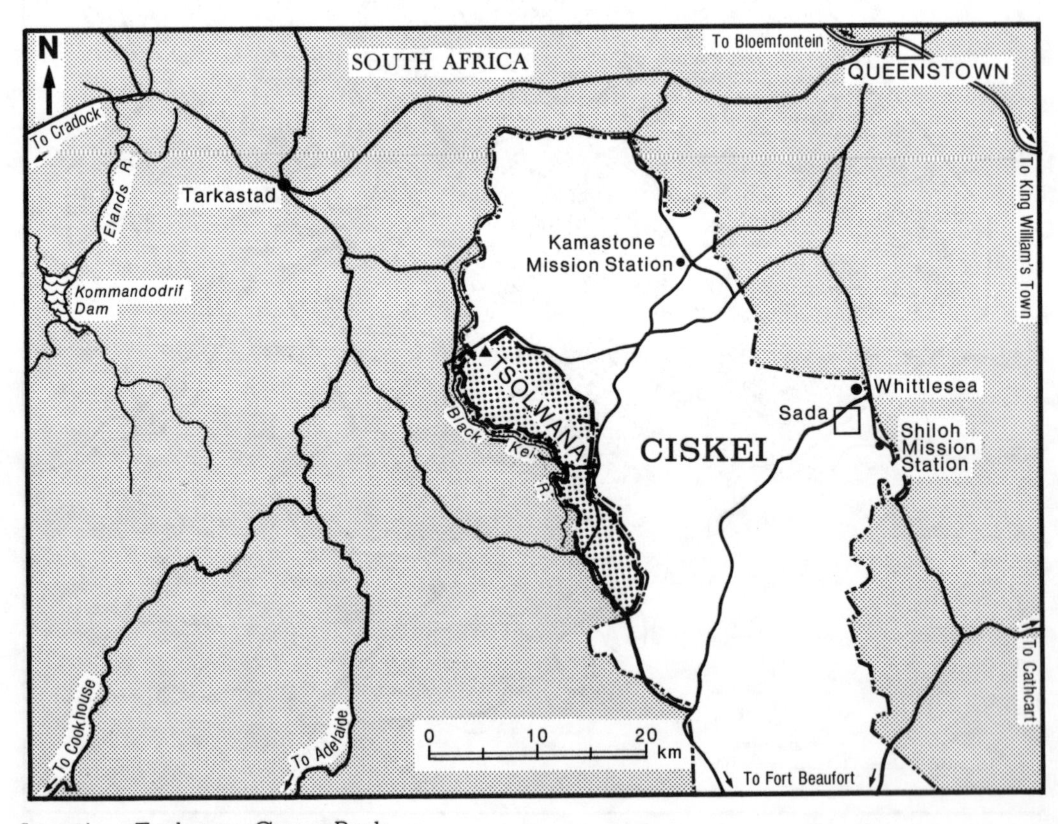


*Location: Tsolwana Game Park*

## Distance and Classification

30 km (approximately), 2-3 days
A grade

## Permits

Reservations should be made three months in advance by writing to The Manager, Tsolwana Game Park, P O Box 87, Tarkastad 5370, Telephone (04582) 5402. Groups are usually limited to 10 people, but larger groups can be accommodated provided prior arrangements have been made.

## Maps

Trails are conducted by professional game rangers and scouts and do not follow specific routes. Those who wish to obtain detailed maps of the area are advised to obtain the relevant 1:50 000 topographical maps 3226AB, 3226BA and 3226BC.

## Relevant Information

- Guided trails are conducted between September and March. These trails can range from a few hours to three days and can be arranged to suit your personal interests.
- Trailists must provide their own equipment and food.
- A daypack is useful for carrying your lunch, water-bottle, bird guide and warm clothing on trail.
- Trout fishing can be enjoyed in the park.

## Facilities

There are various types of accommodation in the park, which allows you to choose the most suitable type for your requirements. Accommodation ranges from camping sites with ablutions to self-catering lodges and fully inclusive accommodation with the professional staff of the park.

Accommodation on the trail is provided in a log cabin/tent at the Empolweni bush camp, where facilities include fireplaces, firewood, running water and toilets.

## Climate

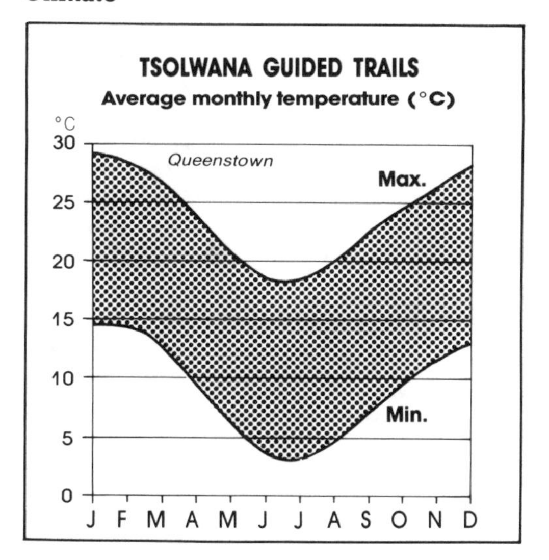


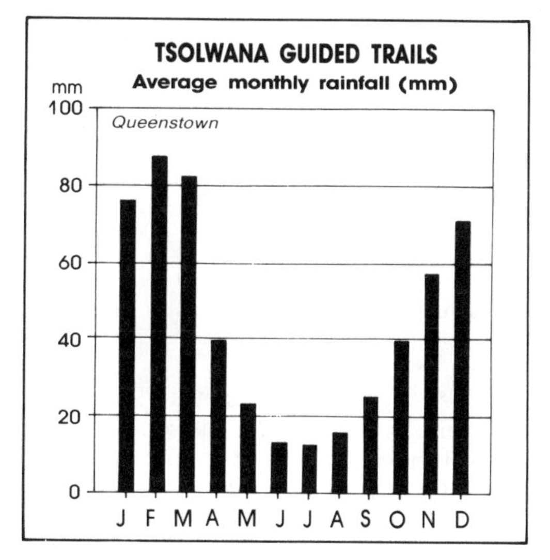


## Flora

The vegetation of the park has been classified by Acocks as Dry Cymbopogon-Themeda Veld (Veld Type 50). This type is one of the 13 pure grassveld types identified by Acocks and occurs on the upper plateaux and mountain tops of regions that are either too dry or too frosty, or both, for the development of forests. The name is derived from two of the grass species that occur, *Cymbopogon plurinodis* and *Themeda triandra*. Acocks distinguished four variations in this veld type. The south-eastern variation which occurs in the park is confined to the Upper White and Black

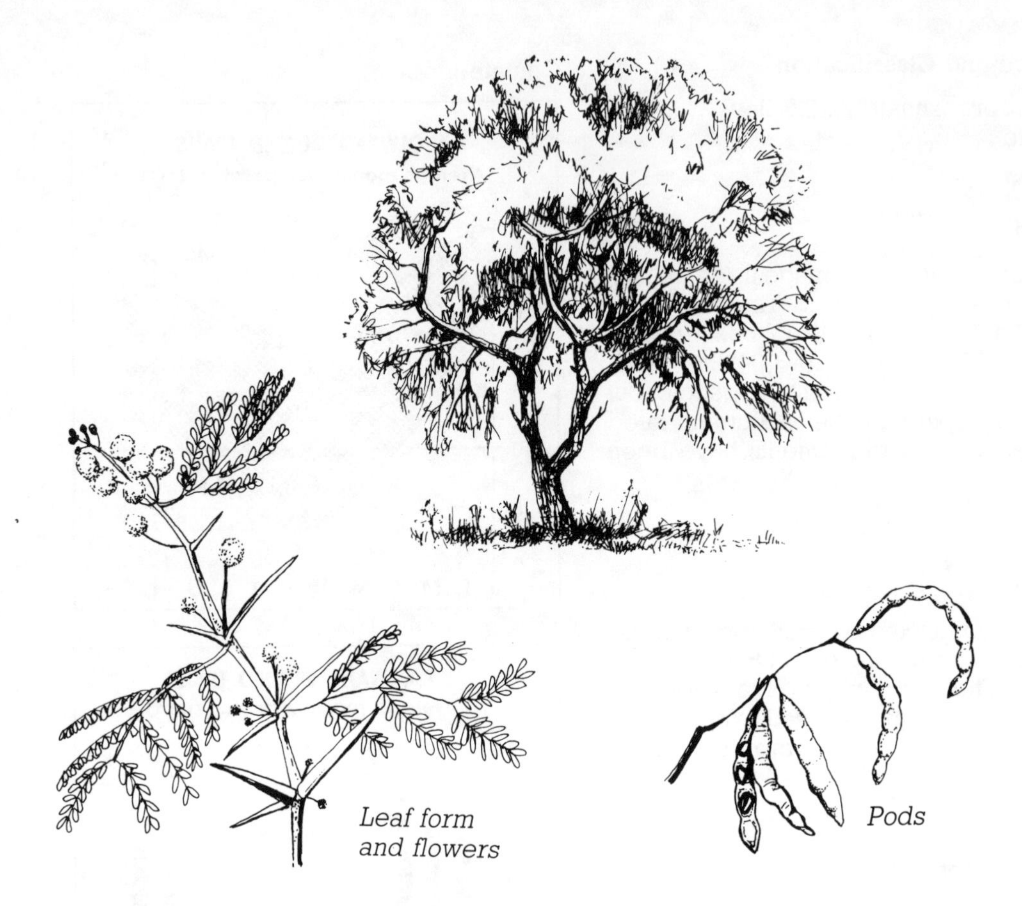


*The sweet thorn is the acacia with the widest distribution in South Africa*

Kei basin in the Queenstown, Tarkastad and Sterkstroom districts. The southern variation stretches from south of Burgersdorp to the Orange River, where it becomes known as the central variation, continuing northwards to the Vaal River. The northern variation occurs from the Vaal River to north-west of Lichtenburg in the western Transvaal.

The *Cymbopogon-Themeda* grassland comprises dominant species such as redgrass (*T. triandra*), narrow-leaved turpentine grass (*C. plurinodis*), *Eragrostis curvula, E. plana* and *Aristida junciformis*. Karoo dwarf shrub, thornveld and fynbos communities also occur in the park. The Karoo dwarf shrub communities include typical Karoo species such as sweet thorn (172), broom karree (383), Karoo bush (*Chrysocoma tenuifolia*), blue Karoo daisy (*Felicia filifolia*) and various *Senecio* and everlasting (*Helichrysum*) species.

**Fauna**

The Tsolwana Game Park is home to some 48 mammal species. Some of the smaller species occurred naturally in the area before the proclamation of the park, while others, including a number of exotic species, were reintroduced. The park embodies the concept of environmental conservation coupled with resource management and hunting is, consequently, one of the main sources of revenue. The hunting season is between 1 March and 15 October, but owing to the suitable weather conditions hunting is occasionally conducted outside these dates for specific trophies. Hunting is conducted either on foot or from hides and conventional, handgun and bow hunting are permitted.

Surplus meat from hunting and culling as well as skins and bones are sold to the rural people living close to Tsolwana, while all

*Horns of (a) mountain reedbuck (b) reedbuck*

revenue from the park is paid over to the Ciskei Agricultural Corporation.

The most abundant species is the mountain reedbuck, which numbers about 1 500 and occurs mainly on the north-facing mountain slopes and in *Acacia* thickets. Other species favouring the mountainous habitat include grey rhebok, which inhabits the southern mountainous areas of the park adjoining the Swart Kei River, chacma baboon and rock dassie. Springbok, kudu, blesbok, eland, red hartebeest and black wildebeest can be seen on the plains.

Among the smaller antelope you might encounter are steenbok and common duiker. Various smaller mammals such as caracal, black-backed jackal, Cape fox and vervet monkey also occur.

Animals such as bontebok, red lechwe, white (square-lipped) rhinoceros and giraffe, which did not occur in the area historically, have also been introduced into the park — a move that has raised the eyebrows of many conservationists. Perhaps even more disturbing to some conservationists has been the introduction of exotic species such as fallow deer, Himalayan tahr, Barbary sheep and mouflon, all of which have been introduced solely for the benefit of hunters. The question can rightly be asked whether the introduction of species that did not occur in the area historically and alien species has not created a totally artificial situation — a kind of free-range zoo.

To date some 117 bird species have been identified in the park. Among the species

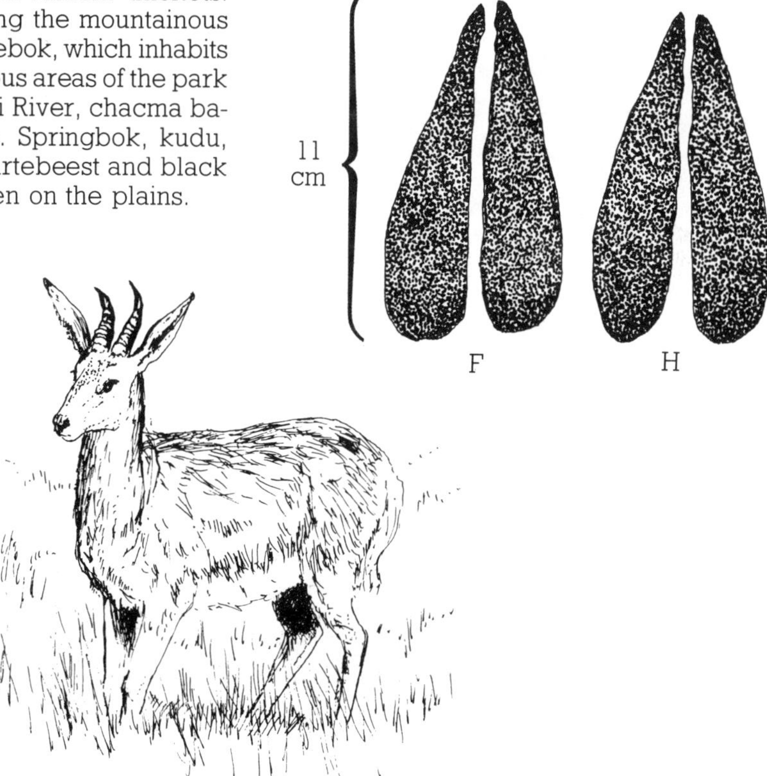


*Mountain reedbuck – the most abundant species in Tsolwana*

*Kudu usually occur in well-wooded areas*

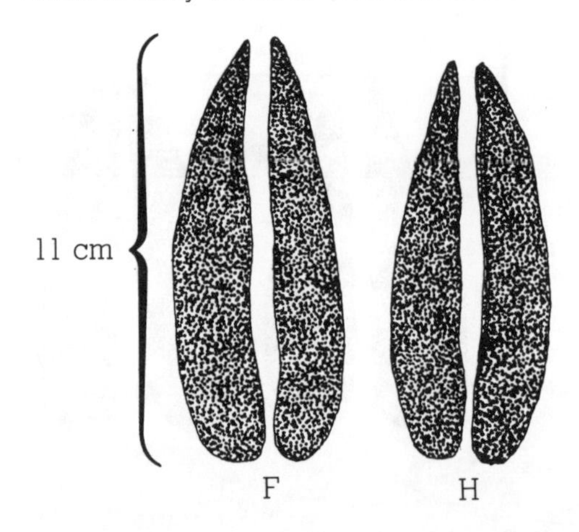


you might spot are woollynecked stork (86), Cape vulture (122), martial eagle (140), African fish eagle (148), Stanley's bustard (231), giant kingfisher (429) and ostrich (1).

Adjoining Tsolwana in the north is the Hinana Tribal Resource Area, the first such area to be established in the Ciskei. The area has been fenced and stocked with game, which is owned by the local tribal people. Hunting is permitted in the resource area and except for licence fees, all revenue goes directly to the tribe. The money derived in this way is used to build schools and fund health projects. In addition the local people are permitted to collect firewood and herbs and are allowed to graze their domestic stock in the resource area during the winter months. By performing tribal dances for visitors to Tsolwana they are able to generate further income.

*Kudu cows are hornless*

Because tangible benefits are derived from the area the concept has proved to be so successful that five more resource areas are planned for the Ciskei.

**History**

From the distribution of rock painting sites in the Ciskei it is clear that the last of the Stone Age people, the San (Bushmen), favoured the area inland of the Amatola Mountains. Later Stone Age sites in the Klipplaat River basin and rock paintings in the vicinity of Tsolwana testify to the inhabitation of the area by the San. According to the historian C W Stow, a San group led by Madura inhabited the Klipplaat and Upper Black Kei river until about 1835, when they moved north-east. A painting in a cave near Whittlesea was reported by Stow to be a portrayal of the missionary Dr Van der Kemp.

Arrangements can be made with the park management to see rock paintings in the vicinity of Tsolwana should you be interested.

During the 1820s new arrivals, the Xhosa-speaking Thembu, settled in the Stormberg, Drakensberg and the present-day district of Queenstown. Prior to their westward migration the Thembu inhabited the area between the Mtata and Mbashe rivers. Their migration to the uplands further west followed in the wake of Shaka's campaigns, one of which was directed against them. Relations between the San and the Thembu varied between peaceful co-existence and acculturation to conflict as the numbers of the new arrivals grew and competition for grazing and hunting grounds increased.

Several mission stations were established in the area during the first half of the nineteenth century. The Shiloh Mission Station near Whittlesea, west of Tsolwana, was established by the Moravian Mission Society in 1828 to serve the Thembu. The ruins of an old water-driven mill dating from 1849 can be seen behind the village. Other mission stations are the eNgotini Moravian Mission Church near Sada, which was built in 1821, and the Kamastone Mission Church, which was founded in 1849 by the Reverend William Shepstone of the Wesleyan Methodist Church. The building was designed by the well-known artist-explorer, Thomas Baines.

The nineteenth-century history of the area is closely linked to that of the fierce frontier wars which raged for a century in the eastern Cape. Following the seventh Frontier War (1846-1847), white control was extended over the area between the Amatola Mountains and the Black Kei River in 1847, when Sir Harry Smith annexed the land between the Fish and Keiskamma rivers as the district of Victoria East. The territory between the Kei and the Keiskamma rivers was proclaimed as the crown colony of British Kaffraria.

A resident magistrate was posted at Whittlesea in 1847 and a town established two years later. A defence post was established in 1849, a year before the eighth Frontier War (1850-1853) broke out and four of the town's main buildings were fortified by a certain Captain Tylden. Two of these buildings — Fort Loxton and Fort Luxary — are still in existence. During the Katberg Rebellion of 1851 the outpost was attacked by a combined Khoikhoi/Thembu force, but the attack was repulsed.

At the end of the eighth Frontier War white control over the area was extended towards the Stormberg and Victoria East was incorporated into the new district of Queenstown, which was proclaimed on 22 September 1853 by the Cape Governor, Sir George Cathcart. Farms were allotted to some 200 settlers of British and Dutch origin and by settling neutral Mfengu around the mission stations at Lesseyton and Oxkraal it was hoped to create a buffer zone between the Colony and the eastern frontier.

In 1865 the area was annexed by the Cape Colony and the Thembu were relocated in the Glen Grey, Cala and Cofimvaba districts. These people became known as the Emigrant Thembu.

Before consolidation into the Ciskei, the Hewu region was occupied by white farmers. However, since 1977 there has been an influx of immigrants from the Glen Grey and Herschel districts which were incorporated into the Transkei. The people inhabiting the area today belong mainly to the Hlubi, Bhele and Jwarha groups. These groups fled southwards in the wake of the expan-

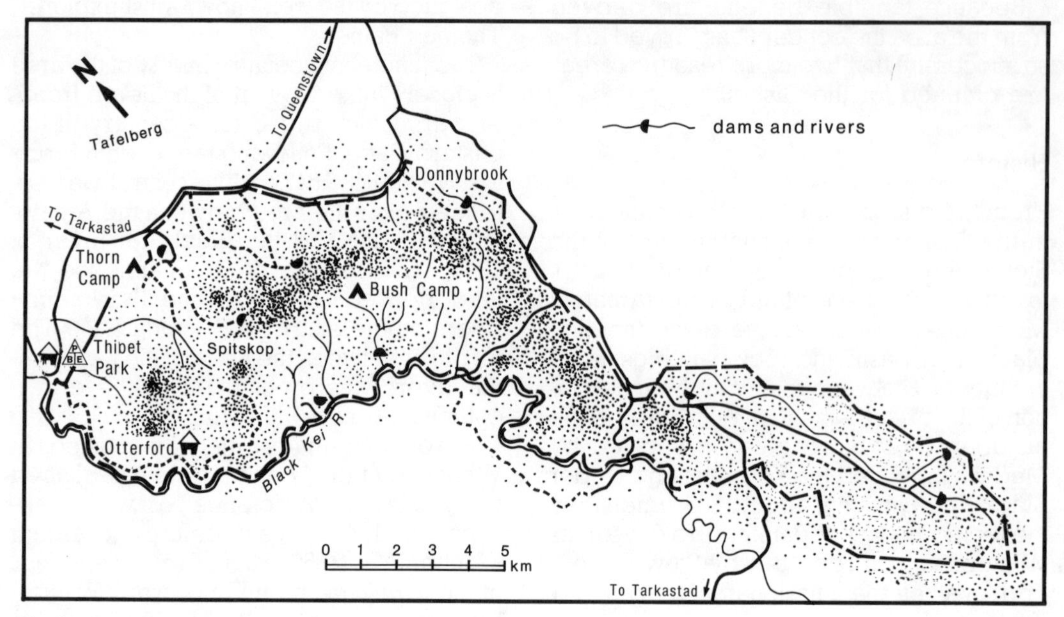


*Tsolwana Guided Trails*

sion of the Zulu kingdom and the *Difaqane* wars and became known as the Mfengu, a Xhosa word meaning beggar or scavenger.

## Trail Synopsis

Tsolwana offers a wide range of activities ranging from guided walks of a few hours to guided trails lasting two or three days. An added attraction is that you can combine your guided trail with day or night game-viewing excursions in a four-wheel-drive vehicle. Your options are almost unlimited! Nocturnal animals you might be fortunate to see on night drives include antbear, aardwolf, porcupine, springhares and Cape fox. Trails are conducted by professional rangers or game scouts, from a bush camp on the southern slopes of Tsolwana Mountain overlooking the Swart Kei River valley.

As with other guided wilderness trails, the trails in Tsolwana are flexible to suit trailists' interests and levels of fitness. Unlike most other guided trails, however, you must provide all the necessary equipment and food for the duration of the trail.

## DON'T MISS

- the numerous places of interest in the area, such as the Shiloh Mission Station, Fort Loxton in Whittlesea and the Kammastone Mission Church. Obtain the pamphlet *Motoring Trails in Ciskei — The Northern Circuit (4)* from the Ciskei Tourist Board, P O Box 56, Bisho, Ciskei and explore the area from the comfort of your car.

# Part 4
# Lesotho

# 10 Sehlabathebe Backpacking Area

Situated high on the Drakensberg escarpment, Sehlabathebe National Park is dominated by the triple peaks, Baroa-ba-Bararo, the Three Bushmen. The park has several rare and unusual features, including weird sandstone formations, the rare *Aponogeton* waterlily, which is almost exclusively found in the rock pools of Sehlabathebe, and *Oreodaimon*, a rare minnow which was rediscovered in 1970 in the Tsoelikane River after last being seen in 1938.

## Location

The park is in south-eastern Lesotho and is surrounded by east Griqualand, Transkei, Natal and the rest of Lesotho. You follow the Drakensberg Gardens/Bushman's Nek road from Underberg for 4 km, after which you turn left and continue for approximately another 1 km before turning right at the next junction. After 26 km you will reach a T-junction where you turn right and continue for 8 km to the Bushman's Nek Hotel. About 3 km beyond the hotel you reach the SAP border post. From here you can continue on foot to the Bushman's Nek footpass. The route follows a well-defined path to the Ngoangoana border post and the lodge in Sehlabathebe.

## Distance and Classification

Bushman's Nek to Sehlabathebe Lodge and back: approximately 30 km, 2 days
B+ grade

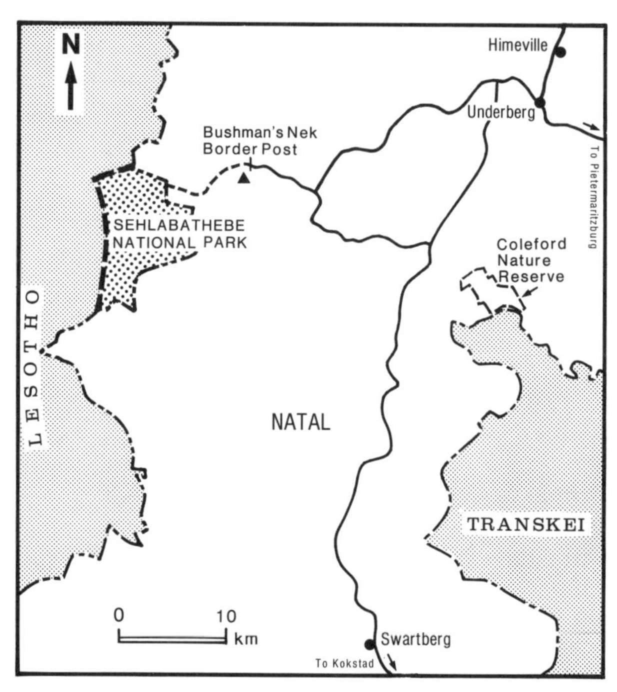


*Location: Sehlabathebe Backpacking Area*

Several day walks of varying length are also possible in the park.

### Permits

At present permits are not required to backpack in the park.

### Maps

A photocopy of the 1:50 000 topographical map covering the area is available in the park but it is advisable to obtain the 1:50 000 topographical map 2929CC which is available from the South African Government Printer.

### Relevant Information

- South African citizens require a valid passport to enter Lesotho while non-South Africans must enquire at their nearest consulate regarding passports and other travel documents, as well as re-entry visas which may be required to return to South Africa. Such applications should be made to the nearest regional representative of the Department of Home Affairs.
- Thick mist can descend very suddenly in the park and reduce visibility to almost zero. Unless you are familiar with the park you must remain where you are until the mist lifts.
- Lightning is a danger in the park and normally occurs with thunderstorms.
- Snow can occur at any time of the year, even during summer, making it essential to pack suitable clothing. A good-quality tent and sleeping-bag are necessary for camping.

### Facilities

The Bushman's Nek Hotel is conveniently situated near the start but it does not have caravan or camping facilities. The nearest campsite and caravan park is some 39 km away in the Himeville Nature Reserve.

Accommodation in the Sehlabathebe National Park ranges from campsites to a luxury lodge fully equipped with beds, bedding, fridge, stove, cooking utensils, crockery and cutlery. All you need to supply in the lodge is your own food. You can also stay in the nearby hostel, where bunk-beds, a fridge, cooking utensils, crockery and cutlery are provided. There are also unlimited campsites, without facilities, wherever you choose to overnight.

Campsites do not have to be reserved but it is advisable to book well in advance for the lodge or hostel with the Lesotho National Parks Board, P O Box 92, Maseru 100, Lesotho, Telephone (050) 323600.

### Climate

The climate is generally cool to cold, with the annual average maximum and minimum temperatures fluctuating between 16 °C and 9 °C. During December and January the average maximum daily temperature is 23 °C, dropping to average minimum daily temperatures of 2,5 °C and lower between May and July.

The average rainfall of Sehlabathebe is 1 300 mm, 80 per cent of which occurs between December and March when thick mist, often lasting several days, is also common.

Snow falls on an average of 17 days a year and can occur in any month. Between May and October it snows twice a month on average. Strong, cold winds are common throughout the year.

### Flora

The vegetation of the park is classified as sub-alpine grassland, redgrass (*Themeda triandra*) being the dominant species.

The pride of the park is the aquatic plant *Aponogeton ranunculiflorus,* also known as the Crown Jewels of Sehlabathebe. This plant was discovered in 1970 by the British botanist Kate Williamson and it is confined to the rock pools along the northern border of the park as well as a few pools on the Natal side of the Drakensberg. The plants grow in the humid mud of cave sandstone pools with a depth of 200 mm to 3 m and the white buttercup-like flowers float on the surface of the water. Be on the lookout for the flowers from November to January.

*The lip-flower sugarbush is widespread on the Natal side of the Drakensberg, but only a single plant grows in Sehlabathebe*

In the park is a single survivor of the lip-flower sugarbush (98), a species which is common and widespread on the Natal side of the Drakensberg at heights up to 2 300 m. The specimen in the park grows at an approximate altitude of 2 400 m and both colour varieties, rose pink and cream, occur. To withstand extremes of temperature the leaves and stems are slightly woolly, a characteristic from which the plant derives the species name *subvestita*, meaning 'partly clothed'.

**Fauna**

Twenty-six mammal species have been identified in the park, of which three are classified as abundant, ten as common, five as uncommon, four as transient and one as uncertain.

The animal you are most likely to see is the grey rhebok, which is common in all areas of the park. They have excellent eyesight, hearing and sense of smell and will normally retreat to a safe distance with a sharp alarm call, a coughing snort, as you approach. On the run they are easily identified by their white bushy tails.

Oribi are frequently sighted in the Tsoelikane Valley in the central portion of the park and eland have been spotted along the park's eastern border in early summer when the grazing is favourable.

In the vicinity of the research centre, a number of black wildebeest are kept in an enclosure to determine their influence on the vegetation before they are released. They are predominantly localised grazers and this could be harmful to the vegetation. These animals probably occurred here naturally in earlier times during the summer months when the sour grassveld is more palatable.

Black wildebeest are mainly active in the coolness of early morning and late afternoon and during the day they can be seen resting in the open. There are three distinct social groups — females, bachelor herds and territorial males — which remain in the same area for long periods. You will be able to recognise the older males in the herd because they become almost black compared to the usually buffish-brown colouring of younger males.

Black wildebeest give birth to a single calf after a gestation period of eight and a half months, usually during summer. This calf remains with its mother until the arrival of the next calf, upon which the first is driven away.

Most of the other mammals in the park are nocturnal and are therefore seldom seen, but there is abundant evidence of their presence in the form of tracks and droppings. An informative booklet entitled *Mammals of the Sehlabathebe National Park* containing line drawings of the various tracks and droppings can be purchased in the park.

Approximately 110 bird species have been recorded in Sehlabathebe National Park, but owing to the harsh environment at this altitude they are not concentrated in any particular area and the casual visitor is unlikely to tick off more than a few species. Among the more common and conspicuous species are the whitenecked raven (550), black crow (547), Cape bunting (885) and greywing francolin (190). Thirteen birds of prey have been identified, including the rare bearded vulture (119), which in South Africa has virtually disappeared with the advance of civilisation. Today it is confined to the Drakensberg range where no more than about 120 pairs survive. In flight it can be identified by its long, diamond-shaped tail.

The streams of Sehlabathebe are the habitat of a small minnow that was last observed in 1938 before being rediscovered in the Tsoelikane River in 1970. Known as the Mountain Spirit of the Drakensberg (*Oreodaimon quathlambae*), this rare species has adapted to survive in the cold mountain streams of the park which are frequently covered by ice during winter. It is endemic to the park.

Sehlabathebe is a paradise for trout fishermen and it was in this area that a Southern Africa record rainbow trout of 4,2 kg was taken some years ago. The 'King of the Trout', a giant trout of 7 kg or more, is rumoured to be lurking somewhere in the streams of Sehlabathebe. Fishing is permitted in the park below the waterfall in the Tsoelikane River and licences can be obtained from the superintendent at the lodge. The ponds below the lodge are well stocked with trout but are reserved for registered trout anglers only.

### History

Excavations in south-eastern Lesotho have confirmed the former occupation of the region by people of the Middle and Later Stone Ages. Deposits at Moshebi Shelter, a few kilometres outside the park, were found to contain Middle as well as Later Stone Age artefacts. Two successive Middle Stone Age layers were overlain by Later Stone Age material, which has been dated at about 2180 BP. Excavations in the upper layers of the Later Stone Age deposits have revealed hearths dated at between 2210 BP and 290 BP.

Upstream from Moshebi Shelter, at Ha Soloja, the deposits throughout contain Middle Stone Age artefacts and the upper part of the excavation dates back more than 45 000 years.

At Sehonghong, about 40 km north-west of Sehlabathebe, the Middle Stone Age has been dated at between 32 150 BP and 20 900 BP and the Later Stone Age at 1400 BP. Among the interesting artefacts from this site are about 20 marine shells which have been dated at about 1430 BP. As the site is about 240 km from the Indian Ocean, this provides proof of early trading contact between inland and coastal groups.

From the numerous rock paintings in caves and overhangs in the park and the surrounding areas it is clear that it must have been a popular hunting ground of the San (Bushmen).

Initial relations between the San and immigrant Basotho[1] during the last century were of peaceful co-existence, and some of the San were even protected by Basotho chiefs such as Moorosi. However, as the number of immigrants in the area began to increase, the denser populations inevitably led to conflict. This reached its climax when the San raided cattle from the Basotho. One of the San bands in the Sehonghong area was exterminated in the 1870s and according to oral tradition the last of the San on the Leqoa and Tsoelike rivers were exterminated in about 1886. By the early 1890s there were few free San remaining in Lesotho.

To date more than 60 rock painting sites where San artists recreated tribal ceremonies, hunting scenes and daily life have been located in the park.

The origin of the name Sehlabathebe — Plateau of the Shield — is obscure, but it is

---

1 Refer to the Lesotho Pony Trekking Safari for a more detailed history of the Basotho.

*One of the numerous rock paintings in Sehlabathebe National Park*

thought to be derived from a popular tale relating to a great battle where a victorious tribe pierced the shield of the enemy. According to the Basotho of the area it was named after Chief Sehlabathebe, who was apparently given this name after a victorious battle.

The park was established in 1970 for the preservation of Lesotho's unique natural and cultural heritage and covers an area of 6 805 ha. The International Union for the Conservation of Nature (IUCN) and the World Wildlife Fund through the Southern African Nature Foundation played an important role with a grant of R45 000 for its development, including fencing, the erection of a research centre, equipment and research facilities for the laboratories.

As a result of the high altitude and severe winter climate, the park is suitable only for truly montane animal species. It is also too small to maintain large numbers of animals permanently and is rather being developed as a scenic, recreational and fishing area.

**Trail Synopsis**

**Day 1: Bushman's Nek Border Post to Sehlabathebe Lodge**

After passing through the border post a forestry road is followed for a short while before you turn left onto a jeep track. Shortly after the turn you cross the Ngwangwane River, which is followed for about 4 km before you have the choice of either continuing along the jeep track, which follows an easier gradient, or taking a more direct, steeper route.

A short distance further you reach the end of the jeep track and the route continues along a bridle path. It is a fairly steep ascent and over the next 2,5 km you gain about 500 m in altitude. Once the cutline is reached it is an easy 3 km walk over a flat grassy plateau to the Lesotho border post, which is reached after four to five hours. The post was unmanned at the time of writing.

The park is entered through a gate north

of the border post and you follow the park road for about 3 km before reaching a short-cut leading off to the left. The lodge is about 2 km away and can be seen clearly with the Three Bushmen, also known as the Devil's Knuckles, forming an impressive backdrop.

The total distance covered is about 15 km should you use the short-cut in the park and is normally covered in six to seven hours.

### Suggested Trail Routes in the Park

There is no integrated trail system in the park but there are numerous footpaths and disused cattle tracks that you can follow.

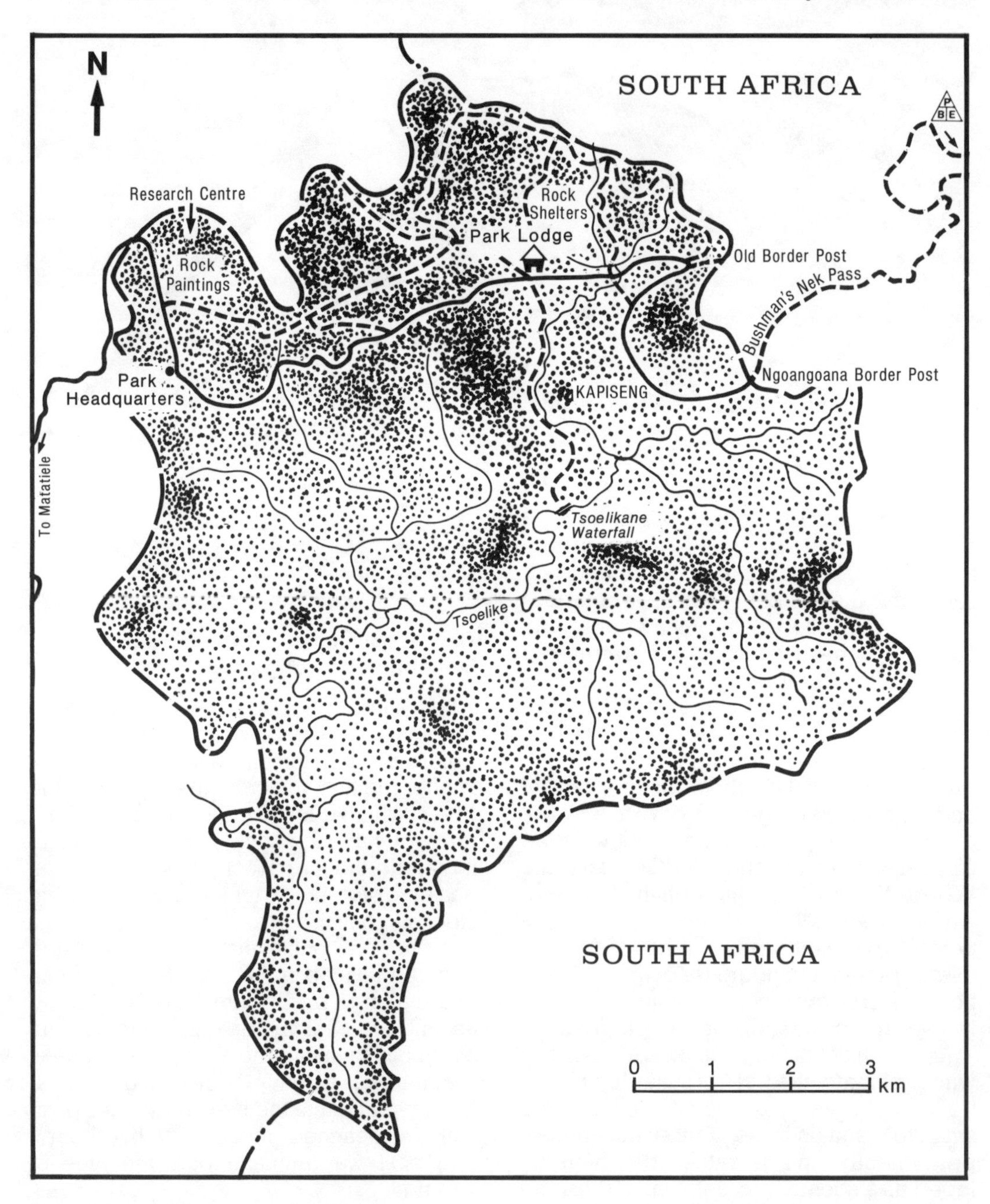


*Sehlabathebe Backpacking Area*

*The Three Bushmen Peaks dominate the scenery in Sehlabathebe. Note the stone-built shelter in the natural recess of the rocks to the left*

A gravel road leads from the lodge to the research centre and the park headquarters at the western border of the park where one of the most accessible rock paintings in the park is situated in an overhang. The shelter contains over 130 individual paintings, ranging from the usual eland and grey rhebok to a hunter who appears to be wearing a mask and a most interesting panel of six African-like figures dressed in wide shapeless dresses with bangles around their necks.

The distance from the lodge to the research centre is about 9 km. Sehlabathebe trading store, where it is possible to stock up with basic foodstuffs, is a short distance outside the park.

Of particular interest in Sehlabathebe are the many extraordinary sandstone formations which have been shaped into fascinating caves, pillars, arches and potholes by centuries of wind, rain and extremes of temperature. The contact of the sandstone with the Drakensberg basalt here lies at 2 380 m above sea level, which is probably responsible for the greater exposure of the rock. These are said to be the highest exposed sandstone formations in Southern Africa.

There are several natural rock arches that have been gouged out by the forces of nature, one of which forms a complete circle, with the Three Bushmen etched in the background.

In the vicinity of the lodge several former dwellings of Basotho herdsmen can be seen. Before the proclamation of the park these people used to migrate to Sehlabathebe from the Quachas Nek area during the summer months when the grazing is more nutritious in the highlands. By extending stone dwellings from the natural recesses in the rocks they were able to gain protection from storms and possible enemies.

Among these former dwellings are games engraved into flat rocks and domestic implements such as grinding stones can still be found lying about.

The former inhabitation of these rock shelters and the use of the larger ones elsewhere in the park to shelter animals during inclement weather has unfortunately damaged or destroyed a large number of rock paintings. Some have been obliterated by greasy animals rubbing against them, while others have been scribbled over by herdsmen or damaged by soot from fires lit near the walls.

An interesting day excursion from the lodge is to follow the Tsoelikane River downstream. After a short while you will reach an overhanging rock formation, which is known to the local people as Kepiseng or The Cap. The climb to the base of this imposing formation is steep but rewarding and takes about 15 to 20 minutes.

Looking down onto the Tsoelikane River you will immediately be struck by its wandering course. This phenomenon is known as meandering, a name derived from the River Meander in Asia. During its early development a river normally follows a straight course down the steepest gradient, cutting straight down into the underlying rock. In later stages the lower gradient causes the flow to diminish and the river starts to cut into its own banks, carving out a winding course. Oxbow lakes are caused when a meander cuts through its own bank to form small lakes and these normally contain water only after floods. One of the best examples of meandering in Southern Africa is the well-known Colley Wobbles on the Mbashe River in the Transkei.

About 1 to 1,5 km further downstream the Tsoelikane River suddenly swings sharply to the right and after 15 to 20 minutes of walking you reach the Tsoelikane Waterfall. The 20 m high fall drops into a large pool and if the water temperature allows you can cool down before returning to the base camp.

The rock pools north of the lodge are also worth exploring and you may be fortunate enough to catch a glimpse of the rare water lily *Aponogeton ranunculiflorus*, mentioned earlier, which flowers between November and January.

A rewarding trail for fit and energetic backpackers leads to the Three Bushmen Peaks. From the peaks you have an impressive view of Lesotho to the west and low-lying Natal to the east, with the sheer cliffs plunging nearly 400 m below you. Looking north you can clearly see Walker's Peak with the unmistakable Rhino Peak about 7 km beyond.

Although it is only about 4 to 5 km to the first of the three peaks, about 550 m is gained in altitude and this walk is therefore not recommended for backpackers who are not entirely fit.

# 11 Lesotho Pony Trek

The rugged mountains of Lesotho can best be experienced from the back of a Basotho pony, one of the main means of transport in the country. A pony trek is the most exciting way of discovering this unspoilt country with its awe-inspiring vistas, dramatic mountain peaks, deep river gorges, crystal clear pools and spectacular waterfalls. You will also have many opportunities to experience authentic tribal village culture.

### Location

Treks are usually conducted eastwards from the western edge of the Maloti Mountains.

Treks arranged by the **Lesotho Tourist Board** start at Qaba, about 80 km south of Maseru, and transport from Maseru to the starting point is provided by the Board.

Treks conducted by **Basotho Pony Trekking** depart from the Trekking Centre near Molimo Nthuse, which is about 45 minutes drive (58 km) on the tarred Mountain Road from Maseru. You travel east from Maseru, reaching Mazenod after 15 km. Here you take the Roma road, which is followed for approximately 10 km to St Michaels where the Mountain Road branches off to the left. A spectacular route over Bushman's Pass (2 260 m) and then Molimo Nthuse Pass (God Help Me Pass) is followed. The Trekking Centre is about five minutes beyond Molimo Nthuse Lodge.

### Distance and Classification

Six to seven hours of riding are done each day.

A grade — you need not be an experienced rider but novices will discover that muscles are used even when sitting on a pony!

### Permits

No permits are required for pony trekking safaris in the Maloti. Treks can be booked through either the **Lesotho Tourist Board,** P O Box 1378, Maseru 100, Lesotho, Telephone (050) 32 2896 or 32 3760 or **Basotho Pony Trekking,** P O Box 1027, Maseru 100, Lesotho, Telephone (050) 32 2896 or 32 3760.

### Maps

The country is covered by 1:50 000 topographical maps obtainable from the Department of Lands, Surveys and Physical Planning, Ministry of the Interior, P O Box MS 876, Maseru 100, Lesotho. However, the two-part 1:250 000 maps of Lesotho are a more manageable size and are sufficient.

### Relevant Information

- Treks conducted by the **Lesotho Tourist Board** are fully inclusive of planning, reservations and food as well as a guide, ponies and tack. *These trails are inclusive of transport from Maseru to Qaba, the return flight from Semonkong to Maseru and transfers from the airport to the city on completion of the trek.* Reservations can be made with the Lesotho Tourist Board, P O Box 1378, Maseru 100, Lesotho, Telephone (050) 32 2896 or 32 3760.
- Treks that only include ponies, saddles, saddle bags, pack horses, pack saddles and a guide can be booked through **Basotho Pony Trekking,** P O Box 1027, Maseru 100, Lesotho, Telephone (050) 32 2896 or 32 3760. Trekkers must supply their own food and arrange their own accommodation and transport to and from the Trekking Centre, as well as their return flights from Semonkong to Maseru or road transport from Qaba to Maseru, depending on where the trek terminates.
- South African citizens require a valid passport, while foreigners should en-

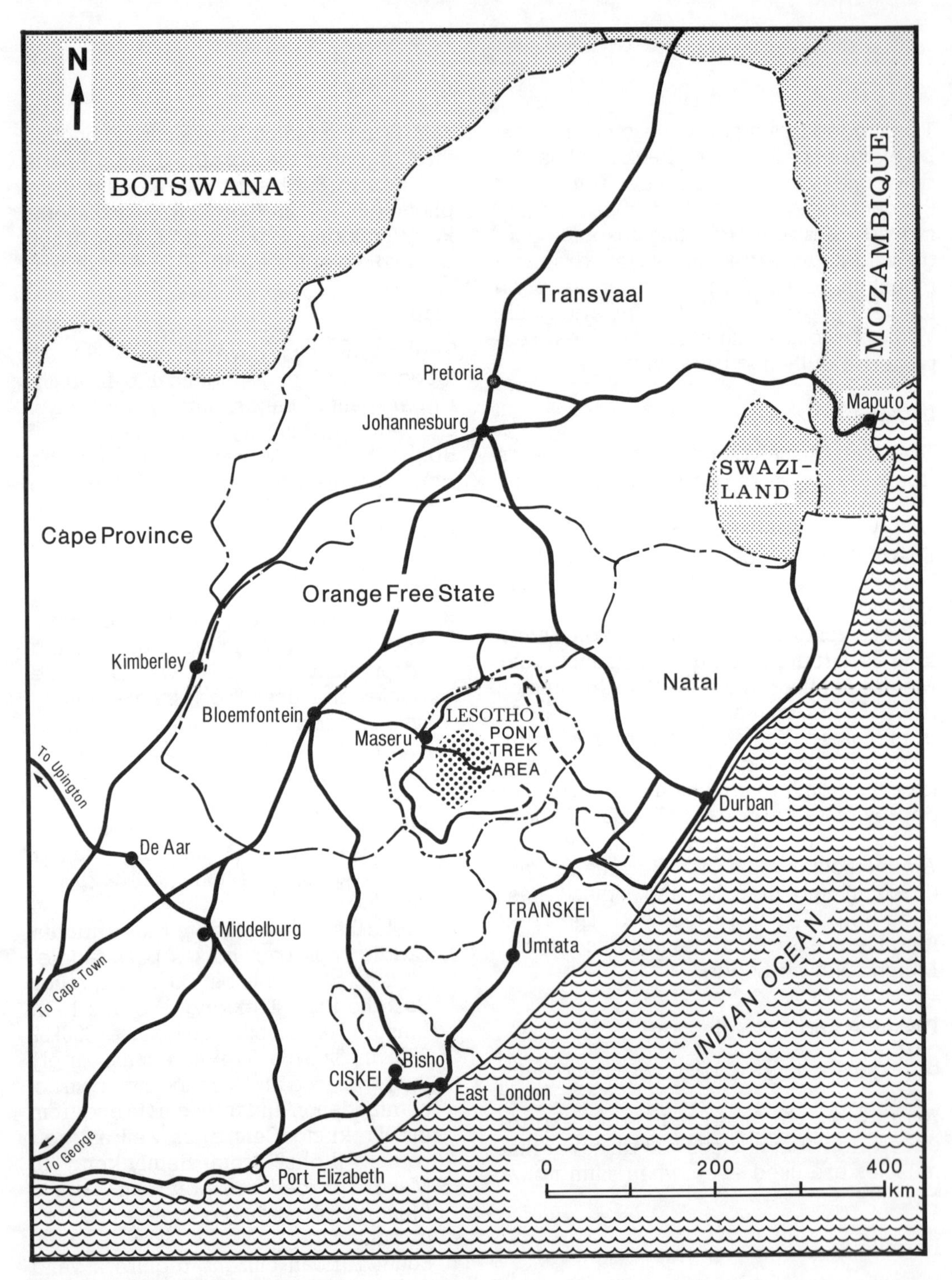


*Location: Lesotho Pony Trekking*

representative of the Department of Home Affairs.
- Be well prepared for any sudden changes in weather. Both scorching sun and violent thunderstorms can be experienced on the same day during the summer months.
- A daypack is useful for keeping water and other necessary items close at hand whilst riding.
- Trekkers must supply their own sleeping-bags, camping mattresses and rain gear.

## Facilities

If you are booked on the fully inclusive **Lesotho Tourist Board** trek leaving from Qaba Lodge, the night prior to the departure of the trek can be spent in any of several tourist hotels in Maseru. On the trek itself you will have lodging and meals in local rondavels.

Trekkers booked with **Basotho Pony Trekking** can reserve accommodation at the Molimo Nthuse Lodge, which is only five minutes from the Trekking Centre. Facilities include 15 rooms with bathrooms, a restaurant and bar. On the trek itself trekkers have a choice of pitching their own tents or renting village rondavels at the overnight stops at reasonable rates. On trails which terminate at Qaba and Semonkong it is possible to book lodges that are run by Frasers. Facilities include beds, gas cookers, a kitchen and cooking utensils, and a bathroom. Soft drinks and liquor can be purchased. Reservations can be made with Frasers Lodges, P O Box MS 5, Maseru 100, Lesotho, Telephone (050) 32 2601.

## Climate

Trekkers should be prepared for afternoon thunderstorms between October and April. Over 85 per cent of the annual rainfall occurs during these seven months. Although fog occurs throughout the year, the summer months are notorious for dense fog, which could last for several days.

Snow is not confined to winter and can be expected during any month. At higher altitudes frost is common throughout the year.

January is the hottest month, when the daily maximum temperature sometimes exceeds 30 °C. The minimum daily temperature usually drops to 15 °C below the maximum, and nights are cool. Winter nights are cold and temperatures below freezing point are not uncommon. Winter days are cloudless and generally pleasantly warm.

## Flora

Lesotho is virtually treeless, the vegetation being grassland with typical alpine flower species such as everlastings (*Helichrysum*), *Dianthus*, *Senecio*, *Scabiosa*, red hot pokers (*Kniphofia* spp.), *Myosotis* and *Valeriana*.

The grasslands consist mainly of two types. *Themeda* occurs up to about 2 700 m on north-facing slopes, while the hardier *Festuca-Merxmuellera* dominates the south-facing slopes above 2 100 and 2 300 m.

Although Lesotho has never had extensive forests to speak of, a large number of trees were cut down by missionaries and early white settlers some 150 years ago and used for building houses. The Basotho also felled many trees for roof timbers and the remaining woody vegetation suffered severely during the cold winters of the late 1800s when dung for burning was in short supply because of the rinderpest. However, the missionaries and white settlers introduced several alien species such as the weeping willow (*Salix babylonica*) and the white poplar (*Populus alba*). Today these trees are not only an important source of timber and fuel, but also play an important role in preventing erosion.

The indigenous trees are limited to inaccessible kloofs and slopes and include oldwood (145), wild olive (617) and Vaal willow (35).

An interesting feature often seen in the riverheads of many valleys is the bright green patches of vegetation known as bogs. They vary in size and some cover several square kilometres. Botanical and geological research has shown that they originated some 8 000 years ago as a result of the increase in temperature following the last ice age when the higher parts of the mountains were covered in snow for long periods. Conditions subsequently again became favourable for the growth of the first plants in the barren mountains above 3 000 m. The formation of the bogs was encouraged by groundwater from springs and seepage in the screes, and in the course of time peat deposits accumulated around these springs, creating an ideal habitat for a number of miniature plants. These peat deposits are of a great ecological importance as they not only serve as purifying filters which produce clear water, but most important, they act as sponges which release water in regular flows. The characteristic hummocks on the sponges are known as thufur, which are caused by needle-ice forcing soil particles upwards.

*The rare spiral aloe is endemic to Lesotho It occurs as either left- or right-handed spirals*

The area in the vicinity of Molimo Nthuse, as well as certain other areas in the Maloti, are the habitat of the rare spiral aloe (*Aloe polyphylla*). This species is restricted to the steep basalt slopes high in the Maloti and its most fascinating aspect is that it occurs as either left- or right-handed spirals, with both forms existing in almost equal numbers. Also of interest is that split plants will divide into one right-handed and one left-handed spiral. Occasionally they divide into two or three rosettes but they reproduce mainly from seeds. Unfortunately the numbers of spiral aloe are declining rapidly because of plundering by the local population for sale to tourists.

Among the other *Aloe* species are *A. ferox*, which creates a colourful display with tall red flowers in southern Lesotho during spring, and *A. striatula*.

**Fauna**

From the accounts of the early missionaries it appears that game was abundant in Lesotho 150 years ago. As a result of the spread of the population and hunting by both whites and Sotho, most of the game has sadly disappeared.

A large number of smaller mammals have managed to survive, but as they are mainly nocturnal, they are seldom seen. The grey rhebok is still common, and mountain reedbuck still occur. The status of klipspringer is uncertain.

Chacma baboon are present but are limited to the remoter areas, although in autumn you are likely to see them raiding maize fields. Rock dassie are still plentiful and mongoose, genets, otters (Cape clawless and spotted necked) and hares as well as rodents occur.

Among the predators, the black-backed jackal and the Cape fox are still widespread but are more often heard than seen. A few leopard still survive in the Maloti while caracal also occur but are rarely seen.

Lesotho is rich in lowland cliff-breeding birds and boasts a remarkable concentration of the rare bearded vulture (119) as well as small numbers of bald ibis (92).

Among the more than 270 bird species recorded in Lesotho are several montane endemics which will delight bird-watchers. The orangebreasted rockjumper (612) is normally found on boulder-strewn slopes or hills in pairs or small parties, and is usually seen hopping from rock to rock as its name implies. The yellowbreasted pipit (725) occurs singly or in pairs in the shorter grass of the flats and valleys. Another uncommon species to keep an eye open for is the Drakensberg siskin (875), a species which is restricted to the high mountain areas of the eastern Cape, Griqualand East, Lesotho and the Natal Drakensberg.

The rocky outcrops are the habitat of mountain (586) and familiar (589) chat, while small parties of ground woodpecker (480) might be spotted near rocky hillsides.

Grassland species include greywing francolin (190), thickbilled lark (512), wailing cisticola (670) and orangethroated longclaw (727).

Black crow (547) and whitenecked raven (550) are commonly seen, while the malachite sunbird (775) is often observed feeding on the nectar of aloes and red-hot pokers (*Kniphofia* spp.). Of the three kingfisher species recorded in Lesotho the giant kingfisher (429) is the most common.

Lesotho is criss-crossed by hundreds of kilometres of crystal-clear streams and for many years has been renowned for its excellent trout fishing. Unfortunately cultivation and overgrazing in many mountain areas have caused siltation and consequently a decline in the fish population, but fishing remains reasonably good. The rivers have been stocked with both brown and rainbow trout but remember that you require a fishing licence. The closed season is from 1 June to 31 August and you can obtain further information from the Fisheries Officer, Ministry of Agriculture, P O Box 24, Maseru 100, Lesotho.

## History

Archaeological excavations in and around Lesotho have confirmed the presence of early man more than 50 000 years ago. Research at Rose Cottage Cave near Ladybrand, close to Lesotho's western border, has revealed occupation of the

*The bald ibis occurs in flocks of up to 100 birds in high-altitude grasslands*

cave by both Middle and Later Stone Age people. A date of 6850 BP has been obtained from Later Stone Age material from this site.

Several sites have been excavated in south-eastern Lesotho, some of which are described in more detail in the history of the Sehlabathebe National Park on p. 130.

The earliest reliable date for rock paintings comes from Sehonghong, where a painting has been dated at 1560 BP. It is, however, certain that the San (Bushmen) arrived in the Drakensberg some 11 000 years ago. Several hundred sites with rock paintings have been located throughout the country and more than 10 000 individual paintings have been recorded from some 100 sites. An analysis of a sample of 20 sites from north-western Lesotho has shown that almost 65 per cent of the paintings were of people, while just over 25 per cent depicted animals.

Archaeological excavations show that the earliest Iron Age settlements in the highlands south of the Vaal River were established about 600 BP. The first black tribes that migrated into what is now Lesotho — the Pethla, Polane and the Phuthi — were of Nguni origin. They initially settled in the lowlands but later retreated into the mountainous regions to the south.

These tribes were later followed by Sotho-speaking people, whose ancestors had established large states in the western Transvaal. The history of these groups, which slowly dispersed south of the Vaal River, is marked by a great degree of fragmentation. The first Sotho-speaking group to settle in the area was the Fokeng, who are regarded by most oral historians as the most senior of the Sotho-speaking people. The Fokeng were followed by the Kwena, Sia, Taung and several other Sotho-speaking groups.

The expansion of certain Nguni clans, notably the Ndwandwe, the Ngwane and the Mthethwa, towards the end of the eighteenth century and the rise of Shaka and the Zulu kingdom, triggered off a chain of events which became known as the *Difaqane* or *Lifaqane*.[1]

Following the defeat of the Ngwane in 1818 by Dingiswayo's Mthethwa, the Ngwane fled to the foothills of the Drakensberg, where they ousted the Hlubi. A section of the Hlubi fled over the Drakensberg into Sotho country where they attacked the Tlokwa.

In 1822 the Ngwane fled over the Drakensberg following an attack by the Zulu and once again they fell upon the Hlubi. To obtain food, the Ngwane, Hlubi and Tlokwa raided the southern Sotho chiefdoms who were unable to withstand the raids and consequently broke up.

The young Kwena chief Moshweshwe and his followers occupied Butha-Buthe Hill in the north-east of Lesotho in 1820, moving southwards four years later to the natural fortress at Thaba Bosiu, from where they successfully repulsed several attacks. From his mountain capital Moshweshwe built up the Basotho nation by providing cattle and land to the chiefs of fragmented tribes who sought his protection.

In 1880 the Cape Government passed the Peace Preservation Act, which required the Basotho to surrender all their firearms. This led to the Gun War (1880-1881), which cost the Cape Government dearly in both money and men. In 1884 the Cape Government relinquished control over Basotholand and Britain resumed control.

During the Anglo-Boer War (1899-1902) Britain used Basotholand as a base and bought thousands of ponies from the Basotho for use as remounts. In 1910 Basotholand requested to be excluded from the Union of South Africa which was then being formed and in 1966 the country became independent under King Moshweshwe II.

### Trek Synopsis

The Basotho pony has been an important means of transport in Lesotho for more than a century, which accounts for the large number of bridle paths that criss-cross the country. Horses were first brought into the country by explorers and missionaries from the Cape and were predominantly of eastern origin, including Barb and Arab. The ponies of Javanese origin can be traced back to the Russian Steppes and even to Genghis Khan in Mongolia. During the Anglo-Boer War (1899-1902) these surefooted, reliable ponies were in great demand and as much as £80 was paid for a Basotho pony.

Basotho ponies are renowned for their sturdiness and two made world headlines when they travelled overland from Lesotho to the 1976 Olympic Games in Munich. An interest in conventional horses, such as the boerperd, at one stage almost resulted in the Basotho pony becoming extinct. In 1978 the government of Ireland started to fund and provide the expertise to establish the First National Pony Stud at Thaba Tseka. The best possible specimens of Basotho ponies were located and bred with Irish and Arab studs. (This is an ongoing project.)

The treks not only offer you dramatic views but also the opportunity to experience traditional African village culture. You will exchange the customary greeting *Lumela* with smiling Basotho men and wom-

1 The Sotho-speaking peoples use the names *Difaqane* or *Lifaqane*, while the Nguni-speaking peoples use the name *Mfecane*.

en in their colourful blankets, which you will soon realise play a fundamental role in Basotho family life and social traditions. Blankets were first introduced in about 1860, and rapidly replaced the old sheepskin or kaross in popularity. No other nation has developed the blanket cult to the same degree as the Basotho.

Young men undergoing the initiation ceremony wear a special ochre blanket called the *Moholobela* and carry decorated knobkieries. After the ceremony they are entitled to wear the *Lekhokolo*, a blanket which signifies that they have reached manhood.

On special occasions men of substance may wear not one but three blankets — the torch, Victoria and the Sandringham. The Victoria blanket was introduced in 1897 and is still the hallmark of the well-dressed Basotho, although the Seanamarena has been developed from the Victoria. For marriages there is, of course, yet another blanket, and when the first child is born to the first wife, the proud father presents her with a special blanket called a *Serope sa Motsoetse*.

Both the colour and design of the blankets are very important. The colour of a stripe can dictate whether a blanket is to be worn during the day or at night. The stripe is always worn vertically because a horizontal stripe is believed to retard growth. The crocodile, totem of the Kwena, is popular

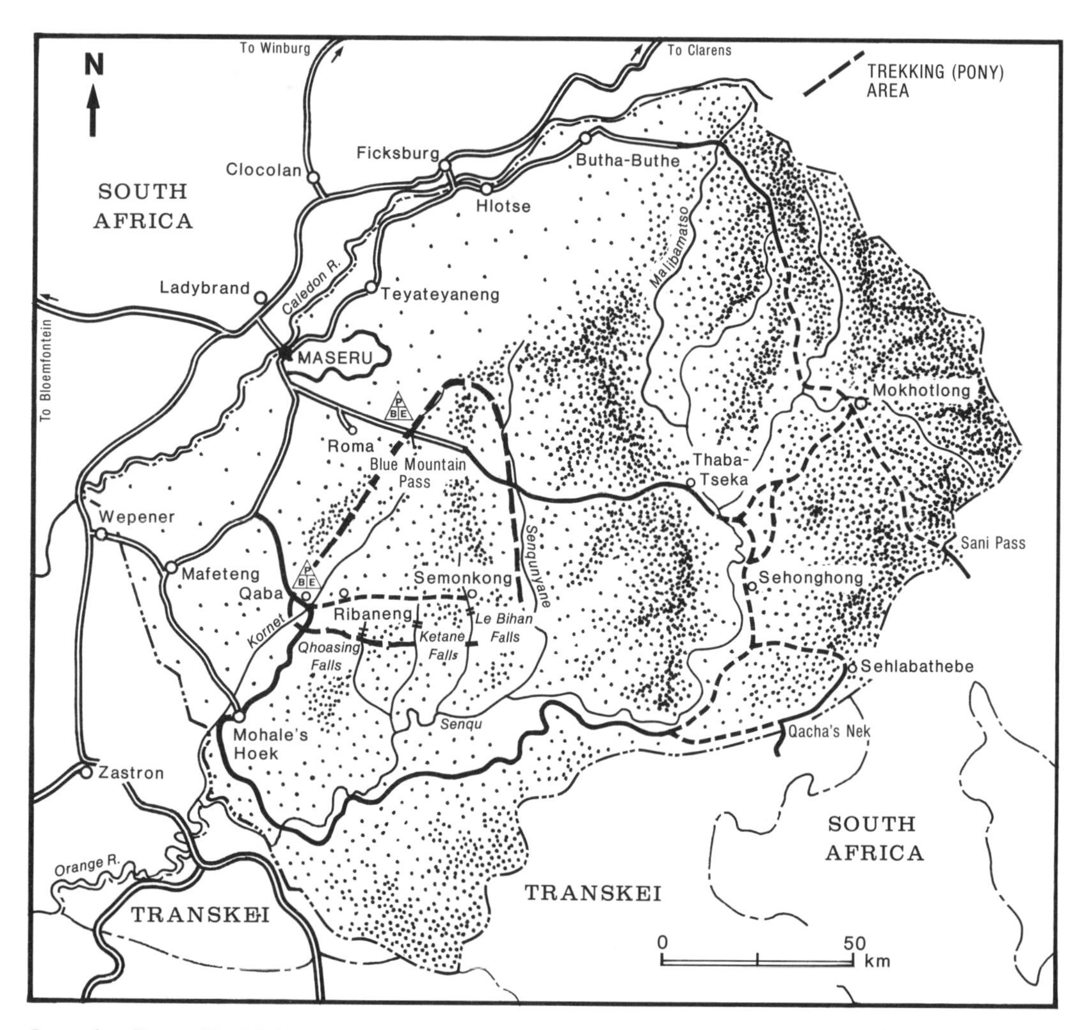


*Lesotho Pony Trekking Area*

*A typical village scene encountered by trekkers taking part in a pony trekking safari in Lesotho's Maloti Mountains*

with members of that tribe, while the lion is popular among the Taung. During the visit of the British royal family to Basotholand in 1947 the crown and sceptre became a popular emblem on the blankets of loyal subjects but since independence in 1966 this has been replaced mostly by the freedom torch.

Should you wish to sample traditional Sotho dishes such as wheat samp, wild spinach, papa (hard porridge) and sorghum beer, arrangements can be made with your guide. The food is cooked over a dung fire, which is made in a depression in the floor of the hut.

You will also learn early on in the trek that a white flag outside a hut means it is a traditional beer shop where yellow, green, and hops beer, as well as commercial brands, are sold.

Following are brief outlines of two typical four-day pony treks offered by the Lesotho Tourist Board and Basotho Pony Trekking.

### Qaba Lodge to Semonkong (Lesotho Tourist Board)

This popular trek arranged by the **Lesotho Tourist Board** departs from Maseru at 06h00 on the day of the trek. The trek starts after breakfast and a briefing session at Qaba Lodge, and on the first day your ride will take you past rock paintings.

On the second day you will pass through the exciting Rasebetsane Pass and visit two of the country's three great waterfalls. Ribaneng Falls are the lowest of the three and are passed first, followed by the second highest in Lesotho, Ketane Falls.

By the third day you will be at the highest

point of the trek, from where there are awe-inspiring vistas in all directions. From here the ponies cross a marshy area known as Mohlakaoatuka, and after lunch on the soft grasses of the valley the last few remaining kilometres to Semonkong Lodge are completed. A hot bath and a comfortable bed await you at the lodge.

An early start is made on the fourth day with a short ride to the 192 m high Lebihan Falls (also known as Semonkong Falls), which tumble down into a huge pool. The ruggedness of the gorge, the beauty of the falls and the chorus of birdsong make the last day of the trek truly memorable. Later in the day you fly back to Maseru.

The trek described above is all inclusive, but should you prefer a less expensive, circular expedition where you supply your own food and tent, consult the brochure *Pony Trekking in Lesotho* issued by Basotho Pony Trekking. They arrange rides ranging from a few hours (which do not have to be booked) to weekend and five-day treks.

### Molimo Nthuse Circular Trek (Basotho Pony Trekking)

This four-day trek departs from the Trekking Centre at 10h00 and the first day takes you on a relaxing climb to the top of the Blue Mountain Pass before descending to Ha Matlapu. There is an ideal lunch spot alongside the Bkoaneng River where you can cool off in one of the inviting rock pools. After lunch you continue to the overnight stop at the village of Matsiring.

On the second day you pass through the villages of Ha Matsoai, Ha Mphakho and Takatso before stopping for lunch, once again at a river. After lunch the Jorotane River is crossed and you continue to Molikaliko, the overnight stop, where you can freshen up in the Senqunyane River. If you are energetic enough you can also attempt an early morning dip here before setting off to Ha Seotsa, where you recross the Jorotane River. After cooling off in the river and having lunch, the trek continues to your overnight stop at Rapolakane. *En route* you pass through the village of Ha Likomisi and some of the most beautiful scenery in Lesotho unfolds before you. Without the burden of a heavy pack and having to watch where you are walking you will be able to enjoy the spectacular scenery to its fullest.

On the fourth day you leave the Jorotane Valley and ascend to the pass leading to the Sosa cattle post area. You then cross the Maine Pass and descend to the Makhaleng Valley and the Qiloane Falls, where you can enjoy a swim and lunch in the shade. The falls are close to Molimo Nthuse, so if you are not in a hurry you can relax here for a few hours before remounting and completing the trail.

# Part 5
# Drakensberg and Natal

# *Introduction to the Natal Drakensberg*

Stretching for some 200 km, from the Sentinel in the north to Bushman's Nek in the south, the Drakensberg is a paradise of waterfalls, spectacular sandstone cliffs, towering, often snow-capped peaks and soaring buttresses, and is the home of the rare bearded vulture. Little wonder then that it is South Africa's most popular backpacking and mountaineering area.

For the purpose of this book the Drakensberg has been divided into three sections — southern, central and northern — based on the recreational series of maps compiled by the Forestry Branch.

As the climate, flora, fauna, general history and geology of the Natal Drakensberg are similar in most respects for the various areas, these are dealt with in this introductory section. However, aspects particularly relevant to a specific area will be dealt with in more detail in that area.

**It is *essential* to refer to the General Rules of Access to Drakensberg Areas on pages 154-156.**

## Climate

Summer temperatures in the foothills of the northern Berg range between 13 °C and 32 °C, while winter temperatures vary between 5 °C and 16 °C. Temperatures do, however, often drop to well below freezing point and are generally lower in the southern Berg.

Although some areas have up to 1 500 mm of rain a year, the average rainfall over most of the Drakensberg is 1 250 mm. It increases from the valleys to the upper part of the Little Berg, but rainfall on the escarpment is lower than that of the upper part of the Little Berg. About 85 per cent of the rain falls between October and March in the form of heavy afternoon thunderstorms.

During summer the Little Berg and summit are often blanketed by heavy cloud and mist which lasts for anything up to two weeks before lifting. Frost occurs about 150 nights a year.

Snow occurs 6 to 12 times a year and although it can be expected any time of the year, it generally occurs between April and September. In the southern Berg snowfalls are generally more frequent and heavier than in the northern Berg. Although snow is usually restricted to the summit and near summit, it occasionally reaches down to 1 800 m.

## Flora

According to Acocks, three veld types occur in the Natal Drakensberg: Themeda Festuca Alpine Veld (Veld Type 56), Highland Sourveld (Veld Type 44 [a] ) and Southern Tall Grassveld (Veld Type 65).

During his study of the plant ecology of the Cathedral Peak area, Killick[1] categorised three vegetation belts.

### *Montane belt*

This belt covers the vegetation from the valley floors to the lowermost basalt cliffs at the edge of the Little Berg between altitudes of 1 250 and 2 000 m. It consists mainly of grassland dominated by redgrass (*Themeda triandra*) with scattered *Protea* stands which form *Protea* savanna. The dominant species are the common sugarbush (87) and

1 Killick, D.J.B. 1963. An Account of the Plant Ecology of the Cathedral Peak Area of the Natal Drakensberg. *Botanical Survey of South Africa* 34: 24, 27.

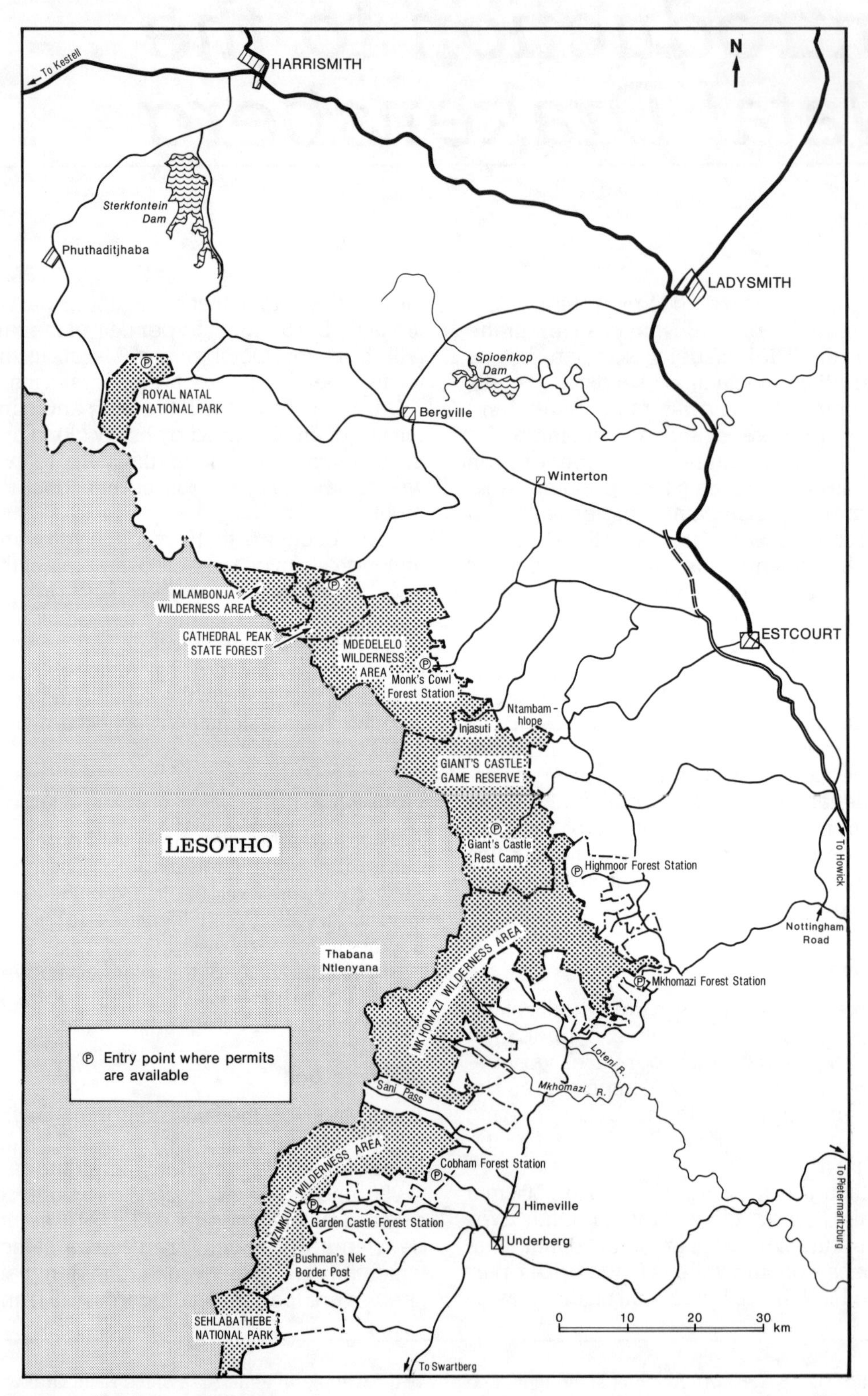


*Location: Southern, Central and*

the silver sugarbush (96), while the lip-flowered sugarbush (98), *P. simplex* and *P. dracomontana* also occur.

Those accustomed to the rich floral wealth of the western Cape are often disappointed by the apparent absence of flowering plants in the area. However, Killick recorded more than 900 flowering species in a small area of Cathedral Peak and the total number of species in the Drakensberg is likely to be far greater. Many species are obscured by the grasslands or grow in protected places and are therefore easily missed, so take your time and you will be surprised by the wide variety of flowers. Species you are likely to encounter are the beautiful white *Anemone fanninii*, the dark pink *Graderia scabra*, black-eyed Susan (*Callilepis laureola*), the blue scilla (*Scilla natalensis*), watsonia (*Watsonia densiflora*) and various *Helichrysum* and *Agapanthus* species.

Yellowwood (*Podocarpus*) forests are limited to protected valleys and kloofs and south-, south-east- and east-facing slopes. The forests are mixed in character, comprising some 20 species. These include Outeniqua yellowwood (16) and real yellowwood (18), as well as white candlewood (405), red pear (496), assegai (570) and white stinkwood (39). Species occurring along the forest margins include oldwood (145), sagewood (637) and tree fuchsia (670).

Oldwood and sagewood form dense scrub communities in gullies and stream beds where they are protected from fires. A species characteristic of the area between the Clarens Sandstone and the lowermost basalt cliffs is the mountain cypress (20), which grows between 3 and 4,6 m high. The Clarens Sandstone and the lowermost basalt cliffs are the habitat of the krantz aloe (28.1), Natal bottlebrush (446) and the mountain cabbage tree (563).

### *Sub-alpine belt*

This belt extends from the edge of the Little Berg (approximately 2 000 m) to just below the Drakensberg summit. Killick identified five major grassland types, of which the redgrass (*Themeda triandra*) grassland type is the most extensive in this belt.

Shrubs and trees of this belt consist mainly of mountain cypress (20), oldwood (145) and sagewood (637).

The climax community of the Sub-alpine Belt comprises fynbos dominated by *Passerina filiformis*, *Philippia evansii*, and mountain cypress (20). Other species occurring are *Protea dracomontana* and the lip-flower sugarbush (98). This community is best developed on the steep valley and escarpment slopes at the head of the major rivers.

Flowering plants include *Albuca tricophylla*, *Aster perfoliatus*, the dainty *Nemesia denticulata* and the pineapple flower (*Eucomis* spp.). A large number of orchids can be seen flowering in the summer. Among them you might spot *Satyrium longicauda*, one of the most common ground orchids, the pink-flowering *Disa versicolor* and the lime-green *Eulophia foliosa*.

### *Alpine belt*

This belt occurs above altitudes of 2 865 m and is dominated by *Erica* and *Helichrysum* species interspersed with grasslands consisting mainly of *Festuca*, *Danthonia* and *Pentaschistis* species. The ground on the escarpment plateau is often boggy in the wet summer months, providing an ideal habitat for species like the red hot poker (*Kniphofia northiae* and *K. caulescens*), the Alpine iris (*Moraea spathulata*), the bell-shaped *Dierama igneum* and the yellow *Cyrtanthus flanaganii*. The alpine forbs are seen at their best between summer and early autumn, while several orchids can be seen flowering during January and February.

## Fauna

Although very little remains of the large numbers of game that inhabited the Drakensberg in former times, game numbers are again increasing since most of the Drakensberg now enjoys some form of conservation status.

The species you are most likely to come across is the grey rhebok, which is probably the most common antelope in the Drakensberg. It prefers the more level areas of the Little Berg and is sometimes mistaken for the smaller mountain reedbuck. However, the latter species usually

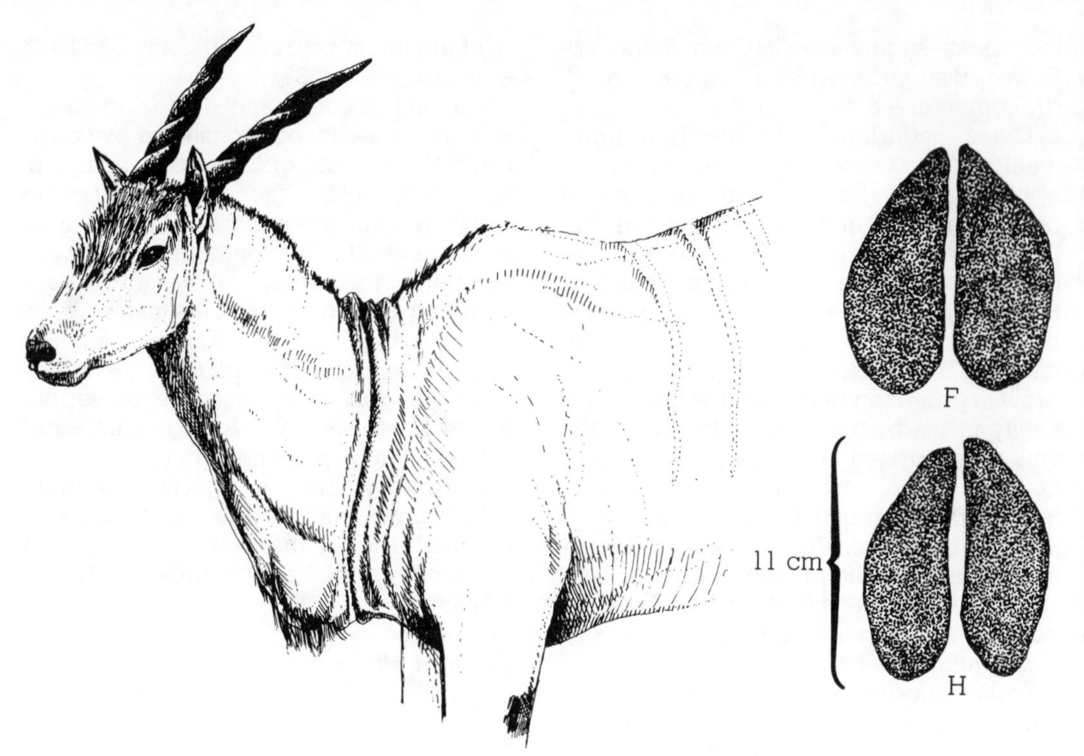


*Eland – the most common large antelope in the Natal Drakensberg*

occurs on slopes near the cover of shrubs, rocks or boulders. Although at a glance these two antelope are similar in appearance, the coat of the mountain reedbuck is less woolly and reddish-brown compared with the greyish-brown, shaggy coat of the grey rhebok. A useful distinguishing feature is the horns, which are straight in the grey rhebok but forwardly curved from the top of the ears in the mountain reedbuck.

Two other common species which frequent the rocky areas of the Drakensberg are the chacma baboon and the rock dassie.

You may spot eland on the Little Berg during the spring and summer when the grasses here are palatable. During winter, however, they move into the river valleys and forest patches where the vegetation is more nutritious.

Other large antelope species occurring are blesbok, red hartebeest and black wildebeest. Smaller antelope include bushbuck, common duiker, oribi and klipspringer. The latter species is confined to basalt krantzes between 2 400 and 2 700 m and is rarely seen.

Several predators occur, but on account of their mostly nocturnal and secretive habits you are unlikely to see any. Predators recorded include the black-backed jackal, African wild cat, serval, caracal, Cape clawless otter, spotted-necked otter and several mongoose species. The status of the leopard is uncertain; although there is no positive proof that this species has disappeared entirely from the Drakensberg, evidence confirming their presence is scant.

More than 213 bird species have been recorded for the Natal Drakensberg, including several species listed in the *South African Red Data Book — Birds.* One of the rarest and most interesting birds of the Drakensberg is the bearded vulture (119). It has long, pointed wings and a wedge-shaped tail and is restricted to the upper elevations of the Drakensberg. Their numbers have been estimated at about 120 pairs. Other birds of prey you might see which are listed in the *Red Data Book* are Cape vulture (122) (vulnerable), cuckoo hawk (128) (indeterminate) and martial eagle (140) (vulnerable).

The summit plateau and the slopes and rockfaces above 2 200 m are sparsely inhabited by species such as the white stork (83) — a summer visitor — and the bald ibis (92), which are listed as rare and out of danger respectively in the *Red Data Book.* More commonly seen species include rock pigeon (349), whitenecked raven (550), sentinel rock thrush (582), familiar chat (589) and redwinged starling (769).

In the open grassland keep an eye open for secretarybird (118), redwing francolin (192), common quail (200), ground woodpecker (480), orangethroated longclaw (727), bokmakierie (746) and the pintailed whydah (860). These species also occur in the *Protea* veld which in addition attracts birds such as Gurney's sugarbird (774), malachite sunbird (775), greater doublecollared sunbird (785) and the fiscal shrike (732).

The patches of indigenous forest provide a suitable habitat for the redchested cuckoo (377), cardinal woodpecker (486), blackheaded oriole (545), blackeyed bulbul (568) and the paradise flycatcher (710).

A large number of species are attracted to the riverine bush and scrub habitat, including the blackheaded heron (63), hamerkop (81), southern boubou (736) and several kingfishers such as the pied (428), giant (429), halfcollared (430), malachite (431) and brownhooded (435) kingfishers.

The vleis, marshes and wetlands are

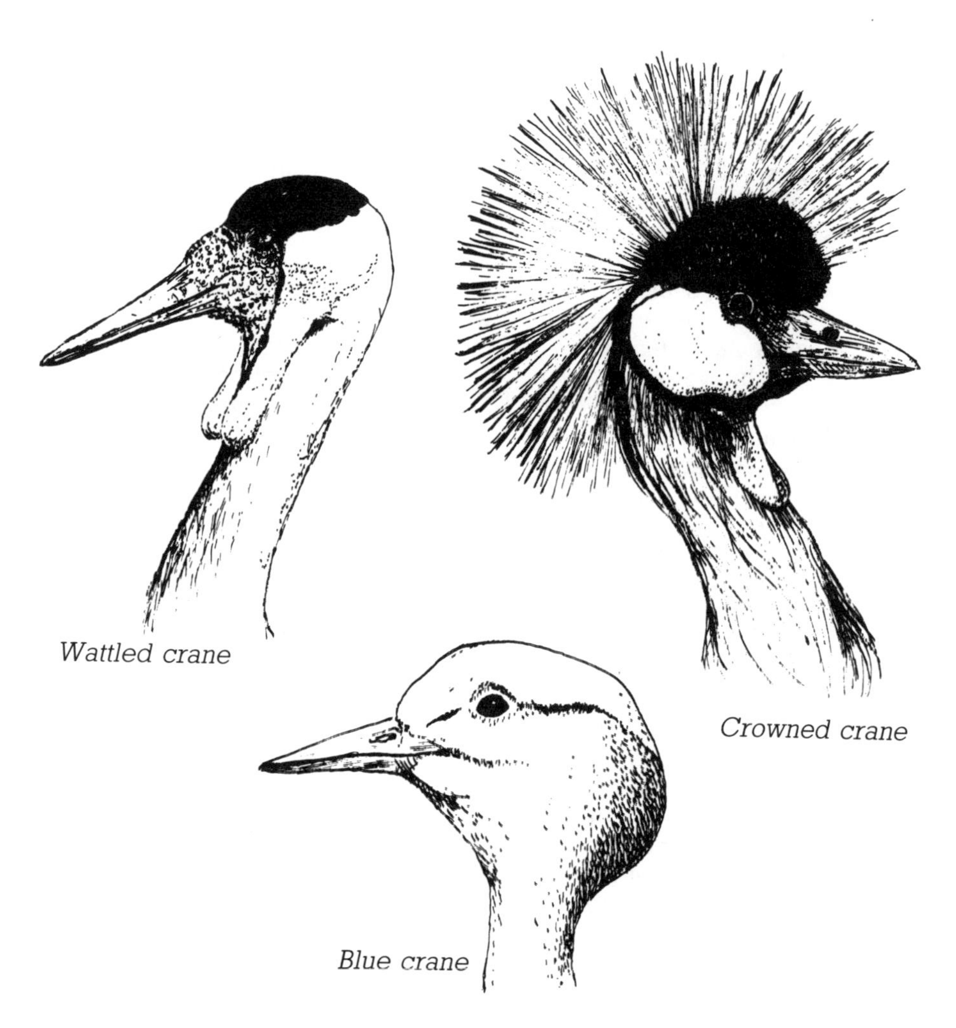


*All three southern African crane species have been recorded in the Natal Drakensberg*

sparsely distributed on flat ground. Typical species here are the hadeda ibis (94), blue crane (208), marsh owl (395) and the long-tailed widow (832).

## History

Archaeological evidence indicates that the San (Bushmen) lived in the caves and shelters of the mountain for thousands of years before the arrival of the first wave of the Nguni people. It has been suggested that they inhabited the Drakensberg in the summer when game and food were plentiful, migrating to the Natal midlands in autumn. Excavations in south-eastern Lesotho have provided evidence of Middle Stone Age inhabitation of caves in the area as far back as 43 000 BP, while Later Stone Age material has been dated at 1 430 BP.

For both quantity and quality, the Drakensberg is considered one of the richest rock art areas in the world and to date more than 600 sites, with a total of more than 22 000 individual paintings, have been recorded. It has been estimated that the Drakensberg contains some 35 per cent of the total number of painted sites in South Africa.

An analysis of some 22 500 paintings recorded by Vinnicombe (southern Drakensberg), Pager (Cathedral Peak area) and Lewis-Williams (Giant's Castle Game Reserve) revealed that 51 per cent of the paintings depicted humans and 36 per cent animals. Thirteen per cent were classified as miscellaneous. Of the animals depicted, 67 per cent represented antelope, with eland constituting 57 per cent of all identifiable antelope.[2]

A clear picture of the settlement of the Nguni people along the east coast is still emerging. The earliest known Nguni people to arrive in the foothills of the Drakensberg were the Zizi who, according to their own history, settled between the Upper Tugela and the Bushman's rivers around AD 1700. It is, however, likely that groups of Iron Age people were already present in the Drakensberg foothills centuries earlier. Relations between the San and the new immigrants varied from absorption and acculturation to conflict.

The expansion of the Ndwandwe, the Ngwane and the Mthethwa chiefdoms and the rise to power of the Zulu kingdom under Shaka caused widespread destruction. In about 1818 the Ngwane under Matiwane were first attacked by Dingiswayo's Mthethwa and shortly afterwards by the Ndwandwe of Zwide. The Ngwane fled westwards, attacking the Hlubi and the Bele tribes. On reaching the Drakensberg they displaced the Zizi and settled in the vicinity of Mdedelelo. Peace was short-lived, however, for in 1822 the armies of Shaka swept as far south as the Umzimvubu River, destroying crops, razing entire villages and uprooting tribes. Tribes fell upon one another and some fugitives sought refuge in the caves and shelters of the Drakensberg, where they clashed with the San. For one such tribe, the Duga clan under Mdavu, the situation was so desperate that they resorted to cannibalism. These events are known as the *Difaqane* or forced migrations.

The first whites to see the Drakensberg were probably the survivors of the Portuguese vessel *Santo Alberto,* which was shipwrecked along the Transkei coast on 24 March 1593. The survivors set out on an epic journey of more than 1 000 km to Delagoa Bay (the present Maputo) and decided to travel further inland to avoid having to cross the wide river mouths along the coast. At the beginning of May they reported seeing a range of snow-covered mountains to the west, which must have been the Drakensberg.

The first white man to explore the remote valleys of the Drakensberg was Captain Allen Francis Gardiner. After being prevented from travelling from Port Natal (Durban) to the Cape early in 1835 by hostile Xhosa-speaking tribes, Gardiner set off on a second journey in September 1835, travelling further inland in the hope of finding a pass over the Drakensberg. On 3 October 1835 the mighty Drakensberg came into view

2 Willcox, A.R. 1984. *The Rock Art of Africa*. Johannesburg: Macmillan, 195.

and a remarkable mountain with '... singularly indented outline ...'[3] induced Gardiner to name it the Giant's Cup. Following the death of Thomas Hodgson during a punitive expedition against San cattle raiders in 1862 the peaks forming the outline of Giant's Cup were named Hodgson's Peaks.

Further south Gardiner was '... quite startled at the appearance of a rugged mountain which I have named the Giant's Castle ... Its resemblance to Edinburgh Castle from one or two points was so striking that for the moment I could almost fancy myself transported to Prince's Street.'[4] The name was later given to the peak known today as Giant's Castle further north and Gardiner's original name changed to Garden Castle.

In October 1836 two French missionaries, Thomas Arbousset and Francis Daumas, reached the summit of the northernmost point of the Maluti Mountains and named it Mont-aux-Sources.

In December the following year the Voortrekkers crossed the Drakensberg and settled in the area of the upper Tugela basin. Following the murder of Piet Retief and the defeat of Dingane, the Voortrekkers declared Natal a republic. Farms of 2 428 ha were allocated to Trekkers who had settled in Natal before 1840 and many settled in the area between the Tugela and Bushman's rivers.

Conflict soon arose between the pastoral Voortrekkers and the San, but the cause has not been satisfactorily explained. According to Vinnicombe, the San were used to domestic animals as the land settled by the Boers had been occupied in pre-Shakan times by cattle-owning Bantu-speakers '... who had apparently remained on comparatively amicable terms with the Bushmen... but whatever understanding they had reached with the black pastoralists was not extended to the white settlers.'[5] She also points out that many of the raids were organised from afar and that black tribes were also involved: 'To what extent these depredations can be attributed to personal vendettas against the white intruders, or simply to lawless banditti, is difficult to assess. It is well established that many of the Bantu-speakers who had been rendered homeless by the chaotic events preceding the Great Trek, adopted cattle rustling as a way of life and the settlers' herds which often grazed unattended over vast areas of unfenced country became an obvious object of cupidity.'[6]

The influx of black refugees into Natal, Commissioner Cloete's land settlement arrangements and repeated raids by the San caused dissatisfaction among the Voortrekkers after Natal became a British colony in 1843. Large numbers of Voortrekkers crossed back into the Free State and it was only through the intervention of Sir Harry Smith that the remaining Trekkers were persuaded in 1848 not to leave Natal. The size of all farms was fixed at 2 428 ha and protection against the blacks, as well as firm action against San raiders, was promised. Many of the farms were laid out along the headwaters of the Tugela River and its tributaries, which were sparsely populated.

Several locations were established in the foothills of the Drakensberg in 1849 to act as a buffer between the white farmers and the raiding San. The number of raids declined steadily and 20 years later, in July 1869, the last recorded San raid against a white farmer in Natal took place. Several raids were carried out after this date against blacks, the last raid specifically attributed to San being in August 1872.

Some San continued their ancient way of life in the mountains of Lesotho. In 1878 a couple who visited the Tugela Valley came across what was considered to be the last group of San seen in the Drakensberg by whites. However, in 1925 a farmer named Anton Lombard discovered a hunting outfit on a high ledge in Eland Cave, a shelter

---

3 Gardiner, A.F. 1966. *Narrative of a Journey to the Zoolu Country in South Africa, Undertaken in 1835.* (Facsimile Reprint), Cape Town: C Struik, 327-8.

4 *Ibid.*, 339.

5 Vinnicombe, P. 1976. *People of the Eland.* Pietermaritzburg: University of Natal Press, 23.

6 *Ibid.*

on the south slope of the Mhlawazini Valley. A few days later the site was visited by another farmer, W Carter Robinson, who noticed sleeping quarters which he estimated were probably not more than six months old. It was presumed that these belonged to a lone San survivor.

English settlers began occupying farms in the foothills of the Drakensberg around 1840, and many of the farms still bear their original names: Castle End, Castledene, Paiseley, Wilander Downs and Snowdon.

## Geology

The scenery is one of the outstanding features of the Drakensberg range and is among the finest in the world. The range is renowned for its spectacular free-standing peaks, towering buttresses, sheer rock faces, deeply eroded river valleys and fascinating sandstone formations.

The geological formations of the Natal Drakensberg belong to the Karoo Sequence which, from the base upwards, consists of the Beaufort Group and the Molteno, Elliot, Clarens Sandstone and Drakensberg Basalt formations.

The Beaufort Group is the older sedimentary formation and therefore the lowest. It was laid down some 200 million years ago under extremely wet conditions when much of South Africa was covered by swamps. It consists of several red, green and maroon shales overlain by yellow fine-grained sandstone with shales.

The beds of the Molteno Formation were deposited about 180 million years ago. They are recognisable as successive beds of sandstone, alternating with layers of blue and grey shales, and are thought to have accumulated in a vast inland lake. These sediments form the terraces and ledges at the foot of the Little Berg and are best seen in the southern Berg.

The Elliot Formation, formerly known as the Red Beds, was laid down about 170 million years ago and consists of alternating beds of red shales and fine-grained sandstone. This formation is rarely exposed and is best seen in the stream beds below the Clarens Sandstone Formation (formerly Cave Sandstone) and along paths. It forms the steeply vegetated slopes below the Clarens Sandstone Formation.

The Clarens Sandstone Formation is the most prominent of the sedimentary units exposed in the Drakensberg. The distinctive creamy-white cliffs are a characteristic feature of the Drakensberg foothills and the sandstone layer forms the Little Berg. These beds are about 160 million years old and were originally laid down as desert dunes in a very arid climate during the Jurassic period. The formation originally took its name from the large number of caves and shallow overhangs occurring at the base of the thick sandstone layer.

The highest part of the Berg was formed by lava flows, and is known as the Drakensberg Basalt Formation. Between the Middle Jurassic and early Cretaceous periods volcanic activity resulted in the outpouring of lava from fissures associated with the break-up of the supercontinent, Gondwana. Individual flows have been traced for more than 32 km and the lava flows varied in thickness from 0,3 m to 45 m and built up to a thickness of over 1 300 m, covering what is today known as Natal. The dolerite dykes and sills associated with the Karoo rocks underlying the Drakensberg lavas represent magma (molten matter) that did not reach the surface to form basalt flows. These vertical sills and horizontal dykes have been exposed through subsequent erosion.

The present rugged landscape of the Drakensberg has been formed by headward erosion of the Great Escarpment following the break-up of Gondwana. The erosion has been aided by seaward tilting of the Natal coastal area and four successive periods of continental uplift.

## General Rules of Access to the Natal Drakensberg

On account of the rugged terrain and the weather, which can change extremely rapidly, the Drakensberg has claimed the lives of numerous backpackers. It is therefore essential to pay special attention to this section, which is applicable to all Drakensberg areas described in this book and should be read in conjunction with each of the various sections.

## PROFILE OF THE GEOLOGICAL STRUCTURE OF THE NATAL DRAKENSBERG

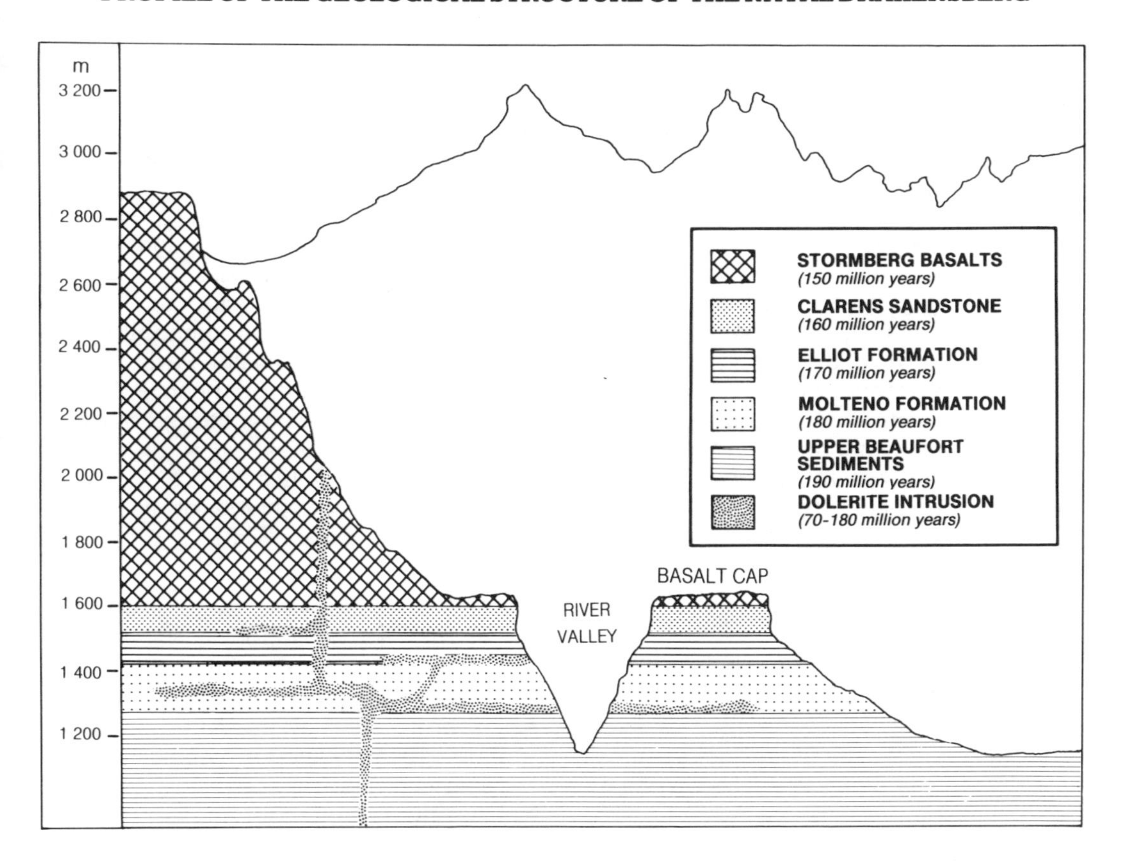


### *Permits*

- Access is by permit only and the permit regulations must be strictly adhered to. The addresses where permits can be obtained are given in the relevant sections.
- When on Natal Provincial Administration property or adjoining Natal Parks Board land, permits must be produced on demand by a provincial conservation or Natal Parks Board officer. Any person not in possession of a permit is liable to be prosecuted. Permits issued by the two authorities are interchangeable.
- Entry permits can be obtained by making a written or telephone reservation in advance or on arrival, provided the number of persons already in the area does not exceed the maximum capacity. The maximum group size is 12, but the number of groups permitted in a particular area is also limited, depending on the size of the area.
- Permits for angling are available upon production of a valid Natal Provincial angling licence.
- A valid passport is required for excursions beyond the escarpment into Lesotho.

### *Equipment*

- Persons wishing to camp in the mountains may be refused a permit unless the following equipment is carried: tent, sleeping-bag, adequate footwear and warm clothing, torch, candle and matches, camping stove and fuel, food — including sufficient emergency rations — and a first aid kit.
- Sunglasses or sun-goggles are advisable in the event of snowfalls, when the glare can be damaging to the eyes.
- Your enjoyment of the Drakensberg will be considerably enhanced by binoculars and field guides to the flora and fauna.

### *Maps*

The entire Drakensberg from Mont-aux-Sources in the north to Sehlabathebe in the south is covered by a three-part recreational map series published by the Forestry Branch. These maps are an invaluable aid to backpackers.

The maps are printed to a scale of 1:50 000 on all-weather plasticised material, which is extremely durable. They provide a wealth of useful information on the Berg such as caves, with their maximum overnight accommodation capacity, perennial streams, dangerous river crossings, major and minor paths, ill-defined 'Ways to Go', difficult sections where a rope may be required, approximate distances between path junctions, nature reserves and so on.

A useful feature of the maps is the numbered intersections of footpaths. It has become standard practice for backpackers completing the mountain register to state the actual junction numbers of their intended routes. Another useful feature is the safety grid, which enables you to pin-point your exact position very quickly.

### *Rescue Register*

- It is compulsory to complete the mountain register upon entering any of the mountain areas. Do this as accurately as possible as this information will speed up assistance or rescue operations should these be necessary. The various mountain register points are listed under the relevant sections.
- It is imperative to note the actual time and date of your return in the rescue register to avoid being held liable for the costs of unnecessary rescue operations. Please inform the Officer-in-Charge upon returning.

### *Emergencies*

- Rescue operations are costly and often extremely hazardous, especially when carried out in adverse weather conditions. You are therefore requested to take the necessary precautions and to avoid taking careless risks.
- In the event of an accident or illness where the victim is immobile, the Officer-in-Charge, Natal Parks Board official or the South African Police in charge of the area concerned must be contacted.
- Refer to general directions for action in the case of serious injuries or disabilities in First Aid, pages 23-31.

### *General*

- Pets are not permitted in Natal Parks Board and provincial nature reserves/wilderness areas.
- Firearms are not permitted in Natal Parks Board and provincial nature reserves/wilderness areas.
- Littering is an offence. All litter must be carried out and should *not* be buried.
- No open fires are permitted and it is an offence to collect firewood.
- Sleeping is not permitted in caves containing rock paintings, except in those caves (with paintings) indicated as such on the recreational map series.
- On arrival at the forest station, certain caves may be reserved for your party. However, this does not ensure exclusive occupation of the cave in the event of inclement weather when it may be necessary to share the cave with other backpackers.

# 12 Mzimkulu Backpacking Area

The southern Berg area is characterised by spectacular sandstone formations, grasslands and numerous streams and rivers. Those seeking to escape from the more popular areas further north will find Mzimkulu a haven of tranquillity. Although the area lacks a well-defined contour path, the northern section has an extensive network of paths, while in the southern part you can ascend the escarpment along several passes.

**Location**

This wilderness area in the southern Drakensberg extends from Sani Pass in the north to Griqualand East in the south.

The main approaches to the area are from Cobham Forest Station in the north, Garden Castle Forest Station in the centre and the Bushman's Nek border post in the south.

The Cobham access point is reached by turning right onto the D7 along the Underberg/Himeville road just outside Himeville. The forest station is situated about 14 km further along this road.

The route to the Garden Castle access point and the Drakensberg Gardens Hotel is well signposted from Underberg. After following the Underberg/Swartberg road (R394) for about 4 km you turn right onto a gravel road. The hotel is reached 29 km on along this road, which ends a short distance further at the forest station.

From Underberg, the Bushman's Nek border post is reached by following the Swartberg road (R394) for about 5 km before turning right onto the Bushman's Nek road. After 25 km you turn right, reaching Bushman's Nek Hotel some 8 km further. The border post is situated a short distance beyond the hotel.

**Distance and Classification**

The wilderness area is traversed by more than 165 km of management paths, with a further 55 km in the adjoining areas. Distance and classification depend on the routes you select.

**Permits**

Groups are limited to a minimum of two and a maximum of 12 people and the number of groups is also restricted. Permits are obtainable from The Forester, Cobham Forest Station, P O Box 116, Himeville 4585, Telephone (03392) 1831, and The Forester, Garden Castle Forest Station, Private Bag X312, Underberg 4590, Telephone (03372) 1722.

**Maps**

The area is covered by two maps in the Drakensberg Recreational Series, which are map 5: Drakensberg South — Vergelegen, Cobham and Garden Castle; and map 6: Drakensberg South — Garden Castle, Bushman's Nek and Sehlabathebe.

**Relevant Information**

- It is *essential* to refer to the General Rules of Access to Drakensberg Areas dealt with on pages 154-156.
- Mountain register points are at Cobham Forest Station, the Drakensberg Gardens Hotel (Garden Castle area) and at the SAP border post at Bushman's Nek.
- The Bushman's Nek border post is open between 08h00 and 16h00.

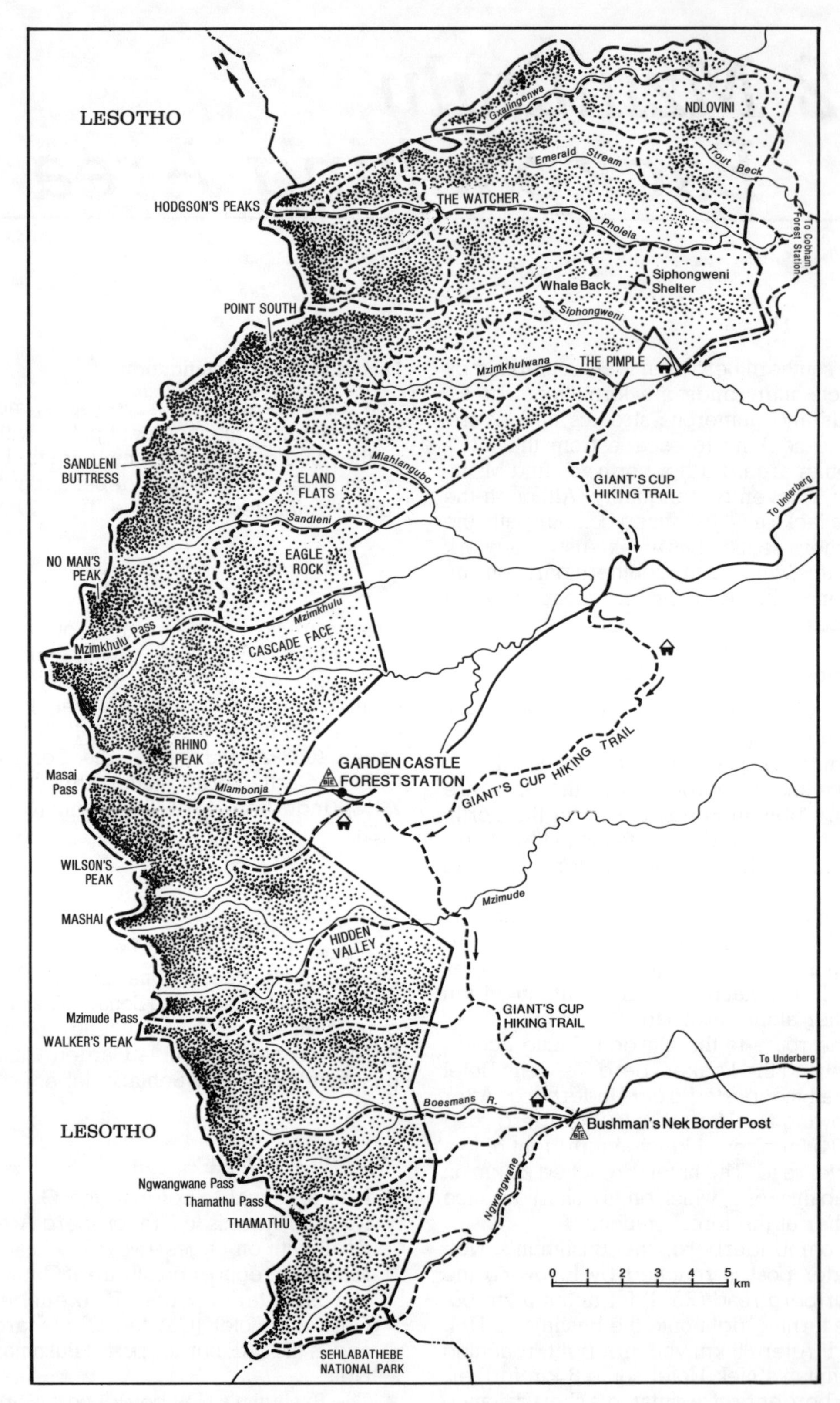


*Mzimkulu Backpacking Area*

### Facilities

Five informal campsites without ablution facilities have been provided at Cobham and Garden Castle forest stations. It is advisable to book these well in advance if you are planning to camp at either venue. Several caves can be used for overnight accommodation in the wilderness area. Refer to page 156 for conditions applying to the occupation of caves.

### Climate, Flora, Fauna, History and Geology

For information regarding the climate, flora, fauna, history and geology of the Drakensberg, refer to the introduction to the Natal Drakensberg on page 147.

*Although not common in the Drakensberg,* Erica cerinthoides *is one of the best known ericas in South Africa*

*Brunsvigia natalensis*

### Trail Synopsis

After stretching south-east for some 250 km, the escarpment swings sharply south-west at Sani Pass. The scenery is similar to that of the Mkhomazi Wilderness Area to the north and although the area lacks the prominent free-standing peaks of the central and northern Berg areas, several unusual buttresses and rock formations create impressive scenery.

To the north of the Mzimkulu Wilderness Area lies Sani Pass, one of the most impressive passes in Southern Africa. (See Don't Miss on page 161.)

Access to the greatest concentration of footpaths is from Cobham Forest Station, which is a convenient base for exploring the northern section of the wilderness area.

The Sipongweni Shelter is situated about 8 km (two to three hours) from Cobham Forest Station and is reached by following the course of the Pholela River upstream for about 7 km before turning left. The shelter is situated about 1 km further along this path. It has been described as possibly one of the best in the Drakensberg, taking into account the number of paintings, their good state of preservation and the interesting themes depicted. The reason for this is

*Rhino Peak is a familiar landmark in the southern Drakensberg*

twofold: owing to its remoteness the shelter was one of the last to be used by the San and for the same reason it has escaped the attention of vandals.

The shelter is perhaps best known for the painting depicting men spearing fish from small canoes. This painting is to the left of the cave and was much sharper when it was first photographed in 1907. The black pigment used by the San is unfortunately not as long-lasting as other pigments and this factor combined with exfoliation has resulted in the gradual deterioration of the paintings.

Another painting in the cave depicts men with feathers on their heads dancing to a rhythm clapped by women on both sides. Near the right-hand end of the shelter is an excellent painting of a San cattle raid. The scene depicts several naked drovers with hats, two saddle horses and a San-like figure riding a horse.

Other paintings include two horsemen racing neck and neck and a dancing scene in which the central figure appears to represent a baboon. Most of the figures appear to wear feathers and horns on their heads, while the woman to the left is speckled with dots of orange and white paint.

Research carried out by Vinnicombe[1] revealed that a high proportion of the animals depicted in the southern Berg are domestic rather than wild animals. Mazel[2] has argued that it is likely that the San ceased living in the northern Drakensberg long before the arrival of white settlers because of black expansion. In the northern Drakensberg mainly sheep, dogs and cattle are depicted and there is only one historical scene. Paintings of horses occur only in the southern Berg, south of 29° 15″ latitude, with only five per cent of the total number of paintings depicting cattle north of this latitude.

About 14 km south of Hodgson's Peaks is one of the most conspicuous peaks in the southern Drakensberg, the 3 051 m high Rhino Peak, which juts out approximately 2 km from the escarpment. The Zulu name, Ntabangcobo, means 'rhino's horn peak'. The peak is reached by following a well-defined path from the forest station at Garden Castle along the Mlambonja River. About 2 km along this path you will reach

---

1 Vinnicombe, P. 1976. *People of the Eland*. Pietermaritzburg: University of Natal Press, 155.

2 Mazel, A. 1982. Distribution of painting themes in the Natal Drakensberg. *Annals of the Natal Museum* 25 (1), 73.

Pillar Cave, which is often used as a base camp for excursions to the escarpment and which can comfortably accommodate 12 people. From here there is an impressive view of the Mashai Fangs south-west of the Mashai Pass.

Over the next 3,5 km you gain some 500 m in altitude, followed by another 400 m gain in height over the final 1,5 km. Once the escarpment is reached the path swings eastwards and about 2 km on you will reach Rhino Peak, which is easily ascended. To the south lies Wilson's Peak (3 276 m), Mashai (3 313 m), Walker's Peak (3 306 m), Thaba Ngwangwane (3 068 m), Thamathu (2 734 m) and the Devil's Knuckles (3 028 m), also known as the Three Bushmen, Thaba-Ntsu or Baroa-Ba-Bararo.

From the Garden Castle Forest Station to Rhino Peak you gain some 1 200 m in altitude and depending on your physical condition the ascent should take about six hours. The total distance is about 18 km and can be completed in a day.

South of Garden Castle the footpaths are restricted to a number of foot passes leading to the escarpment. They are the Mzimude, Ngangwane, Thamathu and Knuckle passes.

The wilderness area borders on the north-western boundary of Lesotho's Sehlabathebe National Park, which can be reached along either Bushman's Nek Pass or a foot pass along the Ngangwane River. (The park is described in detail on pages 128-134.)

## DON'T MISS

- the Sani Pass Summit. The pass is restricted to four-wheel-drive vehicles, but it is possible to reach the South African border post 15 km beyond the Sani Pass Hotel in a sedan car. You will need about two to three hours to hike from the border post to the summit, where the Lesotho border post and a chalet for mountaineers are situated. The 7 km track snakes vigorously up the Mkhomazana Valley, gaining about 1 000 m in altitude and revealing some of the most magnificent scenery in the country. Valid travel documents (a Book of Life is not acceptable) are required to pass through the border posts and it is advisable to make advance reservations for the Mountain Chalet by writing to Sani Top, P O Box 12, Himeville 4585, Telephone (03392) 1302.

# 13 Mkhomazi Backpacking Area

Proclaimed in May 1973, this wilderness area of some 54 000 ha is not as well known as the more popular areas further north. Deeply incised gorges and valleys give the landscape a characteristic rugged appearance. The area is rich in legend and was the scene of many bitter clashes between San (Bushman) cattle raiders and the early white settlers. Some routes to the escarpment are the original passes used by the San and the Basotho across the Drakensberg.

### Location

Mkhomazi in the central and southern Drakensberg stretches between Giant's Castle Game Reserve in the north through Highmoor forestry area and the Loteni and Vergelegen reserves of the Natal Parks Board in the central Berg, to Sani Pass in the south.

Highmoor Forest Station is reached by following the signposted road from Rosetta to Kamberg Nature Reserve. About 30 km beyond Rosetta the route forks. Keep to the right along the road which leads to Ntabamhlope. Almost immediately after this fork, you turn left. Highmoor Forest Station is about 10 km along this road.

Loteni Reserve is situated on the Nottingham Road/Himeville road, the turnoff being signposted about 31 km north of Himeville and 63 km south of Nottingham Road. From the turnoff it is about 16 km to the rest camp.

Access to Vergelegen Nature Reserve is along the Nottingham Road/Himeville route. The turnoff to the reserve is about 15 km north of Himeville, and the reserve is 34 km along a well-signposted road.

### Distance and Classification

The wilderness area is traversed by about 300 km of management paths, with a further 165 km in the adjoining areas. The distance and classification depend on the route you choose.

### Permits

Groups are restricted to a maximum of 12 people and it is necessary to obtain a permit before entering the area. Reservations can be made through The Forester, Highmoor Forest Station, P O Box 51, Rosetta 3301, Telephone (033332) 1322, or The Forester, Mkhomazi Forest Station, P O Box X105, via Nottingham Road 3280, Telephone (033312) 1902.

### Maps

The area is covered by two maps in the Drakensberg Recreational Series, which are map 4: Central Drakensberg — Highmoor, Mzimkulu and Loteni; and map 5: Southern Drakensberg — Vergelegen, Cobham and Garden Castle.

### Relevant Information

- It is *essential* to refer to the General Rules of Access to Drakensberg Areas dealt with on pages 154-156.
- Mountain register points are at the office in Loteni Reserve and at the Sani Pass Hotel. There are no registers at Highmoor Forest Station or Vergelegen Nature Reserve.

### Facilities

Should you wish to overnight in the area before commencing a trail you will have a number of options.

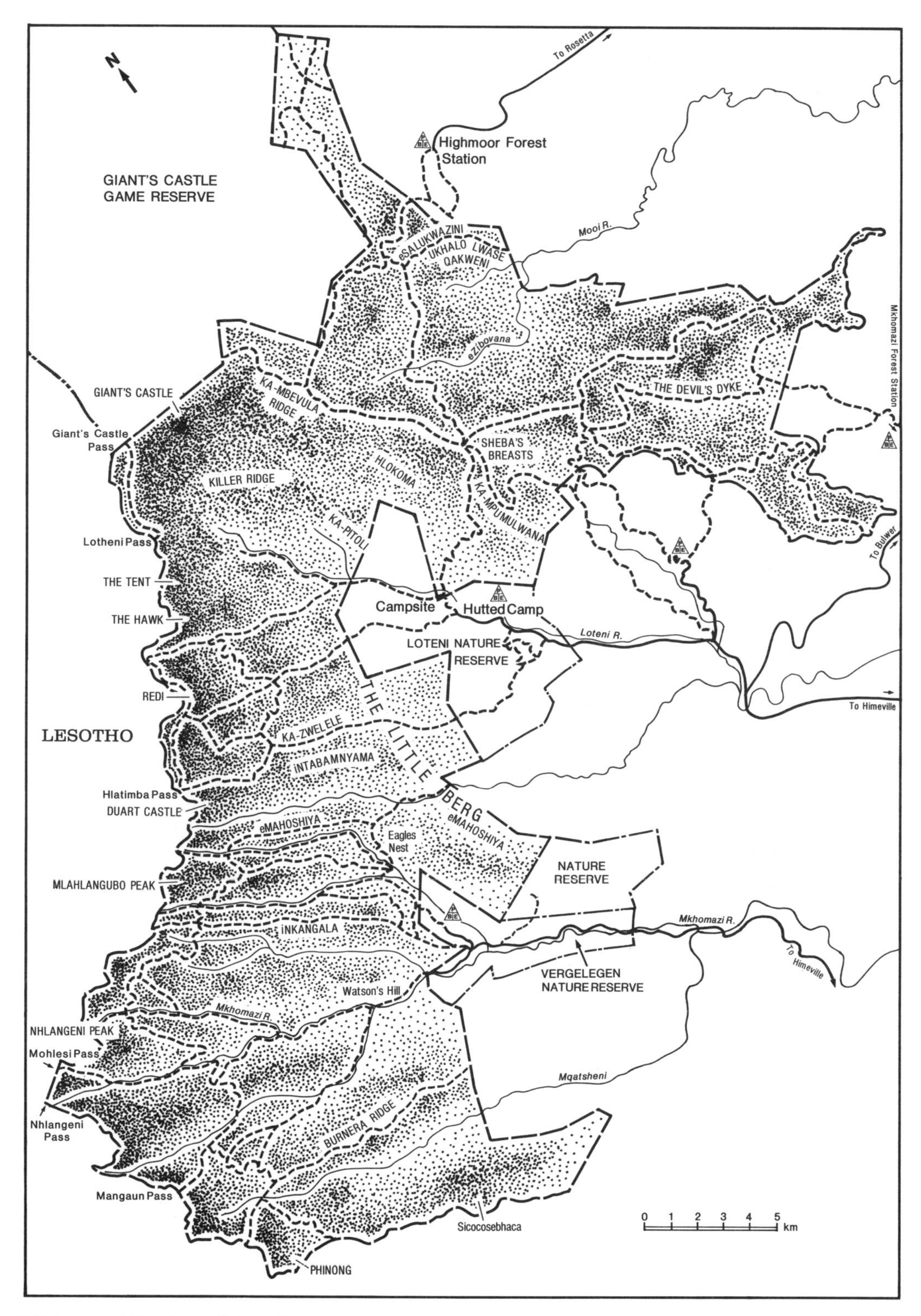


*Mkhomazi Backpacking Area*

Huts are available at Loteni and Vergelegen reserves. As accommodation at Vergelegen consists of only two thatched cottages, it is advisable to book well in advance. Should you prefer to camp, this is possible at Loteni which has a campsite.

Enquiries for hutted accommodation should be directed to the Director, Natal Parks Board, P O Box 662, Pietermaritzburg 3200, Telephone (0331) 471981. Reservations for camping at Loteni must be made with the Camp Superintendent, Loteni Nature Reserve, P O Box 14, Himeville 4585, Telephone (03392) 1521.

An informal campsite with a maximum of five sites, without any facilities, is available at Highmoor Forest Station. Reservations must be made with the forester.

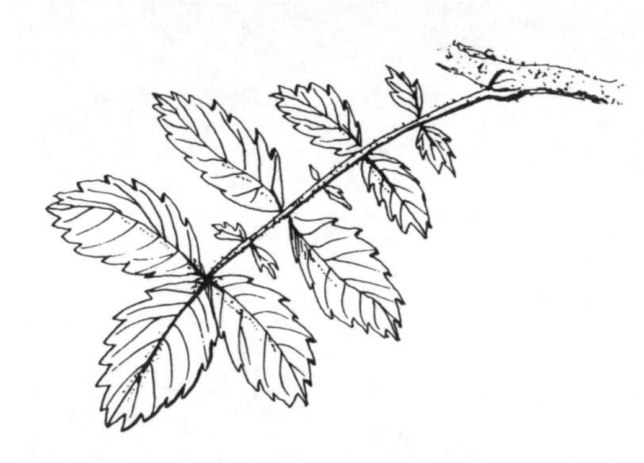

*Old wood trees are commonly found along streams, gullies and kloofs in the Drakensberg*

In the wilderness area there are several caves where you can overnight. Among these are Caracal Cave (12), Yellowwood Cave (8), Sinclair's Shelter, Ash Cave and Runaway Cave (6) and Lotheni and Hlathimba caves (4). (Numbers in brackets indicate the maximum overnight capacity of the caves.) It is, nevertheless, essential to carry a good backpacking tent as caves could be occupied. For conditions applying to the occupation of caves, refer to page 156.

### Climate, Flora, Fauna, History and Geology

For information regarding the climate, flora, fauna, history and geology of the Drakensberg, refer to the introduction to the Natal Drakensberg on page 147.

### Trail Synopsis

Scenically the area is more rugged than the Drakensberg further south. The spurs of the Little Berg extend further east from the escarpment than they do further north and the area is characterised by numerous rivers which have carved deep valleys. Soaring buttresses and several unnamed peaks of over 3 000 m dominate the escarpment.

Despite the rugged nature of the area, there are numerous footpaths. These are mainly restricted to the river valleys and the occasional spur. It is often necessary to boulder-hop up a valley to reach higher ground from where you can enjoy beautiful views of the escarpment. The main access routes to the escarpment are via the Hlatimba, Mohlesi, Nhlangeni and Manguan passes.

The name Loteni is said to be derived from a Zulu word meaning 'ash river', which refers to the grey and black shale deposits which resemble ash.

The area is steeped in history. The Loteni River valley was used as early as 1847 by San stock raiders, who descended from Lesotho via the Hlatimba Pass and raided farms as far away as Karkloof, some 90 km to the east. To escape their pursuers they then drove their booty up the tributaries of the Loteni River. A painting in the upper reaches of the river depicts a commando of 22 horsemen and from the close correspondence between this scene and historic documents it has been suggested that the artist was depicting the Harding Commando, which pursued a group of San up the valley in January 1847.

In 1859 Chief Lugaju and his Putini clan, who fled from Zululand in 1848, were settled in the area as a buffer between the farmers and the San and after 1872 no further raids were reported. Some 18 years later farmers, mainly from the British Isles, began settling on farms in the upper reaches of the Loteni. Names such as Duart Castle, Maitland, Snowdon, Movern and Maylands survive still to remind one of these hardy pioneers.

Many of the San raiders also retreated with their stolen animals to the upper reaches of the Mkhomazi River, roughly 10 km south of the Loteni. The river flows into the Indian Ocean some 48 km south-west of Durban and the Zulu name is said to mean 'she-whale river'.

The Hlatimba Pass was the site of the historic Langalibalele 'Rebellion' of 1873. Langalibalele, Chief of the Hlubi, refused to register his people's arms and his subsequent refusal to report personally in Pietermaritzburg was regarded as an act of rebellion. The Natal Government threw a strong cordon around the Hlubi and it was decided to seal the passes over the Drakensberg to prevent Langalibalele from fleeing into Basotholand. Major Anthony Durnford of the Carbineers was detailed to ascend the escarpment via Giant's Castle Pass, but as no reconnaisance trip had been undertaken, he mistakenly ascended along the Hlatimba Pass, about 10 km south of Giant's Castle Pass. The rugged terrain delayed them and when they arrived at the head of the Bushman's River Pass on the morning of 4 November 1873 they found the Hlubi already in possession. In the ensuing skirmish three Carbineers and two black helpers were killed and the Carbineers retreated.

Among the numerous backpacking options available in the Mkhomazi area is an ascent of the escarpment via the Mohlesi Pass, but this should only be attempted by the physically fit as it is rather demanding. From the escarpment you continue for about 5 km to Thaba Ntlenyana (3 482 m) —

*The black eagle can be identified by its wholly black plumage, except for a narrow V on its back, when perched*

The Beautiful Little Mountain. It is the highest point south of Mount Kilimanjaro and used to be called Thabantshonyana or The Little Black Mountain. As the peak is situated in Lesotho, it is important to take a valid passport along even though you do not pass through a border post.

From Vergelegen Nature Reserve you gain about 1 600 m in altitude to the top of Mohlesi Pass and then another 400 m to Thaba Ntlenyana. The distance from Vergelegen is approximately 25 km.

The peak was first ascended in 1951 by a party of nine mountaineers who established its height and named it the King of Peaks. The view from the summit is indescribably beautiful and on a clear day you can see as far as Mont-aux-Sources and Quachas Nek, some 100 km to the north-west and south-west respectively.

# 14 Giant's Castle Backpacking Area

The pristine beauty of this central Drakensberg reserve can only truly be appreciated on horseback or on foot. Situated on a grassy plateau among deep valleys and below sheer cliffs, Giant's Castle Game Reserve is a backpacker's paradise. The reserve is criss-crossed by paths and riding trails, providing both the serious backpacker and the casual day walker with numerous options. The reserve is reputed to be one of the richest areas in the world for rock art and you might also be lucky enough to spot the rare bearded vulture or one of the large herds of eland.

### Location

The reserve can be approached from either Estcourt or Mooi River. From Estcourt you follow the road signposted to Ntabamhlope, turning left at the White Mountain Resort after about 35 km. Continue for another 12 km until the Mooi River/Giant's Castle Road is reached. Turn right and continue for 19 km to the reserve office.

From Mooi River you take the road signposted to Giant's Castle. After about 37 km turn right onto the Ntabamhlope/Kamberg Road, which you follow for about 12 km to the turnoff to the Giant's Castle Game Reserve. From here it is 19 km to the reserve office.

### Distance and Classification

The reserve is traversed by about 285 km of footpaths and the classification depends on the route taken.

### Permits

Your entry permit obtained at the entrance gate of the reserve allows you to explore the reserve. No additional permits are required.

### Maps

The area is covered by map 3 in the Drakensberg Recreational Series: Central Drakensberg — Injasuti, Giant's Castle and Highmoor.

### Relevant Information

- It is *essential* to read the General Rules of Access to Drakensberg Areas discussed on pages 154-156.
- Mountain register points are located at Injasuti camp and the warden's office at Giant's Castle camp.
- You may *not* camp wherever you want to as overnight accommodation is limited to three mountain huts and a few caves. Rock climbers who need to set up a base camp for a climb can make special arrangements with the warden.
- Fires are not allowed at the huts or caves and you must supply your own backpacking stove.
- If you are a bird enthusiast, take your binoculars along because the reserve is one of the best areas in the Drakensberg for bird-watching.

### Facilities

Accommodation at Giant's Castle camp consists of self-contained cottages and bungalows. You must supply your own food, which is prepared by cooks assigned to each bungalow or cottage. Hutted accommodation is also available at the Injasuti camp in the northern section of the reserve. Reservations for hutted accommodation at both these camps should be addressed to the Reservations Officer, Natal Parks

Board, P O Box 662, Pietermaritzburg 3200, Telephone (0331) 471981.

Camping in the reserve is permitted at the Hillside campsite some 30 km from the main camp, as well as at Injasuti. Reservations should be addressed to the Officer-in-Charge, Hillside Campsite, P O Box 288, Estcourt 3310, Telephone (0361) 24435 and the Camp Superintendent, Injasuti, Private Bag X7010, Estcourt 3310, Telephone (03682) Loskop 1311 respectively.

There are three mountain huts as well as a few caves where you can overnight, all of which are marked on the map. Reservations for the huts and caves should be directed to the Warden, Giant's Castle Game Reserve, Private Bag X7055, Estcourt 3310, Telephone (03631) 24616 between 14h00 and 17h00.

**Climate, Flora, Fauna, History and Geology**

Please refer to the introduction to the Natal Drakensberg on page 147 where these are discussed.

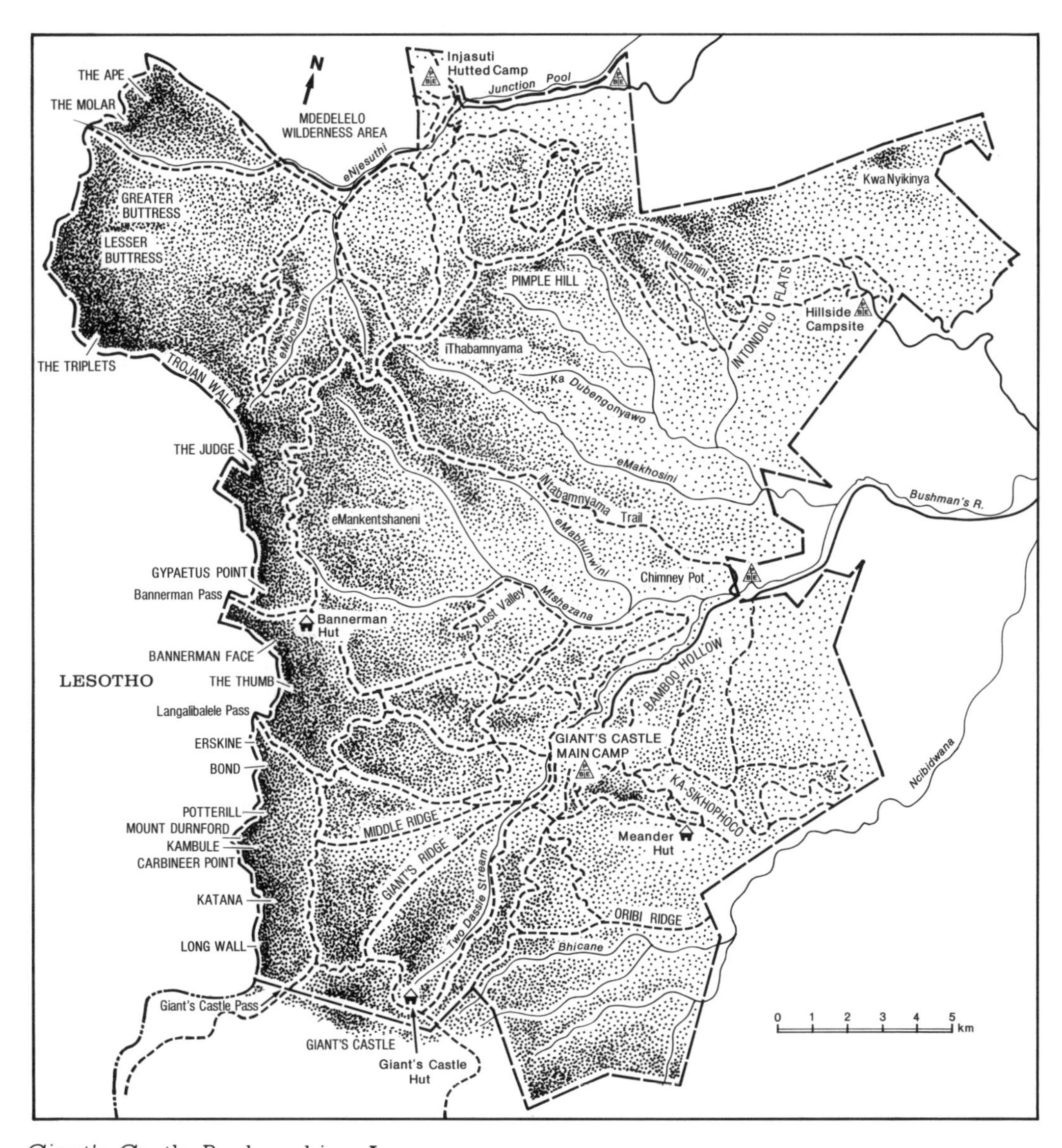


*Giant's Castle Backpacking Area*

**Trail Synopsis**

A four-day route incorporating two of the mountain huts is described here. Depending on time available, this can be varied considerably by consulting the map.

Be on the lookout for *Huttinia woodii*, an extremely rare orchid which has been recorded only in Giant's Castle Game Reserve and on two farms in the Natal midlands. It grows 30 cm high in grasslands at between 1 300 and 2 100 m and produces 15 to 20 small flowers in February. The flowers are either whitish or pale green with purplish markings on the petals.

**Day 1: Giant's Castle Main Camp to Giant's Castle Hut via Two Dassie Stream**

From the camp you follow the path signposted to Main Caves. After about 1,5 km the path winds downhill to an outcrop of boulders. In 1874 a detachment of the 75th Regiment on Foot, commanded by Major Anthony Durnford, established a base camp here while they were engaged in blowing up the entrances to the passes between Oliviershoek and Giant's Castle. These passes were used by cattle rustlers and other troublemakers and were for a long time a thorn in the side of the Natal Government. The figure 75 was carved into one of the boulders, reputedly by the cook of the 75th Regiment on Foot.

The path crosses a footbridge and rises steeply to the Main Caves Museum. The museum has been fenced off but a game guard is present between 08h30 and 16h30. A small entry fee is payable and a recorded commentary on the San (Bushmen), their paintings, culture and history is given hourly. Displayed in the museum is a realistic model of the way of life of the San as well as facsimiles of artefacts and a stratigraphical reconstruction of the excavations of a hearth-site.

According to Willcox the Giant's Castle Game Reserve is one of the richest areas in the world for rock art if both the quality

Blesbok – a typical antelope species of the highveld

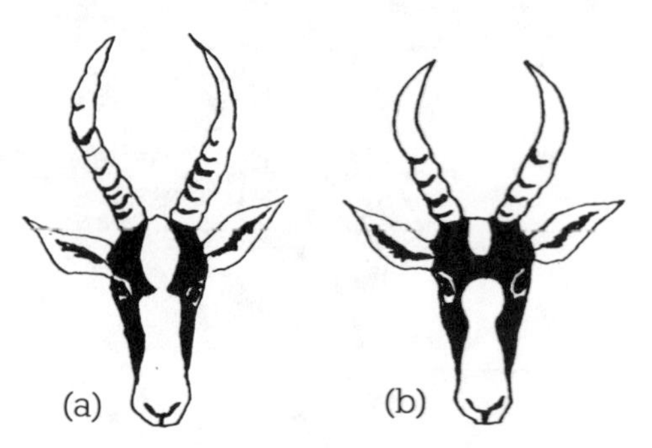


*Difference in facial markings of (a) bontebok and (b) blesbok*

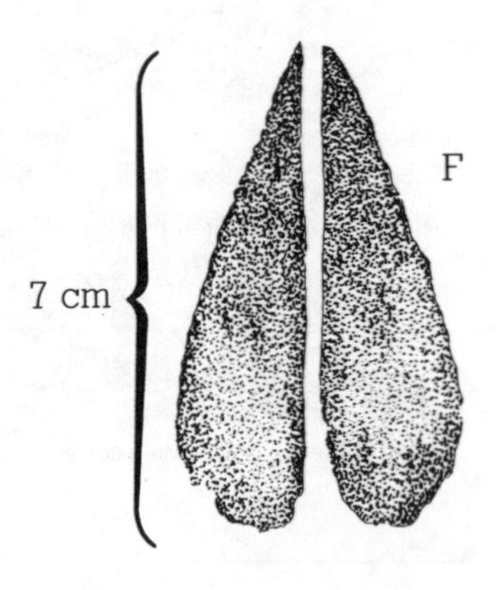

and quantity of paintings are considered.[1] To date more than 50 sites, with a total of more than 5 000 individual paintings, have been recorded in the reserve. The Main Caves contain more than 540 individual paintings.

From the cave a path leads down to the Caves Forest, where you pass through a small patch of forest and join the Giant's Castle route. Two Dassie Stream is crossed several times before you cross over to the right, where you remain until the stream splits. Although the first section of the route is level and fairly easy going, you will nevertheless appreciate the few inviting pools to cool off in. Several boggy areas then have to be crossed, making the going difficult, and as a result of the intervening ridges your view is limited.

After the stream splits you have a fairly steep climb ahead and you gain some 250 m in height before the path levels off just before you join the contour path. Giant's Castle hut is situated a short distance to the west along the contour path. The total distance covered is about 10 km.

Looming behind the hut is the prominent Giant's Castle (3 314 m), which is known to the Zulu as iNtabayikonjwa. There are several explanations for the meaning of the name, one being that pointing at the mountain means disrespect and that it will respond by bringing bad weather.

### Day 2: Giant's Castle Hut to Giant's Castle Peak and Back

Giant's Castle hut is ideally situated should you intend ascending the peak. Three alternative routes for the ascent are described in the guide book on Giant's Castle Game Reserve which is available in the reserve, but only the most clearly defined route is described here.

From the hut you follow the contour path for about 2 km before it is joined by the Giant's Ridge path. Another 2 km further on the contour path brings you to the foot of the Giant's Castle Pass, which was probably the route followed by the party of six who made the first recorded ascent of the Giant in 1864. You continue up the pass for about 2 km, gaining some 770 m in height. The last section of the pass is steep and you must be careful of landslides. Avoid gullies branching off to the left as they are impassable.

From the pass a path leads to the east, reaching the cairn on the summit of Giant's Castle after a gentle ascent of about 230 m. You return along the same route to Giant's Castle hut, a total distance of about 18 km.

### Day 3: Giant's Castle Hut to Bannerman Hut

From Giant's Castle hut it is about 17,5 km to Bannerman hut. The contour path traverses the reserve at an altitude of about 2 300 m and except for crossing numerous mountain streams, where the terrain becomes a little difficult, the walk is fairly easy.

After leaving Giant's Castle Hut the foot of Giant's Castle Pass is reached after 4 km and the contour path then swings in a north-westerly direction. Several streams have to be crossed and this may slow you down. Take your time, however, and enjoy the superb scenery.

To the left several prominent peaks tower above the escarpment. The Long Wall (3 114 m) is the first to be passed, followed by Katana (3 072 m), Carbineer Point (3 154 m), Kambula, Mount Durnford, Potterill (3 159 m), Bond (3 153 m) and Erskine. Far below you in the foothills several other landmarks can be distinguished, including World's View, Oribi Ridge and the Chimney Pot.

About 7 km from the hut the contour path is joined by the Middle Ridge route and about 2,5 km on you reach the base of Langalibalele Pass. At least six hours should be allowed for an ascent and descent of the pass, which is about 3 km long, rising almost 700 m over this distance. A simple stone cairn at the top of the pass marks the graves of Erskine, Bond and Potterill and two local blacks, Kambula and Katana. It was here that Major Durnford's forces were put to flight by Chief Langalibalele's Hlubi on

---

1 Willcox, A.R. 1984. *The Drakensberg Bushmen and their Art.* Winterton: Drakensberg Publicity Association, 61.

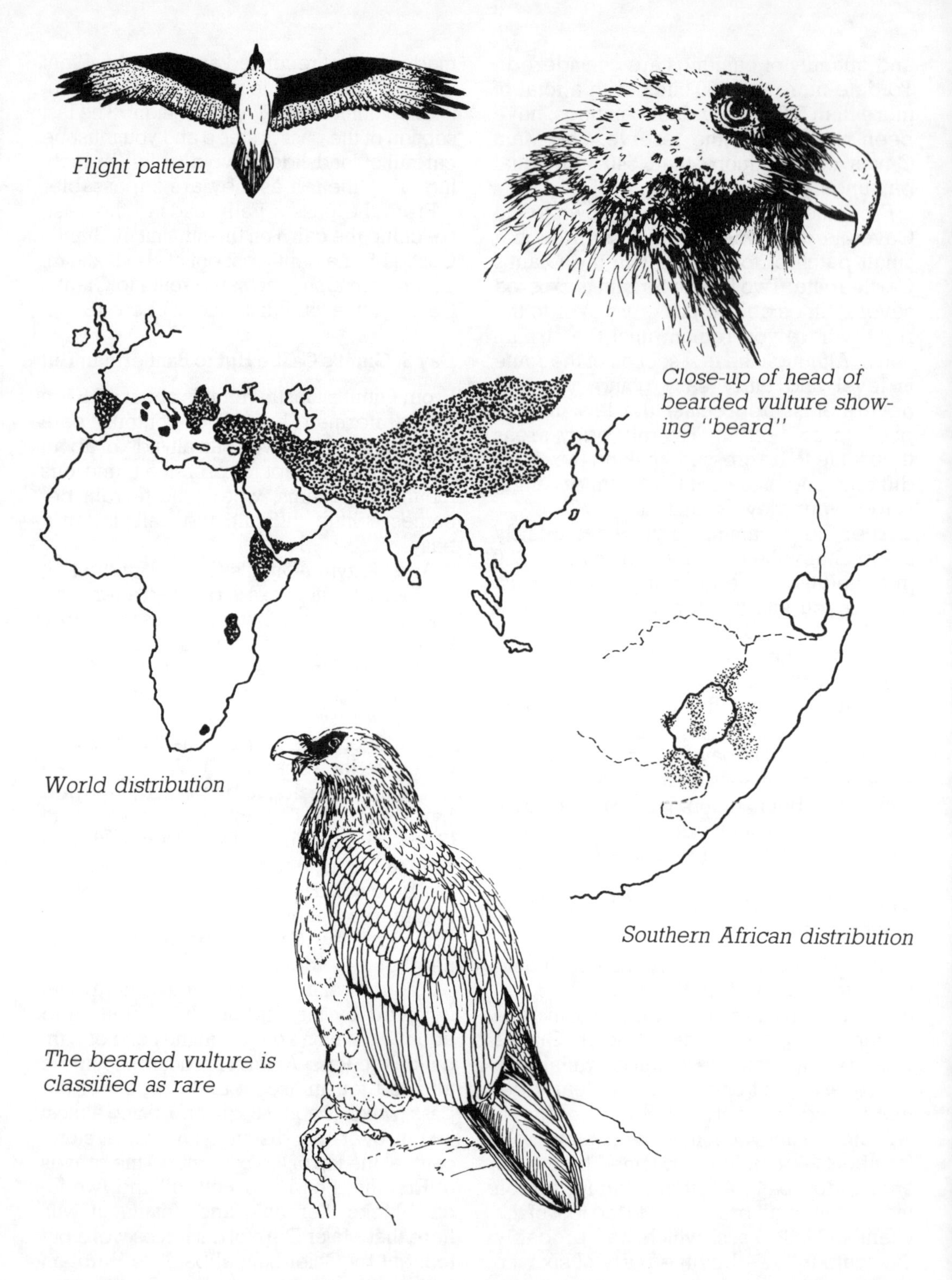
Flight pattern

Close-up of head of bearded vulture showing "beard"

World distribution

Southern African distribution

The bearded vulture is classified as rare

4 November 1873. Five of the peaks passed earlier were named in honour of the men killed during the skirmish.

You continue along the contour path for a further 1 km, where it is joined by the direct route between Giant's Castle Main Camp and Langalibalele Pass. Two and a half kilometres on you pass another junction, reaching a tarn (small vlei) half a kilometre further. The path then traverses below the Thumb and Bannerman Face, which as its name suggests has a distinct resemblance to the profile of Sir Henry Campbell-Bannerman, British Prime Minister from 1905 to 1908.

The hut is situated at the foot of Bannerman Pass, which is about 3 km long, and the ascent requires about two and a half hours. The path is generally well defined with cairns indicating the route in the more difficult places, but boulder scree makes the ascent tricky in the steeper section. From the top of the pass (3 050 m) a short walk along the escarpment brings you to the cairn marking the top of Bannerman Face (3 070 m).

Gypaetus Point, north of Bannerman Pass, is named after the rare bearded vulture or lammergeier (119). The bristly 'beard' of black feathers on the chin gave rise to the common name of the vulture as well as the species name *barbatus.* The bearded vulture is easily recognised by its wedge-shaped tail. It has a wingspan of 2,5 m to 3 m and is extremely powerful on the wing. Gliding speeds of 105 km per hour have been measured.

Historically they occurred from Cape Town along the mountains of the east coast and the Drakensberg as far north as Lydenberg in the Transvaal. In Southern Africa they number only about 120 breeding pairs at present, and are limited to the eastern Orange Free State, Lesotho and the Drakensberg areas of Natal and Griqualand East. Their decline is due to several factors such as better stock management, which has resulted in a storage of carcasses, poisoned meat put out by farmers to trap jackal and other vermin, and persecution by local tribesmen.

Bearded vulture also occur in Kenya, Ethiopia, Egypt,. Sinai Peninsula, southern Arabia, Spain, Greece, the Balkan States and eastwards as far as western China. Breeding populations of the European race have been exterminated compeletely in the Swiss Alps, Bavaria and the Carpathian Mountains.

These highly evolved specialist birds have features of both eagles and vultures and as such have for a long time defied classification. The beak is like that of an eagle, while the long curved claws are vulture-like. Unlike vultures, however, there is no evidence of a large crop for the shortage and transport of food, despite the fact that they feed almost exclusively on carrion.

The major part of their diet consists of bone and they are able to swallow bones as large as the thigh-bone of a lamb. Very large bones are carried in their talons and dropped onto rock slabs — known as ossuaries — from a height of 30 to 40 m, with drops of over 100 m having been recorded (hence their Greek name, *ossfractus* — the bone breaker). Marrow is extracted from the bones with their specially-adapted tongues. Unlike other birds of prey, for example owls, the bearded vulture digests all its food with exceptionally strong gastric juices and no indigestible lumps are regurgitated.

### Day 4: Bannerman Hut to Giant's Castle Main Camp

From Bannerman hut you can either continue along the contour path to the Injasuti Valley, which is roughly 18 km further, or you can return to the Giant's Castle main camp along Secretary Bird Ridge (about 11 km).

### DON'T MISS

- the bearded vulture hide at Bamboo Hollow. In order to supplement the diet of the bearded vulture (119) and to discourage them from foraging on farmlands where they may pick up poisoned bait, meat and bones are put out at a specially constructed hide every Saturday between May and September. Food is not put out during the summer months when it is naturally more readily available.

  The hide is about 3,5 km north of the hutted camp and is reached after an hour's easy walking. From the comfort of the hide you can observe these rare birds as well as other raptors feeding at close range. However, reservations are essential and can be made through the Warden, Private Bag X7055, Estcourt 3310, Telephone (03631) 24616 between 14h00 and 17h00.

# 15 Mdedelelo Backpacking Area

This 29 000 ha wilderness area is characterised by deep valleys, impressive peaks and caves with rock paintings. Familiar landmarks include Cathkin Peak, Champagne Castle, Gatberg and the Dragon's Back, an impressive range of free-standing block-shaped peaks. Backpacking is made easier by a contour path which provides access to the features in the area and links up with several passes leading to the escarpment.

### Location

Mdedelelo Wilderness Area is bordered in the north by the Cathedral Peak Area and in the south by Giant's Castle Game Reserve. The main access point is from Monks Cowl Forest Station. From Bergville you turn right onto the road signposted Cathedral Peak shortly after crossing the Tugela River, east of the town. After about 14 km the Cathedral Peak turnoff is reached but you continue for another 13 km until turning right onto the road signposted Cathkin Peak, Dragon Peaks, Champagne Castle. The Monk's Cowl Forest Station is reached after roughly 21,5 km.

Backpackers can also enter the area from Injasuti in the south and Cathedral Peak to the north.

### Distance and Classification

The wilderness area is traversed by about 185 km of footpaths and the classification depends on the route you choose.

### Permits

The number of people per group is limited to a maximum of 12, while the number of groups is also restricted. Permits can be obtained from The Forester, Monk's Cowl Forest Station, Private Bag X2, Winterton 3340, Telephone (03682) 2204 or The Forester, Cathedral Peak Forest Station, Private Bag X1, Winterton 3340, Telephone (03682) 3621, depending on your point of entry.

### Maps

The area is covered by map 2 in the Drakensberg Recreational Series: Drakensberg North — Cathedral Peak to Injasuti.

### Relevant Information

- It is *essential* to refer to the General Rules of Access to Drakensberg Areas on pages 154-156.
- Depending on your approach route, mountain register points are at the Injasuti Camp, Mike's Pass Gate (Cathedral Peak) and at Monk's Cowl Forest Station.

### Facilities

A pleasant campsite with ablution facilities is provided below the forest station at Monk's Cowl. Access to the campsite remains open until 18h00 on Fridays to accommodate late arrivals.

In the wilderness area you may camp in the Nkosazana (12), Stable (12) and Cowl (6) caves, which can be reserved on arrival at Monk's Cowl for the exclusive use of a party. (The numbers in brackets indicate the maximum number of backpackers who may occupy each cave.) Refer to page 156 for conditions applying to the occupation of caves.

### Climate, Flora, Fauna, History and Geology

For information regarding the climate, flora, fauna, history and geology of the Drakensberg refer to the introduction to the Natal Drakensberg on page 147.

## Trail Synopsis

One of the most popular routes onto the Little Berg from Monk's Cowl Forest Station is via the Sphinx and Verkykerskop. This is the usual route onto the contour path and hence also to the higher peaks and passes. Some 450 m is gained in altitude before the path evens out at Breakfast Stream, and it then ascends gently for about 2 to 3 km to the contour path.

Straight ahead of you the scenery is dominated by Cathkin Peak (3 149 m), from which the area derives its Zulu name, Mdedelelo. The name is translated as 'make room for him', a Zulu expression which is normally used for a bully. This refers to the prominent position of Cathkin,

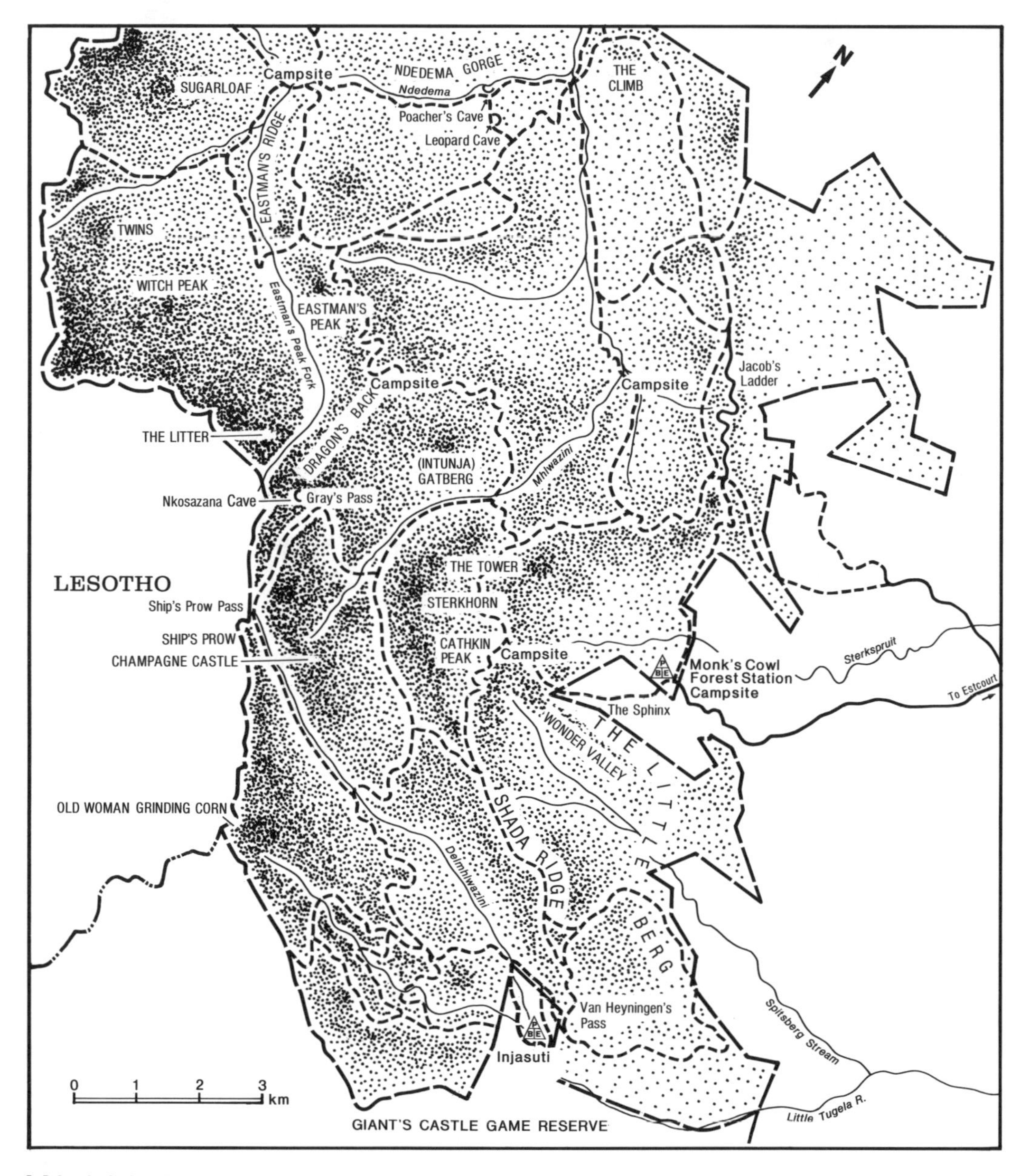


*Mdedelelo Backpacking Area*

*The Cathkin Range. Cathkin Peak (on the left) is also known as Mdedelelo*

which seemingly pushed the other peaks aside to make room for itself.

To the north of Cathkin is another well-known peak, Sterkhorn (2 973 m), also known as Mount Memory. A small cross has been erected on its summit in memory of those who died during World War II. Further north is The Tower (2 670 m) and the Amphlett (2 620 m). The latter peak was named after a well-known Cape climber, G T Amphlett, who spent some time climbing in the Cathkin area. Although Champagne Castle at 3 377 m can lay claim to being the second highest peak in South Africa, it is almost completely obscured by Cathkin Peak when approached from this angle.

Looking further north you are likely to be struck by a peculiar sight — a peak with an enormous hole through its base — the well-known Gatberg. The Zulu name of this unusual formation, Intunja, is variously translated as 'the eye of the needle' and 'the hole in the mountain through which the shepherds can creep'. The gaping hole through the basalt has a diameter of about 9 m.

The contour path is reached about 5,5 km from Monk's Cowl Forest Station and provides access to either the south-eastern parts of Mdedelelo or the north-western parts of the wilderness area. Construction of the contour path to link the Cathkin and Cathedral Peak areas began in 1937 under the guidance of the forester-in-charge of Monk's Cowl at the time, J van Heyningen, and was subsequently extended.

By following the path to the left you can backpack to Injasuti, some 21 km to the south-east. The right-hand route leads to Ndedema Gorge and further afield to the Organ Pipes and to just below Cathedral Peak.

By turning right onto the contour path you have access to the majority of features and backpacking opportunities in the area. Hlatikulu Nek is reached after 2,5 km and here you can turn right if you wish to explore the north-eastern part of Mdedelelo.

Should you continue along the contour path, the turnoff to Gray's Pass is reached on your left 1,5 km on. This path brings you to Keith Bush Camp, a beautiful campsite surrounded by cliffs on three sides at the head of the Mhlawazini River, about 4 km beyond the turnoff. The site was named after Keith Bush, a member of a three-man party who successfully opened a new route on the north face of Cathkin in September 1955. Whilst descending the peak a sling broke and Bush fell to his death. In 1963 mountaineers paid tribute to the able climber when a hut was built on the site of the old base camp and named after him. Following the destruction of the hut by a fire it was decided not to rebuild it as the area had subsequently been proclaimed a wilderness area — a decision in keeping with the policy of minimising human structures in such areas. Between Monk's Cowl Forest Station and Keith Bush Camp, a distance of about 13,5 km, you will gain some 870 m in altitude and depending on your physical condition, about six to seven and a half hours will be required.

Gray's Pass is the most popular route to the escarpment in the area and although it is only 2,5 km long, you will gain roughly 700 m in altitude. The ascent starts a short distance above the camp and as you gain height you have your first uninterrupted view of Monk's Cowl (3 234 m). It is one of the most challenging peaks in the Drakensberg, with some G grade rock climbs, and was first successfully scaled only in 1942.

Nkosazana Cave near the top of the pass is a good place to spend the night on the escarpment. It is situated next to a perennial stream which sometimes flows through the cave in summer, limiting accommodation to about four people. During winter the cave can accommodate up to 10 people, but could be iced up after heavy snow falls.

From the top of the pass it is an easy walk of about 3 km to Champagne Castle (3 377 m). You can either return via Gray's Pass, or descend along Ship's Prow Pass, immediately south of Champagne Castle. Although there are two possible routes down Ship's Prow Pass, the first (shorter) turnoff to your left should be avoided on account of some difficult sections. Continue straight ahead for about 1 km where the easier descent of about 4,5 km to the contour path commences.

Another backpacking option is to follow the contour path to Ndedema Gorge, about 28 km from Monk's Cowl Forest Station. This is a strenuous walk, however, which takes you through two river valleys with long downhills followed by steep ascents. Some 400 m in altitude are lost over the 4 km to Ndedema Gorge. This fascinating area is described in more detail in the following chapter.

*The pineapple flower takes its name from its resemblance to a pineapple*

If you are interested in rock art Eland Cave is well worth visiting. The cave is situated in the north-western part of Mdedelelo but is not indicated on the map and you will have to obtain the necessary directions from the forester at Monk's Cowl. The cave takes its name from the group of eland near the centre of the frieze, which contains more than a thousand individual paintings. A large eland, measuring nearly 1 m in length, was superimposed upon human figures, as well as a roan — an animal rarely portrayed in rock paintings. Other subjects include bushpig, running human figures, two mythological figures that resemble winged buck, and what has been suggested to portray a beehive with bees.

# 16 Cathedral Peak Backpacking Area

Centuries ago large numbers of San (Bushmen) inhabited the Cathedral Peak area, and depicted their lifestyle in the numerous rock shelters. In more recent times Cathedral Peak, with its numerous free-standing peaks and magnificent mountain scenery, has become one of the most favoured parts of the Berg for backpacking and rock-climbing. Popular routes include the spire-like Cathedral Peak, from which the area takes its name, the Organ Pipes and Ndedema Gorge.

### Location

The area is bordered in the north and north-west by the Upper Tugela Location and in the south by the Mdedelelo Wilderness Area. Approaching from Bergville, turn right onto the road signposted Cathedral Peak shortly after crossing the Tugela River, east of Bergville. About 14 km on turn right again, continuing for about 30 km to the forest station and campsite. The Cathedral Peak Hotel is situated a short distance on.

### Distance and Classification

You have a choice of roughly 120 km of footpaths (including the section marked as Mlambonja Wilderness Area, north and north-west of Cathedral Peak Forest Station). Distance and classification depend on the route chosen.

### Permits

Groups are restricted to a maximum of 12 people. As the number of groups permitted into the area is also restricted, it is advisable to obtain a permit in advance. Permits can be obtained from The Forester, Cathedral Peak Forest Station, Private Bag X1, Winterton 3340, Telephone (03682) 3621.

### Maps

The area is covered by map 2 in the Drakensberg Recreational Series: Drakensberg North — Cathedral Peak to Injasuti.

### Climate

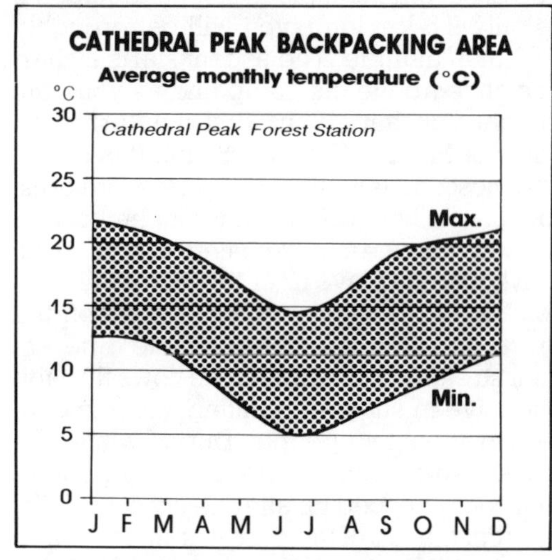


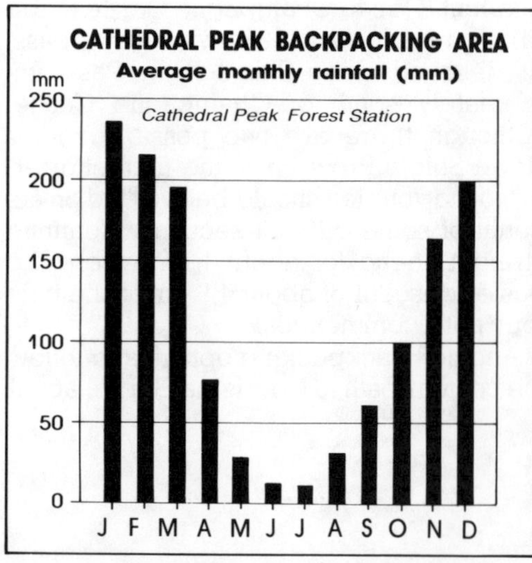

**Relevant Information**

- It is *essential* to refer to the General Rules of Access to Drakensberg Areas dealt with on pages 154-156.

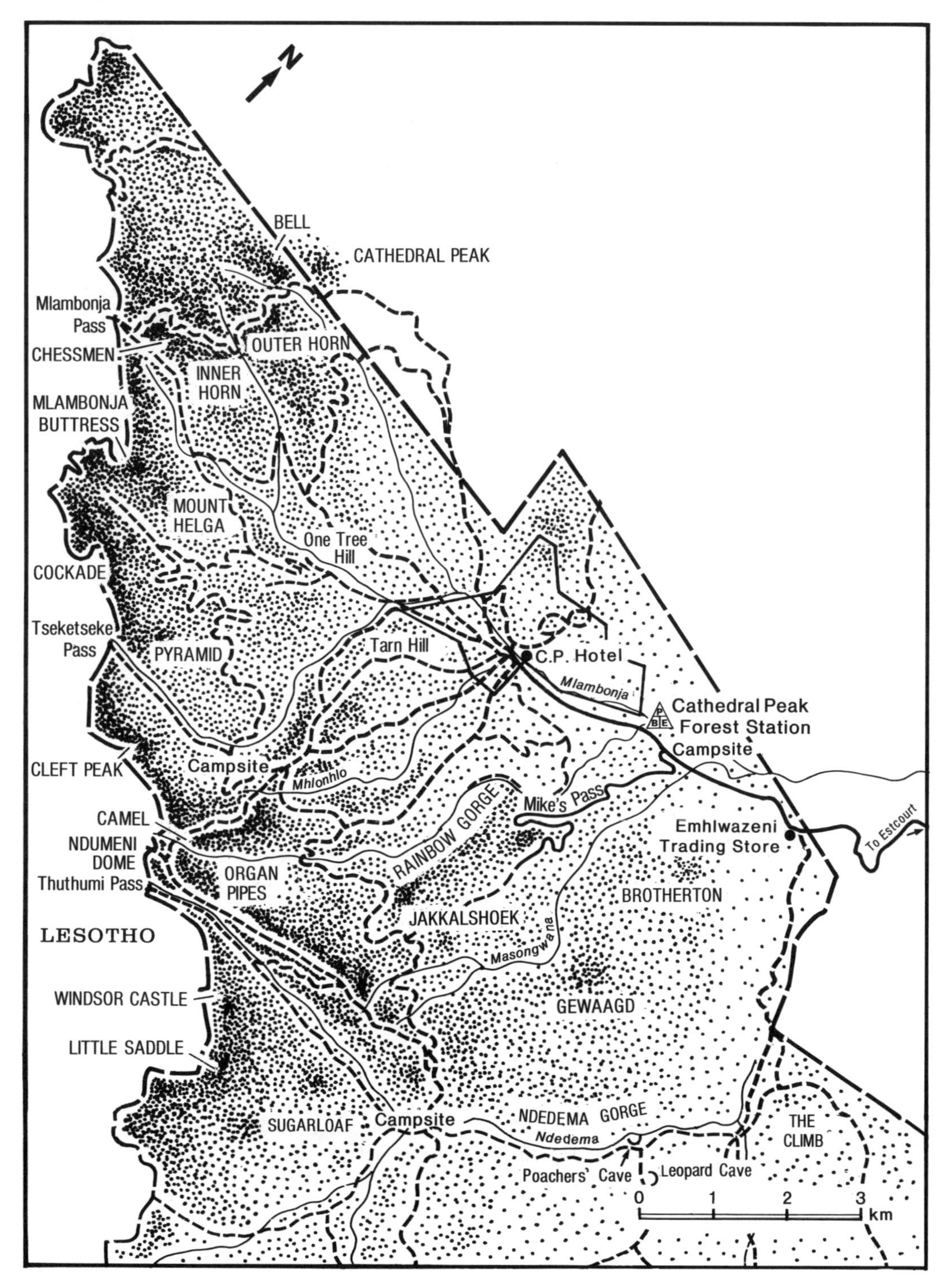


*Cathedral Peak Backpacking Area*

- The mountain register point is at Mike's Pass Gate near the Cathedral Peak Forest Station.

## Facilities

Campsites with ablution facilities are situated a short distance below the forest station.

Backpackers may reserve the exclusive use of the following shelters upon arrival: Ndumeni (4), Barker's Chalet and Bell (5), Ribbon Falls (6), Schoongezicht, Xeni, Zunkels, Drip and Leopard (8), Sherman's and Outer Horn (10) and Twins (12) caves. (The maximum number of visitors who may occupy each shelter is indicated in brackets.) Refer to page 156 for conditions applying to the occupation of caves.

## Flora, Fauna, History and Geology

For information regarding the flora, fauna, history and geology of the area, refer to the introduction to the Natal Drakensberg on page 147.

## Trail Synopsis

The scenery of this area is dominated by the massive Cathedral range, also known as the Ridge of the Horns. This 4 km-long row of free-standing peaks includes some of the most spectacular peaks in South Africa, such as Cathedral Peak (3 004 m), Bell (2 930 m), Outer Horn (3 005 m), Inner Horn (3 005 m) and the Chessmen. Two other well-known spectacular free-standing peaks, the Column (2 926 m) and Pyramid (2 914 m), are situated south-west of Cathedral Peak Forest Station.

The peaks of the escarpment here are all over 3 000 m and include the Ndumeni Dome (3 206 m), Castle Buttress (3 053 m), Cleft Peak (3 281 m), Cockade (3 161 m), Elephant (3 109 m) and Mlambonja Buttress (3 007 m). Access to the escarpment is via any of a number of passes, the most popular being the Organ Pipes, Camel and Thuthumi passes.

One of the most popular excursions in this part of the Berg is an ascent of Cathedral Peak. Approximately eight to nine hours should be allowed for this fairly strenuous

*Sebayeni Cave is renowned for its rock paintings*

*Bark, fruit and male catkins of (above) the common Yellowwood (Podocarpus falcatus) and (below) the real yellowwood (P. latifolius)*

route, which starts at the Cathedral Peak Hotel. The round trip covers approximately 18 km. The final section involves a C grade scramble and is, therefore, not recommended for inexperienced backpackers. On a clear day the view from the peak is magnificent, with Cathkin Peak in the south and Eastern Buttress in the north clearly visible. Immediately below you, to the south-east, the scenery is dominated by the deep valley carved by the Mlambonja River.

Cathedral Peak is the only area where you can drive to the top of the Little Berg, bringing you much closer to the escarpment. Access to the Little Berg is via Mike's Pass, a 10,5 km-long jeep track that was built between 1947 and 1949 by an Italian road construction engineer, G R Monzali. The pass, which climbs some 500 m, ends at the Arendsig Gate and was named after Mike de Villiers, the forestry research officer at the time, who played a major role in establishing the research station and in having the pass built. The Arendsig Gate is the starting point of routes to the renowned Ndedema Gorge, the Organ Pipes and the escarpment.

The head of the Ndedema Valley is about 10 km from the Arendsig Gate along easy terrain. The gorge has been described by the international authority on rock art, Harald Pager, as the richest rock art area in the world. During his survey of the area, Pager recorded over 3 900 individual rock paintings in 17 shelters and published his research findings and life-like tracings in the classical work, *Ndedema*.[1]

1 Pager, H. 1971. *Ndedema — A Documentation of the Rock Paintings of Ndedema Gorge.* Graz, Austria: Akademische Druck-u Verlagsanstalt,

Sebayeni Cave is the first shelter in the sandstone band on the southern side of the valley. It is the largest of the painted shelters in the gorge, containing more than 1 100 individual paintings, a large number of which have unfortunately faded. The site was first discovered by the Frobenius expedition in 1929 but was 'lost' for a number of years before being re-discovered by Alex Willcox, another authority on the rock art of South Africa.

One of the most interesting scenes in the shelter is that of 30 antelope-headed figures. Initially it was fancifully believed that they represented 'foreigners' from the Mediterranean, but according to Willcox there is '... no reason to suppose that the people are not San (Bushmen) wearing their well-known hunting disguise.'[2] Several hundred human figures are also depicted, including running figures, most of them with bows, a row of women overlaid by a white animal and two strange beings with animal ears. The right-hand figure appears to have a tail, while the large object attached to the left-hand figure is thought to be a tail swung around or a flapping apron.

Ndedema means 'place of reverberations', a likely reference to the thundering noise caused by the river when in flood. A footpath follows the upper edge of the gorge for about 5 km, giving you splendid views of the extensive yellowwood (*Podocarpus* spp.) forests on the south-facing slope. The footpath then descends into the forest and in this vicinity there are two shelters — Poacher's Cave and Leopard Cave — with rock paintings where backpackers may overnight.

Poacher's Cave on the southern slopes of the gorge contains more than 200 individual paintings and is one of the few shelters in the Berg depicting reclining rhebok. Other paintings include a swarm of bees, some of them in two colours, and numerous human figures in various poses, including a hunting scene.

The turnoff to Leopard Cave, which can sleep about 12 people, is reached shortly before you start descending into Ndedema Gorge. After turning right you continue for about 1 km before reaching the cave, which faces south-west. The cave takes its name from a painting which depicts a man being chased by a cat-like figure, presumably a leopard. There are well over 100 paintings, mainly of human figures but also of eland, bushbuck and rhebok, but unfortunately they are mainly fragmentary.

Another popular route is to ascend the escarpment via the Organ Pipes Pass, the start of which is signposted some 2,5 km before you reach Ndedema Gorge. Over the following 6,5 km you will gain more than 900 m in altitude, passing an assembly of spires and buttresses known to the Zulu as Qolo la Masoja, the Ridge of the Soldiers. According to Pearse[3] the name could be a reference to the fluted columns which conjure up visions of a regiment of soldiers standing to attention, or may be derived from a tradition which associated it with military action. The columns cause echoes when you shout or yodel and this natural phenomenon is said to have been used to maintain contact between the Zulu and the Basotho.

---

2 Willcox, A.R. 1984. *The Drakensberg Bushmen and their Art.* Winterton: Drakensberg Publicity Association, 89.

3 Pearse, R.O. 1973. *Barrier of Spears — Drama of the Drakensberg.* Cape Town: Howard Timmins, 124.

# 17 Royal Natal Backpacking Area

The Amphitheatre, Mont-aux-Sources, Tugela Falls and the Tugela Tunnel and Gorge are some of the well-known features in the northern part of the Natal Drakensberg. The Natal Parks Board maintains a network of approximately 100 km of paths in the Royal Natal National Park and although these routes are all day-walks, it is possible to plan an overnight route to the top of the Amphitheatre (this is outside of the park).

### Location

The park is situated in the northern Natal Drakensberg and from the north is approached via Harrismith and Oliviershoek Pass — 72 km along a tarred road. Approaching from the south on the N3, turn at the Frere intersection onto the R615 to Winterton and Bergville. From Bergville it is a further 45 km to the Royal Natal National Park.

### Distance and Classification

Mahai campsite to the Amphitheatre via chain ladders: 20 km one way, C grade. Car park to Amphitheatre via chain ladders: 5 km one way, B grade 2 days or longer.

### Permits

Your entry permit, obtained at the entrance gate to the park, allows you to explore the park. No additional permits are required at present to hike in Qwa-Qwa, which controls access to the Amphitheatre as it falls within the homeland, but as this may change in future you should make enquiries at the Witsieshoek Mountain Resort.

### Maps

The area is covered by map 1 of the Drakensberg Recreational Series: Drakensberg North — Mt. Aux Sources to Cathedral Peak.

### Relevant Information

- It is *essential* to read the General Rules of Access to the Drakensberg discussed on pages 154-156.
- The mountain register point is at the warden's office in the park. Backpackers must also sign the register at the hut at the end of the Mountain Road.
- You are advised to take precautions against thieving, especially on or near the escarpment. Some of the caves, such as Crow's Nest Cave, are particularly vulnerable to thieving.
- In the park you may not overnight wherever you choose and have to return to the base camps. However, the Amphitheatre is out of the park and you may pitch camp anywhere. Although there are caves, it is advisable to take a tent as these may be occupied. The caves cannot be reserved and permits are not required.

### Facilities

Accommodation in the Royal Natal National Park consists of bungalows and cottages at Tendele hutted camp, the Royal Natal National Park Hotel and the Mahai and Rugged Glen campsites.

The bungalows and cottages are completely self-contained and a cook is assigned to each bungalow/cottage. Visitors must provide their own food and drink.

Reservations should be made with the Director, Natal Parks Board, P O Box 662, Pietermaritzburg 3200, Telephone (0331) 471981.

Enquiries for reservations at the Royal Natal National Park Hotel, which is a private operation, should be addressed to the Lessee, Royal Natal National Park, P O Mont-aux-Sources 3353, Telephone (03642) Mont-aux-Sources 1.

Reservations for the Mahai and Rugged Glen campsites are made through the Camp Superintendent, P O Mont-aux-Sources 3353, Telephone (03642) Mont-aux-Sources 3.

Facilities at the Witsieshoek Mountain Resort include chalets and a restaurant. A mountain hut at the end of the Mountain Road offers accommodation on a first-come, first-served basis (reservations are not accepted). Sentinel Cave near the summit can accommodate upwards of 12 people, while Crow's Nest Cave can accommodate 6-8 people.

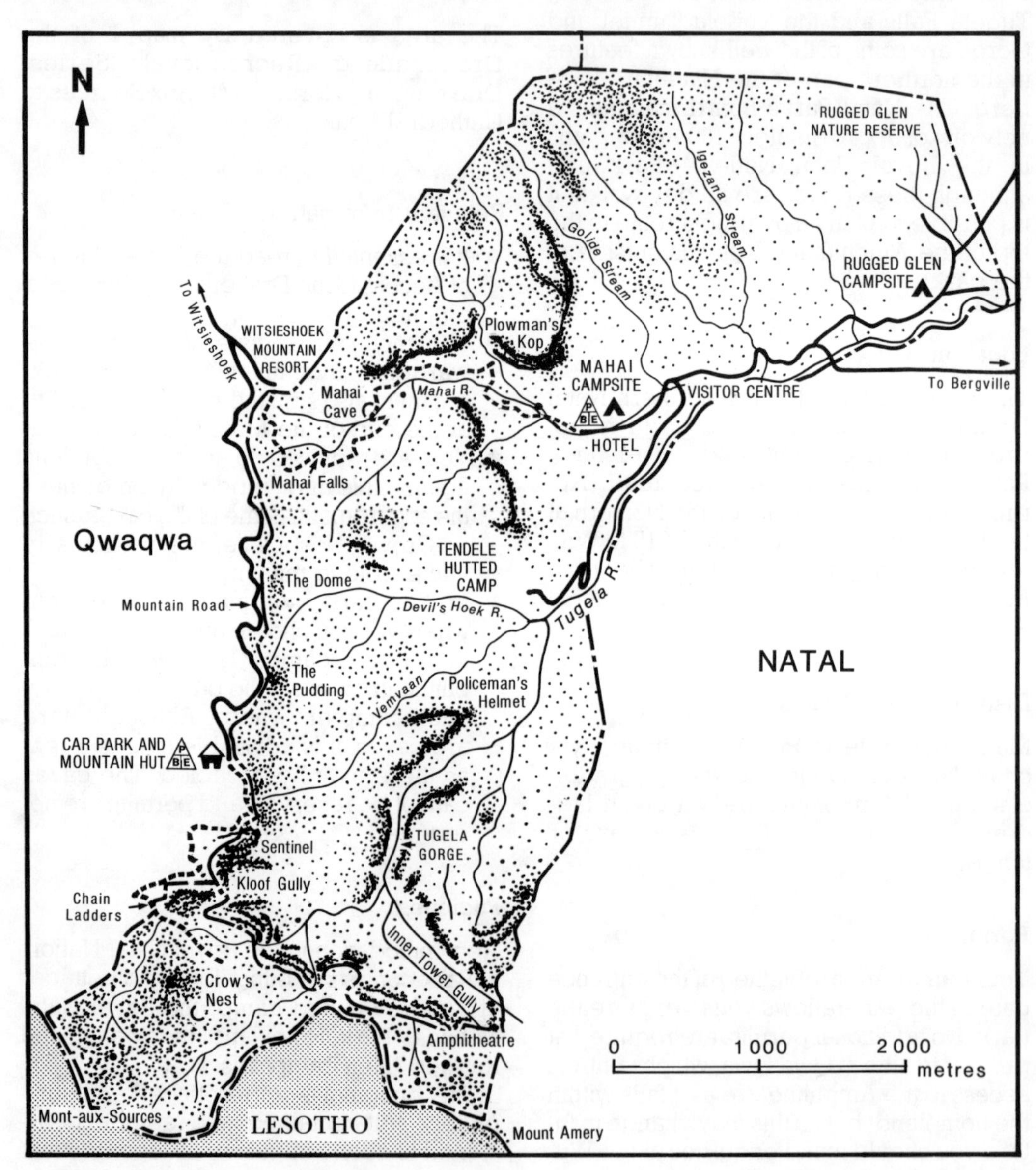


*Royal Natal Backpacking Area*

### Climate, Flora, Fauna and Geology

Please refer to the introduction to the Natal Drakensberg on page 147 where these are discussed.

*Growth form of Natal bottlebrush*

*Leaf and flower of Natal bottlebrush*

### History

The general history of the Drakensberg is described in detail in the introduction to the Natal Drakensberg on page 152 and only the local history is outlined here.

Like the rest of the Drakensberg, the region was inhabited by the San (Bushmen) who hunted here for thousands of years. As a result of poor rock surfaces and the lack of suitable shelters there are generally fewer paintings in this part of the Drakensberg than further south. The San were known to have survived in the area as late as 1878 and this was probably one of the last surviving groups of Drakensberg San.

Much of the present park was offered for sale as farms in the early 1880s. The idea of establishing a park was conceived in 1908 when the area was explored by Senator Frank Churchill, Colonel (later General) Jas S Wylie, Colonel Dick and Mr W O Coventry. It was not until eight years later, in 1916, that the park came into being when the Secretary of Lands authorised the reservation of five farms and certain state land totalling about 3 300 ha. In 1942 the Advisory Committee that had been appointed in 1916 to control the park was abolished and its administration passed into the hands of the Natal Provincial Administration, until the formation of the Natal Parks, Game and Fish Preservation Board on 1 December 1947. In the same year the park had the distinction of being visited by the British royal family during their tour of South Africa.

Although referred to as the Royal Natal *National* Park, it is not a national park in terms of the National Parks Act.

### Trail Synopsis

Described here is the original access route to Mont-aux-Sources before the Mountain Road leading to the base of the Sentinel was built.

### Day 1: Mahai Campsite to the Amphitheatre

It is about 20 km from the park to the chain ladders, with a gain of 1 500 m in altitude. The route should therefore not be attempted by the unfit, who are advised to start from the car park at the end of the Mountain Road.

Setting off from the Mahai campsite, the route leads past the trout hatchery to Lookout Rock and you then continue for about 500 m to Gudu Bush. Shortly before crossing the Igudu River, the path branches off to the left. You continue for about 700 m up the valley before the turnoff to The Crack is passed. Ignore the turnoff on your right and continue straight ahead to reach the Mahai Cave about 2 km on. In years gone by this used to be a popular overnight spot with mountaineers. The cave can accommodate 12 people, and sleeping is permitted here.

A short distance past the cave you cross the Mahai River and shortly afterwards the trail splits, with the path to the left being the route to The Nek. As a result of erosion this path has been closed and you must follow the right-hand path to Basuto Gate. The Mahai Falls are reached about 1 km from the split and from this point it is only about 2 km to Basuto Gate and the Witzieshoek Mountain Resort. The total distance covered to the resort is about 7 km and provided you have made an early start you could stop here for a tea break. Bearded vulture (119) are frequently seen in the vicinity, so keep your binoculars handy.

From the resort it is advisable to take a short-cut over the ridge, where you join the Mountain Road. This is followed for about 7 to 8 km to the car park at the base of the Sentinel (3 165 m). Leaving the car park the path zigzags uphill and you pass the Witches, from where you have a magnificent view of Eastern Buttress (3 047 m) and the Devil's Tooth (3 019 m). The contour path at the foot of the Sentinel is reached after gaining some 300 m in altitude and is followed below Western Buttress (3 121 m).

At Kloof Gully there is a steep, rocky route which leads to Beacon Buttress (2 899 m) on the escarpment, providing an alternative route for those wishing to avoid the chain ladders about 1 km on. However, in winter Kloof Gully is often impassible as it can be blocked with snow and ice. In the early days this was the usual way to the top and climbers often slept in Sentinel Cave, a short way beyond the gully. The cave faces north-west and offers good shelter, although it can be damp at times. It can accommodate about 12 people and you may overnight here as the cave is outside the park. In summer water can be obtained from seepage in the roof.

Two chain ladders, constructed in 1930 by the Natal Section of the Mountain Club of South Africa and the Natal Parks Board, provide access to the summit. The first ladder scales near vertical cliffs and has approximately 50 rungs over about 17 m. This is followed by a second ladder of approximately 45 rungs over about 13 m.

From the top of the ladders it is about 1,5

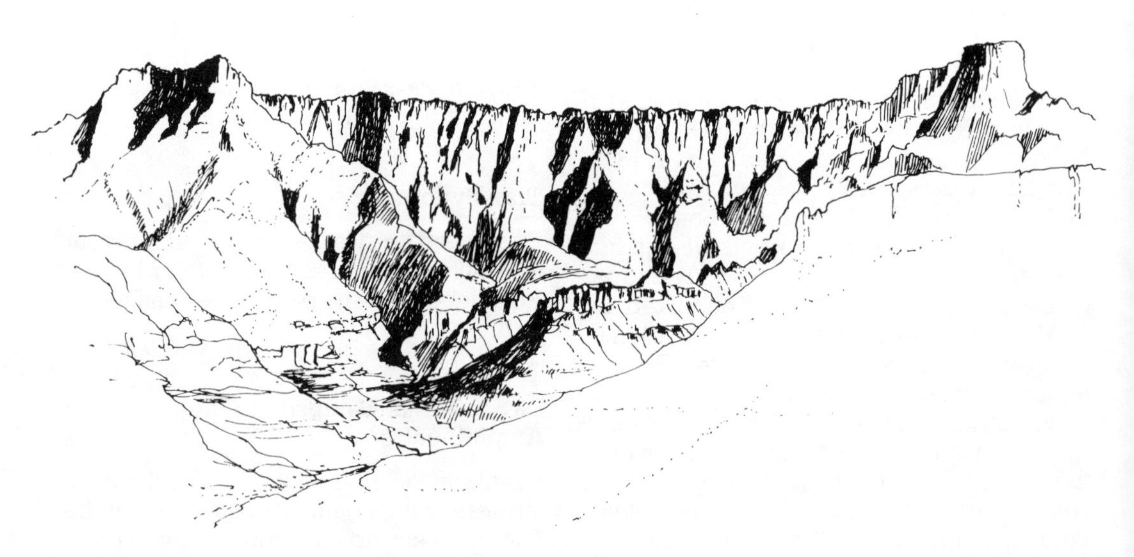

*The Amphitheatre in Royal Natal National Park*

km to the escarpment edge, with the Tugela River crossed *en route*. It is difficult to believe that the Tugela is one of South Africa's major rivers, as it is a mere trickle where you cross it. The meaning of the name is obscure but has been interpreted as 'the startling one', 'the astonishing one' or 'a river that acts with frightening suddenness'.

The Amphitheatre is one of the world's most spectacular examples of the forces of nature and it is still being eroded at an estimated rate of 1 m every 300 years. Stretching for 8 km between the Sentinel in the west and Eastern Buttress in the east, the basalt wall rises more than 1 500 m above the foothills of the Berg. From the Amphitheatre the Tugela Falls, reputed to be among the highest in the world, can be seen plunging 853 m in five gigantic leaps. During winter the upper few hundred metres are sometimes frozen into long columns of ice.

On the escarpment you can sleep in a few small rock shelters behind the Natal Mountain Club hut ruin and in Crow's Nest Cave, which can accommodate six to eight people. The cave is situated about 1 km southwest of the ruin and probably received the name because mountaineers used it as a vantage point.

### Day 2: Exploring the Amphitheatre

There are several peaks on the escarpment that can be reached on foot from the summit plateau. These include Mount Amery, Western Buttress and Mont-aux-Sources itself.

The Natal Mountain Club hut ruin is an important landmark on the escarpment. The hut was erected in 1929 by Otto Zunkel, who took over the lease of the old hostel in the park in 1926. His son, Walter, who succeeded him, also helped with the construction of the hut and all the material, except the stone, was carried from the Royal Natal National Park. Unfortunately the hut was plundered continuously and as a result of disputes over the ownership of the land on which it stood, the hut was totally neglected after it burned down in December 1975. The area is not under the control of the Natal Parks Board at present, but negotiations are in progress for the Board to obtain some form of control over the summit. The Board hopes, in time, to re-roof the MCSA hut.

Mount Amery, another well-known landmark, is situated about 5 km south-east of the ruin and offers a fine view of the distant Berg peaks and Singati Valley to the east.

Mont-aux-Sources (3 282 m) is the highest point of the Amphitheatre and is situated about 4 km south-west of the ruin. It is reached by following the Tugela River upstream to its source and then to the beacon which marks the boundary between Lesotho, Natal and Qwa-Qwa.

The summit was first ascended in 1830 by two French Protestant missionaries, Thomas Arbousset and François Daumas, while they were exploring the highlands of Lesotho. Realising the importance of the peak as the source of five major rivers, they named it 'Mountain of Sources'. The Bilanjil and Tugela rivers flow into Natal, the Western and Eastern Khubedu form the upper source of the Orange River and the Elands River which flows into Qwa-Qwa is seen tumbling over a precipice near the chain ladders.

### Day 3: Amphitheatre to Mahai Campsite

Once you have finished exploring the area or your time has run out, you return to the Royal Natal National Park along the same route followed on Day 1.

### DON'T MISS

- the picturesque Tunnel and Gorge Walk. Although it is only 10 km long, you are advised to make the most of it by setting at least half a day aside. The walk takes you past one of the best-known landmarks in the northern Berg, the Policeman's Helmet. As recently as 1978 a *Protea* species, *P. nubigena*, was discovered on a south-east-facing cliff above Policeman's Helmet ridge. The species name *nubigena* means 'born in the clouds', an apt reference to the high altitude (2 300 m) at which this species grows. It grows as a multi-branched shrub, reaching heights of between 30 and 50 cm, and only two populations are known to occur in the park.

- Otto's Walk. This short (2,6 km) self-guided walk starts close to the visitor's centre. Several interesting features marked along the route are described in a booklet available at the starting point. Your appreciation and understanding of the Drakensberg will be considerably enhanced by doing this walk before setting off on the overnight route.
- several other walks. Details of the walks available are contained in a booklet that can be purchased at the visitors' centre. In addition the ranger/naturalist of the park conducts educational walks to the more popular areas of the park, details of which can also be obtained from the visitors' centre.
- horse rides. These take place three times daily from the stables at Rugged Glen. Information can be obtained from the notice board at the visitors' centre.
- the trout hatchery. It is beyond the Mahai campsite and a nominal admission fee is payable. Full details about trout fishing in the park can be obtained from the hatchery supervisor.

# 18 Ntendeka Backpacking Area

Ntendeka — the Place of Precipitous Heights — is a wonder-world of spectacular cliffs, tropical indigenous forests, lowland grassland and highland savanna grassland. Although it lacks an extensive trail network, several bridle paths established by the early inhabitants of the area lead into the forest, which has been described as the most beautiful in Zululand. The forest is the habitat of rare and beautiful epiphytic orchids and ferns, as well as colourful bird species. Ntendeka is the smallest of South Africa's wilderness areas and was proclaimed in 1975.

### Location

The Ntendeka Wilderness Area in northern Natal was originally a portion of Ngome State Forest, which after the consolidation of KwaZulu remained under the control of the Forestry Branch.

Approaching from Vryheid, take the Louwsburg road (R69) and after about 27 km turn right onto the R618 signposted to Nongoma. Continue until a signpost indicates that it is 40 km to Nongoma and just after this turn right, at the Ngome signboard. The office is about 600 m on.

### Distance and Classification

25 km of footpaths in total. Various options are possible, but visitors must ensure that they are back at the campsite by nightfall as camping is not permitted in the wilderness area.
A and B grade

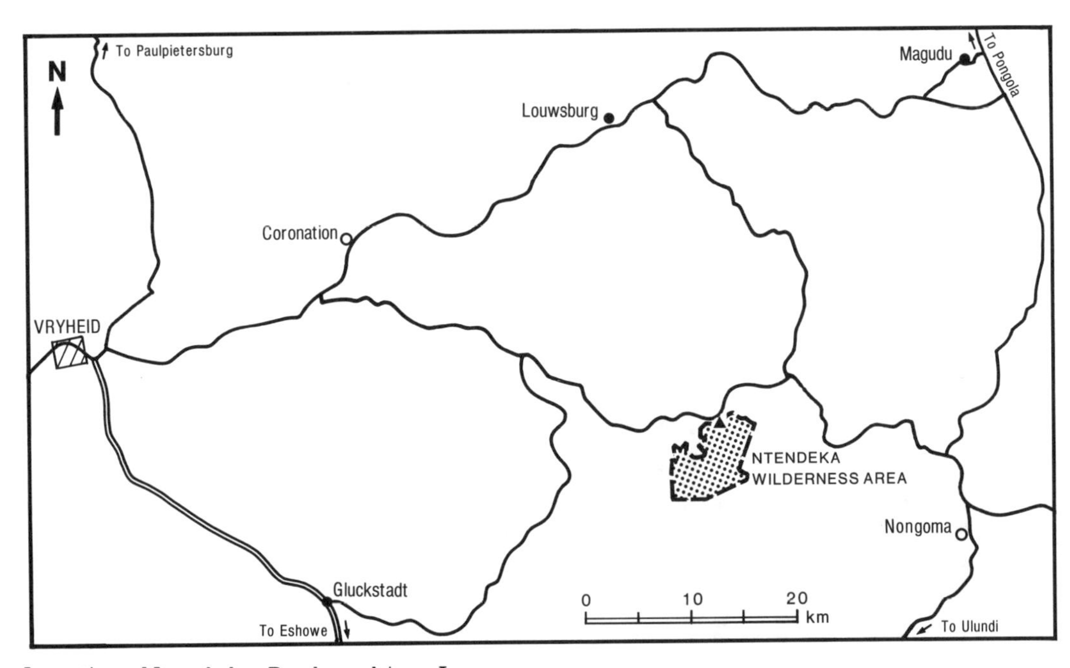


*Location: Ntendeka Backpacking Area*

### Permits

Permits can be obtained from The Forester, Private Bag X9306, Vryheid 3100, Telephone (0386) 883. The maximum group size is 12 and no more than 25 people are allowed in the wilderness area per day.

### Maps

A sketch map of the area is available but serves only to orientate you and it is advisable to obtain the 1:50 000 topographical map section 2731CD.

### Climate

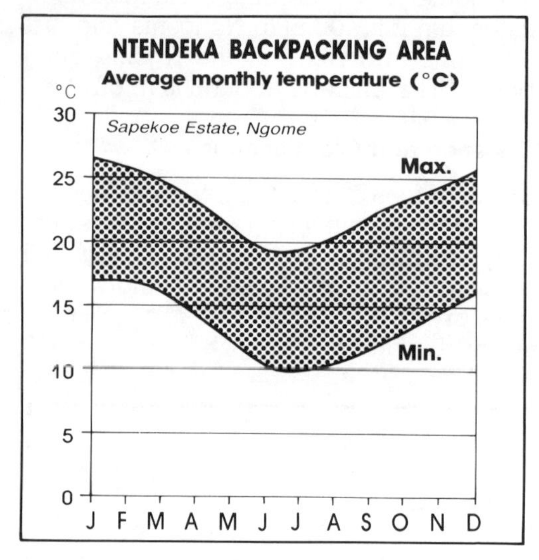


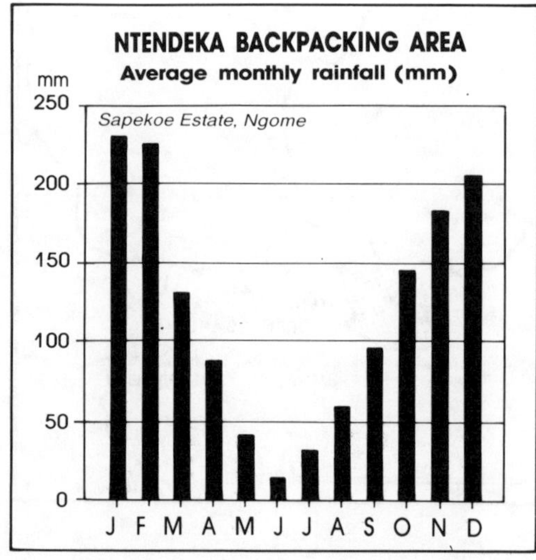


### Relevant Information

- Fires are permitted at the campsite near the forest station but nowhere else in the wilderness area.

### Facilities

A campsite has been provided near the forest station. It is situated in an indigenous forest and fireplaces, firewood, water and ablutions are available. Camping is not permitted in the wilderness area.

### Flora

Ngome forest has a rich, tropical atmosphere and is classified by Acocks as Inland Tropical Forest of the North Eastern Mountain Sourveld (Veld Type 8). The vegetation consists of indigenous forest, which covers about 2 636 ha, and highland grassland and lowland savanna grasslands, which cover approximately 2 594 ha.

South of Ngome the tropical forest types are confined mainly to the coastal belt, but extensive patches have survived from Ngome northwards to Louwsberg, the mountains of Swaziland, the mountains south and west of Barberton, the Transvaal Drakensberg and continuing to the Soutpansberg.

To date some 89 tree and shrub species have been identified and a provisional list of shrubs and trees is appended to a pamphlet on Ntendeka available from the forest station. The six most common large forest species are the myrtle quince (115), knobwood (254), red currant (380), forest bushwillow (540), forest waterwood (556) and the forest silver oak (731). Other typical forest species that you are likely to notice include both the Outeniqua yellowwood (16) and the real yellowwood (18), lemonwood (111) and the tree fuchsia (670).

An interesting species is the Terblanz beech (*Faurea macnaughtonii*) (74), which is widely distributed in small, isolated areas from the Transvaal to Knysna in the Cape as well as in Tanzania and Madagascar. In South Africa the genus *Faurea,* a member of the family Proteaceae, is represented by four species. This tall tree (20 to 25 m high) with its hard, attractive pale brown to dark red wood was overlooked by early woodcutters and first worked by a certain Terblanz, hence the common name.

The forest is the habitat of more than 60 fern species, many of which are rarely found elsewhere in South Africa. One of the most striking of these is *Didymochlaena truncatula*, a large fern with fronds of up to 2,5 m in length. This species, with its beautiful dark green, glossy fronds, is common throughout Ngome in wet, shady ravines. Another species you will most certainly notice is the forest tree fern (2) which reaches heights of over 8 m here. Although this species is also common in the southern Cape forests, it does not reach the same size there as it does in the Ngome Forest.

Several endophytic ferns are found on moss-covered rocks and in the humus of tree forks of Ngome Forest. They are always associated with warm, moist (tropical) climates and the Ngome Forest provides an ideal habitat for a large number of species. They differ from epiphytic orchids, which are common on the trunks or branches of trees, in that the roots of the endophytic fern actually draw all their moisture and nutrients from the bark and mosses of the host, while the epiphytic fern draws no nourishment from its host. Consequently, endophytic ferns will wilt during dry periods as no water is stored in the bark of trees.

Epiphytic orchids have roots which are entirely aerial, absorbing moisture from the atmosphere with a specialised structure to cope with dry periods. To date more than 42 species have been discovered in Southern Africa south of the Limpopo River. The greatest concentration is found in Zululand, which boasts no less than 32 species. Some 19 species are distributed in the Eshowe, Nkandla, Ngotshe and Hlabisa magisterial districts.

In Southern Africa epiphytic orchids are divided into three groups, namely *Polystachyinae, Bulbophyllinae* and *Sarcanthinae. Polystachya cultriformis* was originally named *Polystachya gerrardii* after Mr W T Gerrard, who first discovered the species at Ngome in the nineteenth century. It is the only South African species in the genus with a solitary leaf at the apex of the tall pseudobulbs. If you are in the area between November and February, keep a lookout for the yellow-green flowers of this species.

*Fruit and leaves of knobwood*

*Close-up of stem of knobwood*

Another species that was first discovered in the Ngome Forest is *P. fusiformis*, which you are most likely to see attached to cabbage trees (*Cussonia* spp.). You can identify it by the spindle-shaped pseudobulbs which vary between 8 and 18 cm in length and are less than 1 mm in diameter. Small olive-green flowers appear from October to December. Although this species is widespread elsewhere in Africa and in Madagascar, in South Africa it is restricted to the cool, moist forests of the Ngotshe district and a few areas of the highland forest in the eastern Transvaal.

The giant-leaved *Streptocarpus candidus* is found near water in the lower forest. Also found in the forest is the Ngome lily (*Crinum moorei*) and *Clivea miniata. C. moorei* and

*S. candidus* are endemic to the area. Be on the lookout for *Aloe suprafoliata*, which grows on the exposed sandstone pavements near the edge of the forest.

The forest is replaced on the mountain tops by sour grassland, comprising redgrass (*Themeda triandra*), russet grass (*Loudetia simplex*), *Tristachya leucothrix* and others. In open area of short grass you may see *Scilla natalensis*, with its tiny pale blue flowers borne on a long stem, *S. nervosa*, which is smaller with a greenish-white flower, and *Brunsvigia radulosa*. Other species to look out for are the attractive *Erica cerinthoides* with its coral and white tubular flower, the common tree fern (1) which grows along watercourses in open grassland and the Natal bottlebrush (446), which is especially common on the top of the Ntendeka cliffs. Three *Protea* species occur, namely the common sugarbush (87), African white sugarbush (89) and the silver sugarbush (96).

The savanna vegetation of the warmer, dry valleys includes sweet thorn (172), ankle thorn (183), the common coral tree (245), which favours termitaria, buffalo-thorn (447) and magic guarri (595). Grass species found here include redgrass (*Themeda triandra*), broad-leaved turpentine grass (*Cymbopogon caesius*) and *Eragrostis capensis*.

## Fauna

No detailed survey of the fauna has been completed to date but three of the mammals recorded in the area are listed in the *South African Red Data Book — Terrestrial Mammals* as rare. They are the red duiker, blue duiker and the samango monkey.

Because of its shy and secretive nature and its mainly nocturnal habits, you are unlikely to observe the red duiker. It is a browser, feeding on fruit, seed pods and leaves. This species only occurs where water is available and has been recorded in riverine forests, thickly wooded ravines and dense coastal bush. In Southern Africa the red duiker's distribution is limited to isolated populations in the Soutpansberg and north-eastern Natal. It is thought to have once occurred as far south as Durban and perhaps even the Transkei.

If you do surprise a red duiker it will make off with a loud *tchie-tchie*. They are solitary creatures, unless it is a female with offspring, and you will only see them together in the mating season when they form temporary associations. Both the male and female have short, straight horns. The red duiker is smaller than the common duiker, with an average shoulder height of 43 cm and a mass of 14 kg. As the name implies, it is a deep chestnut red colour with the flanks and underparts a paler chestnut.

Other mammals occurring in the wilderness area include bushpig, porcupine, chacma baboon, vervet monkey, bushbuck, common duiker and caracal.

Some 190 bird species have been recorded in the wilderness area, including 32 typical forest birds and several species listed in the *South African Red Data Book — Birds*. The white stork (83), which prefers the open

*The red duiker is classified as rare and is confined to forests or dense thickets of north-eastern Natal, with isolated populations in the Soutpansberg*

grassland, is listed as rare while the bald ibis (92), which favours a similar habitat, is now out of danger. The wattled crane (207) is attracted to the moist grasslands and is one of only five species listed as endangered.

Delegorgue's pigeon (351) has also been recorded in the area and is listed as indeterminate. It occurs from the coastal forests of the eastern Cape northwards through the Transkei and Natal to the north-eastern Transvaal, and through Africa to southern Sudan. The first scientific description of the bird was published in 1847 by Delegorgue from a specimen collected near Durban. Little is known about their habits and they are seldom seen except when calling. The call has been described as a high-pitched series of 10 to 20 hoots, of which the first three are evenly pitched, the fourth louder and higher pitched and the rest falling in pitch and volume, speeding up towards the end. They occur in pairs or small groups and are usually seen perched in the tops of tall trees, except in the early morning and evening when they flap about noisily while gathering food.

Another inconspicuous forest species is the colourful Narina trogon (427), which perches motionless on high branches for long periods and only betrays its presence by its hooting call. Also be on the lookout for the purplecrested lourie (371), trumpeter hornbill (455), olive woodpecker (488), orange thrush (579) and the gorgeous bush shrike (747).

Some 17 raptor species have been recorded, including the martial eagle (140), which probably numbers fewer than 1 000 pairs in South Africa and has consequently been classified as vulnerable. Between August and April you might see Wahlberg's eagle (135), which migrates from Southern Africa northwards to tropical Africa for the winter months, while the steppe buzzard (149), a non-breeding Palaearctic migrant, occurs from October to April. Other raptors include the crowned eagle (141), forest buzzard (150) and black sparrowhawk (158).

The rocky areas are the habitat of the mountain chat (586), familiar chat (589) and the buffstreaked chat (588), which has a more limited distribution. Species to look out for in the grassland include the secretarybird (118), whitebellied korhaan (233), grassbird (661), wailing cisticola (670) and Richard's pipit (716). Both the orangethroated (727) and the yellowthroated (728) longclaw have been recorded. Amongst stands of proteas you are likely to see Gurney's sugarbird (774), malachite sunbird (775) and greater doublecollared sunbird (785).

*The martial eagle can be identified by its lightly spotted white underparts and flat crown*

Species occurring in the savanna grasslands include the grey lourie (373), brownhooded kingfisher (435), grey penduline tit (558), arrowmarked babbler (560), whitebrowed robin (613), chinspot batis (701), brubru (741) and the orangebreasted bush shrike (748).

### History

Stone implements such as arrowheads and rock paintings have confirmed inhabitation of the Natal bushveld by the last of the Later Stone Age people, the San or Bushmen. In around AD 400 they came into contact with the first wave of the southward migrating Nguni people and indications are that the two cultures initially lived side by side. Increasing competition for living space brought the two groups into conflict and during the eighteenth century the San were either absorbed into Nguni society or were driven out to the more mountainous areas.

The Nguni lived in a large number of autonomous, small-scale communities until the end of the eighteenth century, when certain clans expanded their power. One of the clans that was inevitably drawn into the conflict between the Ndwandwe and the Mthethwa was the Khumalo, who lived in the Ngome area. During this time the Zulu under Shaka began to form a powerful kingdom and Mzilikazi, chieftain of the Khumalo, submitted voluntarily to Shaka.

Mzilikazi was popular with Shaka and became an Induna of two composite Zulu regiments. However, he fell foul of Shaka when he decided to retain cattle won on a successful raiding expedition and returned with his troops to Ngome. The Ngome Forest provided a good refuge and it was only on their second attempt, when Mzilikazi was betrayed, that the Zulu were able to take revenge. After a massacre Mzilikazi escaped, regrouped the survivors of his clan and fled across the Drakensberg.

Shaka had hardly forgotten Mzilikazi when umBeje, leader of the Khumalo clan in Zululand, occupied the forest. He refused to pay tithes or to provide regiments for Shaka's army and many futile attempts were made to dislodge umBeje from his stronghold. Finally, in 1830, when Shaka was returning from a victory over the Ndwandwe in the Transvaal, a sizeable section of his army was detached and literally drove umBeje from the forest.

The forest again became a refuge in 1879. Cetshwayo, the last independent king of the Zulu, sheltered in the forest from the British for seven weeks before being surprised and defeated in the valley below Ngome Forest. According to legend, he took shelter under one of the cliffs in a rock shelter which is today known as Cetshwayo's Refuge.

Dinizulu, who with Boer aid succeeded Cetshwayo as Zulu king, gave the Ngome Forest and surrounds to the Boers. This became part of the New Republic merging with the Vryheid Republic and was eventually absorbed into the Transvaal Republic.

The forests were worked from 1876 until the outbreak of the Anglo-Boer War (1899-1902), when all work ceased. The worst exploitation took place over a period of six to seven years when about 60 woodcutters were living at Ngome. It is estimated that during this period 24 000m³ of timber was felled and sold mainly in the Vryheid area. As a result there are practically no yellowwood trees (*Podocarpus* spp.) surviving in the accessible parts of the forest. The original saw pits are still visible and their size is indicative of how large the felled trees must have been. The woodcutters had to pay a minimal monthly fee of 2/6d for a saw and they were not charged for the number of trees felled.

The first forester to Ntendeka was appointed in 1903 and the area was officially demarcated as a forest reserve in 1905. On 2 October 1975 Ntendeka became South Africa's fourth state wilderness area.

### Trail Synopsis

At 5 230 ha Ntendeka is South Africa's smallest official wilderness area and options for backpacking are not as numerous as in other areas. However, this can be to your advantage as more time is at hand to appreciate the exceptionally rich floral wealth of the area, especially in the forest.

Access to the forest is either from the office at Ngome or from the South African Police station a few kilometres west of the forest station. From these two access points you can follow any of a number of interlinking bridle paths. No set route is described here and only the highlights of the area are described. A popular route is along the 'Zulu Highway', the traditional access route between the coastal plains and the highland. The starting point is at the SAP station and soon after passing through the indigenous forest at Ntendeka Kop you will see a conspicuous stone cairn on your right. These are known in Zulu as *isiVivane* and according to custom, a traveller will always add another stone for *iNtlaka* (good luck). This custom was probably adopted from the Khoikhoi who originally marked their paths by placing stone cairns at deviations in the path and on the summits of hills and passes. At a later stage the cairns were thought to mark the grave of the Khoikhoi hero *Heitsi Eibib*. Similar customs appear to have been practised in several other countries. In Mongolia and Tibet cairns are erected to propitiate the gods and there is also evidence of the custom in England, New Zealand, Borneo and North America south to Guatemala.

In South Africa *isiVivane* occur over a wide area, but are especially common in Zululand. Among the most renowned *isiVivane* is the one on the summit of a grassy hill near Mzumbe in Natal, which is said to have been started by Shaka before he invaded Pondoland. On the road between Weenen and Muden in Natal is a cairn 6 m in diameter and 1,5 m high. In the Soutpansberg the Pedi still practise the custom along the trails their forefathers used to enter the area.

Another place of interest is Cetshwayo's Refuge, from where there are impressive views to the east over the Sikwebezi River, a tributary of the Black Umfolozi River. The shelter is at the base of the Ntendeka Cliffs which were formed when dolerite intruded the sandstones of the Ecca Group some 190-150 million years ago. Further west is one of several spectacular waterfalls that tumble over the cliffs and close by is Ntendeka hill.

While walking in the forest your attention will be drawn to the large saw pits, mentioned earlier, which bear testimony to the exploitation of the forest during the last two decades of the previous century. Another reminder of this period is a stone oven to the west of Ntendeka Hill.

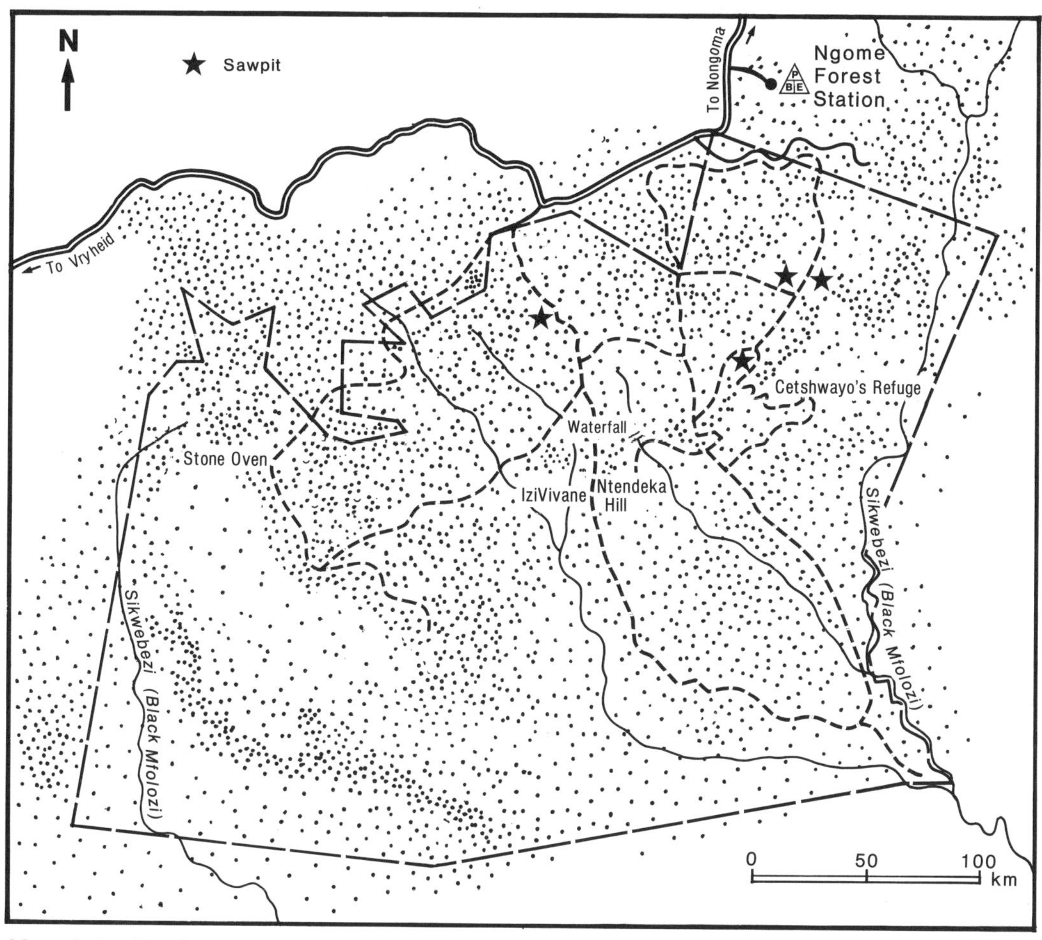


*Ntendeka Backpacking Area*

# 19 Natal Parks Board Guided Wilderness Trails

The Natal Parks Board pioneered the wilderness concept in South Africa by setting aside a portion of the Umfolozi Game Reserve as a wilderness area as early as 1958. At present the board conducts trails in five reserves under its jurisdiction, all of which are immensely popular.

Trails are conducted on foot in the Umfolozi, St Lucia, and Mkuzi game reserves, as well as the Itala Nature Reserve. There is also a horseback trail in the Giant's Castle Game Reserve. Experiences vary considerably on the various trails and a specific description is therefore not given here.

### Distance and Classification

No set distances are covered and routes are adapted to suit each group's needs. A grade, except Umfolozi Primitive Trails — B grade.

### Permits

Reservations are accepted six full calendar months in advance, although applications may be submitted nine months in advance. Reservations are made through the Reservations Officer, Natal Parks Board, P O Box 662, Pietermaritzburg 3200, Telephone (0331) 471981.

Trails on foot are limited to six people and the minimum age of trailists is 16. Groups are limited to eight on the Giant's Castle horse trail and the minimum age is 12.

### Relevant Information

- You are required to bring your own food and personal requirements. All necessary trailing equipment (daypacks, kitbags, sleeping-bags, blankets, groundsheets, stretchers, tents and cooking and eating utensils) is provided by the board. Riding equipment is provided on the Giant's Castle horseback trail.
- Although the choice of food is left to the individual, you are generally asked to pool supplies to make the preparation of meals easier. About 1 kg of food should be allowed per person per day. Where possible, perishables should be avoided on trails where there are no refrigeration facilities and fresh meat should be brought for your first night only. The number of meals to be catered for varies according to the trail and is mentioned in the description of each trail.
- Personal toiletries and clothing should be kept to a minimum and footwear should be comfortable, light, sturdy and well worn-in.
- Precautions against malaria are essential on all the trails except the Giant's Castle Game Reserve Horseback Trail.
- Precautions against ticks are essential on all the trails.
- Game spotting and bird-watching are an integral part of all the trails included in this section, making it advisable for you to take binoculars.
- You are required to sign an indemnity form before departing on a trail, while minors must have the written consent of their parents or legal guardian.
- Information relevant only to a particular trail is included under **Trail Information** in the description of that trail.

Each of the five areas in which the Natal Parks Board conducts guided wilderness trails is discussed individually on the following pages. As these are *guided* wilderness trails, your guide will be at hand to broaden your knowledge or highlight any particularly interesting aspect of the area you are walking through.

## UMFOLOZI GAME RESERVE

### Location

The reserve is about 270 km north of Durban in the Zululand area. The turnoff to the reserve is signposted 3 km north of the Mtubatuba turnoff on the N2. Turn left onto the Nongoma Road (R618) and continue for about 24 km before turning left onto the road signposted Umfolozi Game Reserve. Mambeni Gate, the eastern gate to the reserve, is reached about 5 km further and you will reach Masinda Camp 7 km on.

### Trail Information

- Trails are conducted between March and November.
- Facilities consist of four wilderness trail camps and a trails base camp.
- You must arrive in the reserve by 15h30 on the date indicated on your reservation voucher and report to the camp superintendent at Masinda Camp, who will direct you to the base camp.
- The first night is spent in the base camp, followed by two nights in the wilderness. The last night at the base camp is optional.
- You must cater for two suppers and two breakfasts at the base camp, where mass and bulk are not important and as refrigerators are provided here, fresh meat can be kept. On the trail two breakfasts, three light snack lunches and two suppers must be provided for. Food is transported between the trail camps in pack saddles by donkeys.
- On the trail you need carry only your camera and binoculars, while the responsibility of carrying water and the day's lunch is shared.

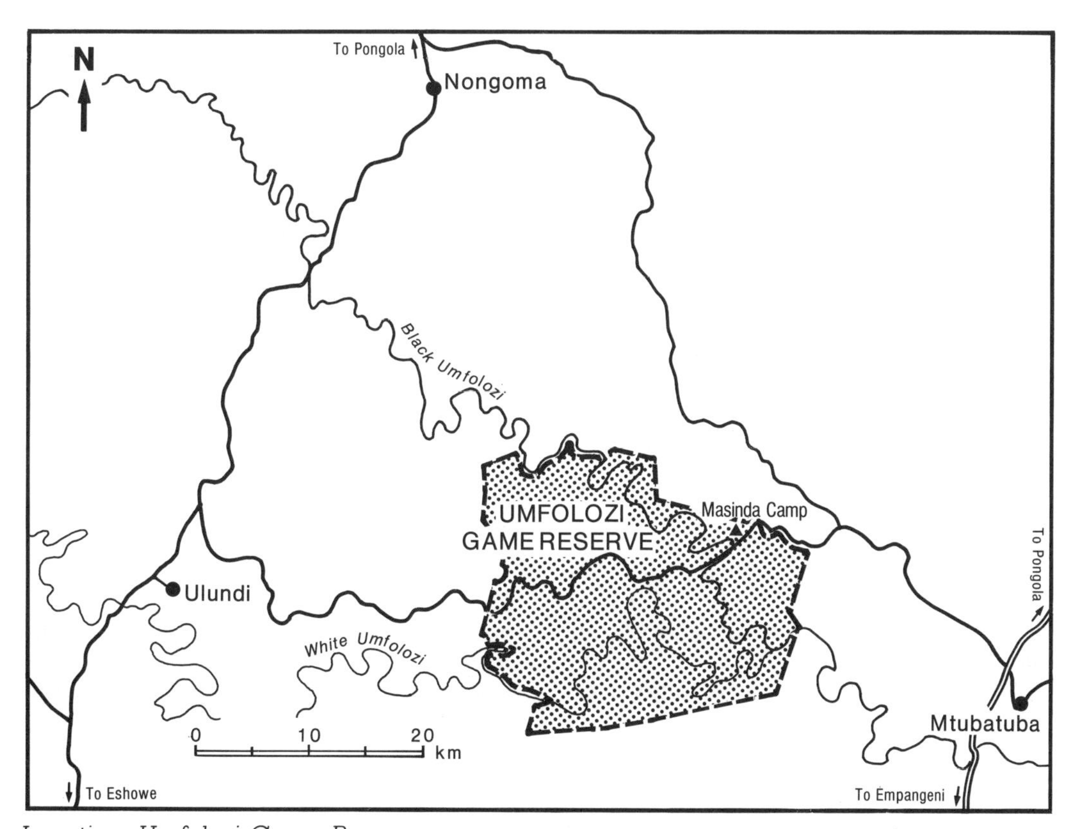


*Location: Umfolozi Game Reserve*

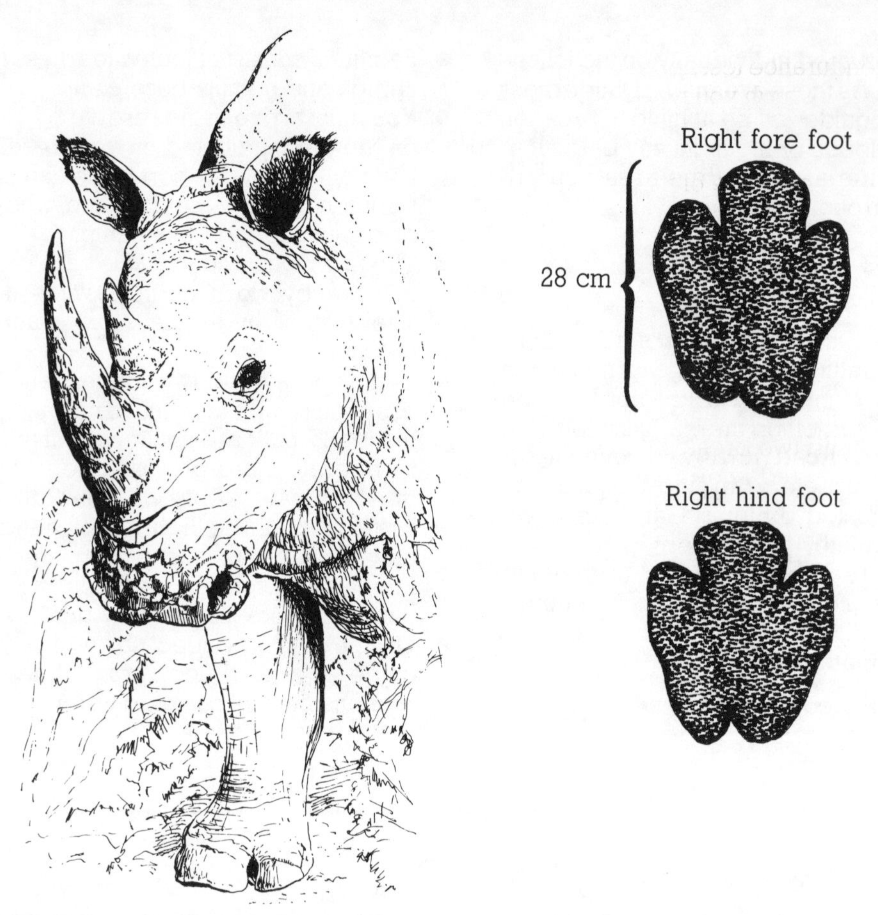


*The efforts of the Natal Parks Board to preserve the white rhino have been proclaimed world-wide*

**Trail Synopsis**

About 24 000 ha of the reserve, which covers 47 753 ha, have been set aside as a wilderness area. It is one of the finest big game areas of Zululand and is traditional game country of yesteryear. The reserve is generally associated with the white (square-lipped) rhinoceros, which was once threatened with extinction but now numbers some 900 in the reserve.

In addition to the white rhinoceros you may also see black (hook-lipped) rhinoceros, buffalo, blue wildebeest, Burchell's zebra, giraffe, impala, nyala and several other antelope and smaller mammal species. The predators are represented by lion, leopard, cheetah, spotted hyaena and black-backed jackal.

The birdlife is typical of the bushveld and more than 300 species have been recorded in the reserve. A comprehensive description of the avifauna has been published in *Lammergeyer*[1], the scientific journal of the Natal Parks Board.

***Primitive trails***

These are conducted in the Umfolozi Game Reserve between March and November. The months between April and September are generally cooler and more suitable for walking. The trails combine the features of a guided wilderness trail and a backpacking trail. However, the primitive trail is

1 Macdonald, I.A.W. and Birkenstock, P.J. 1980. Birds of the Hluhluwe-Umfolozi Game Reserve Complex. *Lammergeyer* 29, 1-56.

neither an endurance test nor a hike around the reserve, although you need to be fairly fit as you must carry all your own equipment.

Because of the nature of these trails it is preferable to make up your own party of six in advance. The daily distance covered depends on the fitness of the group as well as climatic conditions. Your route is chosen by the trails officer and you will sleep in caves, bush enclosures, under krantzes or on other suitable sites *en route*.

On trail you must cater for three lunches, two dinners and two breakfasts, as well as for two dinners and two breakfasts at the base camp.

All your equipment (including a tent, which is optional) must be provided, although sleeping-bags, backpacks, ground sheets and water-bottles can be hired from the warden at Umfolozi. Arrangements in this regard should be made well in advance by telephoning the warden at Mfolozi Reserve number 4.

## ST LUCIA GAME RESERVE AND PARK

### Location

The park is on the central Zululand coast, extending from St Lucia Estuary for 72 km northwards. The water and islands of the lake form the game reserve and cover 36 826 ha, while St Lucia Reserve, which covers 12 545 ha, is formed by a 1 km strip of land around most of the lake.

Follow the main North Coast Road (N2) and take the Mtubatuba turnoff. Continue for about 29 km along the R620 to the St Lucia Resort.

Cape Vidal, where the trail begins, is about 35 km north of the village at St. Lucia. After crossing the estuary bridge, you turn left at the T-junction and continue past the Crocodile Centre and along a gravel road to Cape Vidal.

*Note:* The entrance gate near the Crocodile Centre is closed between 21h00 and 06h00 in winter and 05h00 in summer.

### Trail Information

- Trails last for five days from Friday to Tuesday and are conducted only from April to October, when it is cooler.
- You must report to the Cape Vidal reception office at 14h00 on the Friday, where you are met by the trails officer.
- From the reception office you are transported to the base camp where the first night is spent. On the Saturday morning

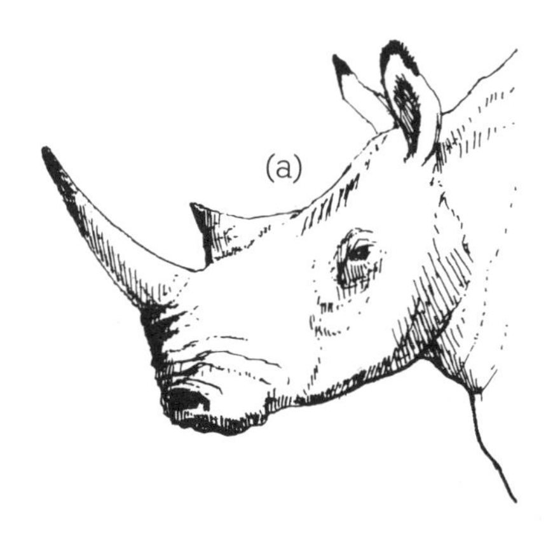

*Outline of heads of (a) white (square-lipped) rhinoceros and (b) black (hook-lipped) rhinoceros*

you will set out and the following two nights are spent in a tented trail camp, from where day walks are undertaken. On the Monday afternoon you return to the base camp where the last night is spent. Should the missile range be in use, all the nights may be spent at the base camp.

- Although donkeys are used to transport you luggage to the trail camp, weight must still be carefully considered.
- You must cater for four breakfasts, lunches and suppers.
- A fair amount of wading is done in the pans, for which a pair of takkies is recommended, while a second pair of comfortable shoes to wear in the evening at the camp is advisable.

**Trail Synopsis**

St Lucia is one of Southern Africa's richest ecological areas and offers you an infinitely varied wilderness experience. Some of the higlights include the second highest forested coastal dunes in the world, fascinating swamp forests, the lake itself, incredibly rich birdlife and a variety of mammals.

Although St Lucia is generally referred to as a lake, it is in fact a large estuary with only a narrow outlet to the sea. It covers

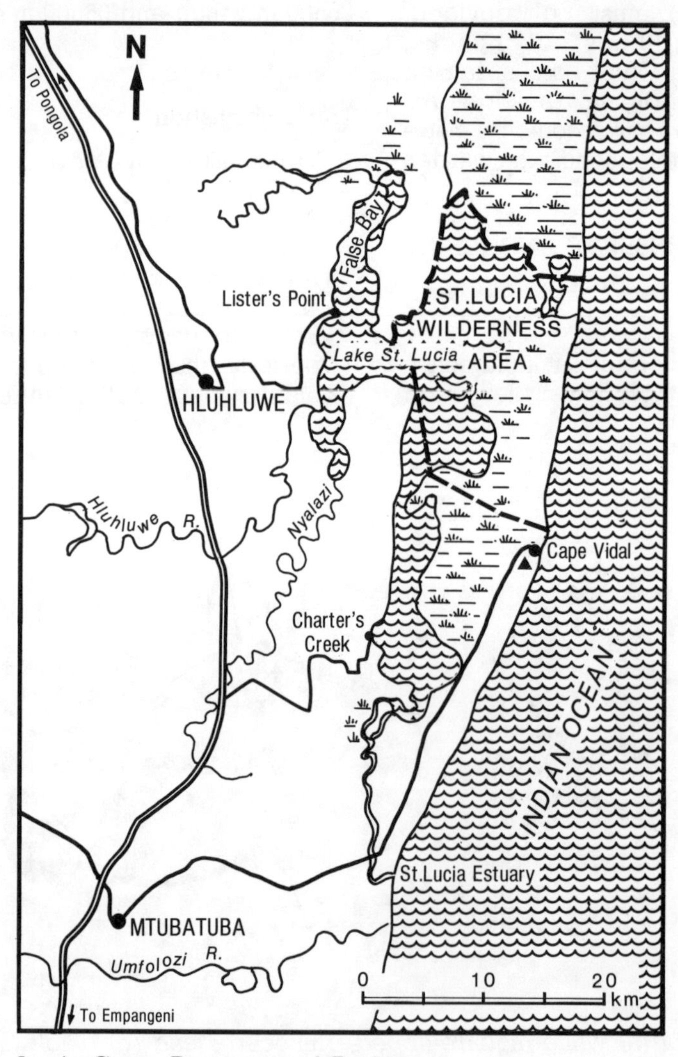


*Location: St. Lucia Game Reserve and Park*

some 300 km² and is at its widest at False Bay, the north-western arm of the H-shaped lake. Nowhere does the depth of the lake exceed 2 m.

Four major rivers, the Mzeneni, Hluhluwe, Nyalazi and the Mkuzi, as well as 50 smaller rivers and streams, contribute 80 per cent of the lake's freshwater. Two other sources supply the remaining 20 per cent, and are especially important during winter when the rivers usually do not flow. In the summer the vast papyrus swamp which blocks the flow of the Mkuzi River allows freshwater to seep slowly into the lake. The network of swamps and pans between the lake and the sea is seasonally filled with more than 1 000 mm of rain and is the second reserve supply of freshwater to the lake.

During summer the rivers usually come down in flood and the level of the lake may rise to 1 m above sea level. At the same time the salinity of the water in the lake drops to around zero. Conversely, in winter there is much less rain, reducing the inflow of freshwater, and the level of the lake may drop to below sea level. Seawater then flows into the lake, increasing the salinity of the water.

A prolonged drought will result in an increase of salinity to such a degree that animals will not be able to survive. In 1969 the highest recorded salinity was measured: the concentration of salt was three times that of seawater. Crocodiles and fish became dehydrated and died, while waterbirds were forced to migrate elsewhere in search of food. However, after good rains the lake is flushed out and the balance is restored.

As more than 50 per cent of the Lake St Lucia complex is covered in water, aquatic life is of special interest. In South Africa, this area is considered the most important prawn habitat and the white prawn, *Penaeus indicus,* is the most common of the five species recorded here. The prawn is of fundamental importance to the food chain of Lake St Lucia.

To date some 120 fish species have been recorded in the lake, including four shark species, one stingray species, one sawfish species, and six species of freshwater fish.

The area was primarily proclaimed to conserve hippo, which number about 600 at present. Nile crocodile (*Crocodylus niloticus*) are also abundant in the lake, particularly at the river mouths flowing into the lake.

The Eastern Shores Nature Reserve boasts the largest population of reedbuck in South Africa. Their distribution is restricted to areas where there is open water with suitable cover close by. Nyala, bushbuck, suni, common duiker, red duiker, steenbok and bushpig might also be seen.

St Lucia is a bird-watcher's paradise and species you will easily identify are the greater and lesser flamingoes (96 and 97), the white and pinkbacked pelicans (49 and 50), the Goliath heron (64) and the saddlebilled stork (88) with its distinctive red and black bill with a yellow saddle.

The waterlogged grassland is an ideal habitat for the pinkthroated longclaw (730), and even if you do not see this species, you can identify it by its characteristic squeaky

*The bill of the greater flamingo (a) is pink with a black tip, compared with the dark red bill of the lesser flamingo (b). The latter species is considerably smaller and pinker than the greater flamingo*

whistle. Green coucal (387) are common in the bush along the western shore, while the blackbellied korhaan (238) inhabits a wide range of habitats.

Species of the dune forest include the Knysna lourie (370) and the white-eared barbet (466). The woodlands are favoured by the purplecrested lourie (371) and the scalythroated honeyguide (475), to mention the most obvious species.

The orchid *Angraecum cultriforme* grows in dense masses close to the ground in the shady coastal forest and bush surrounding the lake. Although this species has also been recorded in Zimbabwe, Zambia, Malawi, Tanzania and Kenya, this is the only area where it occurs in South Africa. Slender, pinkish-beige flowers are produced during summer.

## MKUZI GAME RESERVE

### Location

The reserve is 335 km north of Durban in northern Zululand. Approaching from the south along the N2 you turn right onto a gravel road about 28 km north of Hluhluwe interchange. The turnoff to the reserve is signposted and you continue for 3 km to the old main road. Here you turn left and continue for 11 km, after which you turn right at the reserve signpost. From here it is 8 km along a road leading through the Lebombo Mountains to the gate, and a further 8 km to the camp.

From the north the reserve is approached by turning off to Mkuze village, from where you turn right onto the old main road. The turnoff to the reserve is clearly signposted about 9 km south of Mkuze village.

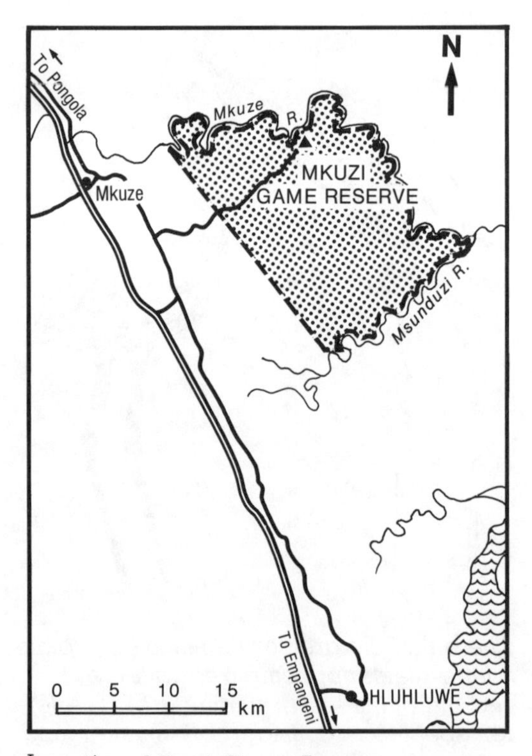

*Location: Mkuzi Game Reserve*

### Trail Information

- Trails are conducted between April and the end of October, starting on Fridays and returning on Mondays.
- You must report to the camp superintendent before 12h00 on the Friday.
- All three nights are spent in the trails camp established in the gorge area of the Mkuze River. From here you are transported to the game viewing areas where walks varying from 6 to 15 km are undertaken.
- Three breakfasts and suppers and four lunches must be catered for. Take fresh meat for the first day only as there are no refrigeration facilities at the camp.
- Although your luggage is transported by vehicle to the trails camp, weight should be kept to a reasonable level.

### Trail Synopsis

Bushveld trails are conducted in this 25 091 ha reserve which, unlike the other Zululand and Natal reserves, consists largely of flat, open country which is advantageous for game viewing. The vegetation varies considerably, resulting in an abundance of birds.

The reserve is well known for its large herds of impala. Kudu, nyala and reedbuck occur in smaller numbers, as well as smaller species such as steenbok, suni and red and common duiker.

Both the white (square-lipped) and black (hook-lipped) rhinoceros occur in the reserve, and you might also see hippo and crocodile. Predators such as leopard,

*Impala. The females are hornless*

cheetah, spotted hyaena, black-backed jackal and side-striped jackal also occur, but are less frequently seen.

To date more than 300 species of bushveld birds have been identified. A seasonal wealth of water birds inhabit the 5 km-long Nsumu Pan, including the lesser jacana (241), pygmy goose (114) and the rufousbellied heron (75), as well as large flocks of various duck species.

The vegetation is equally varied and includes species such as the common cluster fig (66), which dominates the forests along the Mkuze River, *Acacia* spp., and the Natal flame bush (701) with its striking, brilliant red to crimson flowers which can be seen between January and April. The mottled yellow stems of the fever tree (189) create an unforgettable display during winter and early spring.

## ITALA NATURE RESERVE

### Location

The reserve is situated near Louwsburg in northern Natal, close to the Transvaal border. Approaching from the south (Durban) take the N2 to Ladysmith and continue via Dundee to Vryheid. From here continue via Hlobane to Louwsburg along the tarred road. The entrance to the reserve is via Louwsburg village.

The best approach from the Transvaal is along the R29 to Piet Retief and from here along the R33 to Vryheid via Paulpietersburg.

From the Natal north coast continue along the main road to Pongola where you turn left to Magudu and then right on the Louwsburg/Vryheid road. Access to the reserve is through the village of Louwsburg.

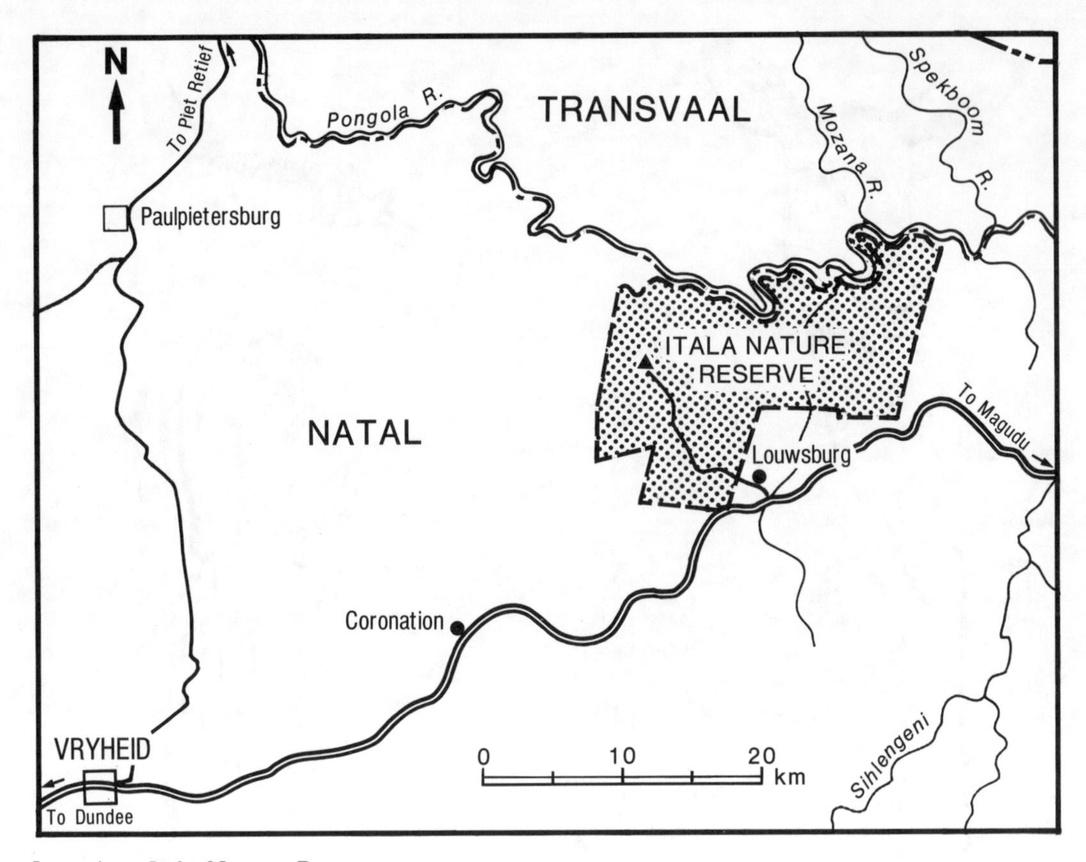


*Location: Itala Nature Reserve*

**Trail Information**

- Trails are conducted from March to October, starting on Fridays and returning on Mondays.
- You must arrive in the reserve before sunset on the Friday and report to the Officer-in-Charge, who will direct you to the base camp.
- The first night is spent at the base camp, the second in the wilderness and the third at either of the two, depending on the trailists' preference.
- Three breakfasts, lunches and suppers must be catered for. There is a fridge at the base camp for perishables.
- Donkeys will carry your food and luggage to the camp.
- When packing your clothing bear in mind that during winter early-morning temperatures often fall below zero and the trails are conducted along the Pongola River, while in summer you keep to higher ground.

**Trail Synopsis**

Steep river valleys characterise this beautiful, rugged reserve, which covers 25 896 ha. No less than six rivers flow through the reserve before joining the Pongola River, which forms the northern boundary of the reserve. Impressive rock formations and interesting vegetation create a true wilderness atmosphere.

Since the reserve was established in 1973, a wide variety of animals have been re-introduced, including 18 species of antelope and both the white (square-lipped) and black (hook-lipped) rhinoceros. The reserve also boasts the largest concentrations of klipspringer as well as the only herd of tsessebe in Natal. Giraffe, roan, eland, kudu, waterbuck, reedbuck and warthog also occur.

The nocturnal pangolin, listed as vulnerable in the *South African Red Data — Terrestrial Mammals,* occurs but is unlikely to be seen as it lies up during the day con-

*The nocturnal pangolin is classfied as vulnerable. When in danger it rolls itself into a tight ball*

cealed under fallen leaves. If you should come across it, however, it is easily recognised by the armour-like brown scales covering its body, except for the underparts.

Leopard occurred naturally when the reserve was established, and cheetah have been re-introduced.

Bird-watching in the reserve can be rewarding as a variety of birds are attracted to the different vegetation types. To date more than 200 species have been recorded in the reserve.

Four different vegetation communities have been identified in the reserve. The montane grassland consists of species such as broom cluster fig (50), oldwood (145) and bush guarri (600). The other communities are riverine and scrub forest, woodlands and various grassveld types, including the sour and mixed plateau grasslands.

## GIANT'S CASTLE GAME RESERVE HORSEBACK TRAIL

### Location

The reserve is situated on the grassy plateau below the sheer face of the central Drakensberg. The base camp for the horseback trails is at Hillside in the north-west of the reserve, which can be approached from either Estcourt or Mooi River.

From Estcourt, turn off at the post office and continue over the railway bridge, following the signs to Ntabamhlope. After about 5 km the road forks, and you follow the right fork. About 30 km on you turn left at the White Mountain resort and continue for roughly 4 km until you reach a signboard indicating the turnoff to Hillside on your right.

From Mooi River the base camp is reached by taking the signposted road to Giant's Castle Game Reserve leading west out of the town. After about 38 km you turn right onto the Ntabamhlope/Kamberg road and continue for about 15 km to where a signpost indicates the turnoff to Hillside on the left. Hillside is about 5 km on.

### Trail Information

- As the trails are carried out on horseback, only accomplished riders should apply for this trail. The minimum age limit is 12 years, unless the child is a proven expert rider.
- Trails are either two, three or four days long and are conducted throughout the year, except during July and August.
- On the trail you will sleep in caves in the foothills of the Drakensberg.
- Free hutted accommodation is available to riders wishing to spend the night preceding and following the trail at Hillside. If you intend making use of this facility, indicate the dates and your re-

quirements when returning your provisional advice forms.

- Report to the warden at Hillside by 09h00 on the morning of departure as the trails set off an hour later. Trails return at about 15h00 on the last day.
- Food and clothing are carried in saddlebags and it is advisable to avoid bulky items, breakables and perishable food.
- When packing remember that irrespective of the season sufficient warm clothing is essential, especially in winter when frost and snow are a distinct possibility. In summer thunderstorms can be expected, making a waterproof garment essential.

**Trail Synopsis**

Giant's Castle Game Reserve is renowned for its beautiful mountain scenery, large herds of eland, the rare bearded vulture (119) and numerous rock painting sites. Refer to the Giant's Castle Backpacking Area on page 166 where these are discussed.

# 20 Wilderness Leadership School Guided Trails

The concept of guided wilderness trails was pioneered in South Africa by Dr Ian Player, one of the country's most distinguished conservationists. Dr Player conceived the idea in 1957 after taking a group of schoolboys on an educational tour to Lake St Lucia to make them aware of the need for conservation. Two years later he set up the first wilderness trail in the country in the Umfolozi Game Reserve in Zululand. In 1963 the Wilderness Leadership School was formally registered as a trust, and since its inception the school has taken more than 10 000 people into the wilderness areas of Zululand, Natal, the Transvaal and, more recently, the Cape.

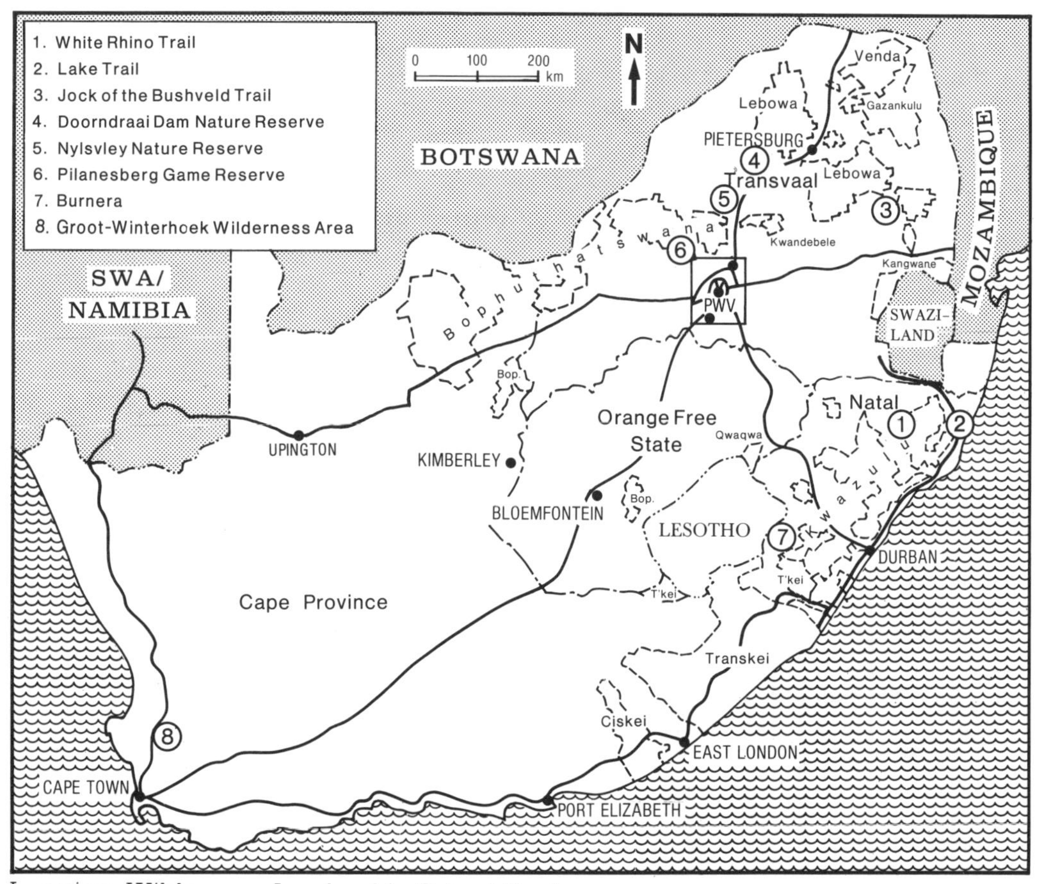


*Location: Wilderness Leadership School Trails*

The school initially focused its efforts on leaders and potential leaders, but has since opened its doors to a wide variety of groups, and endeavours to encourage as many multiracial groups as possible. The trailing areas are carefully selected, and to ensure minimum impact on nature each trail is limited to six participants. Trail parties are led by an experienced field officer who is not only responsible for the group's safety but is also knowledgeable about the environment. Subjects covered include zoology, botany, anthropology, history and geology.

Each day's programme varies according to prevailing local circumstances, but activities usually include following spoor, stalking game and learning more about the environment.

Overnight camps are purposely kept simple and parties sleep in open bush camps or under the stars. At night you will take turns to keep the hourly watch, an experience that the city-dweller will not easily forget.

As trail experiences vary considerably, only a brief outline of the various trails is given below. Your experienced field officer will be at hand on the trail to point out anything that might interest you.

### Distance and Classification

No set distances are covered (except on Cape Weekend Trail in Groot-Winterhoek) and trails are adapted to suit each group's needs.
A grade; Groot-Winterhoek — A+ grade.

### Relevant Information

- On all Wilderness Leadership School trails the school provides transport, backpacks, tents, sleeping-bags, groundsheets, cooking and eating utensils, as well as all meals and hot beverages, from after breakfast on the first day till after lunch on the last day.
- On weekend trails transport, food and all camping equipment except sleeping-bags are supplied. Backpacks are not required except for Groot-Winterhoek but you will find a daypack useful.

### *What to bring*

- Practical outdoor clothing of inconspicuous colouring (*avoid white or brightly coloured articles*)
- Underwear sufficient for the duration of the trail
- Tracksuit or slacks for nightwear
- Jersey or pullover
- Lightweight rainproof garment
- Bathing costume
- A hat of inconspicuous colouring
- Woollen cap and gloves during winter
- Pair of comfortable walking shoes or boots in good condition, and socks
- Toiletries and a towel
- Sunscreen lotion, insect repellent and plaster
- Torch, spare batteries and bulb
- Camera, extra film, binoculars, notebook, pencil and reading material (optional)
- Anti-malaria precautions are necessary in certain areas — check when making your reservation
- The school supplies a basic first aid kit but any specialised medication must be remembered

## WHITE RHINO TRAIL

### Location

The White Rhino Trail is conducted in part of the 24 000 ha wilderness area in the Umfolozi Game Reserve. The reserve is situated about 270 km north of Durban in the bushveld of Zululand, which is traditional big game country. Transport is provided from Durban.

### Duration

Adults 4 and 5 days
Scholars 5 days

### Reservations

Reservations can be made with The Director, Wilderness Leadership School, P O Box 153058, Yellowwood Park 4011, Telephone (031) 42 8642.

*The giraffe is one of several larger mammal species trailists might encounter on the White Rhino Trail*

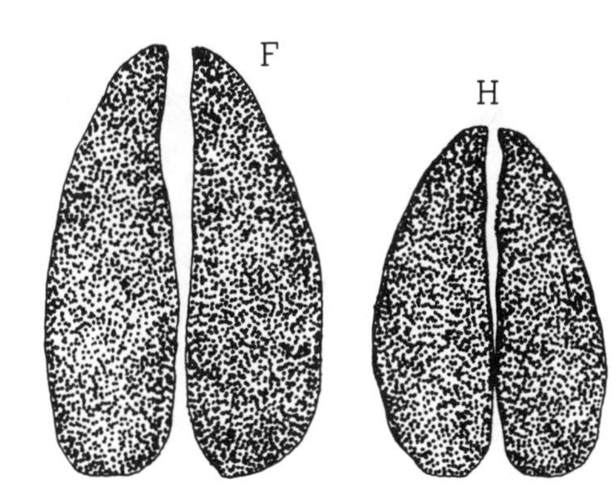


#### Trail Synopsis

On the White Rhino Trail you will be able to explore on foot one of the few remaining big game areas in South Africa. The trail takes you to the Black Umfolozi River over rolling hills steeped in the legends and traditions of the Zulu people who inhabited the area. Place names, old kraal sites and relics such as Shaka's game pits near the confluence of the White and the Black Umfolozi rivers serve as reminders of these people.

The trees in the reserve consist mainly of mixed *Acacia* woodlands with species such as black monkey thorn (161), common hookthorn (162), horned thorn (168.1), knob thorn (178) and umbrella thorn (188). Along the rivers you will see the wild date palm (22) and the water berry (555). Redgrass (*Themeda triandra*) is the dominant grass species.

By 1929 the number of white (square-lipped) rhino in South Africa had declined to less than 150 and a concerted campaign was launched to save the few surviving white rhinos in Zululand, their last stronghold.

Umfolozi became a breeding core for white rhino and by the early 1960s the numbers of this species in the reserve had increased to such an extent that 'Operation Rhino' was initiated by Dr Ian Player, then the senior ranger in charge of Umfolozi. This involved the capture and translocation of animals with a view to re-establishing viable breeding populations in suitable reserves in Southern and Central Africa. Several hundred animals were also exported to zoological gardens in Europe and the United States. To date nearly 4 000 animals have been translocated to all parts of the globe. A population of about 900 animals is maintained in Umfolozi and it is very likely that you will come across white rhino while trailing in the reserve.

Other mammals you are likely to see include blue wildebeest, Burchell's zebra, buffalo and giraffe, as well as black (hook-lipped) rhinoceros, impala, waterbuck, reedbuck, nyala and kudu. Smaller antelope species such as blue duiker, common

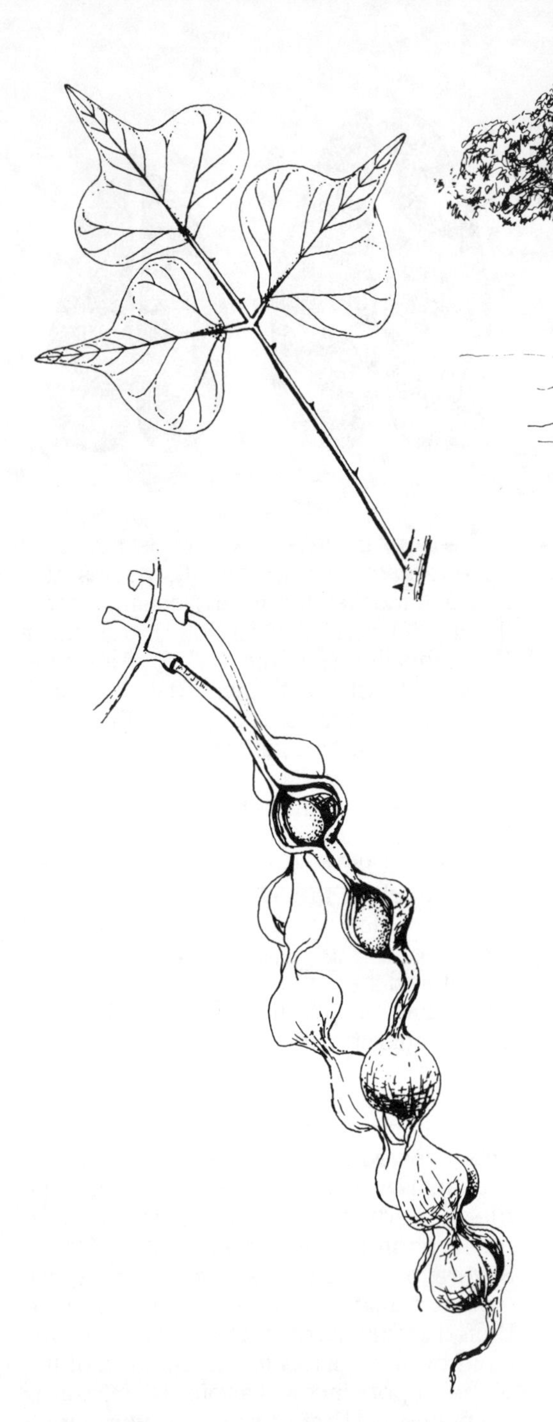

*Leaf and fruit of coast coral tree*

duiker and steenbok also occur. Elephant have recently been re-introduced into the reserve. Predators include lion, spotted hyaena and cheetah as well as wild dog, leopard and brown hyaena, the latter three being listed as *Red Data Book* species.

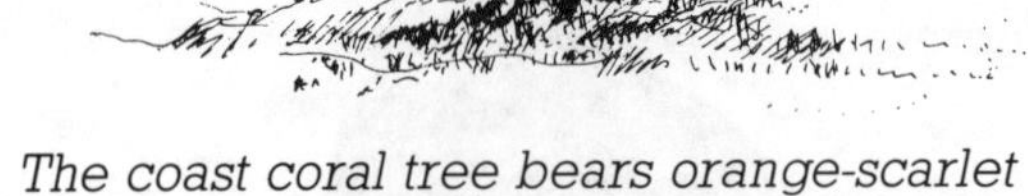

*The coast coral tree bears orange-scarlet flowers during August and September*

The reserve is the home of a large variety of birds and to date some 336 species have been recorded. If you are interested in butterflies you will also not be disappointed, as some 136 species have been recorded in the area.

## THE LAKE TRAIL

### Location

The Lake Trail is conducted in the wilderness area on the eastern shores of Lake St Lucia and offers you the opportunity to explore on foot and by canoe the largest lagoon-estuary complex of its kind in South Africa. The lake is situated about 200 km north-east of Durban. Transport is provided from Durban.

### Duration

Adults 4 and 5 days
Scholars 5 days

### Reservations

Reservations for this trail can be made with the Director, Wilderness Leadership School, P O Box 53058, Yellowwood Park 4011, Telephone (031) 42 8642.

### Trail Synopsis

Experiences on the Lake Trail are as varied

as the trail itself and you will be able to explore not only the land areas, but also the lake itself.

Vegetation on the eastern shores of the lake consists mainly of open, rolling grassland with occasional clumps of palms and other trees, including the common coral tree (245), marula (360) and the Lowveld mangosteen (486). Well-preserved swamp forests cover the banks of the lake, and the coastal dunes are among the tallest forested dunes in the world.

Among the antelope you might come across are reedbuck, waterbuck, impala, kudu and bushbuck. Other mammal species occurring in the area include black (hook-lipped) rhinoceros, leopard, cheetah, antbear (erdvark), bushpig, warthog and numerous smaller mammals. St Lucia supports about 600 hippo, which is the world's largest population of hippo this far south. During the day they often lie up in the swamp forests where you will have to be on the lookout for them. Another inhabitant of the rivers and the lake you are certain to see is the Nile crocodile (*Crocodylus niloticus*). Almost all of the surviving crocodiles in Natal are confined to Lake St Lucia.

Lake St Lucia is a haven for bird-watchers and to date more than 350 species have been recorded, of which about one third are waterbirds. The lake is famous for its large numbers of white pelican (49), Goliath heron (64), African spoonbill (95), African jacana (240), avocet (294) and African fish eagle (148), to mention but a few of the notable species.

For more information on Lake St Lucia refer to page 197.

*Lake St Lucia is possibly the most important breeding area for waterbirds in South Africa, including large numbers of white pelican*

## BURNERA — NATAL DRAKENSBERG

Burnera is in the foothills of the Drakensberg, about 35 km north-west of Himeville. It adjoins the Vergelegen Nature Reserve, which is administered by the Natal Parks Board. The old farmhouse is ideally suited for small groups of up to nine people and is leased from the Forestry Branch. It is used by educational and business groups as a mountain trail centre and for special environmental conferences. The duration and programme can be arranged to suit the requirements of the group. Reservations must be made through the school's Natal office, P O Box 53058, Yellowwood Park 4011, Telephone (031) 42 8642.

## JOCK OF THE BUSHVELD TRAIL

### Location

The Jock of the Bushveld Trail is conducted in the 20 000 ha Hans Hoheisen Private

Game Reserve bordering the Kruger National Park in the eastern Transvaal. The reserve is situated near the Orpen Gate entrance to the Kruger National Park and the Timbavati River flows through the reserve. Transport is provided from White River.

### Duration

Adults and scholars 5 days

### Reservations

Reservations can be made with The Director, Wilderness Leadership School, P O Box 87230, Houghton 2041, Telephone (011) 782-1613.

### Trail Synopsis

The reserve is the home of most of the big game species of the Lowveld, including white (square-lipped) rhinoceros, elephant, lion, leopard, cheetah, spotted hyaena, wild dog and giraffe. Members of the antelope family include buffalo, blue wildebeest, waterbuck, kudu, sable, roan and impala as well as several smaller species. The trail area surrounding the Timbavati River has several permanent waterholes, which encourage animals to frequent the area.

The reserve is also the habitat of a large number of bird species.

## TRANSVAAL WEEKEND TRAILS

A number of weekend trails are conducted in three provincial nature reserves in the Transvaal by dedicated volunteer field guides. Trails depart from Johannesburg at 17h45 on Fridays, returning at 18h00 on Sundays. Reservations for any of these trails should be directed to The Director, Wilderness Leadership School, P O Box 87230, Houghton 2041, Telephone (011) 782 1613.

## DOORNDRAAI DAM NATURE RESERVE

### Location

The Doorndraai Dam Nature Reserve covers about 7 000 ha and is situated about 50 km north of Naboomspruit on the N1 between Naboomspruit and Potgietersrus. Transport is provided by the Wilderness Leadership School.

### Trail Synopsis

The reserve is situated in the foothills of the Waterberg in undulating terrain varying from open hillsides to deep kloofs.

The vegetation consists of highveld-sourveld species such as Transvaal beech (75), common sugarbush (87), common hook-thorn (162), sweet thorn (172), wild

*Buffalo are restricted to suitable habitats in Zululand*

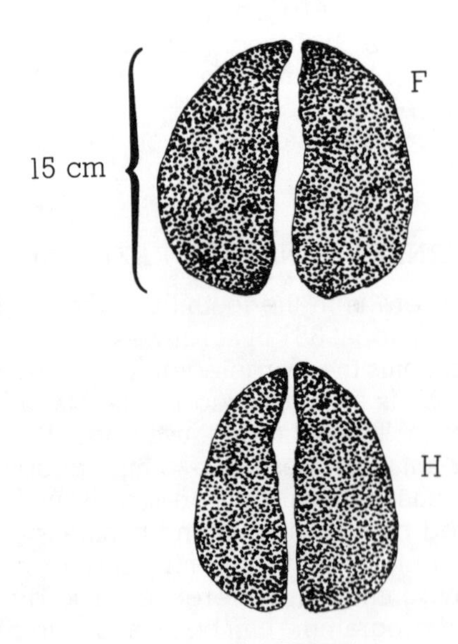

seringa (197), several bushwillow (*Combretum*) species, and the silver cluster-leaf (551).

Among the dominant mammal species occurring are Burchell's zebra, blue wildebeest, waterbuck, kudu and impala. Several mammals listed in the *South African Red Data Book — Terrestrial Mammals* also occur, including roan and sable, which are classified as endangered and vulnerable respectively. The numbers of sable are estimated at about 3 500 in the Transvaal. Other uncommon species you might come across are leopard, aardwolf, brown hyaena and tsessebe, all of which are also listed in the *Red Data Book*.

Several birds of prey inhabit the reserve, such as black eagle (131), martial eagle (140) and African fish eagle (148), as well as a number of falcon species. The 577 ha Doorndraai Dam in the Sterk River Valley attracts numerous water birds, making the reserve a delight for bird-watchers.

*Leaf, fruit and growth form of silver cluster-leaf*

## NYLSVLEY NATURE RESERVE

### Location

The 3 121 ha Nylsvley Nature Reserve is about 20 km south of Naboomspruit on the Boekenhout road, 33 km north of Nylstroom. Transport is provided by the Wilderness Leadership School.

### Trail Synopsis

The reserve is situated on the Nyl River in almost pristine surroundings. Nylsvley is the largest natural vlei in the Transvaal and is well known for its prolific birdlife, with more than 400 species having been recorded from the Nyl River floodplain. Over its total length of about 70 km, an average of 7 800 ha of grasslands are flooded annually, but in years of high rainfall the inundated area can increase to about 16 200 ha.

The months between February and May are the most rewarding for bird-watching. At least 93 aquatic species, of which 51 species are known to breed on the Nyl River, have been recorded from the area. Thirteen heron species, 10 duck and geese species and at least 6 members of the rail family are known to breed on the Nyl River. During years of extensive flooding, you may be fortunate enough to see certain tropical species which are seldom seen in South Africa, including rufousbellied heron (75), dwarf bittern (79) and lesser gallinule (224).

The Nyl River supports the largest known South African breeding populations of several species, namely great white egret

*Crimsonbreasted shrike*

*Spoonbill*

(66) (about 200 pairs), black egret (69) (40 to 50 pairs) and squacco heron (72) (about 250 pairs). In suitable years the little bittern (78), a species which probably numbers less than 100 breeding pairs in South Africa, also breeds on the Nyl River (less than 30 pairs).

The wetland is also the habitat of reasonable numbers of migrant waders. In addition to the aquatic birds there are also a large variety of woodland species, such as Bennett's woodpecker (481), Meyer's parrot (364) and crimsonbreasted shrike (739), to mention but a few.

The vegetation varies from broadleaf deciduous woodlands and savannas dominated by wild seringa (197), peeling plane (483), silver cluster-leaf (551) and various bushwillow (*Combretum*) species to *Acacia* savannas, woodlands and grasslands.

Among the animals you are likely to come across are blue wildebeest, Burchell's zebra, kudu, waterbuck, reedbuck and giraffe. There is also a chance that you might spot roan or tsessebe.

## PILANESBERG GAME RESERVE

### Location

The Pilanesberg Game Reserve is situated in Bophuthatswana about 50 km north-west of the western Transvaal town of Rustenberg some 150 km west of Johannesburg. Transport is provided by the Wilderness Leadership School.

### Trail Synopsis

The reserve lies within one of the most geologically fascinating areas in Southern Africa and boasts a rich diversity of larger mammal species and over 300 bird species. The scenery is superb, with steep slopes and impressive mountain peaks, rolling plains and deep valleys. The mountain, which rises abruptly some 300 to 600 m above the surrounding plains, is a rare feature (other examples are in the USSR and Greenland) in which the roots of an old volcanic formation have been exposed by erosion. It consists of a near-circular series of concentric hills and ring valleys.

The vegetation varies from savannas to open grassland and densely wooded valleys. Trees of the summits and slopes include Transvaal beech (75), common hook-thorn (162), sweet thorn (172) and common wild pear (471). Spike-flowered black-thorn (176.1), umbrella thorn (188), karree (386) and wild olive (617) are the dominant species of the valley floors. The Pilanesberg is the habitat of the endemic Transvaal red balloon (436.2), a species with a total world population of only a few hundred specimens.

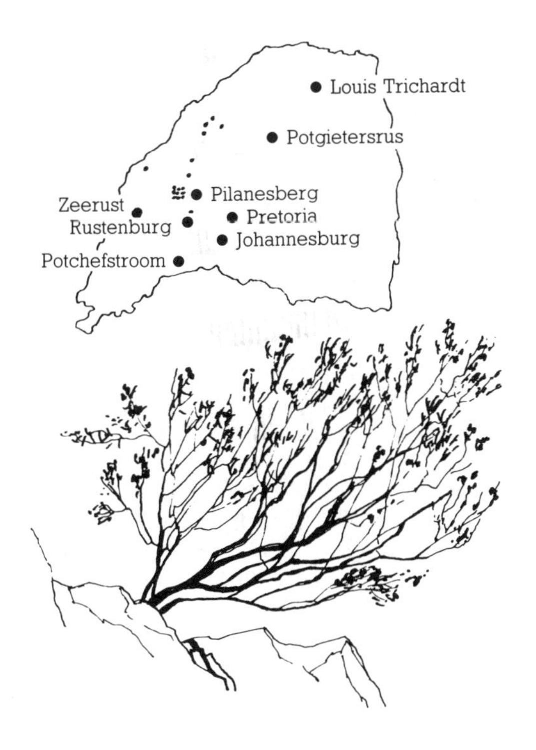


*Distribution and growth form of the Transvaal red balloon*

To date more than 50 mammal species, excluding bats, rodents and smaller carnivores, have been recorded in the reserve. The reserve has made an important contribution to the conservation of the white (square-lipped) rhinoceros by establishing the third largest population (240) of these animals in the world. It also supports large numbers of impala, mountain reedbuck, red hartebeest, blue wildebeest and Burchell's zebra, while elephant, black rhino, leopard and brown hyaena also occur.

Some 320 bird species have been recorded, including no less than 32 species of birds of prey. The grey lourie (373) is most likely to attract your attention with its distinctive alarm call, as is the attractive lilac-breasted roller (447), which displays its beautiful blue wings in flight.

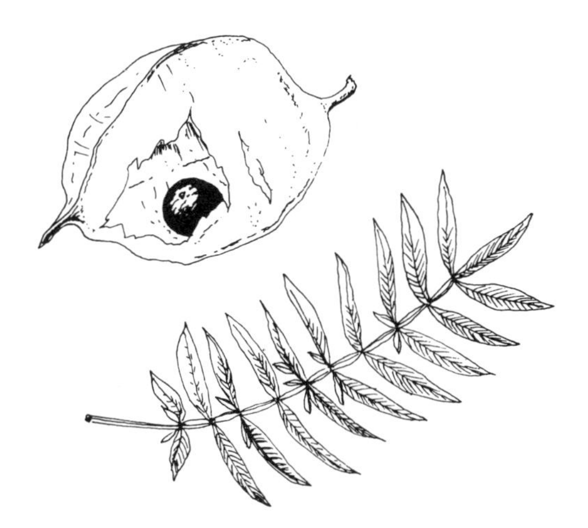

*Bladder-like seed-pod and leaves of the Transvaal red balloon – a species largely restricted to the Pilanesberg Game Reserve*

## CAPE WEEKEND TRAILS

### GROOT-WINTERHOEK WILDERNESS AREA

Weekend and four-day trails are conducted from Cape Town, by volunteer field guides, to the Groot-Winterhoek Wilderness Area, which is characterised by beautiful mountain scenery, rich fynbos vegetation and numerous crystal clear pools.

#### Location

The trails are conducted in the Groot-Winterhoek Wilderness Area near Porterville in the western Cape. The wilderness area covers some 19 468 ha of magnificent mountain scenery.

#### Reservations

Reservations must be directed to the Secretary, Wilderness Leadership School, 22 Park Road, Rondebosch 7700, Telephone (021) 66 6622.

#### Trail Synopsis

Groot-Winterhoek is a naturalist's paradise. Few people are aware of the floral wealth of the western and south-western Cape, and this trail offers you the opportunity to find out more about the Cape Floral Kingdom, which is the richest of the six floral kingdoms in the world although it only covers 0,04 per cent of the world's surface.

The vegetation varies from patches of virgin riverine forest to open fynbos with masses of *Erica* and Proteaceae species. The

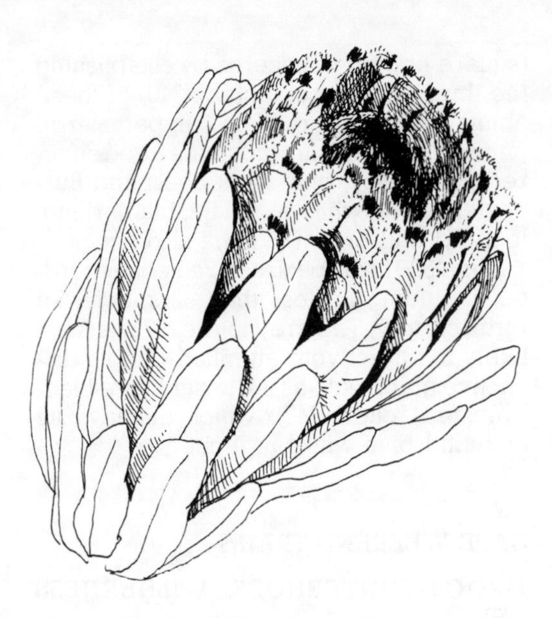

*The bearded sugarbush*

area is also the home of a number of uncommon plant species such as the yellow variety of *Disa uniflora,* as well as a number of Proteaceae species, including *Spatalla tulbaghensis* and *Sorocephalus scabridus.*

The mountains of the western Cape do not support a large variety of mammals. The species you are most likely to encounter are grey rhebok, klipspringer, chacma baboon and perhaps grysbok. Although it is most unlikely that you will spot the shy and elusive leopard, you are almost certain to come across its spoor.

Birds often seen in the area are greywing francolin (190), Cape francolin (195), ground woodpecker (480), Cape rock thrush (581), mountain chat (586), Cape rockjumper (611), redwinged starling (769), Cape sugarbird (773), orangebreasted sunbird (777), lesser doublecollared sunbird (783), Cape siskin (874) and Cape bunting (885).

# *Part 6*
# *Transvaal*

# 21 Kruger National Park Guided Wilderness Trails

Four guided wilderness trails are conducted in the 19 485 ha Kruger National Park, offering you the opportunity to experience the beauty of the bushveld on foot. Apart from game spotting, which is not the major objective of these wilderness trails, time is spent learning more about the environment, visiting archaeological and anthropological sites, bird-watching and appreciating the natural beauty about you. Listening to the call of the animals at night, watching the sun setting, pausing at a spider's web glistening in the early morning dew or watching the antics of a bateleur are as much part of the experience as coming breathtakingly close to a herd of elephant.

### Location

The park is situated roughly 400 km north-east of Johannesburg, and your entrance point will depend on which trail you are doing.

- The Wolhuter Trail in the south of the park departs from the Skukuza reception office, and Kruger Gate on the R536 is the most convenient entry point.
- The Bushman Trail, also in the south of the park, departs from the Berg-en-dal reception office and the closest entry point is Malelane Gate, 3 km off the N4.
- The Olifants Trail in the centre of the park departs from the Letaba reception office, 50 km from Phalaborwa Gate.
- The Nyalaland Trail in the north of the park departs from the Punda Maria reception office, which is reached on the R524.

### Distance and Classification

No set distances are covered and routes are adapted to suit each group's needs.
A grade

### Permits

Reservations can be made a year in advance with The Chief Director, National Parks Board, P O Box 787, Pretoria 0001, Telephone (012) 44 1191/-9 or P O Box 7400, Roggebaai 8012, Telephone (021) 419 5365. Groups are limited to a maximum of eight people with a minimum age restriction of 12 and a maximum of 60, although those older than 45 must be 'walking fit'.

### Maps

You will find the tourist map of the Kruger National Park useful for orientation. Owing to the nature of these trails, the standard 1:50 000 topographical maps are of little use.

### Relevant Information

- Trails leave on Mondays and Fridays and trailists must report to the respective reception offices before 15h00 on the day of departure. After a short briefing you are transported to the base camp.
- Trails last for two days and three nights, returning to the rest camp after breakfast on the final day.
- Clothing must be in dull, inconspicuous tones such as green, brown or khaki. A tracksuit is ideal for evening wear.
- Comfortable footwear is essential.

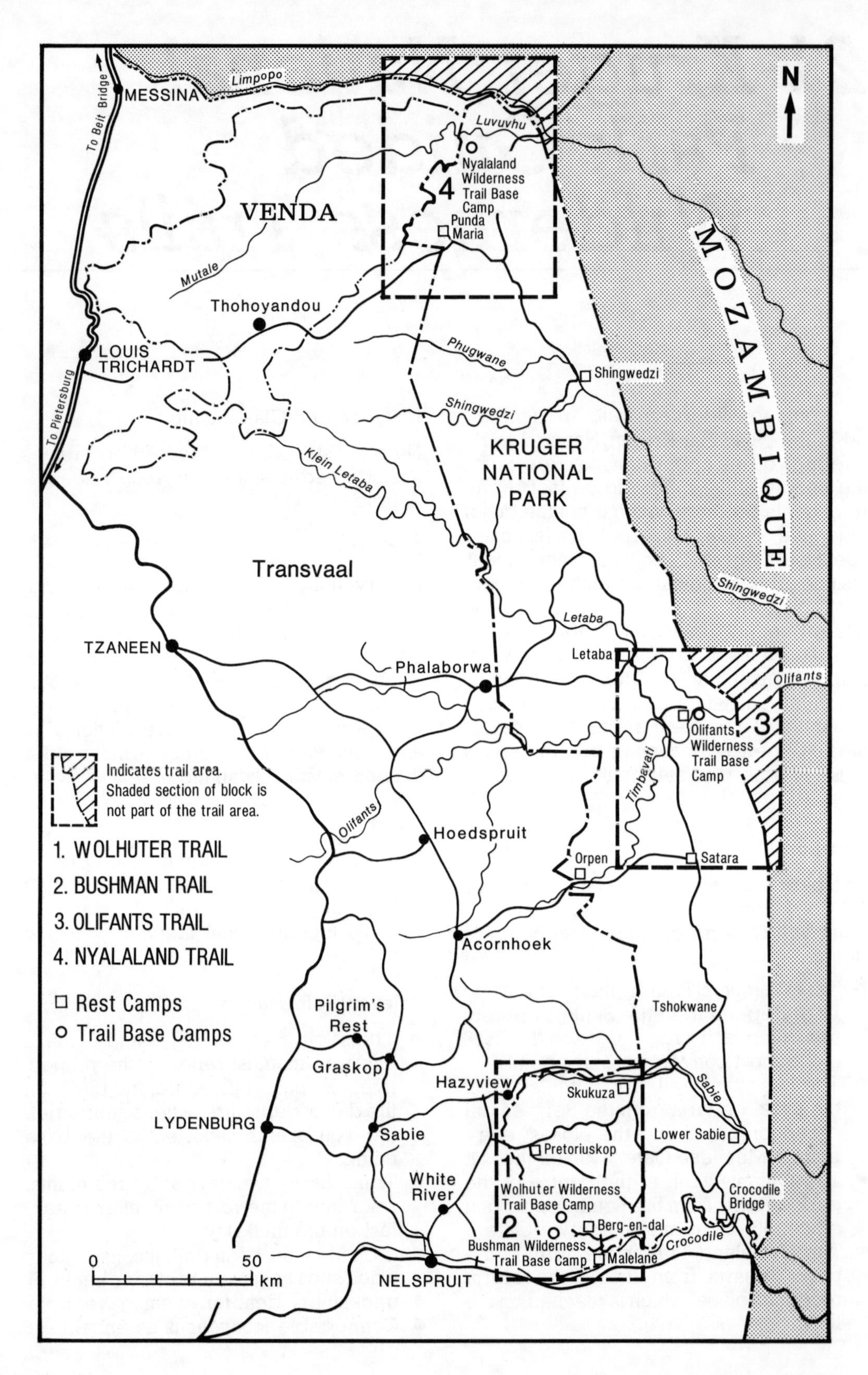

N
MESSINA
Limpopo
To Beit Bridge
Luvuvhu
Nyalaland
Wilderness
Trail Base
Camp
4
VENDA
Punda
Maria
MOZAMBIQUE
Mutale
Thohoyandou
LOUIS
TRICHARDT
Phugwane
Shingwedzi
To Pietersburg
Shingwedzi
KRUGER
NATIONAL
PARK
Klein Letaba
Transvaal
Shingwedzi
Letaba
TZANEEN
Letaba
Phalaborwa
Olifants
Olifants
Wilderness
Trail Base
Camp
3
Timbavati
Indicates trail area.
Shaded section of block is
not part of the trail area.
Olifants
Hoedspruit
1. WOLHUTER TRAIL
2. BUSHMAN TRAIL
3. OLIFANTS TRAIL
4. NYALALAND TRAIL
Orpen
Satara
Acornhoek
Rest Camps
Trail Base Camps
Pilgrim's
Rest
Tshokwane
Graskop
Hazyview
Skukuza
Sabie
LYDENBURG
Sabie
Lower Sabie
Pretoriuskop
1
White
River
Wolhuter Wilderness
Trail Base Camp
Crocodile
Bridge
2
Berg-en-dal
Bushman Wilderness
Trail Base Camp
Crocodile
Malelane
0
50
km
NELSPRUIT

- Anti-malaria precautions and sunscreen lotion are essential.
- All meals and soft drinks are provided on the trail. Alcohol is not included but you may supply your own.
- Daypacks, water-bottles, bedding, towels and eating utensils are supplied by the board.
- Binoculars are essential for game spotting and bird-watching. Smithers *Land Mammals of Southern Africa — A Field Guide* and Newman's *Birds of the Kruger National Park* are useful for identification and make interesting reading.
- During summer the hottest part of the day is spent relaxing at the base camp so remember to take some reading material.
- Although you will not be exposed to any unnecessary danger, it must be borne in mind that there is always an element of danger in the wild.
- All trailists must complete an indemnity form prior to departure and minors must be in possession of a form or letter signed by their parents or legal guardian.

### Facilities

Hutted accommodation, stretchers with bedding, cooking bomas, bush showers and toilets are provided at the base camps.

Enquiries and reservations for accommodation before and after your trail can be made when booking the trail. Caravan and camping sites, as well as a variety of hutted accommodation, are available. The larger camps have restaurants, cafeterias and shops where most commodities can be obtained, including wine, beer and spirits.

### Flora and Fauna

These form an integral part of each trail and are discussed under the relevant trail synopses.

### History

It is only since the early 1970s that archaeologists and anthropologists have turned their attention to the early history of the Kruger National Park and as a result a clear picture of the early inhabitants of the area is still emerging. However, it is known that Middle Stone Age man was present in the area some 100 000 to 30 000 years ago. They were followed by the Later Stone Age people and the San (Bushmen). To date 300 archaeological sites from the different ages have been recorded in the park.

Excavations revealing San spears, arrows, stone tools and ostrich eggshell beads, and numerous rock paintings (nearly 100 known sites) would suggest that San inhabited the area until only a few centuries ago. The south of the park is particularly rich in rock paintings, some of which can be seen on the Bushman Trail, which also takes you past other sites of archaeological interest.

In about 1755 BP Iron Age migrants entered the Lowveld, and between 1255 and 1155 BP several other groups passed through the area, with some settling there. Initially these communities depended on hunting and agriculture. Although livestock was later introduced, it could not have been too successful because of tsetse fly.

Among these Sotho-speaking Iron Age people were the Phalaborwa, who were adept at mining and extracted copper at Lolwe Hill (now Phalaborwa). Copper and its alloys were treasured for making ornaments and the value attached to the metal by these people is evident from the lengths to which they went to extract it. Mine shafts, adits and trenches reached down into the earth at least 20 m in places. Underground fires were made to crack the rock and iron chisels and stone hammers were tools used by the miners.

Iron smelting is believed to have taken place at Phalaborwa from AD 800, but the old network of mines has now been destroyed by modern day mining. Phalaborwa people also lived in the hills of Shikhumbu near the Phalaborwa entrance gate to the park, as well as at Masorini, another Iron Age site inside the park. The village at Masorini has been reconstructed and creates a good impression of how these people lived. An interesting feature is that the living area, smelting works and forging works are unusually close to each other. Although no copper smelting furnaces have been located at Masorini, good examples

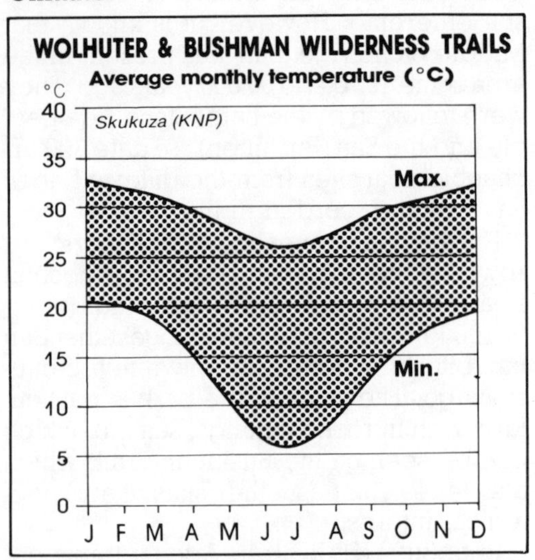
WOLHUTER & BUSHMAN WILDERNESS TRAILS
Average monthly temperature (°C)
°C
Skukuza (KNP)
Max.
Min.
40
35
30
25
20
15
10
5
0
J F M A M J J A S O N D

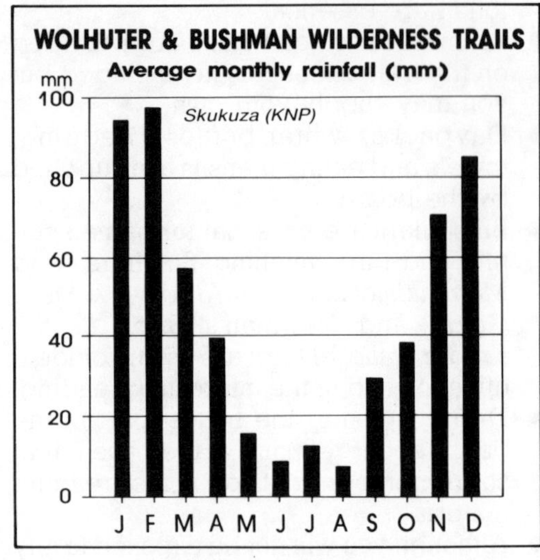
WOLHUTER & BUSHMAN WILDERNESS TRAILS
Average monthly rainfall (mm)
mm
Skukuza (KNP)
100
80
60
40
20
0
J F M A M J J A S O N D

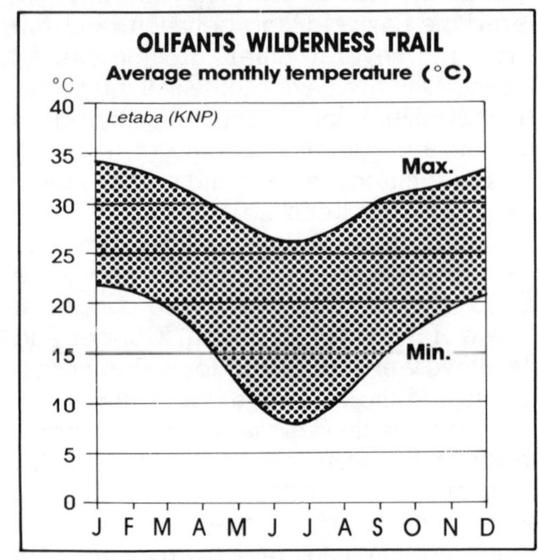
OLIFANTS WILDERNESS TRAIL
Average monthly temperature (°C)
°C
Letaba (KNP)
Max.
Min.
40
35
30
25
20
15
10
5
0
J F M A M J J A S O N D

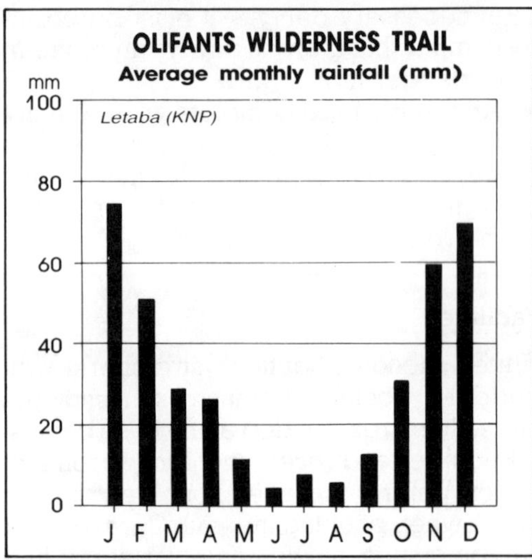
OLIFANTS WILDERNESS TRAIL
Average monthly rainfall (mm)
mm
Letaba (KNP)
100
80
60
40
20
0
J F M A M J J A S O N D

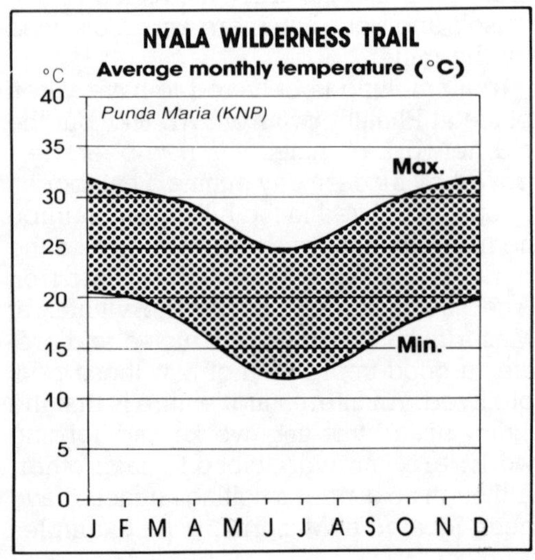
NYALA WILDERNESS TRAIL
Average monthly temperature (°C)
°C
Punda Maria (KNP)
Max.
Min.
40
35
30
25
20
15
10
5
0
J F M A M J J A S O N D

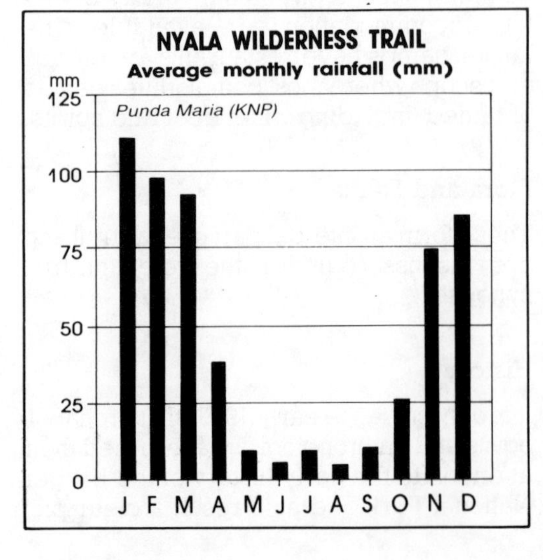
NYALA WILDERNESS TRAIL
Average monthly rainfall (mm)
mm
Punda Maria (KNP)
125
100
75
50
25
0
J F M A M J J A S O N D

of other smelting furnaces have been found at the bottom of Masorinikop.

Also present in the north-eastern Transvaal were the Shangana-Tsonga and the Venda, of whom the Makahane ruins on a hilltop in the north of the park are a reminder.

The first whites recorded to have entered the area were the De Kuiper expedition, who tried to establish a route from Delagoa Bay (now Maputo) to Zimbabwe via the Transvaal Lowveld after the VOC (Dutch East India Company) occupied Delagoa Bay in an attempt to gain control of the reported goldfields of Monomotapa in Zimbabwe. Captain François de Kuiper set off on 27 June 1725 with 31 men and entered the present-day park a few kilometres north of Crocodile Bridge. The expedition camped at a place called Gomondwane for a few days but were attacked by blacks and had to flee.

Although De Kuiper and his men survived their ordeal and returned to Delagoa Bay, the route was not pursued owing to their negative reports and whites did not enter the area for another century.

The next whites to enter the Lowveld were the Voortrekkers under Hans van Rensburg and Louis Tregardt, who were looking for a route to the sea and Delagoa Bay. The Van Rensburg party was massacred by Chief Soshangaan and his warriors, but Tregardt did reach his destination, although many of his party died of malaria. The grave of Willem Pretorius, one of the malaria victims, can be seen near Numbi gate.

The legendary Portuguese trader and adventurer João Albasini came to the Lowveld in 1832 in order to establish trading routes into the interior. On his travels he met up with the Boers and later assisted them in establishing their route to Delagoa Bay. This route is known as the Old Voortrekker Road. Albasini was an avid hunter, and conducted numerous hunting safaris to obtain ivory, sometimes accompanied by as many as 500 men. The ruins of the trading store established by Albasini just north-west of the present-day Pretoriuskop camp are still visible today.

The ruins of Sardelli's shop, another Portuguese trading store, can be seen at Gomondwane close to some old bluegum trees near Crocodile Bridge Camp, while several drifts, campsites and graves serve as reminders of the exploits of other early adventurers in the park.

As the population in the Transvaal increased with fortune seekers trying their luck wherever new discoveries were made, so the game rapidly started vanishing from the Lowveld. It was only in 1884 that Paul Kruger, president of the Zuid Afrikaansche Republiek (Transvaal), proposed to his *Volksraad* that a reserve be set aside in an attempt to conserve this valuable national heritage. Eventually, after much debating, the Pongola Reserve was proclaimed on 13 June 1894. Unfortunately not much game occupied this area and after another four years of ardent opposition, Kruger was able to proclaim the first official government game reserve on 26 March 1898. Known as the Sabie Game Reserve, it covered roughly 4 600 km² between the Sabie and Crocodile rivers.

Major (later Colonel) James Stevenson-Hamilton was appointed in 1902 as the first warden of the reserve. Sabie Bridge, today Skukuza, was selected as the site of the first park headquarters. Skukuza, translated as 'the man who sweeps clean', was the name given by the local blacks to Stevenson-Hamilton, a reference to the unpopular task he had of removing them from the reserve.

In 1903 Shingwedzi, an area of mopane and savanna land north of the Letaba River, was also proclaimed a reserve and placed under the control of Stevenson-Hamilton. A growing awareness of the need to promote conservation resulted in a commission of enquiry recommending in 1918 that more land be protected.

With the change in government in 1924 Piet Grobler, a grand-nephew of Paul Kruger, was appointed Minister of Lands. He presented the National Parks Board Bill in Parliament on 31 May 1926, by which he hoped to institute a central board of honorary trustees to control the two existing reserves and all future reserves countrywide. The bill was unanimously supported and the Kruger National Park, uniting the old Sabie and Shingwedzi game reserves, was proclaimed.

**Trail Synopses**

In July 1978 the dreams of many visitors to the Kruger National Park became a reality with the opening of the Wolhuter Wilderness Trail. For the first time visitors could leave the protection of their cars and absorb the atmosphere of the park on foot.

Four wilderness trails are now conducted in the park, all of which are extremely popular, and there are plans to establish more. Each group is led by an experienced game ranger, whose intimate knowledge of the area will considerably enhance your enjoyment of the trail. As the experiences on each trail are so different, no attempt is made here to give detailed descriptions.

## THE WOLHUTER GUIDED WILDERNESS TRAIL

The trail was named after Harry and Henry Wolhuter, father and son, who controlled the southern section of the park for many years. Harry Wolhuter served the park for more than 40 years and the classic story of how he managed to kill a lion with his pocket-knife after it pounced on his horse in August 1903, is today a legend in Africa and part of the history of the Kruger National Park.

This was the first wilderness trail to be opened and is conducted in the south of the park, between Pretoriuskop and Malelane, from the base camp at Mavukane River in the vicinity of Stolznek Dam. ('Mavukane', 'the one who is wide awake', was the nickname given to the ranger S H Trollope who was stationed at Malelane from 1925 to 1928.) The camp has been constructed to blend in well with the natural surroundings, and welcome shade is provided by indigenous trees and shrubs which were left undisturbed when the camp was built. A waterhole near the edge of the camp may well prove rewarding for game spotting and at night you may be fortunate to catch a glimpse of an African civet that frequently visits the camp.

The topography of the trail area varies from gently undulating plains to valleys, riverine thickets and high granite outcrops such as Mangake Hill. In the south-west of the park the vegetation consists of open broad-leaved species and has been classified as *Terminalia* (silver clusterleaf)/Sicklebush veld. As you progress eastwards it changes to medium-sized trees dominated by red bushwillow (*Combretum* spp.) veld which is frequently interspersed with open grassland.

Two trees that you are likely to notice on both this trail and the Bushman Trail are the marula (360) and the knob thorn (178). As its name implies, the latter is identified by its thorn-tipped knobs, although these are not always present on older branches. During August and September the still leafless knob thorn is covered in sweetly scented,

*Fruit and leaves*

*The marula, with its broadly round canopy, is one of the most widespread trees in the park*

*The southern part of the Kruger National Park is renowned for its rock paintings*

creamy-white flowers which make the tree particularly conspicuous. The medium-sized marula is also a deciduous tree and is well known for its small, round, yellow fruits which are produced between April and June. Potent alcoholic drinks are brewed from the fruit and jam with a distinctive flavour can also be made.

Game favouring the south of the park includes the white (square-lipped) rhinoceros, sable and mountain reedbuck, and on the trail you are likely to see most of the larger mammal species, such as impala, giraffe, blue wildebeest and lion. It is estimated that there are some 900 white rhino and 150 mountain reedbuck in the park. By 1896 white rhino had been hunted to extinction in the Transvaal. In an attempt to reintroduce the white rhino to the Transvaal, two bulls and two cows were translocated from the Umfolozi Game Reserve in Natal and released in the park in October 1961. Further translocations took place and by the end of October 1969 a total of 141 had been translocated, the total number translocated from Natal being more than 340.

Yellowbilled (459) and redbilled (458) hornbills and the crested francolin (189) are common in the camp, where they search for titbits. The crest of the crested francolin is not normally seen as it is raised only when the bird is alarmed.

The area is rich in the history of early adventurers. Twenty five kilometres north of the base camp lies the Old Voortrekker Road, once a regular trade route to Delagoa Bay (Maputo). This was also the route followed by Sir Percy Fitzpatrick, who immortalised the adventures of his dog, Jock, in the classic book, *Jock of the Bushveld.*

## THE BUSHMAN GUIDED WILDERNESS TRAIL

This was the most recent trail to be opened and the trail camp is situated only about 6 km away from the Wolhuter Trail huts. As the name implies, the area is rich in rock paintings, with most of the sites in the park concentrated in this area. Although this trail offers a similar experience to the other trails in the park, more frequent visits are made to rock paintings and other sites of anthropological interest.

The trail is conducted in the same area

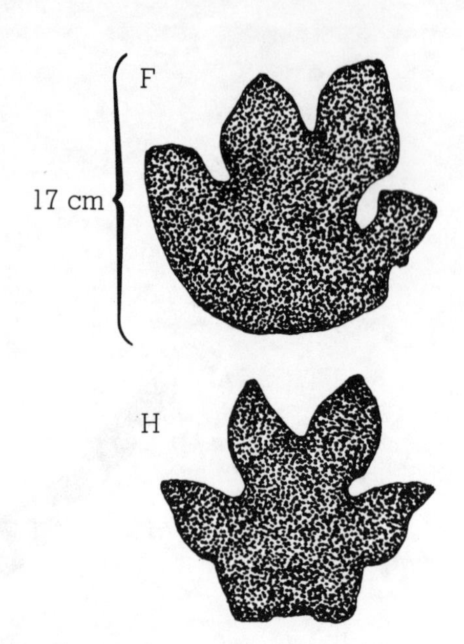


*Hippo are frequently sighted on the Olifants Wilderness Trail*

as the Wolhuter Guided Wilderness Trail, and consequently the vegetation and game described under that trail also apply to this trail.

Five vulture species occur in the park. The Cape vulture (122) is common in the south during summer but is easily confused with the smaller, whitebacked vulture (123), which is the most abundant vulture in the park and easily outnumbers the Cape vulture at carcasses. The hooded vulture (121) is fairly common throughout the park but as it is relatively small and has a weak bill, it does not compete at carcasses but waits for scraps. The lappetfaced vulture (124), the largest of the vultures, is also a fairly common resident in the park, while the fifth species, the whiteheaded vulture (125), is a resident but not common.

## THE OLIFANTS GUIDED WILDERNESS TRAIL

The base camp for the Olifants Guided Wilderness Trail is well positioned on the southern bank of the Olifants River, roughly 4 km west of the confluence of the Olifants and Letaba rivers. Situated above the river gorge, only 300 m from the river, the camp offers a magnificent view of the river and the surrounding countryside stretching to the Lebombo Mountains in the east, which form a natural boundary to the park.

The vegetation of the area has been classified as Lebombo Mountain Communities. Although the trail is unlikely to take you into the mountains, it is interesting to know that they are the habitat of the Lebombo euphorbia (345), a candelabriform tree reaching up to 10 m in height. The tree bears greenish-yellow flowers from June to August and the deep red fruits appear from July to September. Three other euphorbias also occur in the Park: the Transvaal candelabra tree (346), which occurs on rocky outcrops, the common tree euphorbia (351), which is often seen close to termite mounds, and the rubber euphorbia (355), a many-branched tree that grows in various habitats.

The deciduous white seringa (267) is an easily identifiable medium-sized tree and is fairly common in the base camp. The Lebombo wattle (191), a large tree reaching 25 m in height, is restricted to the area at the confluence of the Olifants and Letaba rivers. The tree produces dark red seed pods, about 30 cm long, which turn brown with age, and in winter you may notice the flat, elongated seeds on the ground. They are usually about 6 cm long and have a russet coloured papery wing.

The rivers are the habitat of hippo and crocodile, and you are likely to also see Burchell's zebra, elephant and giraffe. Among the less common bird species in the park which you may be able to tick off here are the jackal buzzard (152), rock martin (529), wailing cisticola (670), cuckoo finch (820) and the Cape canary (872).

It is worth exploring a little way upstream from the camp, where some fantastic natural sculptures have been carved into the rock in a narrow stretch of the river. After passing through these narrow ravines the river widens out again and continues its course on fairly level terrain.

## THE NYALALAND GUIDED WILDERNESS TRAIL

The Nyalaland Guided Wilderness Trail in the Punda Maria region was the third guided wilderness trail to be opened in the park. The base camp is situated among sandstone koppies 8 km south of the confluence of the Mutale and Luvuvhu rivers and alongside the Madzaringwe Spruit. The Punda Maria region is considered one of the most outstanding wilderness areas in Southern Africa. The trail is named after the nyala, which is seldom seen in the southern regions of the park but occurs in significant numbers in the north.

The vegetation on the trail can be broad-

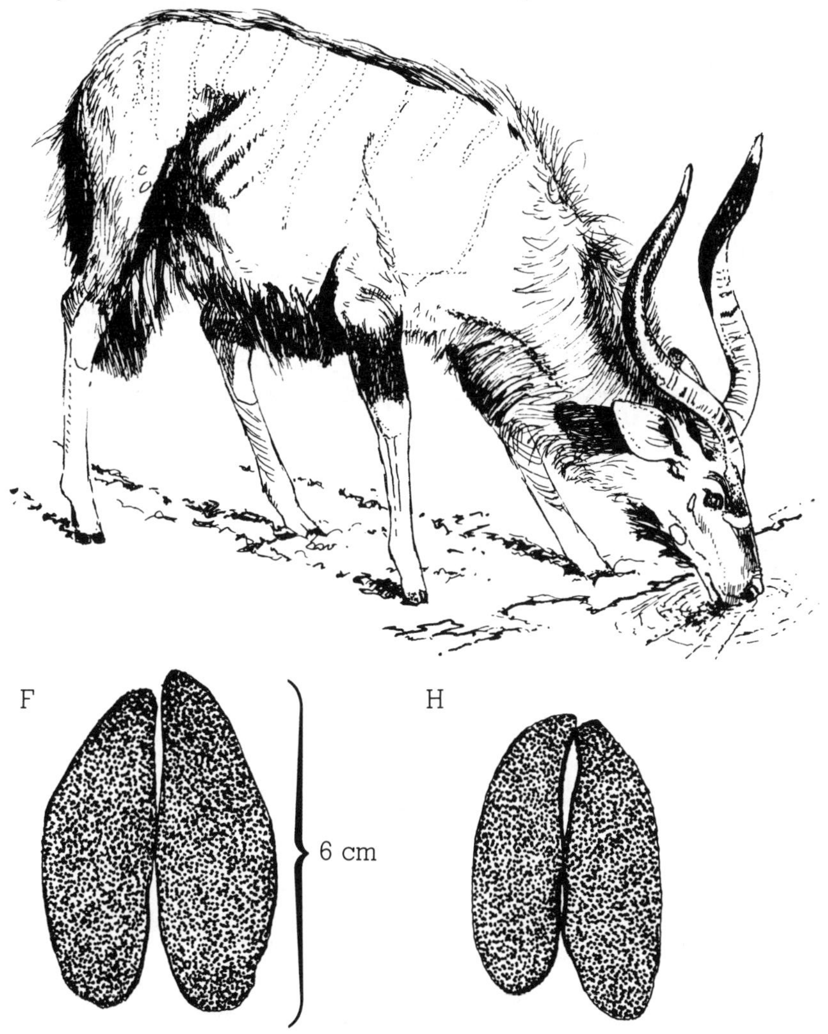


*The nyala favours riverine forest in the northern part of the Kruger National Park*

ly classified as Punda Maria sandveld communities, consisting of dense woodland of medium-sized trees such as *Acacia* spp., apple-leaf (238), Natal mahogany (301), leadwood (539), tamboti (341) and red bushwillow (532). Further eastwards the vegetation changes to mopane veld, consisting mainly of mopane (198) interspersed with large areas of open grassland. Although the baobab (467) occurs as far south as Tshokwane, it is most common in the Pafuri area, where there are extensive baobab 'forests'.

The northern Kruger National Park has the richest variety of flora and fauna in the park, with a large number of species that do not occur in the south. Noteworthy plant species include the Zimbabwe aloe (28.8), Wylliespoort aloe (28.4) and *Euphorbia rowlandii*.

Mammal species that occur only in the north are the rare yellow golden mole and the rufous hairy bat (which are respectively classified as rare and indeterminate in the *South African Red Data Book — Terrestrial Mammals*), Hildebrandt's horseshoe bat and the yellow spotted rock dassie.

The riverine forests of the Luvuvhu River are the habitat of species such as bushbuck and nyala, while Burchell's zebra, impala, buffalo and elephant are frequently encountered in the mopane veld further east.

Several bird species listed in the *South African Red Data Book — Birds* occur only in this part of South Africa, including the rackettailed roller (448) and the longtailed starling (763), which are both indeterminate, while the mottled spinetail (422) and Böhm's spinetail (423) have both been classified as rare. The silverycheeked hornbill (456) is an occasional vagrant into the extreme north of the park. It is distributed from eastern Zimbabwe through East Africa to Ethiopia, but sometimes moves south during the rainy season.

The Makahane ruins are within walking distance of the base camp and are usually visited by trailists. Makahane was the chief of the Lembethu people who preceded the main Venda migration in the seventeenth century. Also known as 'Makahane the Terrible', he was notorious for his cruelty to his subjects and was eventually murdered by his son, Nelombe. He was buried in front of his 'throne', a stone seat (still visible today) built into a wall with a number of steps leading up to it.

The ruins bear an interesting resemblance to structures in the northern Transvaal and Zimbabwe, where the dry-packed walls, built from flat sandstone blocks, show evidence of a passage and several enclosures.

# 22 Wolkberg Backpacking Area

The Wolkberg is an unspoilt area of deep ravines, indigenous forests and high mountain peaks, which are often covered in a fine mist during the summer months, lending an air of mystery and romance. The area abounds with myths and legends, and John Buchan was inspired to use it as a backdrop to his classic adventure story, *Prester John*. Harry Klein, too, came under its spell and immortalised it in his book *Valley of the Mists,* and General Smuts fell in love with it when he visited the area in 1937.

### Location

The Wolkberg forms an arc where the northern extension of the Transvaal Drakensberg joins the eastern extremity of the Strydpoort Mountains.

The nearest major towns are Tzaneen and Pietersburg and the entry point at Serala Forest Station is reached by taking the gravel road which turns south from the main Pietersburg/Tzaneen road (R71), 35 km east of Pietersburg. About 9 km on you come to a four-way intersection, and you continue straight ahead. After 7 km the road forks, and you keep left. After another 14 km the road forks again, with the left fork leading to Serala Forest Station 6 km on.

### Distance and Classification

Depends on the route chosen.
A to C grade options are possible.

### Permits

It is advisable to book well in advance as both the group size and the total number of

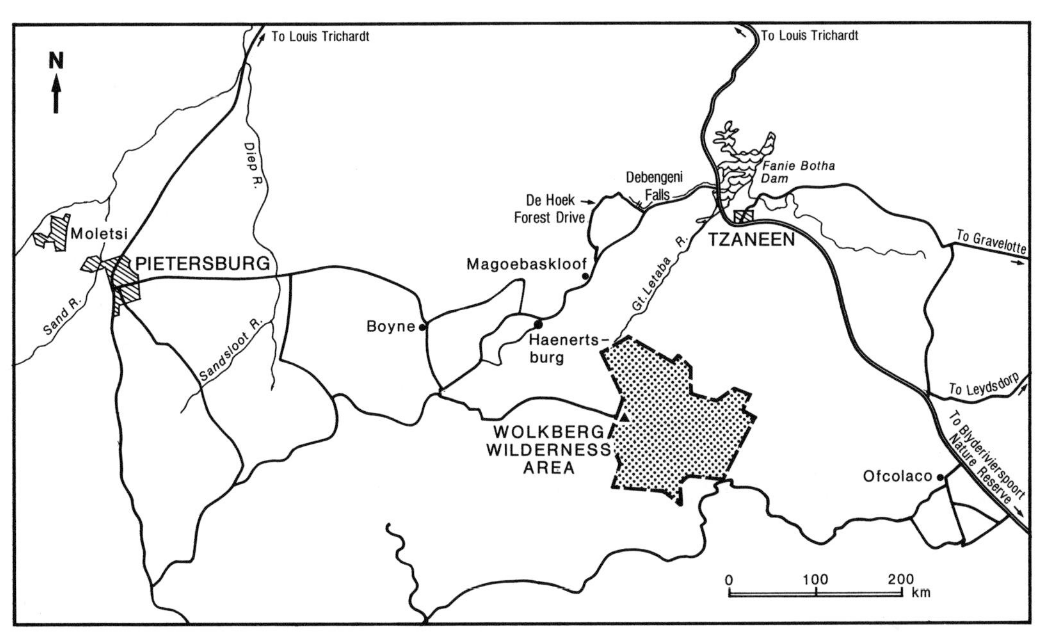


*Wolkberg Backpaking Area.*

people permitted in the wilderness area are restricted. Overnight groups are limited to a maximum of 10 people per group, while the total number of day and overnight visitors is restricted to 60. Reservations can be made with The Officer-in-Charge, Serala Forest Station, Private Bag, Haenertsburg 0730, Telephone (0152222) 1303.

### Maps

A sketch map and an information booklet can be obtained when making reservations. For more detailed information, 1:50 000 topographical maps 2330CC and 2430AA can be obtained.

### Relevant Information

- Fires are not permitted in the wilderness area and a backpacking stove is therefore essential.
- The use of soap and detergents in rivers and streams is strictly prohibited.

### Facilities

There is a small campsite with showers, toilets and parking at the entry point at Serala. Accommodation in the wilderness area is in the open and it is essential to take a backpacking tent as the summits are often covered in mist.

### Climate

At New Agatha Forest Station, north of the wilderness area, the average annual temperature is 18,1 °C. The average annual daily maximum is 22,4 °C, with average maximum daily temperatures of 24 °C to 25 °C between November and February. Average daily minimum temperatures during these months are around 15 °C to 16 °C. During June, July and August average daily minimum and maximum temperatures fluctuate between 11,5 °C and 18,9 °C, 9,9 °C and 18,2 °C and 10,3°C and 20,3 °C. It should, however, be borne in mind that these temperatures are generally lower at higher altitudes where frost often occurs in winter.

Rainfall in the wilderness area varies from 500 mm in the south-west to 1 350 mm in the higher-lying areas in the north-east, the months between November and February being the wettest. Snow can be expected in the wake of a very cold front.

Mist occurs at an altitude of 1 200 m and higher and although it can be expected throughout the year, it is most common during the summer rainfall period.

The prevailing wind is cool and moderate, but strong, dry winds are common between July and October.

### Flora

The vegetation has been classified by Acocks as North-Eastern Mountain Sourveld (Veld Type 8) and Lowveld Sour Bushveld (Veld Type 9). Both of these are classified by Acocks as inland tropical forest types.

The Lowveld Sour Bushveld is limited to the southern part adjacent to the Mohlapitse Valley and consists of sour grassveld with bushveld species such as round-leaved teak (237), wild teak (236), large-fruited bushwillow (546), marula (360) and Transvaal beech (75).

At higher altitudes the Lowveld Sour Bushveld merges into North-Eastern Mountain Sourveld, which consists of sour grassveld dominated by redgrass (*Themeda triandra*). At these higher elevations be on the lookout for the Transvaal mountain sugarbush (97), which is restricted to the mistbelts from near Lydenburg in the Drakensberg escarpment to the Wolkberg. It grows as a small gnarled tree or shrub, although it can reach up to 8 m in areas with high rainfall and frequent mists. Brilliant, rosy-pink flowers are produced in spring. Other *Protea* species also occur in the montane grasslands. Stands of curry bush (484) with their attractive yellow flowers and characteristic spicy fragrance are common on the slopes, while everlastings (*Helichrysum* spp.) can be seen in the higher mountainous areas. The common tree fern (1) occurs beside streams.

Semi-deciduous indigenous forests account for about eight per cent of the vegetation of the wilderness area, while evergreen montane high forest covers about 10 per cent. Patches of indigenous forest are found in the deep valleys and on the higher southern and south-eastern slopes, and are composed of about 40 tree species. Typi-

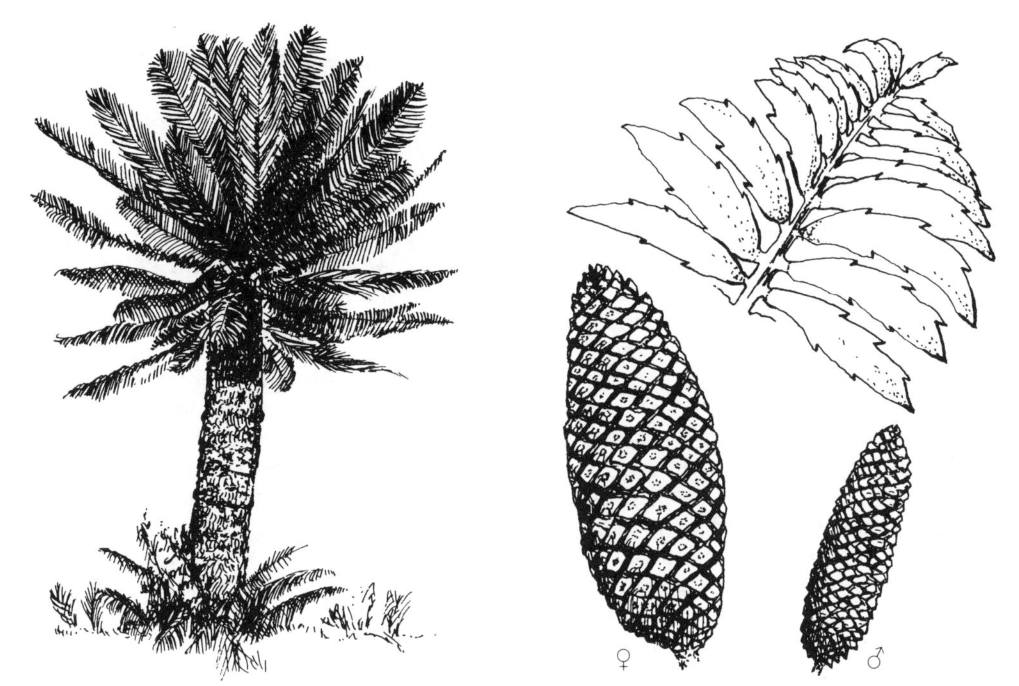


*Growth form, leaf, and female and male cones of the Modjadji cycad, which takes its name from the legendary Rain Queen of the Lobedu*

cal forest species include the common wild fig (48), Cape beech (578), lemonwood (111), Outeniqua (16) and real (18) yellowwoods, forest waterwood (556), forest bushwillow (540) and tree fuchsia (670).

It is estimated that about 4 000 Modjadji cycads (13) occur in the appropriately named Cycad Valley, a very steep valley at the western end of the Devil's Knuckles. The Modjadji cycad is the largest of the 17 South African cycad species, reaching an average height of between 5 and 8 m, although it occasionally reaches up to 13 m. The leaves grow up to 2,5 m in length, and the female cones can weigh as much as 37 kg. The cycad derived its popular name from the Mujaji or Rain Queen of the Lobedu, who lives in the vicinity of Duiwelskloof. According to one theory, the origin of the Lobedu can be traced to Dzugudini, the grand-daughter of a Shona chief, who fled from Zimbabwe in the sixteenth century with her illegitimate son and a number of followers to escape the wrath of her father. With them they brought the sacred rain-making medicines and magic rituals of the chiefdom. Since the early 1800s the Lobedu have been ruled by a dynasty of queens, whose power depended partly on their ability to make rain. The present Rain Queen is the fifth successor to Mujaji I, who inspired Sir Henry Rider Haggard's *She*.

The hill overlooking her kraal is covered with several thousand of these cycads, forming one of the largest cycad forests in the world. The forest enjoyed the protection of succeeding generations of the Rain Queen and was proclaimed a national monument in 1936.

**Fauna**

In days gone by game was generally scarce in the Wolkberg, owing to illegal hunting by farmers and poaching by local dagga growers who lived in the inaccessible kloofs. However, since the area came under the control of the Forestry Branch in 1977 and anti-poaching and hunting measures have been introduced on a regular basis, game is once again on the increase.

The most common antelope are bushbuck and common duiker, but you might also spot grey rhebok, klipspringer and reedbuck. The primates are represented by vervet monkey, lesser bushbaby, chacma baboon and the samango monkey. Predators include leopard, caracal, brown hyaena, Cape clawless otter, African wild cat, black-backed jackal and genets. Bushpig inhabit the forests.

To date some 157 bird species have been recorded in the area. Among the more uncommon species are the bat hawk (129), martial eagle (140) and the blackfronted bush shrike (749), which breeds in the Wonderwoud. The bat hawk is listed as rare in the *South African Red Data Book — Birds* and only two breeding pairs have been recorded in the north-eastern Transvaal. However, this species and its nest are so unobtrusive that the breeding population could well be more extensive. Nonbreeding birds wander extensively and their present distribution includes the eastern Transvaal, Witwatersrand and the lowveld of Zululand. It is a medium-sized dark brown to blackish bird with pale-yellow, owl-like eyes and the wings of a falcon. During the day it perches in shady trees, emerging only before or during dusk or in heavily overcast weather to hunt. Bats and small birds, especially swallows and swifts, are caught and eaten in flight. They normally roost and build their nests close to bat colonies or communal roosts of small birds.

*Lesser bushbaby – a nocturnal inhabitant of the indigenous forest of the Wolkberg*

In addition to the bat hawk and martial eagle, other raptors include blackshouldered kite (127), black eagle (131), forest buzzard (150) and lanner falcon (172). Other interesting species to look out for are the Goliath heron (64), yellow wagtail (714) and the crested guineafowl (204), which can be distinguished from the more common helmeted guineafowl (203) by the tuft of feathers on the crest. Although they have a limited distribution — from Umhlanga Rocks and Karkloof northwards through Zululand to the eastern Transvaal and the Soutpansberg — they are not considered rare. The yellow wagtail is a summer visitor from North Africa, Europe, North Asia and Alaska (October to April) which favours moist short grassland and the edges of vleis and pans.

The numerous rivers and streams of the area are the habitat of species such as Egyptian goose (102), yellowbilled duck (104), black crake (213) and moorhen (226). In riverine bush look out for Burchell's coucal (391), brownhooded kingfisher (435), southern boubou (736) and glossy starling (764).

In the wooded savanna and grassland you might see secretarybird (118) and redcrested korhaan (237). Among the other species occurring in the wilderness area are speckled mousebird (424), lilacbreasted roller (447), clapper lark (495), blackeyed bulbul (568), longtailed wagtail (712), Marico sunbird (779) and swee waxbill (850).

Snakes are represented by species such as the berg adder (*Bitis atropos*), puff adder (*Bitis arietans arietans*), both the black mamba (*Dendroaspis polylepis*) and the green mamba (*D. angusticeps*) and the African python (*Python sebae*). The status of the latter species is listed in the *South African Red Data Book — Reptiles and Amphibians* as vulnerable outside game reserves.

**History**

Archaeological finds in the north-eastern Transvaal have provided abundant evidence that the Wolkberg was inhabited by Early Iron Age man during the late third

*The crested guineafowl – one of more than 157 bird species recorded in the Wolkberg Wilderness Area*

and early fourth centuries. These early inhabitants, the ancestors of the Sotho, were not only pastoralists, but also cultivated crops, worked metal and manufactured pottery. They preferred the open, grassy areas where they lived in fairly large settlements.

The oldest Iron Age site in South Africa, 16 km east of Tzaneen, has been dated to the late third and early fourth centuries. An interesting feature of the pottery unearthed at this site is that it does not closely resemble that of any other Early Iron Age site in South Africa, but displays features corresponding with pottery from East Africa and Malawi. The site is also of importance because it provided the oldest direct evidence of cereal (*Penisetum americanum*) cultivation in the Transvaal.

Stone walls in the wilderness area and place names such as Mampa's Kloof (named after a local Sotho chief) serve as reminders of the Sotho-speaking people who inhabited the area. Other Sotho chiefs who lived in the area when whites started settling there included Motshutli, Tsolobolo, Magoboya and Mamathola, after whom the 3 011 m high peak to the south-east of the wilderness area was named. Further west lived the Tlou tribe of chief Magoeba.

Whites began taking an interest in the area after Edward Button and James Sutherland reported traces of gold in the Murchison Range 40 km south-east of Tzaneen in 1870. The earliest find of gold was the discovery of Ellen's Fortune Reef at the foot of the Iron Crown (2 126 m) by C F Haenert in 1887. Haenertsburg was established in the same year.

However, the Woodbush Gold Fields — as they were known — proved disappointing and after the discovery of richer deposits in the Murchison Range in the early 1880s, the miners turned their attention eastwards. In 1890 the mining settlement

*Heads of (a) crested guineafowl and (b) helmeted guineafowl*

south of the Murchison Range was proclaimed a town and given the name Leydsdorp after the then State Secretary of the Transvaal Republic, Dr W Leyds. The government administrative centre for the goldfields was originally situated near Thabina in the Lowveld. It was named Agatha, after the wife of Dr Leyds. The site was badly chosen, however, and malaria and bilharzia forced the settlers to relocate the centre in the foothills of the mountains. The new centre was named New Agatha, a name that still exists today.

The hotel at New Agatha was originally a coach house on the route between Pietersburg and Leydsdorp. The descent of the precipitous Drakensberg escarpment must have been a nightmare and in parts the gradient was three in one. Some stretches were so steep that the rear wheels of wagons and coaches had to be locked and after rain the red clay soil made the track impassable.

The coach service was run by the coaching firm of C H Zeederberg which, after the discovery of gold in the eastern Transvaal, moved their headquarters from Pietermaritzburg to Pretoria. They operated regular wagon services to Pietermaritzburg and Kimberley and stage coach services to Barberton, Pietersburg and Leydsdorp.

It was a four-and-a-half-day journey from Pretoria to Leydsdorp with passengers sleeping over *en route* first at Nylstroom, then Pietersburg, followed by Haenertsburg and finally, Thabina — now New Agatha. The coach eventually arrived at Leydsdorp at noon on the fifth day, a Saturday. For this journey of roughly 500 km the single fare was £15. Mules were mainly used to haul the coaches, although the Zeederbergs became well known for the domesticated zebras that were also employed!

The more recent history of the area is closely linked to that of Orrie Baragwanath who, in the early 1900s, settled in the highlands south of the wilderness area known as the Downs. He and his ex-hunting partner, Frank Lewis, bought land from the government and began farming sheep and seed potatoes. The area was sparsely inhabited by small groups of Sotho with the closest white neighbours over 60 km distant at Leydsdorp and Thabina. No roads led into the mountains until Baragwanath and Lewis constructed a track up the Asberg from the Mohlapitse River and later a route down the northern face of the mountains was surveyed.

Two Afrikaans farmers, Du Toit and Van Der Gryp, who had lost their farms during the Anglo-Boer War (1899-1902) subsequently settled on the farms Fertillis and Mampa's Kloof respectively. The latter now forms part of the wilderness area and the site of the homestead is marked by a grove of bluegum (*Eucalyptus* spp.) trees.

As part of the government's consolidations scheme, the Downs has been incorporated into Lebowa and now forms part of the Lekgalameetse Nature Reserve. On 28 October 1977 the Wolkberg was declared South Africa's seventh proclaimed wilderness area. It covers some 17 390 ha and is renowned for its spectacular mountain scenery and beautiful indigenous forests.

**Trail Synopsis**

Like other wilderness areas, the Wolkberg allows you to create your own experience. No trails are formally laid out but backpackers have a large choice of management paths and jeep tracks to follow. Only the main features are highlighted here, leaving you to discover the rest.

Prior to the area being transferred to the Nature Conservation Division of the Transvaal Provincial Administration, backpackers could approach the wilderness area from either the New Agatha or Serala forest stations. Backpackers may now enter the area only from the office at Serala from where various options are possible, depending on time available. It is best to consult both the sketch map and the 1:50 000 topographical map and to check with the Officer-in-Charge if you are unfamiliar with the area.

From the office a jeep track descends to the Mohlapitse River, running partly along the Klipdraai River. There are several lovely waterfalls in the Klipdraai River on the way and it is well worth the extra time and effort to visit these. On reaching the Mohlapitse it is a good idea to explore the area to view the fascinating potholes that have been scoured into the solid rock by the swirling waters of the river.

Over countless aeons the Mohlapitse and its tributaries carved deep valleys into the Wolkberg, resulting in the separation of the northern Drakensberg from the Strydpoort Mountains. The Mohlapitse, which is said to mean either 'guardian', 'herd' or 'the pot which is always full', is a tributary of the Letaba River and is an interesting example of river piracy. According to geologists, the Letaba River once flowed through the present Mohlapitse Valley, joining the Olifants River south-west of the Downs. In the course of time the Letaba River cut through its own bank and intercepted the upper reaches of what became known as the Mohlapitse River. As a result the upper reaches of the Mohlapitse River are without running water today.

After exploring the area around the river you have a number of backpacking options, depending on the time available. One is to continue along the jeep track which follows the river downstream until its junction with the Mogwatse River at Mampa's Kloof. The jeep track crosses the river numerous times and one is reminded of the determination of Orrie Baragwanath, who crossed the river no less than 45 times in one day between Haenertsburg and the Downs when he first explored the area. Along this section you will reach the lowest point of the wilderness area — 795 m compared to the 2 050 m of Serala Peak.

By following the footpath up Mampa's Kloof you can join up with the network of footpaths leading to the Thabina Falls, the Wonderwoud and Serala Peak. A detour to the Thabina Falls is well worth the effort.

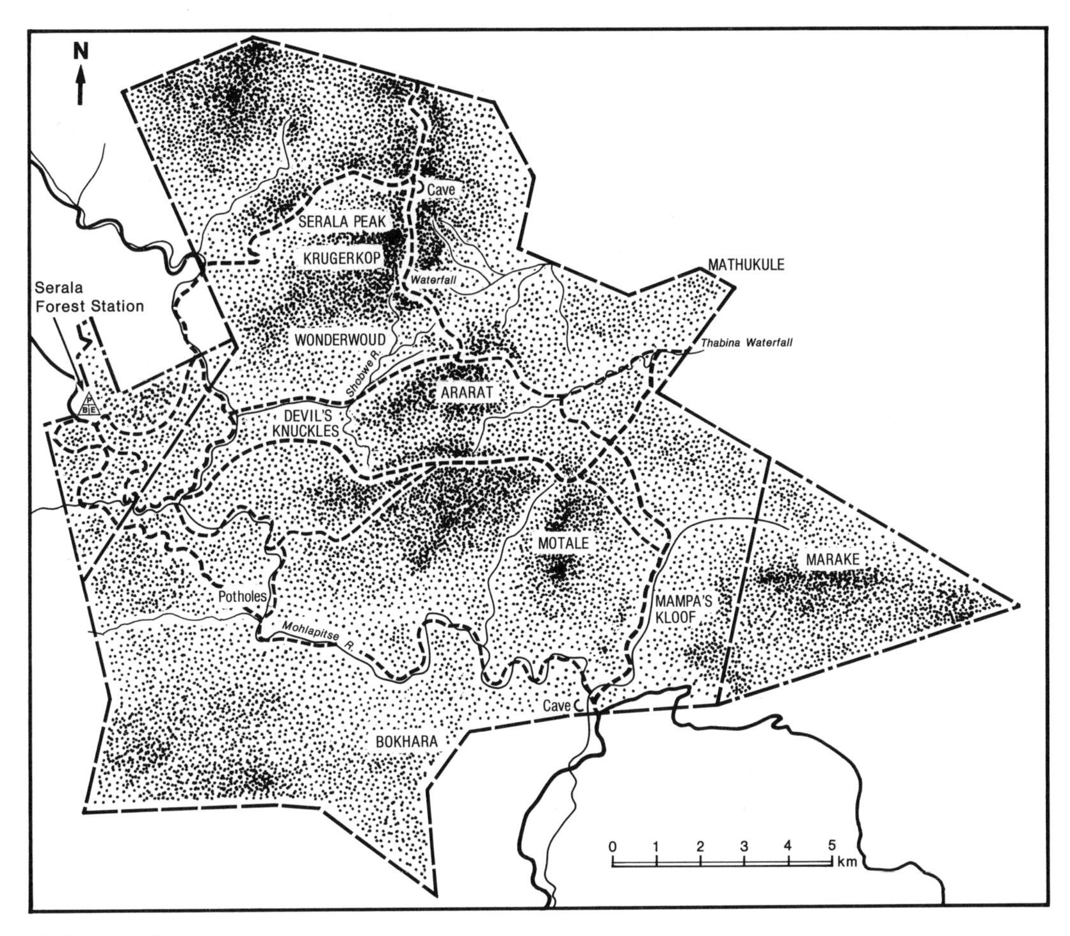


*Wolkberg Backpacking Area*

Over thousands of years the Thabina River and its tributaries have carved deep valleys between the grassy hills and on the edge of the escarpment the river plunges over a magnificent waterfall. Further downstream this water is captured in a dam in Lebowa.

Instead of following the jeep track as described, an alternative is to follow the Mohlapitse upstream until you reach the Shobwe River, where you can join a footpath leading up to Wonderwoud. The river has cut a fairly wide valley between Serala Peak and the Devil's Knuckles (also known as Tandberg or Ararat), a row of quartzite cliffs which initially face north-east for about 2 km but then dwindle in a westerly direction for about 6 km until they end in the Mohlapitse Valley. The route over the Devil's Knuckles involves rock-climbing of C grade standard and is thus not recommended for inexperienced backpackers. If you do intend doing it, it is advisable to take a rope along.

A large part of the Shobwe catchment area is covered by the largest indigenous forest (500 ha) in the wilderness area, the Wonderwoud. Here you will be impressed by the towering yellowwoods (*Podocarpus* spp.), some with a trunk circumference of 5 m.

A fairly steep ascent to the Serala Plateau via Kruger's Nose awaits you on leaving the coolness of the forest. The Letsitele River has its origin above Kruger's Nose and is known here as Motlhaka Semeeste, a North Sotho name which has variously been translated as 'hasty waters' or the 'water which makes light', perhaps a reference to the rainbows that are often seen over the waterfalls. Shortly after it rises, the Motlhaka Semeeste plunges over a high waterfall in a narrow ravine between two peaks, and further north another tributary of the river plunges over the sheer cliffs of the escarpment into a forested kloof. Further downstream the Motlhaka Semeeste becomes known as the Letsitele River. During the nineteenth century the Letsitele Valley was known to the white pioneers as Death Valley, because of the malaria which was common until as late as 1945.

Below Serala Peak is Krugerkop, which as its name implies is said to bear a resemblance to the Zuid-Afrikaansche Republiek president, Paul Kruger, with the forest at the foot of the dome forming his beard! Further south-east the scenery is dominated by Mamotswiri (1 838 m) and to the east you look across the Lowveld. Serala Peak (2 050 m), a long, flat mountain, is the highest point in the wilderness area, although the Iron Crown (2 126 m) which is south of Haenertsburg is the highest point in the area. From Serala Peak you are rewarded with a magnificent view back over the Devil's Knuckles and the Wonderwoud.

From here you can either return along the same route to the office at Serala or, on reaching the Devil's Knuckles, follow a footpath leading to the Thabina Falls, Mampa's Kloof and the Mohlapitse River.

# Part 7
# Botswana and Malawi

# 23 Okavango Delta Mokoro Safari

The Okavango Delta is an unspoilt world of intricate papyrus-fringed waterways, waterlily-carpeted channels and blazing African sunsets. Although strictly speaking the delta is not backpacking territory, it lends itself to a trail with a difference. Harassed city dwellers will soon forget their anxieties as they glide effortlessly through the waterways in a mokoro (dugout) and become enchanted by the beauty and diversity of the delta.

### Location

The delta is in north-western Botswana. Maun, on the eastern edge of the delta, is your gateway should you arrive by road or air from Johannesburg, Gaborone or Francistown. It is 500 km by road from Francistown via Nata, the last 300 km of which is gravel. The condition of the road is generally fair and with careful driving should be negotiable in any vehicle.

### Distance and Classification

Backpacking in the area is limited. Day walks are possible on Chief's Island and shorter walks on other smaller islands.
A grade

### Permits

Permits are not required for the delta should you remain outside the boundaries of the Moremi Wildlife Reserve. However, should you wish to explore the reserve, which includes Chief's Island, you are required to pay the prescribed entry and camping fees which are normally charged when booking a mokoro.

### Maps

The best maps covering the delta are topographical maps: Maun 1:50 000, Sheet SE 34-16, Series DOS 647P and Okavango Delta 1:350 000. They are available from the Department of Surveys and Lands, Private Bag 0037, Gaborone, Botswana.

### Relevant Information

- Exploring the Okavango Delta is limited to either an overland safari or a mokoro trip on the delta's waterways. Opportunities for backpacking are limited and not advisable without a guide. There are several companies offering organised mokoro and walking expeditions. Those wishing to explore the area on their own can hire mekoro (plural of mokoro) or canoes with guides from agents in Maun.
- At present (1988) immunisation/vaccination certificates are not required for yellow fever, smallpox or cholera. However, it is advisable to consult your local health authority at least one month prior to departure as to current health requirements.
- The Okavango Delta is situated in a malaria endemic area and anti-malaria precautions must be taken. (Daraprim and Paludrine tablets are not recommended.)
- South African citizens require a valid passport. Other nationals should enquire at their nearest consulate as to present regulations. A re-entry visa or permit to return to South Africa may also be required and applications should be made to the nearest regional representative of the South African Department of Home Affairs.

- Always be aware of the inherent dangers of being in the wild. Most accidents and fatalities are a result of careless disrespect for wild animals. Never swim unless your poler has decided that the area is safe from hippos and crocodiles. When camping on Chief's Island you should sleep in a tent with a sewn-in groundsheet. Never leave food outside the tent as this is likely to attract animals, especially predators. A small fire kept alive throughout the night will help to keep animals at bay.
- Mosquito repellent and sun protection are essential.
- Beware of leeches attaching themselves to you in shallow water while getting in or out of the mokoro.
- Binoculars are useful for game viewing or bird-watching.
- Remember to take your daypack for a few essentials on short walks.

**Facilities**

Accommodation and camping facilities in Maun are available at Matlapaneng, approximately 12 km north/north-east of the town. Island Safari Lodge is situated on the Maun side of the Thamalakane River and comprises thatched chalets and campsites with ablutions. Restaurant and bar facilities are also available. Okavango Lodge, Koro Safari Lodge and Crocodile Camp Safaris, on the opposite bank of the river, offer similar facilities. Enquiries can be made to the following addresses:

- Island Safari Lodge, P O Box 116, Maun, Telephone 260300.
- Okavango River Lodge, P O Box 32, Maun, Telephone 260298.
- Crocodile Camp Safaris, P O Box 46, Maun, Telephone 260265.
- Koro Safari Lodge, Private Bag 22, Maun, Telephone 260205/260222.

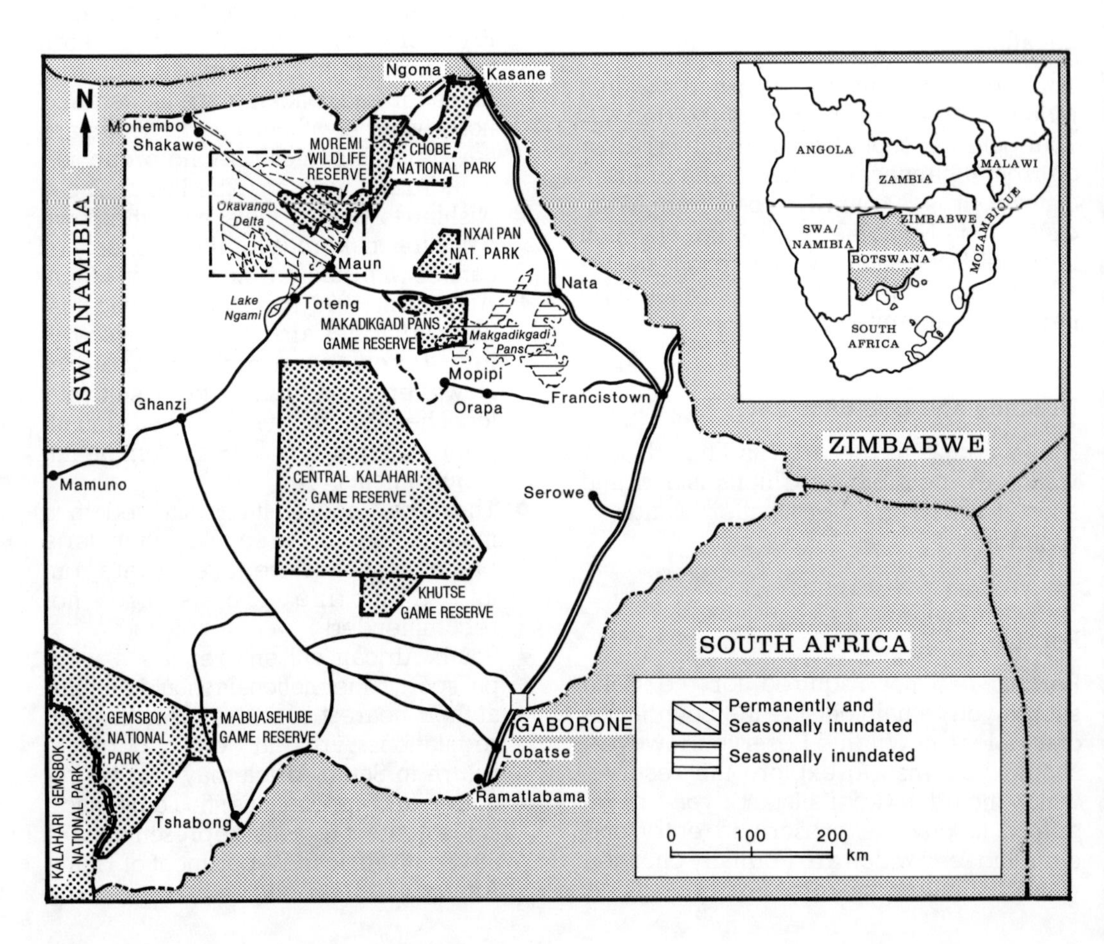

It is not advisable to consider staying at any of these places, however, unless you are in a four-wheel-drive vehicle. Riley's Hotel in Maun, situated fairly close to the airport, is accessible by sedan cars. The address is P O Box 1, Maun, Telephone 260204.

In the delta there are several exclusive luxury camps that provide a fully inclusive service. People making their own arrangements can camp wherever the mokoro takes them. On the same island as Delta Camp, some 60 km north-west of Maun, is a camp catering for those seeking less sophisticated accommodation at very affordable prices. The camp comprises a small shop, bar, camping site with fireplaces, hot showers and toilets. Reservations (including your flight there) can be made c/o Bushman Curio Shop, P O Box 39, Maun, Telephone 260220.

## Climate

The average annual temperature at Maun is 22,2 °C, while the average annual daily maximum is 30,4 °C. The months with the highest maximum temperatures are October, November and December with averages of 35 °C, 34 °C and 33 °C. Average minimum temperatures during these months are 19 °C, 20 °C and 20 °C respectively. Frost occurs during winter when temperatures range from 6 °C to 25/26 °C in June and July.

Maun has an average annual rainfall of 525 mm, but the rainfall is extremely variable from one year to the next. The rainy season usually begins in October and, after reaching a peak in January/February, tapers off in May. During the rainy season the humidity is generally high.

## Flora

The vegetation of Chief's Island and the adjacent floodplain system can be divided into five main vegetation types. Each type can be further divided into several communities, of which only the most prominent are described here.

### *Aquatic vegetation types*

The Boro River from below the Xo Flats and some of the smaller channels of the eastern floodplains are classified as outlet channel communities. In the permanent swamps they are perennial watercourses but lower in the delta they are only subjected to seasonal flow. The dominant marginal vegetation consists of bulrushes (*Miscanthidium* spp.), sedges (*Cyperus articulatis*) and *Seirpus* spp., as well as grasses such as *Vossia cuspidata*. The most common floating plant is the waterlily (*Nymphaea* spp.), which is abundant on the margins of channels and lagoons. Its delicate flowers are found in various shades of white, pink, yellow and blue and are a favourite subject of photographers.

### *Floodplain vegetation types*

The floodplains can be divided into primary communities (the melapo) and secondary communities. Inundated for between five months and a year — depending on the volume of the flood — the primary communities occur in the middle and lower Boro River floodplains. The vegetation consists mainly of semi-aquatic sedges and grasses.

The vegetation of the secondary floodplain communities is typically grasslands, which can be inundated for up to seven months during a flood season or not at all in a poor flood season.

### *Riverine vegetation types*

This vegetation type occurs throughout the delta but is more developed in the proximity of permanent water. It is situated on the margins of islands adjacent to channels and on islands in the floodplains and occupies slightly elevated flat ground.

The lower perennial and wetter seasonal swamp island edges are characterised by species such as the water fig (67.1) and the river bitter-tea (723.3), a bushy shrub or small tree often associated with termite mounds. Other prominent species include apple-leaf (238), Lowveld mangosteen (486), jackal-berry (606) and common cluster fig (66).

### *Marginal riverine vegetation types*

This vegetation type occurs adjacent to riverine woodland on elevated ground that is never flooded. Three main communities can be distinguished.

Knob thorn and fever-berry woodland

and savanna woodland consists of knob thorn (178) and large fever-berry (329), which are the dominant species of the smaller islands and form large communities on Chief's Island. They are often associated with species such as common false-thorn (155), camel thorn (168), apple-leaf and live-long (362).

Mokolwane/fever-berry palm woodland and palm savanna woodland can easily be distinguished by the characteristic real fan palm (24), locally known as mokolwane. They occur either as single-boled trees or as a short scrub growth. Common species within this community include the buffalo-thorn (447), Lowveld mangosteen and the sausage tree (678).

Leadwood/fever-berry woodland and savanna woodland is characterised by the leadwood (539), a species favouring alluvial soils and found in association with the apple-leaf, which forms a sub-dominant community. Species of lesser abundance include the umbrella thorn (188), sickle bush (190) and *Grewia* spp.

On your visit to the delta you are likely to be impressed or perhaps even intrigued by at least three tree species commonly seen in the delta. The real fan palm or mokolwane is very common on most islands and is perhaps the most conspicuous tree in the delta. Single-boled trees reach a height of up to 20 m, while trees growing as a short scrub reach up to 4 m. The fruits are produced in large quantities and a fully grown tree can bear up to 2 000 fruits at a time, which take about two years to mature. Young fruits produce a little milk which is similar to that of a coconut and is relished by the local people. Chacma baboon chew off the husks of the palm fruit, as do elephant, which also favour the newly formed leaves which are crisp at their base and also have a coconut flavour. Palm wine, locally known as busulu, is another favourite derived from the tree. The tree is tapped near the growing tip and the sap is collected in a container and drunk either fresh or fermented. The wine is sweet and only mildly intoxicating and an average tree will yield 60 to 70 litres.

The sausage tree is easily recognised by its very unusual sausage-like fruits, which can weigh up to 10 kg and are up to 1 m long. They are said to be poisonous but in times of drought the seeds are roasted and eaten by the local people. Chacma baboon have also been observed chewing the husks of the fruit. The sausage tree is a medium-sized tree of up to 18 m in height and normally occurs on riverine fringes. The cup-shaped flowers are dark maroon with yellow veining on the outside and are at their best between August and October. Bats visit the flowers and the leaves and fallen flowers are eaten by antelope, making the tree a favourite lair for leopard. The whitish to yellow wood is soft but durable, making this tree (locally known as the moporota) one of the species preferred by the Bayei for making their mekoro or dugouts.

About 14 *Acacia* species occur in the Okavango Delta, of which the knob thorn is the most conspicuous. It is a common, dominant floodplain woodland tree and is easily recognised by its knobby thorns and its few large leaflets, which are the largest in the *Acacia* genus. The knobs tend to disappear on older trees and during winter the tree is often bare for several months. It has an average height of 10 m, but can reach up to 30 m under favourable conditions. The knob thorn is particularly conspicuous between September and November, when long spikes of cream-white flowers appear — usually before the leaves.

### Fauna

As a result of the interdigitation between wet and dry lands, the delta boasts a wide variety of larger animals, ranging from almost totally aquatic species such as the Nile crocodile (*Crocodylus niloticus*) and hippo to semi-aquatic species such as sitatunga and red lechwe, to totally dryland species such as giraffe and Burchell's zebra.

Visitors to the permanently inundated areas of the delta should not expect to see large herds of animals, which occur mainly in the north-eastern parts of Botswana (Moremi, Savuti and Chobe). The permanently inundated area of the delta is mainly inhabited by hippo, crocodile, and Cape clawless and spotted-necked otters, while buffalo inhabit the larger islands.

*The sitatunga is a semi-aquatic species which inhabits the permanent papyrus and reed swamps of the Okavango Delta*

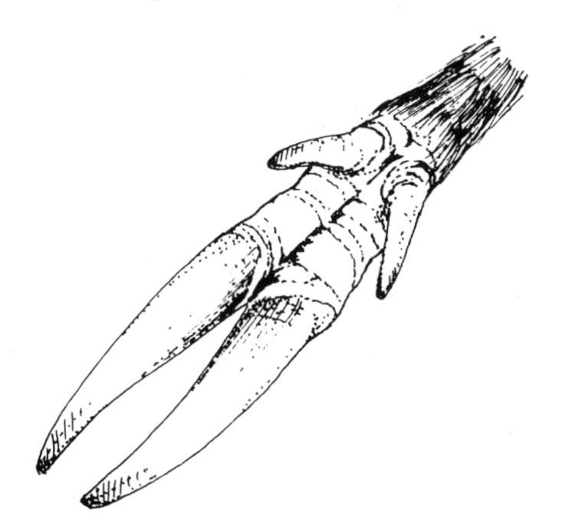

*The distinctive elongated hoof of the sitatunga*

An interesting species of this area is the sitatunga, a member of the tribe Tragelaphini, which includes the kudu, bushbuck and nyala. They are found in the Caprivi in SWA/Namibia, the Okavango Delta and along the Zambezi River above the Victoria Falls, usually singly or in pairs, but sometimes in small groups. They are confined to the permanent papyrus and reed swamps and spend most of their day in the water or on floating platforms of papyrus. When disturbed these shy animals will submerge themselves completely, leaving only their noses visible.

The sitatunga is a medium-sized antelope with an average shoulder height of 90 cm for males and 80 cm for females and a mass

*The African fish eagle is frequently seen perched atop trees lining the waterways of the Okavango Delta*

of up to 115 kg for males and about 80 kg for females. The colour of the fairly long, shaggy coat varies from drab grey-brown through a reddish brown to chocolate with faint white side stripes and white spots on the flanks and the top of the legs. It has a distinctive elongated hoof which splays out, making movement easy through marshy vegetation, mud and silt. They feed during the morning, late afternoon and at night, grazing on swamp grasses and browsing on the leaves, twigs and fruit of semi-aquatic vegetation. They are preyed upon mainly by crocodiles, and occasionally by leopard and lion.

Twenty herbivore species occur, ranging in size from the 10 kg steenbok to the African elephant, which can weigh up to 6 000 kg. Of the estimated 100 000 animals in the delta over 60 per cent are buffalo, red lechwe and impala.

On Chief's Island an early morning or late afternoon walk is almost certain to be rewarded with sightings of kudu, tsessebe, waterbuck and giraffe. You may also observe buffalo and — if you are extremely lucky — lion.

On the waterways you are likely to see red lechwe splashing through the melapo (floodplains) in search of cover. They favour flooded grass plains but are very wary and take cover as soon as they are disturbed.

To date more than 450 bird species have been recorded in the delta. Among the species of the waterways you are likely to see are reed cormorant (58), squacco heron (72) and a host of egret and heron species. Among the duck species you might identify is the pygmy goose (114). From a distance its orange and white underparts are obvious, and in flight the wings have a conspicuous white line down the centre. Species like the African jacana (or lilytrotter) (240) and the black crake (213) have long toes to enable them to walk across the floating vegetation.

The woodlands of the larger islands are the habitat of the grey lourie (373), with its harsh 'go away' call. Three hornbill species occur, namely grey (457), redbilled (458) and yellowbilled (459) hornbills. The blue wings of the lilacbreasted roller (447) are likely to catch your attention as they are particularly beautiful in flight. Woodpeckers (Picidae) are also heard but are difficult to see.

An interesting species is the palm swift (421), which is closely associated with the mokolwane palms. Their swift flight, long thin wings and deeply forked tails make identification easy. Nests are built on vertical dead palm leaves from feathers which are glued onto the leaves with saliva. The eggs are then attached to the nest with salivary glue to prevent them from falling out in windy weather.

Perhaps the most spectacular species of the delta is the African fish eagle (148), which is usually seen perched in high trees at the water's edge. It is identified by its white head, breast and back, chestnut belly and black wings. The call, which is described as '... a loud challenging, yelping kow, kow, kowkowjow uttered with the head thrown right back',[1] is one of the most characteristic sounds of Africa.

## History

Stone Age implements have confirmed habitation of the delta by early man as long ago as 100 000 BP. The last of the Stone Age people to inhabit the delta were the San (Bushmen) who settled along the delta fringes probably thousands of years ago and used reed craft for fishing and as a means of transport.

In about AD 1750 the first Bantu-speaking immigrants, the Bayei, began moving south from their home on Diyei or Ngasa near the confluence of the Chobe and Zambezi rivers following a series of conquests against them by the Lozi king, Ngombela. Punting their mekoro along the water courses which then linked the Chobe and Okavango rivers, they penetrated the delta and settled on the islands and delta fringes. They are now the largest population group in Ngamiland.

About 50 years later the Tswana-speaking Batawana settled in the area but twice, in the late 1820s and 1830s, their state was temporarily destroyed by the Makololo. Towards the end of the 1840s they returned to the area and expanded until they practically ruled all the groups in north-western Botswana.

The Batawana were followed by the Hambukushu, who emigrated from their home near Katimo Mulilo westwards to the Kwando River in Angola to escape from the Lozi wars of conquest. However, as the Lozi continued to extract tribute from them, they moved even further westwards to Andara during the nineteenth century. The mid 1800s saw a major migration of the Hambukushu into the panhandle area of the delta following the introduction of the slave trade by the Portuguese in Angola, and more recently, in the 1970s, there was another mass migration of Hambukushu from Angola as a result of the war in that country. Although the Hambukushu were fishermen and hunters, their main activity was agriculture, which they practised in the riparian areas. Like the Bayei they used the mokoro for transport, but because of the deeper water where they came from, they paddled and did not stand and heave themselves forward with a pole like the Bayei.

Although small numbers of Herero crossed into Botswana in the early 1800s, the major migration of these people from SWA/Namibia into Ngamiland came after General Lothar von Trotha issued his notorious extermination order against the Herero in 1904. They fled to Botswana, leaving their cattle behind, although they were traditionally pastoralists. Their ingrained knowledge of cattle farming was not forgotten, however, and by the 1930s they had regained their independence and they once again own large herds. In Maun the women can still be seen in their colourful dresses and headgear, a tradition inherited from the German missionaries in SWA/Namibia in the nineteenth century.

## Geology and General Background to the Delta

It is believed that prior to the general warping of the earth's crust during the final period of continental uplift some 15 million years ago, the water from the Okavango Delta area drained into the Atlantic Ocean via a deep crack extending westwards from Zambia. This was thought to be an extension of the Great Rift Valley which stretches from the Dead Sea in Israel southwards through eastern and central Africa and finally swings westwards to disappear beneath the sands of the Namib. Over aeons, winds shifting back and forth and

1 McLachlan, G.R. and Liversidge, R. 1981. *Roberts' Birds of South Africa*. Cape Town: John Voelcker Bird Book Fund.

sediments carried by the Okavango River have filled the rift with Kalahari sands to a depth of 300 m in places.

The Okavango is one of the world's largest deltas. No definite conclusions have yet been reached as to how and why the Delta was formed nor exactly what geological processes are taking place today. Many theories have been advanced as to why the Okavango River fans into a delta with only a small percentage of the water leaving it, via the Boteti River, and never reaching the sea.

One theory, put forward by Du Toit in 1926, is that originally the Okavango River flowed via the Boteti River across the Mak

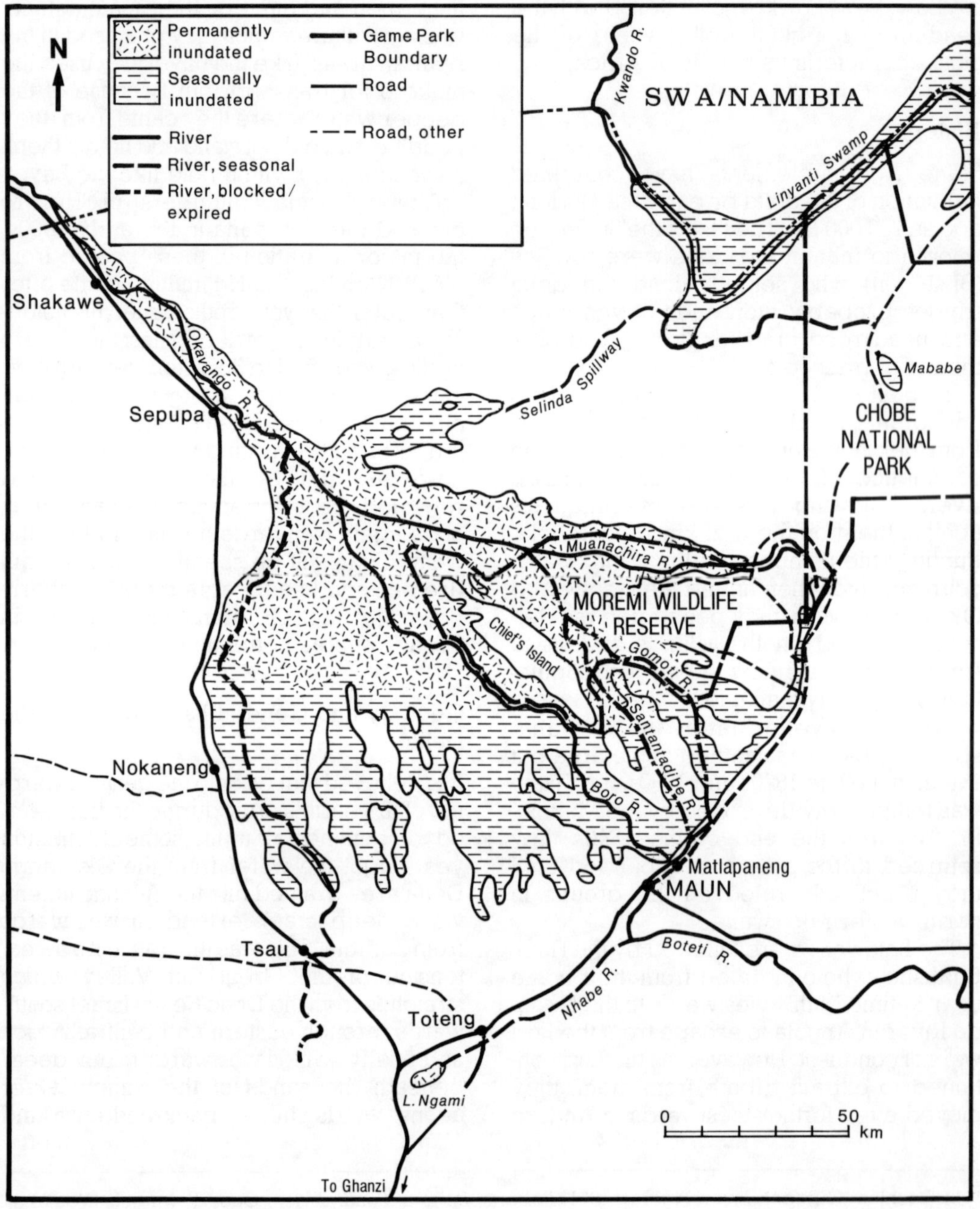


*Okavango Delta*

*Visitors to the Okavango Delta can explore the waterways in a mokoro (dugout canoe), which has been the traditional mode of transport in the Delta for centuries.*

gadikgadi depression and joined the Limpopo River via the Macloutsie Valley. Slowly the earth's crust sank and at the same time the river flow slowed down and also deposited sediments which eventually resulted in the present delta. North-eastern Botswana rose, causing the outlet to the sea via the Limpopo River to be cut off. The supply of water to Makgadikgadi was also cut off from the west.

The Okavango is the third largest river in Southern Africa. It rises in the Bie Plateau in the highlands of Angola, descending rapidly until it reaches the flat northern borders of the Kalahari. It enters Botswana at Mohembo and flows as a fairly narrow river along the panhandle until it reaches Seronga where it broadens into the classical triangular delta shape.

The extent of the annual flood of the delta depends on the rainfall in the catchment area. By late November the Okavango River is in full flood at Shakawe, the north-western extremity of the delta. Flowing at a speed of 3 km per day, the water is spread over an area of 15 000 km$^2$ by way of the Boro, Santantadibe and Muanachira rivers, reaching Maun on the eastern edge of the delta only in June.

It has been estimated that the total capacity of the delta is 16 thousand million m$^3$, with 15,4 thousand million m$^3$ of the water lost through evaporation, transpiration of vegetation and seepage into the soil as ground water. Only three to four per cent flows into the Thamalakane River at Maun from where it continues into the Boteti River which occasionally flows into Lake Ngami.

The delta comprises three major ecosystems, namely the permanent swamp, the seasonally inundated areas and the dry land masses. The permanently inundated area covers much of the north-western part of the delta and is characterised by deep-flowing permanent channels, oxbow lakes, extensive reed and papyrus beds and numerous small islands, which become more frequent further south.

The seasonally inundated areas cover most of the lower delta. The extent of flood ing depends on the rainfall in Angola and, to a much lesser extent, the local rainfall. This ecotype is characterised by a network of shallow channels, floodplains and larger islands.

Three major land masses make up the third major ecotype, the western sandveld tongue or Matsebi, Chief's Island in the centre and Moremi — particularly Mboma Island — in the east.

**Trail Synopsis**

Experiences in the delta vary so much from one trip to another that no attempt is made here to give a day by day description. Instead, a typical day in the delta is briefly described.

The day usually begins with an early morning game walk on Chief's Island. Then, after breakfast, it is time to take to your mokoro and explore the waterways, a journey of discovery where each day brings new surprises. One day you might see the African jacana (240) padding gracefully over the waterlily leaves in search of insects, or a pair of pied kingfishers (428) resting in the reeds, while the next you might see the Cape clawless or spotted-necked otter frolicking alongside your mokoro. Gliding quietly through the reed channels is an unforgettable experience, with the silence only occasionally pierced by the haunting cry of an African fish eagle (148) or the splash of a crocodile as it takes to the water.

During the heat of the day camp is usually established on an island selected by the polers. Late afternoon is again a good time for a short game walk. However, your poler will not stay out too late for he knows that the waterways are dangerous towards sunset when hippos leave the water to graze. One of the most memorable sights on your trip will undoubtedly be the magnificent Okavango sunsets, when mokolwane or real fan palms are etched against a sinking blood red sun. Then follow the sounds of the African night — the grunting of hippos grazing not too far away, the call of the fierynecked nightjar (405) or perhaps the roar of a lion.

While drifting through this world impenetrable to any other mode of transport (except, nowadays, motorboats) you will soon realise how indispensible the mokoro is for long distance travel, fishing, hunting and the gathering of reeds for building. The average mokoro is less than a metre wide and sometimes more than 6 m long, and a larger mokoro can carry a small family and its possessions. In the past the price of a mokoro was determined by the number of average sized persons it could carry before it sank, with a price of one pound sterling for every person it could hold!

The building of a mokoro is a specialised art, requiring at least one month's labour. Initially, a suitable tree with a reasonably straight trunk without branches and a suitable girth is located, the most commonly used trees being the sausage tree, appleleaf and jackal-berry. After the tree has been felled the end nearest the roots, being the heaviest, is shaped into the prow. The branch end is removed and the trunk rolled over until the main weight is at the bottom. Using axes, the two ends are tapered and the trunk is then mounted on branches with the bottom uppermost. Once the outside shape has been roughly formed, the hull is righted and the hollowing-out commences. An axe is used at first until the rough but final shape of the canoe takes form and the sides and bottom are then carefully finished with an adze.

Finally, the mokoro is launched and the keel is checked and leaks pinpointed. Leaks are sealed with molten resin and covered with bundles of thin reeds. If the mokoro is unbalanced, it is hauled ashore and the lopsided side worked down until the boat is completely balanced.

A poler stands in the stern of the mokoro and skilfully guides the boat through the incredible maze of waterways using a three- to four-metre-long pole.

# 24 Mulanje Mountain Backpacking Area

Although Malawi is strictly speaking not in Southern Africa, it has been included in this book as it is one of the few countries in Africa accessible to South Africans and has enormous appeal for backpackers. Unlike the other backpacking trails discussed, Mulanje has the luxury of overnight huts, some of them constructed of fragrant cedar, and some of the routes are marked. However, you decide on your own route and there are numerous mountain peaks to explore. On clear days you have expansive views of the yellow-green tea plantations at the south-western base of the massif and, further afield to the east, Mozambique.

## Location

Mulanje Mountain is situated in south-eastern Malawi, near the Mozambican border. The usual access point is from the forestry office and rest house at Likhubula (sometimes spelt Likabula) on the western side of the mountain.

Should you fly to Malawi, there are local and express bus services operating between Blantyre and Mulanje town. From Mulanje it is 15 km to the Likhubula Forest Station. Two local buses leave from Blantyre each day and pass Likhubula Forest Station. Disembark from this bus at the Likhubula Bus Stage, from where you have a 1,5 km walk to the forest station. Do not rely on this bus during the rainy season, however, as the service is sometimes suspended.

Cars can be hired in most of the major centres. Approaching from Limbe, take the M1 — a single strip tarred road. Travelling via Thyalo, the town of Chitakali is reached after roughly 70 km. Turn left here and continue for a few kilometres to Likhubula. You can also use the Midima road, which includes a 24 km untarred section. This route is 16 km shorter as it cuts across the cultivated Phalombe Plain.

## Distance and Classification

Depends on route taken.
For maximum enjoyment, at least one week is required.
B+ grade

## Permits

Reservations should be made well in advance by writing to the Chief Forester, P O Box 50, Mulanje, Malawi. Include the following information: date of arrival, hut(s) required and for which nights, name of group's leader, address and telephone number, and whether you are a member of the Mountain Club of Malawi. At present, group size depends on the huts used (refer to Facilities for the numbers each hut can accommodate).

## Maps

A 1:30 000 topographical map is available from the Department of Surveys, Map Sales Office, P O Box 349, Blantyre, Malawi. A map indicating the various routes with average backpacking times to the plateaux is included in the booklet *Mulanje Mountain Visitors' Guide* issued by the Ministry of Forestry and Natural Resources, Department of Forestry.

## Relevant Information

- At present (1988) South African passport holders do not require visas. However, it is advisable to enquire about current entry regulations as these could change.

- Advance enquiries should be made with the Department of Health as to whether any vaccinations are required.
- Precautions against malaria are necessary in Malawi.
- Traditionally it is illegal for women to appear in public wearing shorts, trousers or a dress/skirt that does not completely cover the knees. It is advisable to adhere to this custom, which is still well enforced today and applies to visitors as well as residents.
- Long hair (below the collar or covering your ears) is illegal for men.
- The most favourable time for hiking is from mid-April to the end of September. Two disadvantages during this period, however, are cold nights and Chiperone — a thick, cold mist that can blanket the entire mountain for three to five days. From August to October the spectacular views for which Mulanje is renowned are obscured by haze and smoke from veld fires. The rainy season (December to March/April) is considered to be best for photography, but you should be prepared for sudden downpours.
- The main routes routes to the plateau

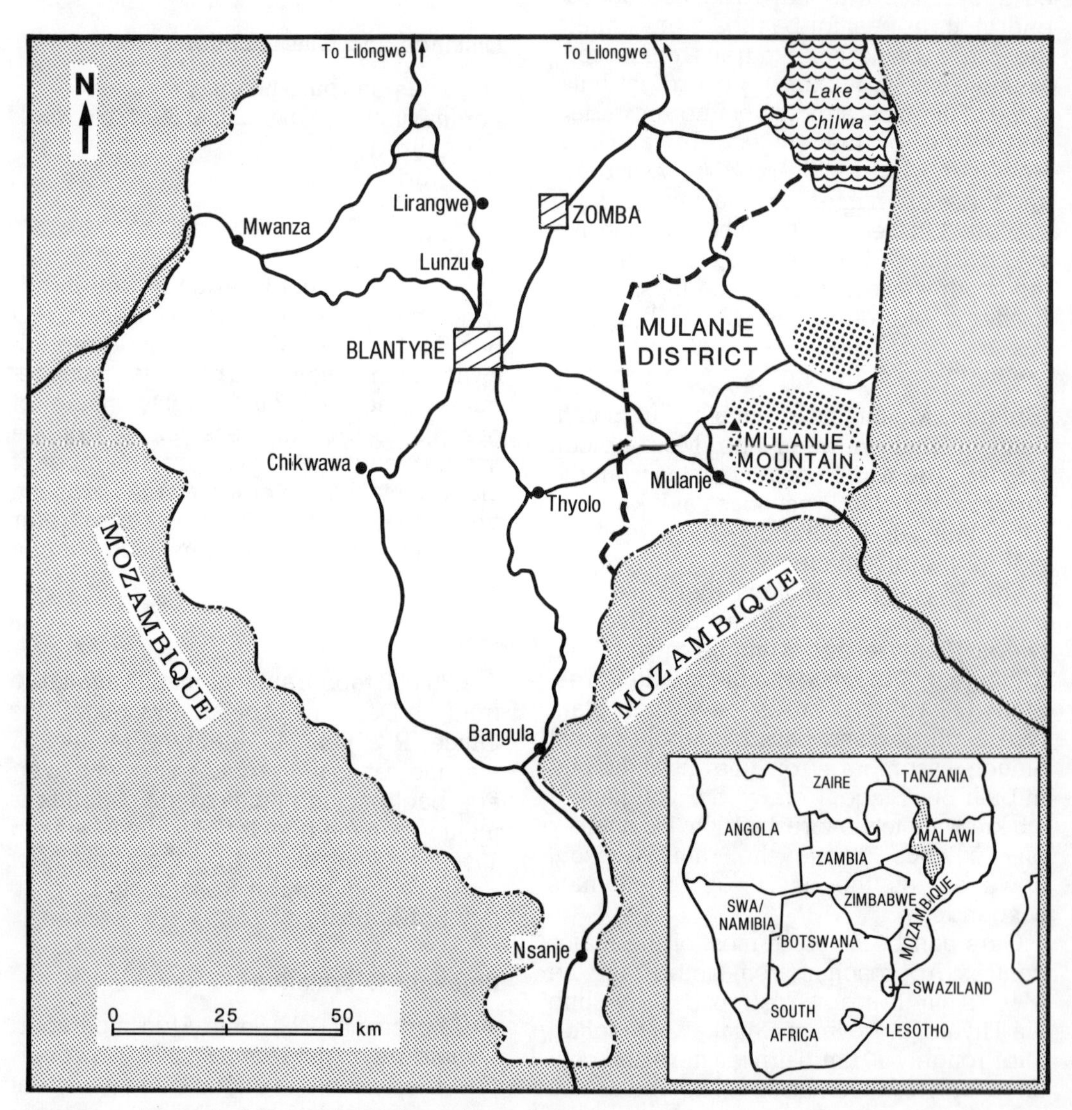


*Location: Mulanje Mountain Backpacking Area*

commence at the Likhubula Forest Station where you must report before setting out. Vehicles can be left here in a guarded car-park. The use of other access routes is permissible provided the forestry officer is advised and you have obtained the necessary permit.

- Porters can be arranged to carry packs from Likhubula and Fort Lister. Should you require this service, it is advisable to inform the forester when making your reservation and state the number of porters required and the period for which they are required. Charges are based on distance and in addition you will have to supply your porter(s) with rations for each day. One porter's rations would be 450 g of maize meal or rice, salt, 200 g meat or fish, and cigarettes. If the porter is required late in the afternoon or to stay overnight, blankets must be supplied. Ensure that equipment is packed in manageable headloads.
- Open fires are prohibited from August to December when dry conditions increase the risk of runaway fires. However, fires are still permitted at the huts.
- Details of routes and your expected time of arrival should be discussed with the hut caretaker and recorded in the book provided at each hut.
- Searches and rescue operations are coordinated by the forestry officers at Likhubula and Fort Lister.
- A daypack is useful for carrying water, snacks, field guides, warm clothing, etc when ascending and descending with a porter, and if you intend to make day excursions from the huts.
- Never set out, even on short walks, without taking warm clothing along. Rapid changes of weather are common on Mulanje.
- During the rainy season (December to April) a rope could prove useful for crossing rivers and streams, which can change from mere trickles to raging torrents.
- Trout fishing is possible in the streams on the Chambe and Lichenya plateaux from September to April. Permits are obtainable from the forestry officer.

### Facilities

There is a small campsite in the grounds of the Likhubula Forestry Office. Camping is not permitted elsewhere unless permission from the forestry officer is obtained. A rest house with three double bedrooms can be reserved in the beautiful Likhubula Valley. You must supply your own food.

There are six mountain huts – Chambe (10), Lichenya (14), Thuchila (16), Chinzama (12), Sombani (8) and Madzeka (8). (The figures in brackets indicate the number of people each hut can accommodate.) Facilities at the huts include a table and chairs, a stove or fireplace, firewood and water. You must supply your own cooking utensils. There is a caretaker at each hut who keeps the keys, and he also cleans the huts, fetches wood and water, and can be paid a small fee if required to assist with the washing of dishes.

Members of the Mountain Club of Malawi or guests and reciprocal members can make use of additional equipment, including beds, mattresses, lamps, utensils and porters' blankets, which are kept in a locked storeroom at each hut.

### Climate

The average annual rainfall on Litchenya Plateau at 2 000 m is 3 300 mm, while the Ruo Valley and other valley shelves have an average of over 2 540 mm. On the south-eastern slopes at altitudes of 600 to 850 m the average annual rainfall is between 2 000 and 3 300 mm. There is, however, a sharp decrease to about 1 500 mm to the north of the main peaks. Western and northern slopes experience a lower rainfall and in the Palombe area there is a well-marked rain shadow where the average rainfall is 965 mm.

The most favourable time for backpacking is from mid-April to the end of September. Do prepare yourself, however, for cold nights and the Chiperone, a thick, cold mist that can blanket the entire mountain for three to five days. Visibility is reduced to almost nil by the Chiperone, and it is advisable to remain at you hut should it set in.

## Flora

The vegetation on Mount Mulanje consists of open montane grassland and small patches of evergreen forest. *Loudetia simple, Exotheca abysinica* and *Andropogon schirensis* are the most dominant species of the grasslands, which provide an ideal habitat for numerous alpine plants that are seen at their best between March and October. Everlastings (*Helichrysum* spp.) are one of the most conspicuous genera and over 15 species have been recorded on Mulanje Mountain. *Helichrysum whyteanum* is endemic to Mulanje and is restricted to rocky outcrops at higher altitudes, where the glistening white or pink flowers will attract your attention. Two more common species are the yellow-flowering *H. densiflorum* and *H. lastii.*

Other alpine species include aloes, flame lilies, iris, gladioli, stag horn lily (*Xerophyta splendens*) and several orchid species. Count yourself fortunate if you spot the attractive, deep blue *Aristea alata* as the flowers, which open one at a time, remain open for only a few hours. The flowering period is between February and March. This species reaches an average height of 18 cm and usually occurs in open grassland or light woodland.

Between May and September large striking clusters of purple flowers among the rocky outcrops will certainly attract your attention. They belong to *Dissotis melleri,* a small shrub endemic to Mulanje and Zomba. On closer inspection you will notice the red filaments and navy anthers of these flowers, which are gathered at the ends of brown, leafless stems.

Should your route take you onto the Lichenya Plateau, the flame-red tubular flowers of the *Cyrtanthus welwitschii* are likely to be seen in the marshy areas. Another member of the family Amaryllidaceae occurring on Mulanje is *Crinum pedicellatum,* a large bulbous plant with white or pink-striped white, trumpet-shaped flowers.

The aromatic curry bush (*Hypericum revolutum*) with its buttercup-like, yellow flowers grows along the forest edge. The flowers can be seen at any time during the year. It grows as a shrub or small tree up to 4 m in height.

*The curry bush occurs at high altitudes in open grasslands, at forest margins and along streams*

The forest patches are remnants of more extensive forests which have been destroyed by fires and subsequently replaced by grasslands. They occur between elevations of 1 500 m and 2 100 m and are limited to isolated stands at the heads of river valleys, plateau edges and the crests of ridges. Characteristic of the forests are the lichen-clad canopies, while the forest floors are covered in a dense undergrowth of ferns, mosses and creepers. Soft, delicate fronds are often draped over the forest tree fern (*Cyathea capensis*), and you will be enchanted in the moist ravines of the south where trees on stream banks are covered in a wealth of various epiphytic ferns and orchids.

One of the most magnificent trees of Mulanje Mountain is the Mulanje cedar (*Widdringtonia nodiflora*), which reaches heights of over 40 m here, compared with an average height of 4-6 m in other areas of its distribution. It occurs in mountainous habitats from the western Cape to the Transvaal Drakensberg, and in eastern Zimbabwe. Mulanje Mountain is its northernmost limit of distribution. At one time it was classified as a separate species (*Widdringtonia whytei*) and believed to be endemic to Mount Mulanje. However, as the scientific name indicates, this original classification was incorrect.

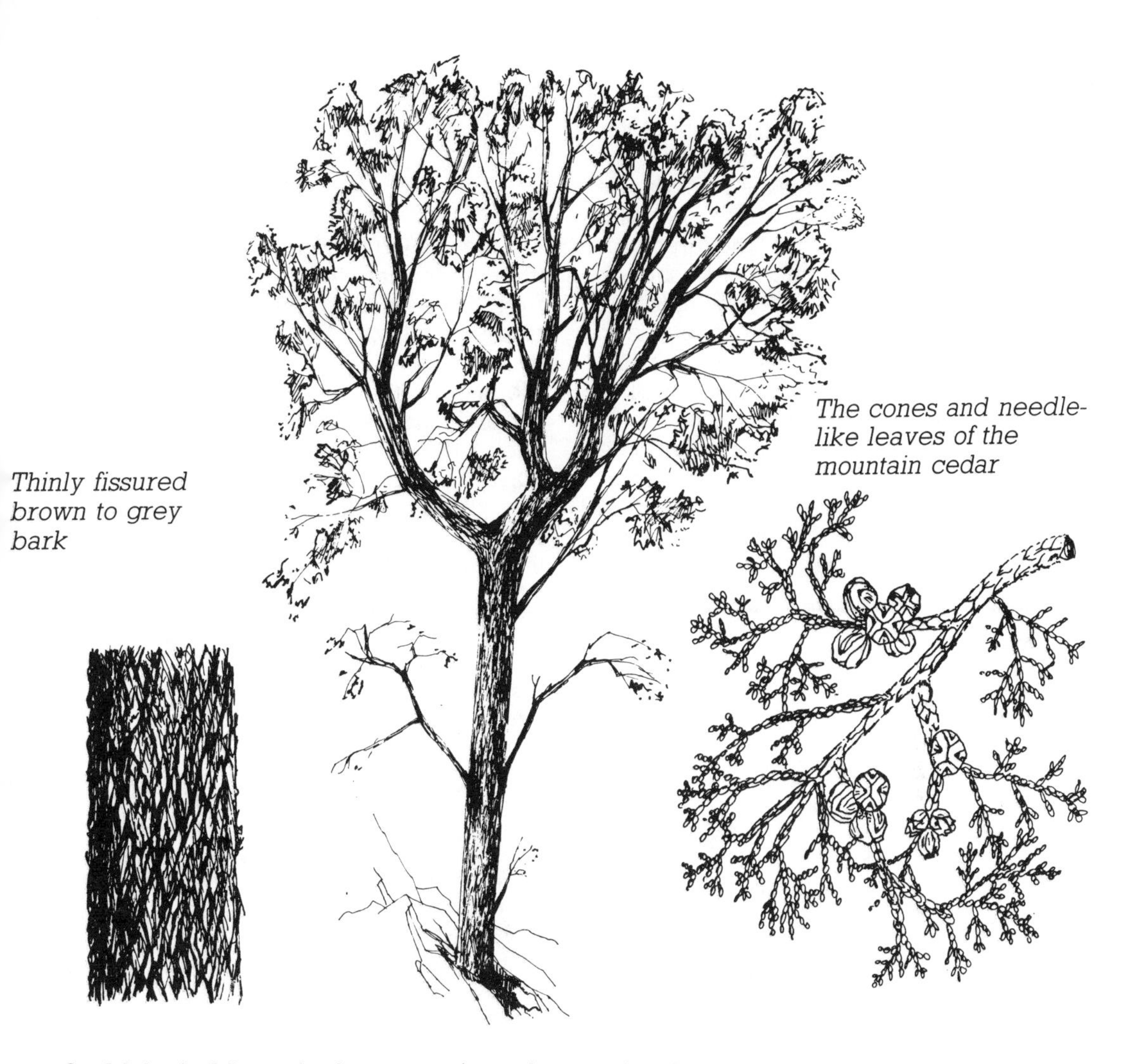


*On Mulanje Mountain the mountain cedar reaches heights of over 40 m*

In open country the Mulanje cedar towers well above the canopies of mixed stands of broad-leaved trees, while on steep slopes and the sides of ravines they dominate the forests in pure stands. Trees with a diameter of 1,8 m at the base are not uncommon. Enormous saw-pits where the trees are sawn into planks with cross-cut saws before being carried down the mountain can be seen in the cedar forests and on your ascent it is not uncommon to see some of the workers speedily making their way down the mountainside with long planks skilfully balanced on their heads.

Among the forest species that will be familiar to South Africans are the real yellowwood (*Podocarpus latifolius*), previously classified as *P. milanjianus*, waterwood (*Syzygium* spp.), flat-crown (*Albizia adianthifolia*) and wild mahogany (*Entandrophragma* spp.). Several tropical species which only occur from Zimbabwe northwards will also be encountered. These include the parasol tree (*Polyscias fulva*), craibia (*Craibia brevicaudata*) and the forest garcinia (*Garcinia kingaensis*).

The Ruo Gorge is renowned for its forests where brown-berry fluted milkwood (*Chrysophyllum gorungosanum*), forest Newtonia (*Newtonia buchananii*), craibia (*Craibia brevicaudata*), parasol tree (*Polyscias fulva*) and big-leaf (*Anthocleista grandiflora*) are some of the most noticeable trees.

## Fauna

The mountain does not support a large variety of mammals and the species you are most likely to encounter is the rock dassie. If you are alert you might also spot klipspringer in the rocky areas. The forests are the habitat of species such as bushbuck, vervet monkey and red duiker. Leopard also occur, but are extremely rarely seen.

The birdlife of the area is more rewarding than the mammalian life and over 90 species have been recorded above 1 800 m with several other species occurring below this altitude.

Of the various habitats — montane grasslands, rocky ridges and krantzes, bracken and brier and evergreen forests — the latter is the most important habitat with some 73 species, 37 of which occur at about 1 800 m.

## History

During the 1860s many people in Malawi (then Nyasaland) fell victim to slave traders from the east coast, one of whose regular trade routes was the Fort Lister Pass between the Mulanje massif and Mchese Mountain to the north. British forces began suppressing the slave traders around 1887 and in 1893 (two years after the proclamation of a British Protectorate over what is today known as Malawi) a fort was built by Alfred Sharpe at the top of the pass to guard the Mulanje/Phalombe area against them.

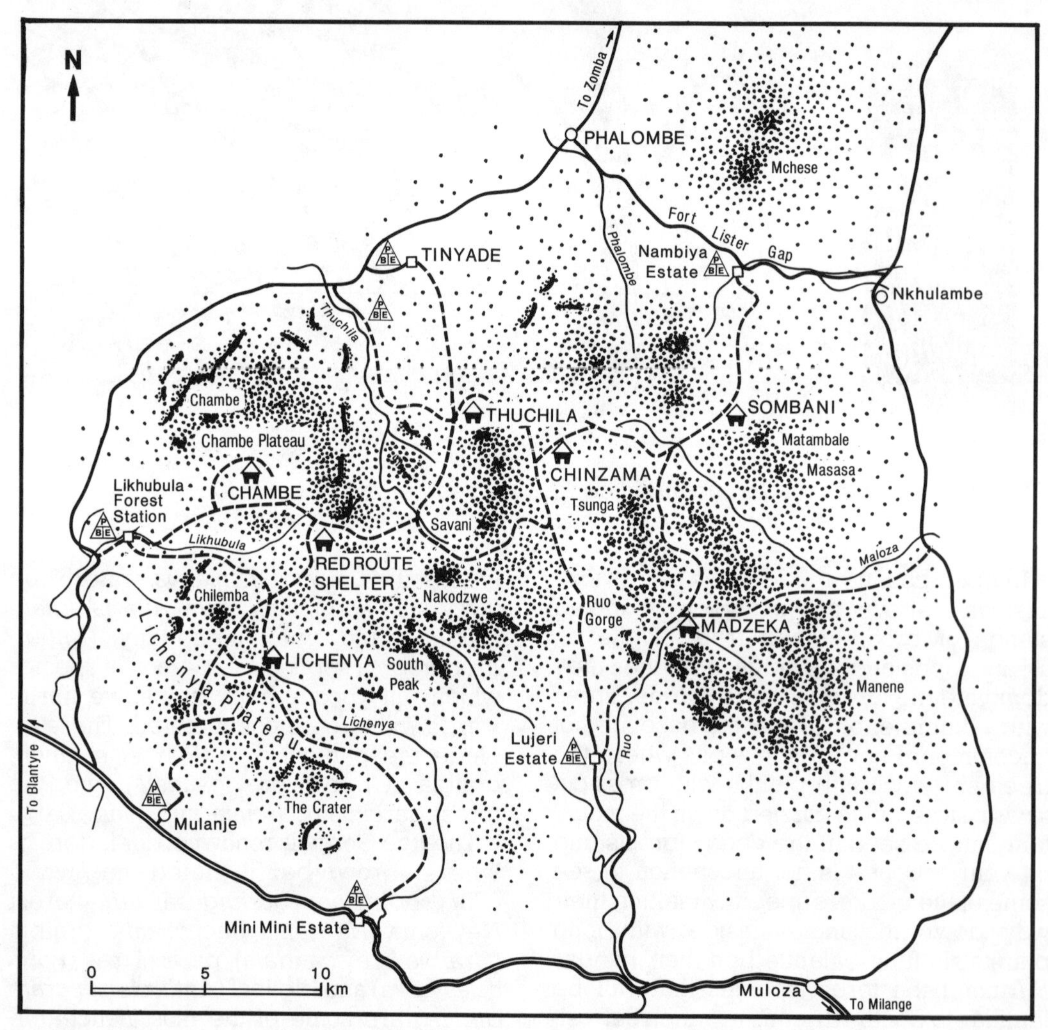


*Mulanje Mountain Backpacking Trail*

After it was abandoned in 1902 the building fell into disrepair and extensive restoration work was recently carried out to preserve the extensive ruins and the graves of two officials who died there. One of the officials, Gilbert Stevenson, was a cousin of the famous Scottish novelist and poet, Robert Louis Stevenson.

### Trail Synopsis

Access to the mountain plateaux is along a number of moderately steep footpaths from the base of the mountain. Depending on the route, about three to six hours are required to reach the bench-like plateaux, which are situated between about 1 800 m and 2 100 m. Once on top, you can explore the entire massif with relative ease by way of a network of footpaths. The huts can all be reached within five to six hours' walking, which leaves ample time for scrambling up some of the accessible peaks.

The main route to the plateau is from the Likhubula Forest Station, from where you have access to both the Chambe and Lichenya plateaux. The footpath, locally known as the Milk Run, ascends between the granite peaks of Chambe in the north and Chilemba in the south and about five hours are required to reach Lichenya hut. Some 1 200 m is gained in altitude before the hut is reached. One of the best examples of the deep cauldron-like hollows caused by erosion can be seen on the southern flank of Lichenya Plateau. This feature is known as The Crater and its peculiar shape gave rise to the belief amongst early travellers that the mountain was of volcanic origin.

From Lichenya you can hike either to Chambe hut or to Thuchila hut, which is about five to six hours distant. The route between Lichenya and the ridge to the Chambe basin offers fine views of Sapitwa, which at 3 002 m is Central Africa's highest peak. Access to the peak, which is said to mean 'don't go there' in Chichewa, is along a well-marked route which starts at a corrugated steel shelter, known as Red Route shelter, at the base of the peak. The round trip can be completed in a day.

Chambe hut, a pine chalet, is situated alongside a stream inside a large circular amphitheatre. Chambe is one of the two main outliers of the Mulanje massif (the other one is Mchese) and is an excellent example of a classically developed ring structure. The west face of Chambe, a sheer cliff of some 1 700 m, is one of the longest rock faces in Africa, but approached from the east the 2 556 m peak can be reached along what has been described as a moderate scramble. Unlike Mchese, which has been substantially affected by erosion and is separated from the Mulanje massif by the Fort Lister Gap, Chambe is still connected to the massif by a narrow ridge which forms the watershed between the western branch of the Thuchila and the Likabula rivers.

To the north-east of Chambe lies the Thuchila hut, from where it is possible to backpack to the Sombani and Madzeka huts in the eastern part of the massif. The only evidence that the massif was once covered by rocks of Karoo age can be seen on the Thuchila plateau. Another option is to hike down the gorge carved by the Ruo River, the largest tributary of the Shire River. From Thuchila the trail ascends, passing the turnoff to the Chinzama hut before reaching the Minunu logging camp on the edge of the Ruo Plateau. The path descends steeply from here and the route is not advisable during the rainy season. The descent from Chinzama hut to the Lujeri Tea Estate takes about five hours, with a 10 km walk remaining to the main road to Blantyre.

### DON'T MISS

- the Zomba Plateau, where numerous short walks revealing spectacular views are possible. The colourful market at Zomba is also interesting.
- relaxing on the shores of Lake Malawi. Take your goggles with you and discover this underwater world of brightly coloured fish. There are over 220 species, many of which are endemic to the lake.
- a boat trip on Lake Malawi. Three lake steamers transport passengers and cargo between Monkey Bay and Karongo, calling at 12 ports. The round trip takes a week.
- Malawi's beautiful game parks and reserves.

# 25 Nyika Guided Wilderness Trail

The Nyika Guided Wilderness Trail is the first guided wilderness trail to be established in Malawi. Situated in northern Malawi, the 3 200 km² Nyika National Park is on the highest continuous plateau in the country and is considered the most scenic of the country's national parks, with undulating grasslands, deep valleys, rugged escarpments, waterfalls and herds of game. The plateau is the source of four major rivers, which plunge over the escarpment in a series of spectacular waterfalls.

### Location

To reach the park you travel through Mzuzu, which is 384 km north of Lilongwe and is the main town in northern Malawi. The entrance to the park is 135 km from Mzuzu. The final 67 km between Rumphi and the park entrance at Thazima is untarred and can be difficult to negotiate during the rainy season. Chelinda Camp is about 56 km from the park entrance.

### Distance and Classification

Trails range from one to five days, depending on your requirements.
A grade

### Permits

It is necessary to make reservations well in advance with The Chief Parks and Wildlife Officer, Department of National Parks and Wildlife, P O Box 30131, Lilongwe 3, Malawi, Telephone Lilongwe 730853.

### Maps

As the trails are guided and no set routes are followed, a topographical map of the area is not required.

### Relevant Information

- At present (1988) South Africans require only a valid passport but it is advisable for both South Africans and foreigners to enquire about current entry regulations.
- Advance enquiries should be made with the Department of Health as to whether any vaccinations are required.
- Precautions against malaria are necessary in Malawi.
- Traditionally it is illegal for women to appear in public wearing shorts, trousers or a dress/skirt that does not completely cover the knees. It is advisable to adhere to this custom, which is still enforced today and applies to visitors as well as local residents.
- Long hair (below the collar or covering your ears) is illegal for men.
- You must provide *all* your equipment, including a tent.
- Unlike the situation on most guided wilderness trails, you must be self-sufficient and carry all your equipment in your backpack, although porters can be hired.
- You can either hire park transport or have your vehicle driven by a park official to the start and from the finish of the trail.
- Before setting off on your trail visit the information centre at Chelinda where you will gain a better understanding of the park's history and ecology.
- The park is criss-crossed by some 220 km of gravel roads, which allows excellent opportunities for game viewing by vehicle.

- Trout fishing is permitted throughout the year in the streams and between September and April in the dams near Chelinda. Licences can be obtained at Chelinda and you must supply your own gear.

### Facilities

Accommodation at Chelinda consists of chalets, each with two bedrooms, a lounge and dining room, shower and toilet, as well as a fully equipped kitchen with a cook to prepare meals. There is also a bedroom

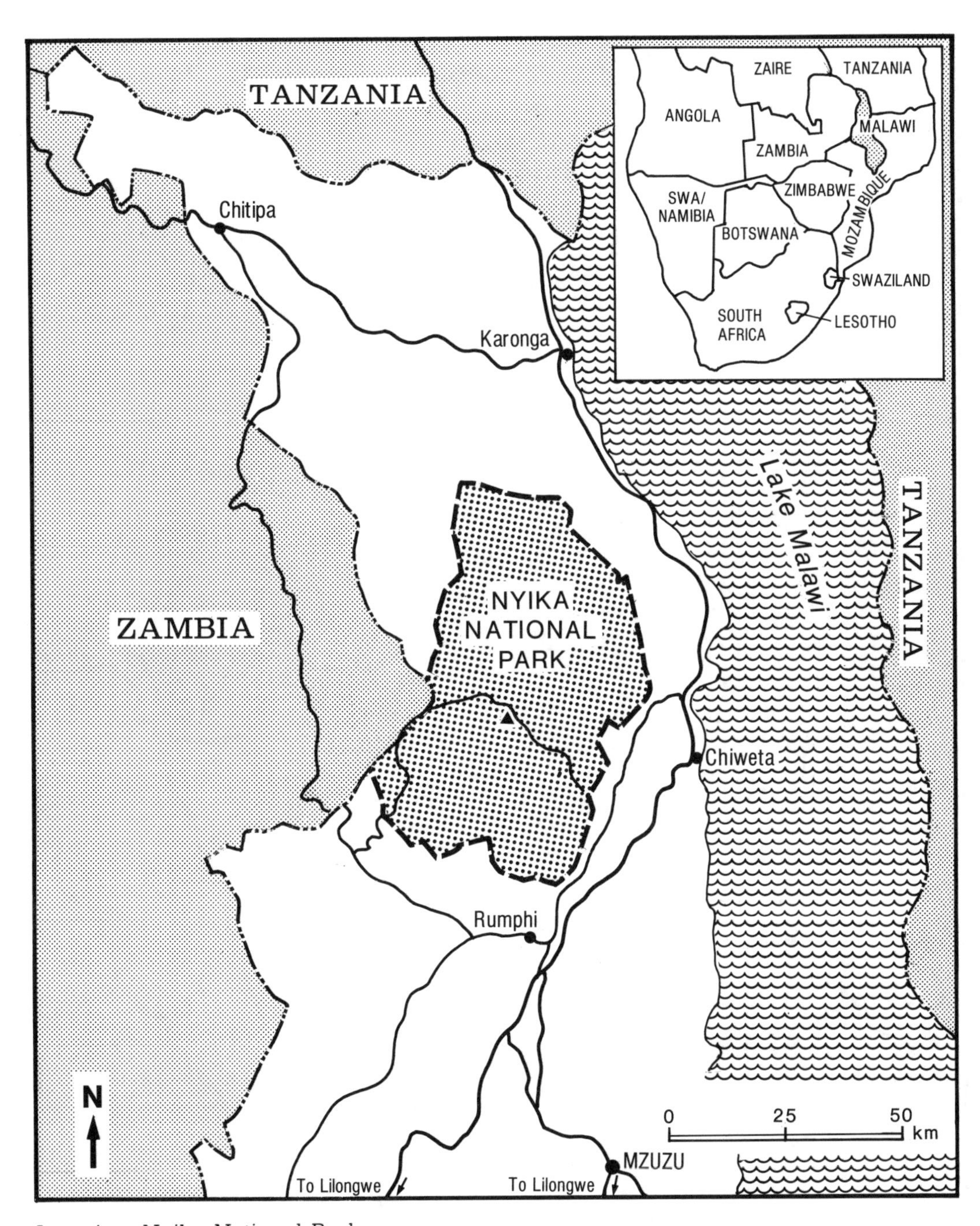


*Location: Nyika National Park*

block consisting of six double bedrooms and a communal dining room.

For those preferring less sophisticated accommodation there is also a campsite at Chelinda with two shelters, fireplaces, water supplied by a water browser and pit

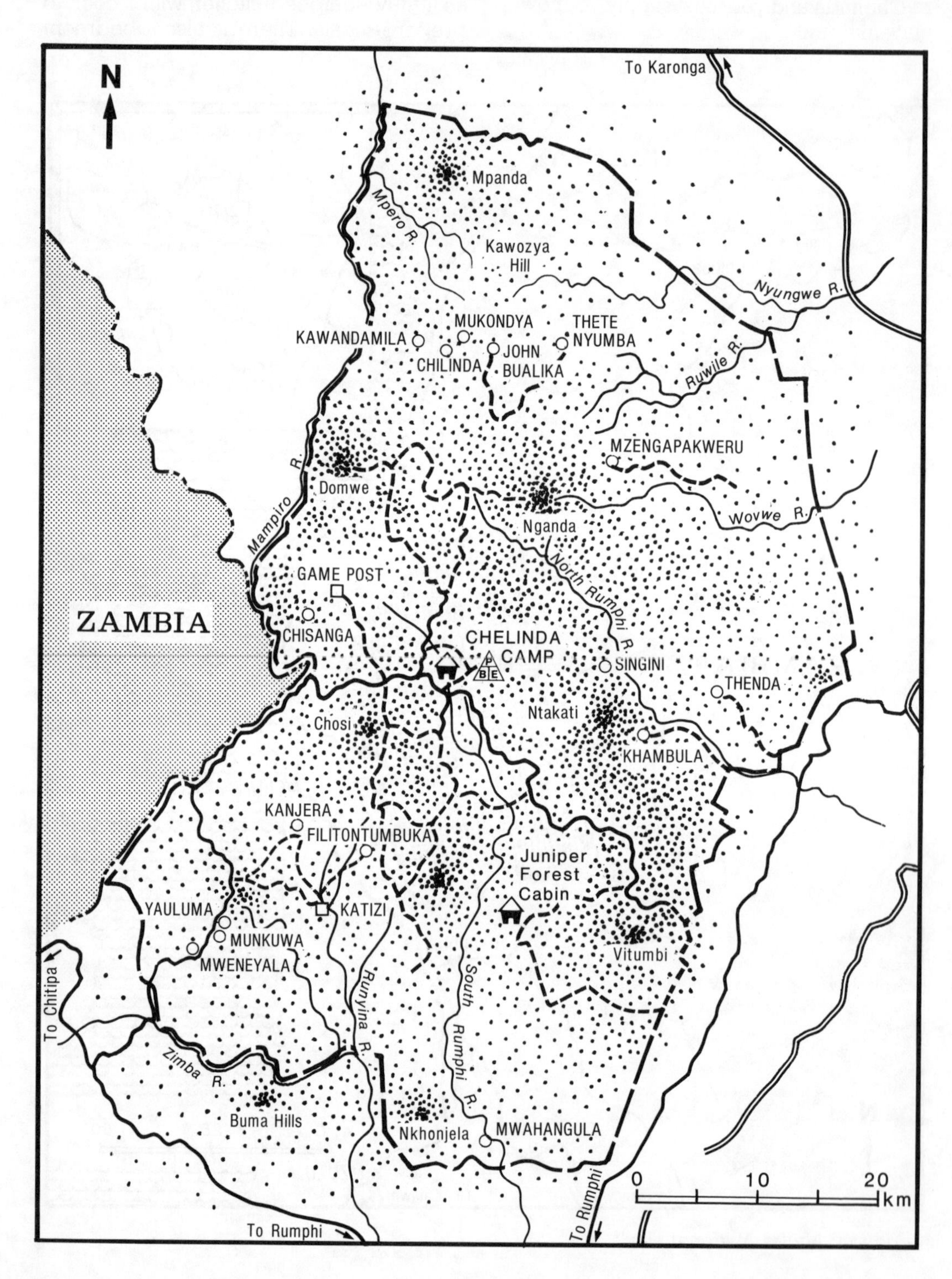

latrines. Visitors must supply their own food as only basic, non-perishable goods can be purchased at the shop in Chelinda. Petrol is usually available at Chelinda, but do not rely on it and ensure that you have adequate fuel for your return journey.

Facilities at the Juniper forest cabin, 35 km south of Chelinda, include four bunk-beds, basic bedding and cooking utensils. There is no running water.

No accommodation facilities are provided on the wilderness trails, making it necessary to provide your own tent.

### Climate

On account of its altitude, Nyika has a bracing and invigorating climate. At elevations of 2 250 m and higher, the temperature rarely exceeds 21 °C, even between September and December, which are generally the hottest months. Frost may occur from July to August. November to March are generally the months with the highest rainfall.

### Flora, Fauna and History

The flora, fauna and history are briefly covered in the Trail Synopsis as they form an integral part of the trail.

### Trail Synopsis

The park covers the entire Nyika plateau, which lies at an altitude of 2 100 to 2 400 m. Above 2 000 m the terrain consists of undulating grasslands intersected by deep river valleys and streams. A feature of the plateau is the grass-covered drainage lines — known locally as *dambos* — which become waterlogged during the rainy season.

Patches of evergreen indigenous forest have survived in the sheltered valleys, while the vegetation of the slopes to the 1 500 m level consists of *miombo (Brachystegia-Julbernardia)* woodlands. *Moraea textilis* is associated with the *Brachystegia* hillsides and the attractive pink to purple flowers of this member of the family Iridaceae can be seen from April to May. The beautifully shaped *Brachystegia spiciformis* and *Julbernardia globiflora,* with which it is often confused, are the dominant species in this mixed deciduous woodland which covers large parts of Zambia, Zimbabwe and Malawi. Neither of these species, nor other trees such as mahobohoba (*Uapaca kirkiana*), occur in South Africa and they will thus be unfamiliar to South African backpackers. The African pencil cedar (*Juniperus procera*) reaches its southernmost limit of distribution in the Uyagaya Valley of eastern Nyika, where it grows as a small remnant forest.

The grasslands are the habitat of a large variety of alpine flowers, as well as orchids which are seen at their best from November to March. A large group of ground orchids are the *Eulophias,* of which *E. coeloglossa* occurs in Nyika and has a wide distribution in tropical East Africa and is also found in Natal and Transkei. This species bears 5 to 10 flowers with pinkish lips between November and January. *Disa erubescens* is fairly common in Nyika and has scarlet or orange eye-catching flowers which should not escape your attention if you are in the park between December and March. *D. ornithantha* is also in bloom during this period and is easily confused with the larger *D. erubescens.* A pink variation of *Gladiolus melleri* flowers between

*The warthog derives its name from the distinctive facial warts. Males have two pairs of warts, while females have only one pair*

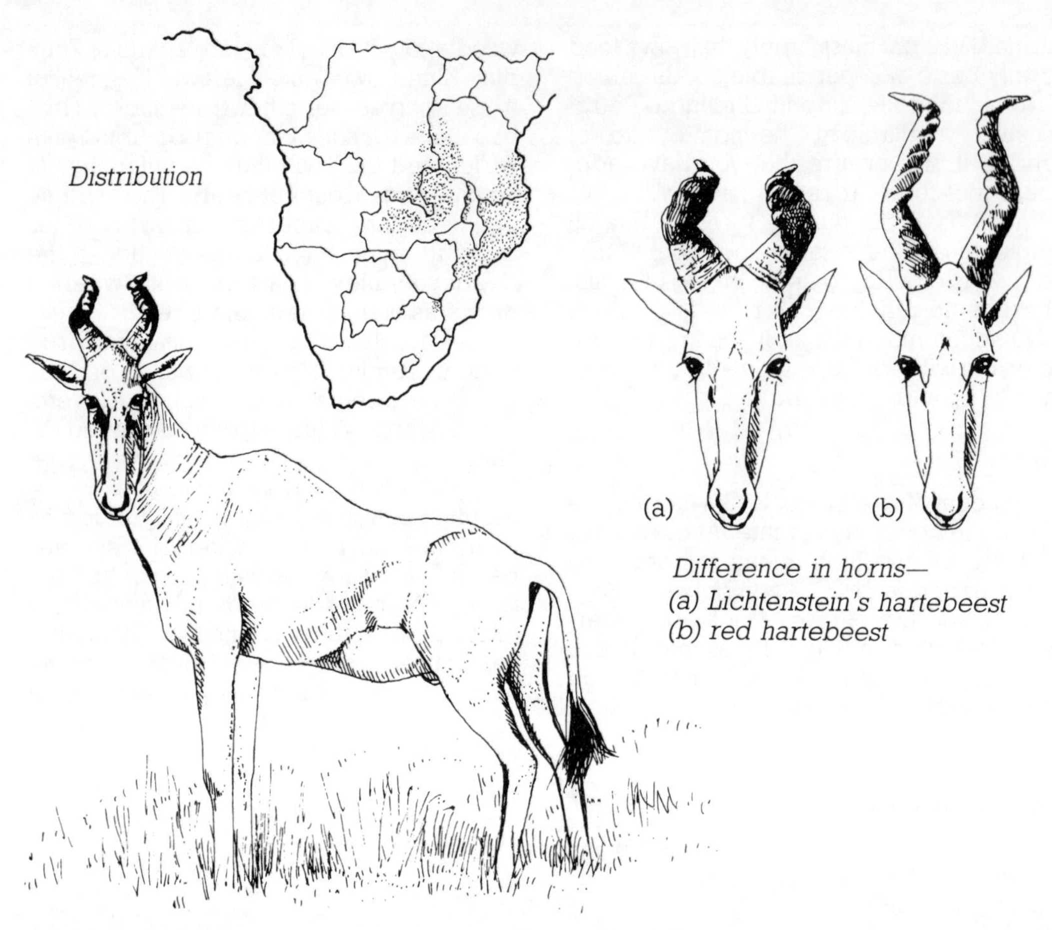


*Difference in horns—*
*(a) Lichtenstein's hartebeest*
*(b) red hartebeest*

*Lichtenstein's hartebeest – a savanna species which occurs in small herds of up to 10 animals*

September and February in the grasslands and amongst rocks. The white and pink flowering *G. atropurpureus* reaches between 30 and 45 cm and adds a touch of colour to the rocky mountain slopes. Proteas can be seen flowering between March and June, while several *Aloe* species flower during the dry winter months.

Antelope of the open grassland include roan, eland, Lichtenstein's hartebeest and reedbuck. Other mammal species you might see are Burchell's zebra, common duiker, warthog and — in the more rocky areas — klipspringer. Leopard and cheetah, as well as several smaller predators, also occur but are very rarely seen. The forest patches are the habitat of red and blue duiker, bushbuck and vervet monkey. As most animals move to the *miombo* woodlands and the forests during the cooler months, November to May are considered the best months for game viewing.

Bird-watching is especially rewarding from October to December when migrants are present. Among the high-altitude species you might observe are redwing francolin (192), wattled crane (207) and Stanley's bustard (231), while several species such as cinnamon dove (360) and starred robin (606) can be spotted in the forests.

Of anthropological interest in the park are a number of small mines and kilns, which were used by Late Iron Age inhabitants who mined and smelted in the area, as well as Later Stone Age sites.

**DON'T MISS**

Refer to Mulanje Mountain Backpacking Area, page 247.

# Part 8
# References

# Part 8
# References

# Tabulated Summary of Backpacking and Guided Wilderness Trails

Following is a tabulated summary, alphabetically arranged, of areas and trails included in this book. The table is intended to assist you in selecting a trail in terrain that appeals to you and with features that interest you. The most outstanding features of each trail are brought to your attention.

An asterisk (*) indicates *guided* wilderness trails.

***Vegetation Key***

B Bushveld D Desert F Fynbos
G Grassland I Indigenous forest
S Savanna Sd Semi-desert
W Woodland

| Trail and where situated | Page number | Vegetation type | Most Outstanding Features of the Area | | | | |
|---|---|---|---|---|---|---|---|
| | | | Spectacular natural features | Flora | Game | Birdlife | Rock paintings |
| **Boosmansbos** Western Cape | 104 | F | ● | ● | | | |
| **Brandberg** Damaraland, SWA/Namibia | 59 | SD | ● | | | | ● |
| ***Burnera** Natal Drakensberg | 209 | G | ● | | | | |
| ***Bushman** Kruger National Park | 223 | B | | | ● | | ● |
| **Cathedral Peak** Northern Drakensberg | 176 | G | ● | | | | ● |
| **Cederberg** Western Cape | 81 | F | ● | ● | | | |
| ***Doorndraai Dam** Waterberg foothills | 210 | B | | | ● | ● | |
| **Fish River Canyon** Southern SWA/Namibia | 69 | SD | ● | | | | |

| Trail and where situated | Page number | Vegetation type | Most Outstanding Features of the Area | | | | |
|---|---|---|---|---|---|---|---|
| | | | Spectacular natural features | Flora | Game | Birdlife | Rock paintings |
| **Giant's Castle**<br>Central Drakensberg | 166 | G | ● | | | | ● |
| ***Giant's Castle — Horseback**<br>Central Drakensberg | 203 | G | ● | | | | ● |
| **Groendal**<br>Eastern Cape | 112 | F/I | ● | ● | | | |
| **Groot-Winterhoek**<br>Western Cape | 96 | F | ● | ● | | | |
| ***Groot-Winterhoek**<br>Western Cape | 213 | F | ● | ● | | | |
| ***Itala Nature Reserve**<br>Northern Natal | 201 | G/W | | | ● | | |
| ***Jock of the Bushveld**<br>Eastern Transvaal | 209 | B | | | ● | | |
| ***Lake Trail**<br>Lake St Lucia | 208 | G/I | | | ● | ● | |
| **Lesotho Pony Trek**<br>Maloti Mountains | 135 | G | ● | | | | |
| **Mdedelelo**<br>Northern Drakensberg | 172 | G | ● | | | | ● |
| **Mkomazi**<br>Central Drakensberg | 162 | G | ● | | | | |
| ***Mkuzi Game Reserve**<br>Zululand | 200 | G/W | | | ● | ● | |
| **Mount Mulanje**<br>South-eastern Malawi | 247 | G/I | ● | ● | | | |
| **Mzimkulu**<br>Southern Drakensberg | 157 | G | ● | | | | ● |
| **Ntendeka**<br>Northern Natal | 187 | G/I | | ● | | | |
| ***Nyalaland**<br>Kruger National Park | 225 | W | | ● | ● | | |
| ***Nyika**<br>Northern Malawi | 254 | W/G | | ● | ● | | |
| ***Nylsvley**<br>Western Transvaal | 211 | W/S | | | ● | ● | |

| Trail and where situated | Page number | Vegetation type | Most Outstanding Features of the Area | | | | |
|---|---|---|---|---|---|---|---|
| | | | Spectacular natural features | Flora | Game | Birdlife | Rock paintings |
| **Okavango Delta** North-western Botswana | 237 | W/S | ● | | | ● | |
| ***Olifants** Kruger National Park | 224 | B | | | ● | | |
| ***Pilanesberg** Bophuthatswana | 212 | S/G | | | ● | ● | |
| **Royal Natal** Northern Drakensberg | 181 | G | ● | | | | |
| **Sehlabathebe** South-eastern Lesotho | 127 | G | ● | | | | ● |
| ***St Lucia Game Reserve** Lake St Lucia | 197 | G/I | ● | | ● | ● | |
| ***Tsolwana** Tsolwana Game Park, Ciskei | 118 | G | | | ● | | |
| ***Ugab River** Skeleton Coast, SWA/Namibia | 52 | D | ● | ● | | | |
| ***Umfolozi Game Reserve** Zululand | 195 | W | | | ● | ● | |
| ***Waterberg Plateau Park** Northern SWA/Namibia | 43 | W/S | ● | | ● | | |
| ***White Rhino** Zululand | 206 | W | | | ● | ● | |
| **Wolkberg** Northern Transvaal | 227 | G/I | ● | ● | | | |

# *Summary of Hiking Trails*

In addition to the backpacking and guided wilderness trails described, there are numerous hiking trails that fall outside the scope of this book. Excluding the more recent trails, they are described in more detail in the *Guide to Hiking Trails of Southern Africa* by the same authors.

Trails marked with a bold dot (●) have been or could be transferred from the Forestry Branch to the conservation division of the relevant provincial administration. It is therefore possible that in the future addresses for reservations for these trails may change.

● ***Alexandria Hiking Trail:*** Regional Director, Eastern Cape Forest Region, Private Bag X7432, King William's Town 5600, Telephone (0433) 2 3445/6 or 2 3475. A two-day trail over 37,5 km passing through beautiful indigenous forests, along the coast and across possibly the largest mobile dune system in South Africa.

***Amatola Hiking Trail:*** Ciskei Tourist Board, P O Box 56, Bisho, Ciskei, Telephone (0401) 9 1131. Covering 105 km, this six-day trail alternates between indigenous forest, plantations and high mountains. Shorter two, three, four or five-day options are also possible.

***Banke Hiking Trail:*** The Secretary, Wildlife Society of Southern Africa, Maluti Centre, P O Box 140, Marquard 9610, Telephone (05272) 21. Here you have three trail options: 43 km over two days for fitter hikers; 43 km over three days; and 33 km over two days, also for the more energetic. Features of this trail include grasslands, views of the Maluti Mountains and rock paintings, as well as a night in traditional huts.

***Blyderivierspoort Hiking Trail:*** The Regional Director, Eastern Transvaal Forest Region, Private Bag X503, Sabie 1260, Telephone (0131512) ask for 307. The beautiful scenery of this part of the eastern Transvaal needs little introduction. An easy 65 km trail which is usually hiked in five days. Shorter options are possible.

● ***Boland: Section Hottentots-Holland:*** The Regional Director, Western Cape Forest Region, Private Bag X9005, Cape Town 8000, Telephone (021) 45 1224. A trail renowned for its floral wealth and magnificent mountain scenery. Three days, 53,7 km, but numerous two-day options are available.

● ***Boland: Section Limietberg:*** The Regional Director, Western Cape Forest Region, Private Bag X9005, Cape Town 8000, Telephone (021) 45 1224. An ideal weekend trail (two days) situated close to Cape Town. Characterised by majestic mountain scenery, inviting mountain pools and fynbos vegetation.

***Brandwater Hiking Trail:*** The Town Clerk, Fouriesburg 9725, Telephone (014332) 14, 88 or 185. This five-day, circular trail of 62 km has a variety of scenery ranging from forested kloofs to unusual sandstone formations. You will overnight either in caves or in a sandstone house.

***Doorndraai Hiking Trail:*** The Officer-in-Charge, Doorndraai Dam Nature Reserve, P O Box 983, Potgietersrus 0060, Telephone (015423) 629. This two-day circular trail of 19 km takes you through lovely deep kloofs and over hillsides. Animals you might see include giraffe, tsessebe, sable and roan.

***Double Drift Hiking Trail:*** Ciskei Tourist Board, P O Box 56, Bisho, Ciskei, Telephone (0401) 9 1131. This 54 km trail passes through an area rich in frontier history. It leads mainly along the Great Fish River, winding through beautiful scenery, and can be completed in either two or three days.

● ***Drakensberg Hiking Trail: Section Giant's Cup:*** The Regional Director, Natal Forest Region, Private Bag X9029, Pietermaritzburg 3200, Telephone (0331) 2 8101. A pleasant, 60 km trail which allows you to explore the beauty of the Drakensberg with relative ease. Usually hiked in five days, although shorter options are possible.

***Dugandlovu Hiking Trail:*** Reservations Officer, Natal Parks Board, P O Box 662, Pietermaritzburg 3200, Telephone (0331) 5 1514. This easy two-day (17 km) hike is ideal for the beginner and family groups. The short distance covered enables you to enjoy the rich plant, bird and animal life of Lake St Lucia at leisure.

***Elandskrans Hiking Trail:*** The Manager, Elandskrans Holiday Resort, Private Bag X03, Waterval Boven 1195, Telephone (013262) 176. A trail rich in the history of the old Zuid-Afrikaansche Republiek. Approximately 24 km are hiked over two days.

***Fanie Botha Hiking Trail:*** The Director, Eastern Transvaal Forest Region, Private Bag X503, Sabie 1260, Telephone (0131512) ask for 307. Pine-scented plantations and beautiful indigenous forests are features of this 76,9 km trail, which takes five days to complete. Shorter options are possible.

***Giraffe Hiking Trail:*** The Officer-in-Charge, Hans Merensky Nature Reserve, Private Bag X502, Letsitele 0885, Telephone (015238) 633/4. An easy, relaxing hike of 35 km laid out in a figure-of-eight. The possibility of spotting game is an added attraction.

***Gold Nugget Hiking Trail:*** Makhonjwa Conservation Foundation, P O Box 221, Barberton 1300, Telephone (01314) 23373. Follow in the footsteps of the early fortune seekers who fossicked in the area in search of gold. Beautiful mountain scenery is a feature of this 46 km trail which is hiked in three days.

***Holkrans Hiking Trail:*** Mr and Mrs D C P van Niekerk, P O Box 2734, Newcastle 2940, Telephone (03435) 600, preferably evenings. A pleasant two-day circular trail (17,5 km) which takes you through indigenous forest patches, grasslands and below overhanging sandstone cliffs.

***Kaapsche Hoop Hiking Trail:*** The Regional Director, Southern Transvaal Forest Region, Private Bag 11201, Nelspruit 1200, Telephone (01311) 2 3244. This plantation trail offers a choice of two two-day hikes (29 and 36 km) with hutted accommodation and a three-day tented route (42 km). The area is rich in reminders of the early gold mining days of the last century.

***Katberg Hiking Trail:*** Ciskei Tourist Board, P O Box 56, Bisho, Ciskei, Telephone (0401) 9 1131. Magnificent mountain scenery, pine plantations and cool indigenous forests are features of this trail which is currently under construction in the Katberg Mountains near Seymour.

***Klipspringer Hiking Trail:*** The Chief Director, National Parks Board, P O Box 787, Pretoria 0001, Telephone (012) 44 1191 or P O Box 7400, Roggebaai 8012, Telephone (021) 419 5365. A pleasant circular hike of 26 km (three days) through lunar landscape scenery which contrasts sharply with the vegetation along the Orange River.

***Kologha Hiking Trail:*** The Regional Director, Eastern Cape Forest Region, Private Bag X7432, King William's Town 5600. Telephone (0433) 2 3445/6 or 2 3475. This two-day trail (34,6 km) takes you through magnificent indigenous forests and pine plantations. Part of the trail winds along the lower slopes of Mount Thomas, affording you magnificent views.

***Koranna Hiking Trail:*** The Secretary, Wildlife Society of Southern Africa, Maluti Centre, P O Box 140, Marquard 9610, Telephone (05272) 21. A two-day, circular trail of approximately 32 km through one of the most beautiful parts of the Orange Free State, with fascinating rock formations, cliffs, waterfalls and wooded gullies. An interesting section through a cave (torches are necessary) will not easily be forgotten.

***Mabudashango Hiking Trail:*** The Director-General, Department of Agriculture and Forestry, Private Bag X2247, Sibasa 0970, Venda, Telephone Sibasa 51 ext 79 or 13 ext 123. A 54 km, circular, four-day trail through splendid scenery, including golden-green tea plantations, pine plantations and indigenous forests, and a glimpse of the sacred lake, Fundudzi.

***Magoebaskloof Hiking Trail: Section Dokolewa:*** The Regional Director, Northern Transvaal Forest Region, Private Bag X2413, Louis Trichardt 0920, Telephone (01551) 2201/2/3. A pleasant 36 km, circular trail which takes you through indigenous forests and pine plantations for three days. Highlights are the large numbers of Knysna louries and trees with clivias.

***Magoebaskloof Hiking Trail: Section Grootbosch:*** The Regional Director, Northern Transvaal Forest Region, Private Bag X2413, Louis Trichardt 0920, Telephone (01551) 2201/2/3. This fairly strenuous three-day trail caters for those who prefer less sophisticated accommodation — only a basic shelter is provided. The 50 km route winds through the largest indigenous forest in the Transvaal.

***Makobolwane Hiking Trail:*** The Officer-in-Charge, Sterkspruit Nature Reserve, P O Box 340, Lydenburg 1120. This circular two-day trail takes you through pine plantations and grasslands, passing streams and waterfalls with large pools. The trail lies south-west of the Long Tom Pass near Lydenburg.

***Mogol Hiking Trail:*** The Officer-in-Charge, Hans Strijdom Nature Reserve, P O Box 473, Ellisras 0555. Situated in the Hans Strijdom Nature Reserve, this 12 km (two-day) trail offers you the opportunity to see uncommon game species such as sable and Sharpe's grysbok. The route passes over mountains and through valleys.

***Mountain Zebra Hiking Trail:*** The Chief Director, National Parks Board, P O Box 787, Pretoria 0001, Telephone (012) 44 1191 or P O Box 7400, Roggebaai 8012, Telephone (021) 419 5365. On this relaxing 25 km, three-day trail you have the opportunity of viewing the Cape mountain zebra and other animals of the Cape midlands in their natural habitat.

***Mziki Hiking Trail:*** The Reservations Officer, Natal Parks Board, P O Box 662, Pietermaritzburg 3200, Telephone (0331) 471981. This three-day, 38 km trail reveals a wealth of flora and fauna as you hike through the southernmost limit of the true tropical and the subtropical regions. Scenery varies from the Indian Ocean to dune forests, grasslands and Lake St Lucia.

***Naukluft Hiking Trail:*** The Director, Directorate of Nature Conservation and Recreation Resorts, Private Bag 13267, Windhoek 9000, SWA/Namibia, Telephone (061) 36975. For either four or eight days you hike through the surprisingly well-watered Naukluft Mountains, refuge to large numbers of Hartmann's mountain zebra. The rugged terrain make this trail best left for the hardier hikers.

***Ngele Hiking Trail:*** The Regional Director, Natal Forest Region, Private Bag X9029, Pietermaritzburg 3200, Telephone (0331) 2 8101. The trail takes you through indigenous forests, grasslands and plantations, including the largest single man-made plantation in South Africa. A circular, five-day trail stretching over 95 km, although shorter variations are possible.

***Op-De-Berg Hiking Trail:*** The Officer-in-Charge, Blyderivierspoort Nature Reserve, P O Box Bourke's Luck 1272, Telephone (0020) ask for Bourke's Luck 15. A four-day circular trail of approximately 35 km in the heart of the Blyderivierspoort Nature Reserve.

***Otter Hiking Trail:*** The Chief Director, National Parks Board, P O Box 787, Pretoria 0001, Telephone (012) 44 1191 or P O Box 7400, Roggebaai 8012, Telephone (021) 419 5365. Features of this well-known five-day trail along the rugged Tsitsikamma coast include coastal forests, plateaux covered in proteas and ericas and beautiful coastal scenery.

***Outeniqua Hiking Trail:*** The Regional Director, Southern Cape Forest Region, Private Bag X12, Knysna 6570, Telephone (0445) 2 3037. The trail covers 137 km in eight or nine days through fynbos, virgin indigenous forests and pine plantations. Shorter variations are possible.

***Prospector's Hiking Trail:*** The Regional Director, Eastern Transvaal Forest Region, Private Bag X503, Sabie 1260, Telephone (0131512) ask for 307. Features of this 69 km, six-day trail include romantic names associated with the gold-mining days of the previous century and the historic village of Pilgrim's Rest, pine plantations and grasslands. Shorter variations are possible.

***Rhebok Hiking Trail:*** The Chief Director, National Parks Board, P O Box 787, Pretoria 0001, Telephone (012) 44 1191 or P O Box 7400, Roggebaai 8012, Telephone (021) 419 5365. Magnificent sandstone formations and the opportunity to spot game typical of the highlands of the north-eastern Free State are the attractions of this two-day, circular trail of approximately 26 km.

***Rustenburg Hiking Trail:*** The Officer-in-Charge, Rustenburg Nature Reserve, P O Box 511, Rustenburg 0300, Telephone (01421) 31050. This trail with two two-day loops enables you to experience the unspoilt Magaliesberg. The reserve is the habitat of several rare and uncommon mammal, bird and plant species.

***Shipwreck Hiking Trail:*** Ciskei Tourist Board, P O Box 56, Bisho, Ciskei, Telephone (0401) 9 1131. This 64 km coastal trail between the Fish River Mouth and the Ncera River near Kidd's Beach follows in the footsteps of many shipwreck victims of yesteryear. Scenery includes stretches of golden beach interspersed with rocky sections, beautiful lagoons and estuaries. Four days or shorter.

***Soutpansberg Hiking Trail: Section Hanglip:*** The Regional Director, Northern Transvaal Forest Region, Private Bag X2413, Louis Trichardt 0920, Telephone (01551) 2201/2/3. Situated in South Africa's northernmost mountain range, this 20,5 km (two-day) trail takes you through plantations and beautiful indigenous forests. The area is a birdlover's paradise.

***Soutpansberg Hiking Trail: Section Entabeni:*** The Regional Director, Northern Transvaal Forest Region, Private Bag X2413, Louis Trichardt 0920, Telephone (01551) 2201/2/3. This circular trail can be hiked as a four-day, three-day or two-day route and passes mainly through plantations and indigenous forests which are the home of troops of samango monkeys.

***Springbok Hiking Trail:*** The Chief Director, National Parks Board, P O Box 787, Pretoria 0001, Telephone (012) 44 1191 or P O Box 7400, Roggebaai 8012, Telephone (021) 419 5365. On this 41 km, three-day, circular trail you can discover the floral wealth and beautiful scenery of the Karoo. Herds of springbok and black wildebeest roam the plains, while gemsbok and red hartebeest also occur.

***Sterkspruit Hiking Trail:*** The Officer-in-Charge, Sterkspruit Nature Reserve, P O Box 340, Lydenburg 1120. A two-day, circular route which leads for 30 km through pine plantations, ravines and grasslands. The trail can be combined with the Makobolwane Hiking Trail into a circular, three-day trail of 33 km.

***Sterkstroom Tent Route:*** The Officer-in-Charge, Doorndraai Nature Reserve, P O Box 983, Potgietersrus 0600, Telephone (015423) 629. A two-day, circular route (30 km) for more experienced hikers. You have to carry a tent and a swim might be necessary at the start of the second day. The reserve is the home of several antelope species and giraffe.

• ***Swartberg Hiking Trail:*** The Regional Director, Southern Cape Forest Region, Private Bag X12, Knysna 6570, Telephone (0445) 2 3037. This trail affords you a number of options and offers magnificent mountain scenery and expansive views of the Little Karoo to the south and the Great Karoo to the north. The trail leads through open fynbos.

• ***Swellendam Hiking Trail:*** The Regional Director, Western Cape Forest Region, Private Bag X9005, Cape Town 8000, Telephone (021) 45 1224. An impressive trail, leading for 81 km through deep ravines and past high krantzes. It offers breathtaking views and a profusion of proteas, ericas and other fynbos flowers. A circular six-day hike, but shorter options are available.

***Suikerbosrand Hiking Trail:*** The Officer-in-Charge, Suikerbosrand Nature Reserve, Private Bag H616, Heidelberg 2400, Telephone (0151) 2181/2/3. This trail on the doorstep of the Vaal Triangle allows you to create your own combination of trails. The reserve has the added attraction of large herds of game. Circular, 66 km trail (six days) with shorter options available.

***Transkei Hiking Trail:*** The Nature Conservation Section, The Department of Agriculture and Forestry, Private Bag X5002, Umtata, Transkei, Telephone (0471) 2 4322 or 24 9309. The Transkei Wild Coast is well known for its unspoilt scenery — secluded beaches, beautiful estuaries and lagoons, and rolling hills dotted with aloes. Several trail sections cover the entire 250 km-long Wild Coast between the Mtamvuna and Great Fish rivers.

***Tsitsikamma Hiking Trail:*** The Regional Director, Tsitsikamma Forest Region, Private Bag X537, Humansdorp 6300, Telephone (04231) 5 1180. Indigenous forests, pine plantations, fynbos and magnificent mountain scenery are the attractions of this 72 km, five-day trail in the southern Cape. Shorter options are possible.

# Useful Addresses

You will find the following addresses useful when making enquiries about backpacking, guided wilderness and hiking trails, permits, joining a hiking or mountaineering club or obtaining maps. Membership of conservation-orientated naturalist societies will broaden your knowledge of nature and therefore enhance your trail experience. A list of some of these societies is included.

**Authorities Associated with Backpacking, Guided Wilderness and Hiking Trails**

Ciskei Tourist Board, P O Box 56, Bisho, Ciskei.

Department of Agriculture and Forestry, Private Bag X5002, Umtata, Transkei.

Department of Agriculture and Forestry, Private Bag X2247, Sibasa 0970, Venda.

Department of Agriculture and Nature Conservation, Private Bag 13267, Windhoek 9000, SWA/Namibia.

Department of Environment Affairs, Private Bag X447, Pretoria 0001.

Department of Forestry (Southern Region), P O Box 5493, Limbe, Malawi.

Department of Nature and Environmental Conservation, Cape Provincial Administration, Private Bag 9086, Cape Town 8000.

Department of Wildlife and National Parks and Tourism, P O Box 131, Gaborone, Botswana.

Division of Nature Conservation, Transvaal Provincial Administration, Private Bag X209, Pretoria 0001.

Lesotho National Parks, P O Box 92, Maseru 100, Lesotho.

Lesotho Tourist Board, P O Box 1378, Maseru, 100, Lesotho.

Natal Parks Board (Natal Parks, Game and Fish Preservation Board), P O Box 662, Pietermaritzburg 3200.

National Hiking Way Board, Private Bag X447, Pretoria 0001.

National Parks Board, P O Box 787, Pretoria 0001.

**Refer to the Summary of Hiking Trails pages 261 to 263 for individual trail addresses. Addresses for the various backpacking and guided wilderness trails are supplied in the actual area description under 'Permits'.**

**Hiking Clubs Affiliated with the Hiking Federation of South Africa**

The following clubs are affiliated with the Hiking Federation of South Africa, which represents the interests of member clubs on the National Hiking Way Board.

*Griqualand West*

Kimberley Hiking Club, 24 Jan Van Zyl Street, Monumenthoogte, Kimberley 8301.

*Orange Free State*

Bloemfontein Hiking Club, c/o Deon Basson, P O Box 7779, Bloemfontein 9300.

Highlands Mountain Club, P O Box 1035, Bethlehem 9700.

*Natal*

Durban Rambling and Hiking Club, P O Box 1623, Durban 4000.

Eshowe Ramblers Club, P O Box 5, Eshowe 3815.

SAP Hiking Club, P O Box 391, Durban 4000.

*Northern Transvaal*

Club International, P O Box 160, Wingate Park 0153.

CSIR Hiking Club, 263 Marais Street, Brooklyn 0181.

ISCOR Hiking Club, P O Box 34048, Erasmia 0023.

Kalender Hiking Club, P O Box 28591, Sunnyside 0132.

Klipspringer Hiking Club, Private Bag X381, Pretoria 0001.

Ndaba Hiking Club, 368 Christoffel Street, Pretoria West 0183.

Nomade Hiking Club, P O Box 2383, Pretoria 0001.

Overtuur, 101 Dikbashof, Kraaistraat, Kwaggasrand 0183.

Pakstappers, 31 Botanica, 2 Malana Avenue, Brumeria 0184.

Panorama Hiking Club, Department of Foreign Affairs, Private Bag X152, Pretoria 0001.

Pietersburg Hiking Club, P O Box 598, Pietersburg 0700.

Pretoria Wandelaars, 711 Ben Swart Street, Rietfontein 0084.

Rugsak en Stewels-voetslaanklub, P O Box 28560, Sunnyside 0132.

SAS Immortelle, Private Bag X104, Pretoria 0001.

Unisa Hiking Club, P O Box 392, Pretoria 0001.

*Southern Transvaal*

East Rand Hiking Club, 44 Dean Crescent, Northmead Ext. 7, Benoni 1500.

Hamba Gahle Hiking Club, P O Box 1775, Alberton 1450.

Harmonie Backpacking Club, P O Box 8859, Minnebron 1549.

IBM Hiking Club, P O Box 70243, Bryanston 2021.

Johannesburg Hiking Club, P O Box 2254, Johannesburg 2000.

Kruinstadstappersklub, Private Bag X30, Roodepoort 1725.

Norkem Park High School Hiking Club, Private Bag X04, Birchleigh 1621.

Ore-Voetslaanklub, P O Box 16041, Atlasville 1465.

Roodepoort Hiking Club, P O Box 21007, Helderkruin 1732.

Sasolburg Bergklimklub, P O Box 725, Sasolburg 9570.

Vlugvoet-voetslaanklub, 39 Rhodes Street, Geduld Extension, Springs 1650.

*Eastern Transvaal*

Cycad Hiking Club, P O Box 93, Middelburg 1050.

Lowveld Hiking Club, P O Box 1929, Nelspruit 1200.

*Western Cape*

Bellville Hiking Club, P O Box 1089, Oakdale 7534.

Breedevallei Hiking Club, P O Box 271, Worcester 6850.

Gantouw Hiking Club, P O Box 316, Strand 7140.

Helderberg Hiking Club, P O Box 857, Somerset West 7130.

Hottentots-Holland Hiking Club, P O Box 5325, Helderberg 7135.

Paarl Hiking Club, P O Box 478, Paarl 7620.

Sanlam Hiking Club, P O Box 1, Sanlamhof 7532.

Stellenbosch Hiking Club, 17 Het Heerenhof, 6 Oudebaan, Stellenbosch 7600.

Swartland Hiking Club, P O Box 283, Malmesbury 7300.

*Eastern Cape*

Algoa Ramblers, 18 Mowbray Street, Newton Park, Port Elizabeth 6045.

### Hiking Clubs not Affiliated with the Hiking Federation of South Africa

Border Outdoor Adventure Association (Hiking Club of East London), P O Box 13200, Vincent, East London 5217.

Peninsula Ramblers, P O Box 982, Cape Town 8000.

Ramblers' Club, Pietermaritzburg, P O Box 10073, Scottsville 3209.

### The Mountain Club of South Africa

*Headquarters:* 97 Hatfield Street, Cape Town 8001.

*Branches*

Cape Town Section, 97 Hatfield Street, Cape Town 8001.

Eastern Province Section, P O Box 1274, Port Elizabeth 6000.

Hottentots-Holland Section, P O Box 1100, Somerset West 7130.

Natal Section, P O Box 4535, Durban 4000.

Northern Natal Section, P O Box 1362, Newcastle 2940.

Northern Transvaal Section, P O Box 1418, Pretoria 0001.

Orange Free State Section, P O Box 1291, Bloemfontein 9300.

Paarl/Wellington Section, P O Box 2645, Paarl 7620.
South West Africa Section, P O Box 2448, Windhoek 9000, SWA/Namibia.
Stellenbosch Section, P O Box 152, Stellenbosch 7600.
Transvaal Section, P O Box 4066, Johannesburg 2000.
Tygerberg Section, P O Box 2125, Bellville 7530.
Worcester Section, P O Box 373, Worcester 6850.

*Miscellaneous*
South African Climbers Club, P O Box 64, Newlands 7700.
The Mountain Club of Malawi, P O Box 240, Blantyre, Malawi.
Western Province Mountain Club, P O Box 54, Crawford 7700.

*Mountain Clubs at Universities*
Membership of university mountain clubs is usually restricted to registered students and university personnel.

Berg-en-Toerklub, University of Stellenbosch, Stellenbosch 7600.
Exploration Stap- en Rotsklimvereniging, Tukkiewerf, University of Pretoria 0002.
Momentum Stap- en Bergklimvereniging, University of the Orange Free State, P O Box 339, Bloemfontein 9300.
UCT Mountain and Ski Club, Sports Union, University of Cape Town, Rondebosch 7700.
University of Natal Mountain Club, Sports Union, P O Box 375, Pietermaritzburg 3200.

**Outdoor Education**

National Outdoor Pursuit Centre, P O Box 42, Clarens 9701 (Associated with Veld and Vlei Leadership Trust of South Africa).
Outward Bound, Private Bag, Leribe, Lesotho.
Veld and Vlei Adventure Trust (Head Office), P O Box 396, Port Elizabeth 6000.
Wilderness Leadership School (Head Office), P O Box 153058, Yellowwood Park 4011.
Wilderness Leadership School (Cape), 22 Park Road, Rondebosch 7700.
Wilderness Leadership School (Transvaal), P O Box 87230, Houghton 2041.

**Conservation-oriented Naturalist Societies**

Botanical Society of South Africa
*Head Office:* Kirstenbosch, Claremont 7735.

*Branches*
There are about 10 branches of the society countrywide. To find out if you have a branch in your area, contact the head office.

Dendrological Society
*Headquarters:* P O Box 104, Pretoria 0001.

*Branches*
The society has various branches countrywide. Contact the head office for further details.

Geological Society of South Africa, P O Box 1017, Johannesburg 2000.
National Veld Trust, P O Box 26192, Arcadia 0007.
Society for the Protection of the Environment, P O Box 370, Stellenbosch 7600.

Southern African Ornithological Society
*Head Office:* P O Box 87234, Houghton 2041, Telephone (011) 782 1547.

*Branches*
Cape Bird Club, P O Box 5022, Cape Town 8000.
Eastern Cape Wild Bird Society, P O Box 27454, Greenacres 6075.
Goldfields Bird Club, P O Box 580, Virginia 9430.
Lowveld Bird Club, P O Box 507, Nelspruit 1200.
Natal Bird Club, P O Box 1218, Durban 4000.
North-eastern Bird Club, P O Box 64, Haenertsburg 0730.
Northern Transvaal Ornithological Society, P O Box 4158, Pretoria 0001.
Orange Free State Ornithological Society, P O Box 6614, Bloemfontein 9300.
Potchefstroom Bird Club, P O Box 2413, Potchefstroom 2520.

Sandton Bird Club, P O Box 65727, Benmore 2010.

SWA/Namibia Bird Club, c/o SWA Scientific Society, P O Box 67, Windhoek 9000, SWA/Namibia.

Witwatersrand Bird Club, P O Box 72091, Parkview 2122.

SANCCOB (SA National Foundation for the Conservation of Coastal Birds), P O Box 11-116, Bloubergrant 7443.

South African Archaeological Society, P O Box 1038, Johannesburg 2000.

Wildlife Society of Southern Africa
*Head Office:* P O Box 44189, Linden 2104.

*Branches*

Border: P O Box 7608, East London 5200.

Eastern Cape: 2c Lawrence Street, Central Hill, Port Elizabeth 6001.

Natal: P O Box 2985, Durban 4000.

Northern Cape: P O Box 316, Kimberley 8300.

OFS: P O Box 2099, Bloemfontein 9300.

Transvaal: P O Box 44344, Linden 2104.

Western Cape: P O Box 145, Tokai 7966.

Wildlife Society of Namibia, P O Box 3508, Windhoek 9000 (affiliated to the Wildlife Society of Southern Africa).

Transkei Wildlife Society, c/o C Shackleton, Botany Department, University of Transkei, Private Bag X5092, Umtata 5100, Transkei (affiliated to the Wildlife Society of Southern Africa).

**Maps and Cartography**

*Botswana*

Department of Surveys and Lands, Private Bag 0037, Gaborone, Botswana.

*Lesotho*

Department of Lands, Surveys and Physical Planning, Ministry of the Interior, P O Box MS 876, Maseru 100, Lesotho.

*Malawi*

Department of Surveys, Map Sales Office, P O Box 349, Blantyre, Malawi.

*South Africa*

Chief Director of Surveys and Mapping, Rhodes Avenue, Private Bag, Mowbray 7705.

Government Printer, Bosman Street, Private Bag X85, Pretoria 0001.

Surveyor-General, Private Bag X20634, Bloemfontein, 9300.

Surveyor-General, P O Box 396, Pietermaritzburg 3200.

*SWA/Namibia*

Surveyor-General, Department of Justice, Private Bag 13182, Windhoek 9000, SWA/Namibia.

# Bibliography

The following sources have been consulted. They will prove useful should you wish to obtain more detailed information and are divided into categories for easy reference. Periodicals and brochures consulted are listed after the books. Books marked with an asterisk (*) have not been consulted but are recommended for further reading.


## Hiking General

*Books*

Bradt, H. 1983. *Backpacker's Africa.* Bucks, England: Bradt Enterprises.
Burman, J. 1980. *Trails and Walks in the Southern Cape.* Cape Town: Human & Rousseau.
Changuion, L. 1977. *Met Rugsak en Stewels.* Johannesburg: Perskor.
Hennig, H. 1983. *The South African Backpacker.* Cape Town: Centaur.
Levy, J. 1982. *Everyone's Guide to Trailing and Mountaineering in Southern Africa.* Cape Town: Struik.
Steyn, A. 1982. *Backpack for Pleasure.* Pretoria: Intergrafix.

## First Aid

*Books*

Ackermann, M. (ed) 1982. *Hiking to Health.* Cape Town: Medical Association of South Africa.
Jackson, J. (ed) 1976. *Safety on Mountains.* Manchester: British Mountain Council.
Mitchell, D. 1979. *Mountaineering First Aid.* Seattle: The Mountaineers.
Pitchford, R.J. 1976. *Bilharzia: Beware.* Pretoria: Department of Health.
Reitz, C.J. 1978. *Poisonous South African Snakes and Snakebite.* Pretoria: Department of Health.
*The South African First Aid Manual — Emergency Procedures for Everyone at Home, at Work or at Leisure* (The authorised Manual of St John Ambulance and the South African Red Cross Society). 1986. Cape Town: C Struik.

## Conservation — General

*Books*

* Du Plessis, A. (ed) 1974. *The Conservation of our Heritage.* Cape Town: Human & Rousseau.
Greyling, T. and Huntley, B.J. (eds) 1984. *Directory of Southern African Conservation Areas.* South African National Scientific Programmes Report No 98, Pretoria: CSIR.
*Martin, V. (ed) 1982. *Wilderness — Proceedings of the Second World Wilderness Congress.* Moray, Scotland: The Findhorn Press.
National Committee for Nature Conservation: Register of Permanent Conservation Areas in South and South West Africa. 1974. *Koedoe* 17, 85-119.
*Player, I. (ed). *Voices of the Wilderness — Proceedings of the Second World Wilderness Congress.* Johannesburg: Jonathan Ball, 1979.
*Richards, D. and Walker, C. 1975. *Walk Through the Wilderness.* Cape Town: Purnell & Sons.

*Periodicals*

Ackerman, D.P. 1977. Nie-Kommersiële Aktiwiteite van die Departement van Bosbou. *South African Forestry Journal* 103, 1-4.
Ackerman, D.P. 1979. The Reservation of Wilderness Areas in South Africa. *South African Forestry Journal* 108, 2-4.

Bands, D.P. 1977. Planning for a Wilderness Area. *South African Forestry Journal* 103, 22-27.

## Southern Africa — General

*Books*

Andersson, C.J. 1974. *Lake Ngami* (Facsimile reprint). Cape Town: Struik.
Clarke, J. and Coulson, D. 1983. *Mountain Odyssey.* Johannesburg: Macmillan.
Duggan, A. (ed) 1983. *Game Parks and Nature Reserves of Southern Africa.* Cape Town: Reader's Digest.
Gardiner, A.F. 1966. *Narrative of a Journey to the Zoolu Country in South Africa* (Facsimile reprint). Cape Town: C. Struik.
Gordon, R. and Bannister, A. 1983. *The National Parks of South Africa.* Cape Town: Struik.
Leigh, M. 1986. *Touring in South Africa.* Cape Town: C Struik.
Oberholster, J.J. 1972. *The Historical Monuments of South Africa.* Stellenbosch: The Rembrandt van Rijn Foundation.
Raper, P.E. 1972. *Streekname in Suid-Afrika en Suidwes.* Cape Town: Tafelberg.
Raper, P.E. 1987. *Directory of Southern African Place Names.* Johannesburg: Lowry Publishers.
Steyn, A. (ed) 1987. *Off The Beaten Track — Selected Day Drives in Southern Africa.* Cape Town: Automobile Association of South Africa.

*References below are generally relevant only to the geographical areas listed.*

## South West Africa/Namibia

*Books*

Bornman, C.H. 1972. *Welwitschia.* Cape Town: Struik.
Jankowitz, W.J. 1975. *Aloes of South West Africa.* Windhoek: Division of Nature Conservation and Tourism, Administration of South West Africa.
Joubert, E. *Meesterplan: Namib-Naukluftpark — 'n Verslag met beleid ten opsigte van doelstellings, sonering en benutting van die Naukluft-Bergkompleks en aangrensende gruisvlaktes, insluitende Sesriem en Sossusvlei.* Windhoek: Division of Nature Conservation and Tourism, Administration of South West Africa.
*Lambrechts, H.A. 1985. *Namibia — A Thirstland Wilderness.* Cape Town: C. Struik.
Muller, M.A.N. 1984. *Grasses of South West Africa/Namibia.* Windhoek: Directorate of Agriculture and Forestry.

*Periodicals*

Broekhuysen, G.J. Broekhuysen, M.G. Winterbottom, J.M. and Winterbottom, M.G. 1966. Birds Recorded from Ai-Ais, Fish River, South West Africa. *The South African Avifauna Series* 42. Cape Town: Percy Fitzpatrick Institute of African Ornithology.
Giess, W. 1971. A Preliminary Vegetation Map of South West Africa. *Dinteria* 4.
Kinahan, J. 1984. The Stratigraphy and Lithic Assemblages of Falls Rock Shelter, Western Damaraland, Namibia. *Cimbebasia* (B) 4 (2).
Kinahan, J. and Kinahan, J.H.A. 1984. Holocene Subsistence and Settlement on the Namib Coast: The Example of the Ugab River. *Cimbebasia* (B) 4 (6): 59-72.
Kinahan, J. 1986. The Archaeological Structure of Pastoral Production in the Central Namib Desert. *South African Archaeological Society Goodwin Series* 5, 69-82.
Kinahan, J. 1987. Archaeological Sites in the Fish River Canyon, Southern SWA/Namibia. *Madoqua* 15 (1), 17-19.
Krynauw, D.W. 1969. Kaap Kruis. *Historical Monuments Commission of South West Africa, Publication No. 4.*
Mienie, J.H. 1979. Cape Cross. *National Monuments Council, Publication No. 4A.*
Nordenstam, B. 1974. The Flora of the Brandberg. *Dinteria* 11.
Shackley, M. 1985. Palaeolithic Archaeology of the Central Namib Desert — A Preliminary Survey of the Chronology, Typology and Site Location. *Cimbebasia* 6.

Simpson, E.S.W. and Hywel Davies, D. 1957. Observations on the Fish River Canyon in South West Africa. *Transactions of the Royal Society of South Africa* 35 (2), 97-108.

Vrey, T. 1983. A Hike into the Unknown. *Custos* 12 (8), 4-5.

### Western Cape

*Books*

Andrag, R.H. 1977. Studies in die Sederberge oor (i) Die Status van die Clanwilliam Seder (*Widdringtonia cedarbergensis* Marsh) (ii) Buitelugontspanning. M.Sc Thesis, University of Stellenbosch.

Cape Bird Club. *A Guide to the Birds of the S W Cape.* Cape Town: Cape Bird Club.

Day, J. Siegfried, W.R. Louw, G.N. and Jarman, M.L. (eds) 1979. *Fynbos Ecology: a preliminary synthesis.* South African National Scientific Programmes Report No 40, Pretoria: CSIR.

*Frandsen, J. 1982. *Birds of the South Western Cape.* Johannesburg: Sable Publishers.

Hall, A.V. and Veldhuis, H.A. 1985. *South African Red Data Book: Plants — Fynbos and Karoo Biomes.* South African National Scientific Programmes Report No 117, Pretoria: CSIR.

Le Roux, A. and Schelpe, E.A.C.L.E. 1981. *Namaqualand and Clanwilliam — South African Wildflower Guide 1.* Cape Town: Botanical Society of SA.

*Periodicals*

Luckhoff, H.A. 1980. The Sederberg Wilderness Area. *Directorate of Forestry and Environmental Conservation, Bulletin* 60.

Minter, M. 1986. Groot-Winterhoek Wilderness Area. *Forestry News* 1, 2 & 3.

Mostert, V. 1976. Die Sneeuprotea. *Veld & Flora* 62 (4). 21 & 22.

Taylor, H.C. 1976. Notes on the Vegetation and Flora of the Cedarberg. *Veld & Flora* 62 (4), 28-30.

Van Rensburg, T.J.F. 1980. Tradouwpas — In die voetspore van die Hottentotte. *Environment RSA* 7 (7), 5.

### Eastern Cape and Ciskei

*Books*

Ciskei Tourist Board. *Ciskei Hiking Trails.* Bisho, Ciskei: Ciskei Tourist Board.

Derricourt, R.M. 1977. *Prehistoric Man in Ciskei and Transkei.* Cape Town: Struik.

Gledhill, E. 1981. *Eastern Cape Veld Flowers.* Cape Town: Department of Nature and Environmental Conservation of the Cape Provincial Administration.

*Godfrey, R. 1941. *Bird-lore of the Eastern Cape Province.* Johannesburg: Witwatersrand University Press.

Page, D. (ed) 1982. *Strategy and Guidelines for the Physical Development of the Republic of Ciskei.* Stellenbosch: Institute for Planning Research, University of Stellenbosch.

Saunders, C. and Derricourt, R.M. (eds) 1974. *Beyond the Cape Frontier — Studies in the History of the Transkei and Ciskei.* London: Longman.

*Periodicals*

Millar, J.C.G. 1968. The Mountain Zebra. *Wildlife of Southern Africa Series.* Mammalogy Seminar, University of Pretoria.

*Von Gadow, K. 1977. 100 Indigenous Trees of the Eastern Cape Border Region — A Leaf Key. *Department of Forestry Pamphlet 195.*

### Lesotho

*Books*

Ambrose, D. 1976. *The Guide to Lesotho.* Johannesburg: Winchester Press.

Associated Research Consultants Limited. *Development Plan for Tourism for Kingdom of Lesotho.* Maseru: Government Printer.

Mc Vean, D.N. 1977. *Nature Conservation in Lesotho — Report on Current Progress and Forward Planning.* Morges, Switzerland: International Union for Conservation of Nature and Natural Resources.

*Periodicals and Brochures*

Anon. 1979. A Kingdom's Culture. *Lesotho — Kingdom in the sky.* 9 & 11.
Anon. 1977. Sehlabathebe — Lesotho's National Park. *African Wildlife* 31 (4), 26-28.
Lesotho National Parks. *Mammals of Sehlabathebe National Park.* Maseru: Government Printer.
Passineau, J.F. 1980. The plateau of the shield. *African Wildlife* 34 (2), 37 & 38.
Smith, K. 1971. Sehlabathebe — Lesotho's First National Park. *African Wildlife* 25 (4), 135-137.
Van Zinderen-Bakker, E.M. 1981. The High Mountains of Lesotho — a Botanical Paradise. *Veld & Flora* 67 (4), 106-109.

**Natal Drakensberg and Natal**

*Books*

Ackhurst, J. Irwin, D. and Irwin, P. 1980. *A Field Guide to the Natal Drakensberg.* Durban: Natal Branch of the Wildlife Society of Southern Africa.
Dodds, D. 1975. *A Cradle of Rivers — The Natal Drakensberg.* Cape Town: Purnell & Sons.
Moll, E. 1981. *Trees of Natal.* Cape Town: University of Cape Town, Eco-Lab Trust Fund.
Pager, H. 1971. *Ndedema — a Documentation of the Rock Paintings of Ndedema Gorge.* Graz, Austria: Akademische Druck-u Verlagsanstalt.
Pearse, R.O. 1973. *Barrier of Spears: Drama of the Drakensberg.* Cape Town: Howard Timmins. (To be republished by Southern Book Publishers in 1988.)
Pearse, R.O. 1978. *Mountain Splendour — The Wild Flowers of the Drakensberg.* Cape Town: Howard Timmins.
*Player, I. 1972. *The White Rhino Saga.* London: Collins.
Vinnicombe, P. 1976. *People of the Eland — Rock Paintings of the Drakensberg Bushmen as a Reflection of their Life and Thought.* Pietermaritzburg: University of Natal Press.
Willcox, A.R. 1984. *The Drakensberg Bushmen and Their Art — With a Guide to the Rock Painting Sites.* Winterton: Drakensberg Publicity Association.

*Periodicals and Brochures*

Burrows, J.E. and Schultz, S.M. 1981. The Ferns of the Ntendeka Wilderness. *Veld & Flora* 67 (4), 118-120.
Day, D.H. 1974. *Giant's Castle Game Reserve.* Pietermaritzburg: Natal Parks Board.
Killick, D.J.B. 1963. An Account of the Plant Ecology of the Cathedral Peak Area of the Natal Drakensberg. *Memoirs of the Botanical Survey No 34.*
Luckhoff, H.A. 1983. The Natal Drakensberg Wilderness Areas. *Forestry News* 3, 21-24.
Mazel, A.D. 1982. Distribution of Painting Themes in the Natal Drakensberg. *Annals Natal Museum* 25 (1), 67-82.
Natal Parks Board. *St Lucia.* Pietermaritzburg: Natal Parks Board.
Natal Parks Board. *Royal Natal National Park.* Natal Parks Board.
Rose, M. 1977/1978. The Oldest Game Reserves in Africa. *African Wildlife* 31 (6), 17-20.
Vincent, J. 1980. The Ecology of Lake St Lucia. *Environment RSA* 7 (1), 4-6.

**Transvaal**

*Books*

Braack, L.E.O. 1983. *The Kruger National Park.* Cape Town: C. Struik.
Bulpin, T.V. 1974. *Lost Trails of the Transvaal.* Cape Town: T V Bulpin.
Fitzpatrick, P. 1976. *Jock of the Bushveld.* Middlesex, England: Puffin Books.
Germishuizen, G. and Fabian, A. 1982. *Transvaal Wild Flowers.* Johannesburg: Macmillan.
Klein, H. 1972. *Valley of the Mists.* Cape Town: Howard Timmins.
Newman, K. 1980. *Birds of Southern Africa 1: Kruger National Park.* Johannesburg: Macmillan.
Nussey, W. and Paynter, D. 1986. *Kruger — Portrait of a National Park.* Johannesburg: Macmillan.
Onderstall, J. 1984. *Transvaal Lowveld and Escarpment Including the Kruger National Park — South African Wild Flower Guide 4.* Cape Town: Botanical Society of South Africa.

Pienaar, U de V. Rautenbach, I.L. and De Graaff, G. 1980. *The Small Mammals of the Kruger National Park.* Pretoria: National Parks Board of South Africa.
Rautenbach, I.L. 1982. *Mammals of the Transvaal.* Pretoria: Ecoplan.

*Periodicals*

Adendorff, G. 1975. João Albasini. *Custos* 4 (5), 17, 19, 21.
Dearlove, T.W. 1978. Bushveld Open to Hikers. *Custos* 7 (6), 6-11.
Dearlove, T.W. 1980. A Third Wilderness Trail for Kruger National Park. *Custos* 9 (8), 5-8.
Dearlove, T.W. 1983. New Hiking Trail for Kruger Park. *Custos* 12 (4), 7-9.
Diederichs, P. 1976. The Rebirth of Masorini. *Custos* 5 (9), 8-12, 26, 27.
Eloff, J.F. and De Vaal, J.B. 1974. The Secrets of Makahane. *Custos* 3 (6), 21-28.
Esterhuyse, C.J. 1986. The Wolkberg Wilderness Area. *Forestry Branch of the Department of Environment Affairs, Pamphlet 361,* Pretoria.
Rosenblatt, D. 1974. Historical Sites of the Kruger National Park. *Custos* 3 (13), 39-41.
Tarboton, W. 1980. The Nyl's birds. *Fauna & Flora* 36, 14-16.
Viljoen, P.J. 1984. Red-list Monkeys Reestablished at Pafuri. *Custos* 13 (6), 29-30.

## Botswana and Malawi

*Books*

Botswana Society. 1976. *Symposium on the Okavango Delta and its Future Utilisation.* Gaborone.
Campbell, A. 1979. *The Guide to Botswana.* Johannesburg: Winchester Press.
Ginn, P. 1979. *Birds of Botswana.* Johannesburg: Chris van Rensburg Publications.
Kippax, F. and Hawkes, M. 1987. *Mulanje Mountain Visitors' Guide.* Lilongwe, Malawi: Department of Forestry.
*Main, M. Fowkes, J. and S. 1987. *Visitors' Guide to Botswana.* Johannesburg: Southern Book Publishers.
Moriarty, A. 1975. *Wild Flowers of Malawi.* Cape Town: Purnell.
Pike, J.G. and Rimmington, G.T. 1965. *Malawi — A Geographical Study.* London: Oxford University Press.
Timberlake, J. 1980. *Handbook of Botswana Acacias.* Gaborone, Botswana: Ministry of Agriculture.
Tinley, K.L. 1966. *An Ecological Reconnaissance of the Moremi Wildlife Reserve Botswana.* Johnnesburg: Okavango Wildlife Society.

*Periodicals*

Burrows, J.E. and S.M. 1987. Mount Mulanje — Last Refuge of the Giants. *Veld & Flora* 73 (4), 122-124.
Campbell, A.C. 1977. The Okavango. *African Wildlife* 31 /5), 13-27.
Games, I. 1983. The Okavango Sitatunga. *African Wildlife* 37 (3), 96-100.

*References below generally cover a large geographical area, ie South Africa or Southern Africa.*

## Flora

*Books*

Coates Palgrave, K. 1977. *Trees of Southern Africa.* Cape Town: Struik.
Eliovson, S. 1965. *Proteas for Pleasure.* Johannesburg: Macmillan.
Harrison, E.R. 1981. *Epiphytic Orchids of Southern Africa.* Durban: Natal Branch of the Wildlife Society of Southern Africa.
Palmer, E. and Pitman, N. 1972/73. *Trees of Southern Africa* (3 vols). Cape Town: A A Balkema.
Reynolds, G.W. 1970. *The Aloes of Southern Africa.* Cape Town: A A Balkema.
Rourke, J.P. 1980. *The Proteas of Southern Africa.* Cape Town: Purnell & Sons.
Stewart, J. Linder, H.P. Schelpe, E.A. and Hall, A.V. 1982. *Wild Orchids of Southern Africa.* Johannesburg: Macmillan.
Vogts, M. 1982. *South Africa's Proteaceae — Know them and Grow them.* Cape Town: Struik.
Von Breitenbach, F. 1986. *National List of Indigenous Trees.* Pretoria: Dendrological Foundation.

*Von Breitenbach, F. 1974. *Southern Cape Forests and Trees.* Pretoria: Government Printer.

*Periodicals*

Acocks, J.H.P. 1975. Veld Types of South Africa. *Memoirs of the Botanical Survey of South Africa* 40.

Edwards, D. 1974. Survey to Determine the Adequacy of Existing Conserved Areas in Relation to Vegetation Types: A Preliminary Report. *Koedoe* 17, 3-38.

Gibbs Russell, G.E. *et al* 1984. List of Species of Southern African Plants. *Memoirs of the Botanical Survey of South Africa* 48.

Smith, C.A. 1966. Common Names of South African Plants. *Memoirs of the Botanical Survey of South Africa* 35.

**Fauna**

*Mammals: Books*

Smithers, R.H.N. 1982. *The Mammals of the Southern African Subregion.* Pretoria: Mammal Research Institute, University of Pretoria.

Smithers, R.H.N. 1986. *South African Red Data Book — Terrestrial Mammals.* South African National Scientific Programmes Report No 125, Pretoria: CSIR.

Smithers, R.H.N. 1986. *Land Mammals of Southern Africa — A Field Guide.* Johannesburg: Macmillan.

Walker, C. 1981. *Signs of the Wild.* Johannesburg: Natural History Publications.

Zaloumis, E.A. and Cross, R.A. 1974. *A Field Guide to the Antelope of Southern Africa.* Durban: Natal Branch of the Wildlife Society of Southern Africa.

*Birds: Books*

Berruti, A. and Sinclair, J.C. 1983. *Where to Watch Birds in Southern Africa.* Cape Town: C. Struik

Brooke, R.K. 1984. *South African Red Data Book — Birds.* South African Scientific Programmes Report No 97, Pretoria: CSIR.

*Johnson, P. 1976. *As Free as a Bird.* Cape Town: C. Struik.

Maclean, G.L. 1985. *Roberts' Birds of Southern Africa.* Cape Town: The Trustees of the John Voelcker Bird Book Fund.

Newman, K. 1983. *Newman's Birds of Southern Africa.* Johannesburg: Macmillan.

Siegfried, W.R. Forest, P.G.H. Cooper, J. and Kemp, A.C. 1976. *South African Red Data Book — Aves.* South African Scientific Programmes Report No 7, Pretoria: CSIR.

*Periodicals*

Brown, C.J. and Rennie, S.E. 1981. Vulture or Eagle? *African Wildlife* 35 (4), 12-14.

*Reptiles and Amphibians: Books*

FitzSimons, V.F.M. 1970. *A Field Guide to the Snakes of Southern Africa.* London: Collins.

McLachlan, G.R. 1978. *South African Red Data Book — Reptiles and Amphibians.* South African National Scientific Programmes Report No 32, Pretoria: CSIR.

Visser, J. and Chapman, D. 1981. *Snakes and Snakebite.* Cape Town: Purnell & Sons.

*Fish: Books*

Salomon, M.G. 1978. *Freshwater Fishing in South Africa.* Johannesburg: Chris van Rensburg Publications.

*Periodicals*

Scott, H.A. 1982. The Olifants River System — Unique Habitat for Rare Cape Fishes. *Cape Conservation Series* 2, Cape Town: Cape Department of Nature and Environment Conservation.

*Marine Fauna: Books*

*Branch, G. 1981. *Living Shores of Southern Africa.* Cape Town: C. Struik.

*Kensley, B. 1973. *Sea-Shells of Southern Africa — Gastropods.* Cape Town: Maskew Miller.

*Richards, D. 1981. *South African Shells — A Collector's Guide.* Cape Town: C. Struik.

**Archaeology, Anthropology and History**

*Books*

Cameron, T. and Spies, S.B. (eds) 1986. *An Illustrated History of South Africa.* Johannesburg: Jonathan Ball Publishers.

Danziger, C. 1979. *The Pioneers (BC-1795).* Cape Town: Purnell & Sons.

Inskeep. R.R. 1978. *The Peopling of Southern Africa.* Cape Town: David Philip.

Levitas, B. 1983. *Ethnology — An Introduction to the Peoples and Cultures of Southern Africa.* Cape Town: Oxford University Press.

Miller, P. 1979. *Myths and Legends of Southern Africa.* Cape Town: T V Bulpin Publications.

Muller, C.F.J. 1980. *500 Jaar Suid Afrikaanse Geskiedenis.* Pretoria: Academica.

Parsons, N. 1982. *A New History of Southern Africa.* London: Macmillan Education Ltd.

Phillipson, D.W. 1977. *The Later Prehistory of Eastern and Southern Africa.* London: Heinemann Education Books.

Tobias, P. (ed) 1978. *The Bushmen: San Hunters and Herders of Southern Africa.* Cape Town: Human & Rousseau.

Willcox, A.R. 1976. *Southern Land — The Prehistory and History of Southern Africa.* Cape Town: Purnell & Sons.

Willcox,, A.R. 1984. *The Rock Art of Africa.* Johannesburg: Macmillan.

Wilson, M. and Thompson, L. (eds) 1982. *A History of South Africa.* Cape Town: David Philip.

*Woodhouse, H.C. 1980. *The Bushman Art of Southern Africa.* Cape Town: Purnell & Sons.

*Woodhouse, H.C. 1984. *When Animals Were People.* Johannesburg: Chris van Rensburg Publications.

**Geology**

*Books*

Mountain, E.D. 1968. *Geology of Southern Africa.* Cape Town: Books of Africa.

All available trail literature was also consulted, but as this is too extensive to list, we suggest that those interested make enquiries to the relevant authorities.

# Scientific, English and Afrikaans names of trees, birds and mammals

## TREES

The following is a list of trees referred to in the text with their *National List of Indigenous Trees* numbers and their scientific, English and Afrikaans names.

| No | Scientific Name | English Name | Afrikaans Name |
|---|---|---|---|
| 1 | *Cyathea dregei* | Common Tree Fern | Gewone Boomvaring |
| 2 | *Cyathea capensis* | Forest Tree Fern | Bosboomvaring |
| 13 | *Encephalartos transvenosus* | Modjadji Cycad | Modjadjebroodboom |
| 15 | *Podocarpus elongatus* | Breede River Yellowwood | Breëriviergeelhout |
| 16 | *Podocarpus falcatus* | Outeniqua Yellowwood | Outeniekwageelhout |
| 17 | *Podocarpus henkelii* | Henkel's Yellowwood | Henkel-se-geelhout |
| 18 | *Podocarpus latifolius* | Real Yellowwood | Opregte Geelhout |
| 19 | *Widdringtonia cedarbergensis* | Clanwilliam Cedar | Clanwilliamseder |
| 20 | *Widdringtonia nodiflora* | Mountain Cypress | Bergsipres |
| 21 | *Widdringtonia schwarzii* | Willowmore Cedar | Baviaanskloofseder |
| 21.1 | *Welwitschia mirabilis* | Welwitschia | Tweeblaarkanniedood |
| 22 | *Phoenix reclinata* | Wild Date Palm | Wildedadelboom |
| 24 | *Hyphaene ventricosa* | Real Fan Palm | Opregte Waaierpalm |
| 28.1 | *Aloe arborescens* | Krantz Aloe | Kransaalwyn |
| 28.4 | *Aloe angelica* | Wylliespoort Aloe | Wylliespoortaalwyn |
| 28.8 | *Aloe excelsa* | Zimbabwe Aloe | Zimbabwe-aalwyn |
| 29 | *Aloe dichotoma* | Quiver Tree | Kokerboom |
| 29.4 | *Aloe littoralis* | Mopane Aloe | Mopanie-aalwyn |
| 35 | *Salix capensis* | Vaal Willow | Vaalwilger |
| 39 | *Celtis africana* | White Stinkwood | Witstinkhout |
| 48 | *Ficus thonningii* | Common Wild Fig | Gewone Wildevy |
| 50 | *Ficus sur* | Broom Cluster Fig | Besemtrosvy |
| 51 | *Ficus cordata* | Namaqua Fig | Namakwavy |
| 66 | *Ficus sycomorus* subsp. *sycomorus* | Common Cluster Fig | Gewone Trosvy |
| 67.1 | *Ficus verruculosa* | Water Fig | Watervy |
| 74 | *Faurea macnaughtonii* | Terblanz Beech | Terblans |
| 75 | *Faurea saligna* | Transvaal Beech | Transvaalboekenhout |
| 81 | *Leucadendron eucalyptifolium* | Tall Yellowbush | Grootgeelbos |
| 84.2 | *Leucospermum cuneiforme* | Common Pincushion | Gewone Luisiesbos |
| 86 | *Protea nitida* | Wagon Tree | Waboom |
| 86.1 | *Protea magnifica* | Bearded Sugarbush | Baardsuikerbos |
| 87 | *Protea caffra* | Common Sugarbush | Gewone Suikerbos |

| No | Scientific Name | English Name | Afrikaans Name |
|---|---|---|---|
| 89 | *Protea gaguedi* | African White Sugarbush | Afrikaanse Witsuikerbos |
| 93.1 | *Protea neriifolia* | Blue Sugarbush | Blousuikerbos |
| 96 | *Protea roupelliae* | Silver Sugarbush | Silwersuikerbos |
| 97 | *Protea rubropilosa* | Transvaal Mountain Sugarbush | Transvaalse Bergsuikerbos |
| 98 | *Protea subvestita* | Lip-flower Sugarbush | Lippeblomsuikerbos |
| 104 | *Portulacaria afra* | Porkbush | Spekboom |
| 111 | *Xymalos monospora* | Lemonwood | Lemoenhout |
| 115 | *Cryptocarya myrtifolia* | Myrtle Quince | Mirtekweper |
| 118 | *Ocotea bullata* | Stinkwood | Stinkhout |
| 122 | *Boscia albitrunca* | Shepherd's Tree | Witgat |
| 130 | *Capparis sepiaria* var. *citrifolia* | Wild Caper-bush | Wildekapperbos |
| 136 | *Maerua schinzii* | Ringwood Tree | Kringboom |
| 137 | *Moringa ovalifolia* | Phantom Tree | Meelsakboom |
| 140 | *Cunonia capensis* | Red Alder | Rooiels |
| 141 | *Platylophus trifoliatus* | White Alder | Witels |
| 145 | *Leucosidea sericea* | Oldwood | Ouhout |
| 155 | *Albizia harveyi* | Common False-thorn | Bleekblaarboom |
| 159 | *Acacia albida* | Ana Tree | Anaboom |
| 161 | *Acacia burkei* | Black Monkey Thorn | Swartapiesdoring |
| 162 | *Acacia caffra* | Common Hook-thorn | Gewone Haakdoring |
| 168 | *Acacia erioloba* | Camel Thorn | Kameeldoring |
| 168.1 | *Acacia grandicornuta* | Horned Thorn | Horingdoring |
| 171 | *Acacia hereroensis* | Mountain Thorn | Bergdoring |
| 172 | *Acacia karroo* | Sweet Thorn | Soetdoring |
| 176 | *Acacia mellifera* subsp. *detinens* | Black Thorn | Swarthaak |
| 177 | *Acacia montis-usti* | Brandberg Thorn | Brandbergdoring |
| 178 | *Acacia nigrescens* | Knob Thorn | Knoppiesdoring |
| 183 | *Acacia robusta* subsp. *robusta* | Ankle Thorn | Enkeldoring |
| 185.1 | *Acacia senegal* var. *rostrata* | Three-hook Thorn | Driehaakdoring |
| 188 | *Acacia tortilis* subsp. *heteracantha* | Umbrella Thorn | Haak-en-steek |
| 189 | *Acacia xanthophloea* | Fever Tree | Koorsboom |
| 190 | *Dichrostachys cinerea* subsp. *africana* | Sickle Bush | Sekelbos |
| 191 | *Newtonia hildebrandtii* var. *hildebrandtii* | Lebombo Wattle | Lebombowattel |
| 197 | *Burkea africana* | Wild Seringa | Wildesering |
| 198 | *Colophospermum mopane* | Mopane | Mopanie |
| 214 | *Parkinsonia africana* | Wild Green-hair Tree | Wildegroenhaarboom |
| 215 | *Peltophorum africanum* | Weeping Wattle | Huilboom |
| 221 | *Virgilia oroboides* | Blossom Tree | Keurboom |
| 226 | *Mundulea sericea* | Cork Bush | Kurkbos |
| 236 | *Pterocarpus angolensis* | Wild Teak | Kiaat |
| 237 | *Pterocarpus rotundifolius* | Round-leaved Teak | Dopperkiaat |
| 238 | *Lonchocarpus capassa* | Apple-leaf | Appelblaar |
| 239 | *Lonchocarpus nelsii* | Kalahari Apple-leaf | Kalahari-appelblaar |
| 242 | *Erythrina caffra* | Coast Coral Tree | Kuskoraalboom |
| 245 | *Erythrina lysistemon* | Common Coral Tree | Gewone Koraalboom |
| 254 | *Zanthoxylum davyi* | Knobwood | Perdepram |
| 256 | *Calodendrum capense* | Cape Chestnut | Wildekastaiing |
| 267 | *Kirkia acuminata* | White Seringa | Witsering |
| 292 | *Ptaeroxylon obliquum* | Sneezewood | Nieshout |
| 301 | *Trichilia emetica* | Natal Mahogany | Rooiessenhout |
| 329 | *Croton megalobotrys* | Large Fever-berry | Grootkoorsbessie |

| No | Scientific Name | English Name | Afrikaans Name |
|---|---|---|---|
| 341 | *Spirostachys africana* | Tamboti | Tambotie |
| 345 | *Euphorbia confinalis* | Lebombo Euphorbia | Lebombonaboom |
| 346 | *Euphorbia cooperi* | Transvaal Candelabra Tree | Transvaalse Kandelaarnaboom |
| 351 | *Euphorbia ingens* | Common Tree Euphorbia | Gewone Naboom |
| 355 | *Euphorbia tirucalli* | Rubber Euphorbia | Kraalnaboom |
| 360 | *Sclerocarya birrea* subsp. *caffra* | Marula | Maroela |
| 361 | *Harpephyllum caffrum* | Wild Plum | Wildepruim |
| 362 | *Lannea discolor* | Live-long | Dikbas |
| 366 | *Laurophyllus capensis* | Iron Martin | Ystermartiens |
| 368 | *Heeria argentea* | Rockwood | Kliphout |
| 380 | *Rhus chirindensis* | Red Currant | Bostaaibos |
| 383 | *Rhus erosa* | Broom Karree | Besemkaree |
| 386 | *Rhus lancea* | Karree | Karee |
| 397 | *Ilex mitis* | Cape Holly | Without |
| 405 | *Pterocelastrus echinatus* | White Candlewood | Witkershout |
| 409 | *Pterocelastrus tricuspidatus* | Candlewood | Kershout |
| 413 | *Cassine eucleiformis* | White Silky Bark | Witsybas |
| 418 | *Hartogiella schinoides* | Spoonwood | Lepelhout |
| 436.2 | *Erythrophysa transvaalensis* | Transvaal Red Balloon | Transvaalse Rooiklapperbos |
| 446 | *Greyia sutherlandii* | Natal Bottlebrush | Natalse Baakhout |
| 447 | *Ziziphus mucronata* subsp. *mucronata* | Buffalo-thorn | Blinkblaarwag-'n-bietjie |
| 451 | *Scutia myrtina* | Cat-thorn | Katdoring |
| 452 | *Rhamnus prinoides* | Dogwood | Blinkblaar |
| 459.1 | *Grewia flava* | Velvet Raisin | Fluweelrosyntjie |
| 467 | *Adansonia digitata* | Baobab | Kremetart |
| 471 | *Dombeya rotundifolia* | Common Wild Pear | Gewone Drolpeer |
| 473 | *Sterculia alexandri* | Cape Star-chestnut | Kaapse Sterkastaiing |
| 474 | *Sterculia africana* | African Star-chestnut | Afrikaanse Sterkastaiing |
| 483 | *Ochna pulchra* | Peeling Plane | Lekkerbreek |
| 484 | *Hypericum revolutum* | Curry Bush | Kerriebos |
| 486 | *Garcinia livingstonei* | Lowveld Mangosteen | Laeveldse Geelmelkhout |
| 487 | *Tamarix usneoides* | Wild Tamarisk | Abiekwasgeelhout |
| 494 | *Kiggelaria africana* | Wild Peach | Wildeperske |
| 496 | *Scolopia mundii* | Red Pear | Rooipeer |
| 499 | *Pseudoscolopia polyantha* | False Red Pear | Valsrooipeer |
| 532 | *Combretum apiculatum* subsp. *apiculatum* | Red Bushwillow | Rooiboswilg |
| 532.1 | *Combretum apiculatum* var. *leutweinii* | Hairy Red Bushwillow | Harige Rooiboswilg |
| 539 | *Combretum imberbe* | Leadwood | Hardekool |
| 540 | *Combretum kraussii* | Forest Bushwillow | Bosvaderlandswilg |
| 546 | *Combretum zeyheri* | Large-fruited Bushwillow | Raasblaar |
| 551 | *Terminalia sericea* | Silver Cluster-leaf | Vaalboom |
| 555 | *Syzygium cordatum* | Water Berry | Waterbessie |
| 556 | *Syzygium gerrardii* | Forest Waterwood | Boswaterhout |
| 559 | *Metrosideros angustifolius* | Lance-leaved Myrtle | Smalblad |
| 563 | *Cussonia paniculata* var. *sinuata* | Mountain Cabbage Tree | Bergkiepersol |
| 570 | *Curtisia dentata* | Assegai | Assegaai |
| 578 | *Rapanea melanophloeos* | Cape Beech | Boekenhout |
| 595 | *Euclea divinorum* | Magic Guarri | Towerghwarrie |
| 598 | *Euclea pseudebenus* | Ebony Tree | Ebbeboom |
| 600 | *Euclea schimperi* subsp. *schimperi* | Bush Guarri | Bosghwarrie |

| No | Scientific Name | English Name | Afrikaans Name |
|---|---|---|---|
| 606 | *Diospyros mespiliformis* | Jackal-berry | Jakkalsbessie |
| 617 | *Olea europaea* subsp. *africana* | Wild Olive | Olienhout |
| 622 | *Salvadora persica* | Real Mustard Tree | Regte Mosterdboom |
| 637 | *Buddleja salviifolia* | Sagewood | Saliehout |
| 669.1 | *Lycium oxycarpum* | Honey-thorn | Kriedoring |
| 670 | *Halleria lucida* | Tree Fuchsia | Notsung |
| 678 | *Kigelia africana* | Sausage Tree | Worsboom |
| 688 | *Burchellia bubalina* | Wild Pomegranate | Wildegranaat |
| 693 | *Rothmannia capensis* | Cape Gardenia | Kaapse Katjiepiering |
| 701 | *Alberta magna* | Natal Flame Bush | Breekhout |
| 723.3 | *Vernonia amygdalina* | River Bitter-tea | Rivierbittertee |
| 731 | *Brachylaena discolor* subsp. *transvaalensis* | Forest Silver Oak | Bosvaalbos |

## BIRDS

The following is a list of birds referred to in the text with their *Roberts'* numbers and their scientific, English and Afrikaans names.

| No | Scientific Name | English Name | Afrikaans Name |
|---|---|---|---|
| 1 | *Struthio camelus* | Ostrich | Volstruis |
| 8 | *Tachybaptus ruficollis* | Dabchick | Kleindobbertjie |
| 49 | *Pelecanus onocrotalus* | White Pelican | Witpelikaan |
| 50 | *Pelecanus rufescens* | Pinkbacked Pelican | Kleinpelikaan |
| 58 | *Phalacrocorax africanus* | Reed Cormorant | Rietduiker |
| 62 | *Ardea cinerea* | Grey Heron | Bloureier |
| 63 | *Ardea melanocephala* | Blackheaded Heron | Swartkopreier |
| 64 | *Ardea goliath* | Goliath Heron | Reuse Reier |
| 66 | *Egretta alba* | Great White Egret | Grootwitreier |
| 69 | *Egretta ardesiaca* | Black Egret | Swartreier |
| 72 | *Ardeola ralloides* | Squacco Heron | Ralreier |
| 75 | *Butorides rufiventris* | Rufousbellied Heron | Rooipensreier |
| 78 | *Ixobrychus minutus* | Little Bittern | Woudapie |
| 79 | *Ixobrychus sturmii* | Dwarf Bittern | Dwergrietreier |
| 80 | *Botaurus stellaris* | Bittern | Grootrietreier |
| 81 | *Scopus umbretta* | Hamerkop | Hamerkop |
| 83 | *Ciconia ciconia* | White Stork | Witooievaar |
| 86 | *Ciconia episcopus* | Woollynecked Stork | Wolnekooievaar |
| 88 | *Ephippiorhynchus senegalensis* | Saddlebilled Stork | Saalbekooievaar |
| 92 | *Geronticus calvus* | Bald Ibis | Kalkoenibis |
| 94 | *Bostrychia hagedash* | Hadeda Ibis | Hadeda |
| 95 | *Platalea alba* | African Spoonbill | Lepelaar |
| 96 | *Phoenicopterus ruber* | Greater Flamingo | Grootflamink |
| 97 | *Phoenicopterus minor* | Lesser Flamingo | Kleinflamink |
| 102 | *Alopochen aegyptiacus* | Egyptian Goose | Kolgans |
| 103 | *Tadorna cana* | South African Shelduck | Kopereend |
| 104 | *Anas undulata* | Yellowbilled Duck | Geelbekeend |
| 105 | *Anas sparsa* | African Black Duck | Swarteend |
| 114 | *Nettapus auritus* | Pygmy Goose | Dwerggans |
| 118 | *Sagittarius serpentarius* | Secretarybird | Sekretarisvoël |
| 119 | *Gypaetus barbatus* | Bearded Vulture | Baardaasvoël |
| 121 | *Necrosyrtes monachus* | Hooded Vulture | Monnikaasvoël |
| 122 | *Gyps coprotheres* | Cape Vulture | Kraansaasvoël |
| 123 | *Gyps africanus* | Whitebacked Vulture | Witrugaasvoël |
| 124 | *Torgos tracheliotus* | Lappetfaced Vulture | Swartaasvoël |
| 125 | *Trigonoceps occipitalis* | Whiteheaded Vulture | Witkopaasvoël |
| 127 | *Elanus caeruleus* | Blackshouldered Kite | Blouvalk |
| 128 | *Aviceda cuculoides* | Cuckoo Hawk | Koekoekvalk |
| 129 | *Macheiramphus alcinus* | Bat Hawk | Vlermuisvalk |
| 131 | *Aquila verreauxii* | Black Eagle | Witkruisarend |
| 135 | *Aquila wahlbergi* | Wahlberg's Eagle | Bruinarend |
| 136 | *Hieraaetus pennatus* | Booted Eagle | Dwergarend |
| 137 | *Hieraaetus fasciatus* | African Hawk Eagle | Grootjagarend |
| 140 | *Polemaetus bellicosus* | Martial Eagle | Breëkoparend |
| 141 | *Stephanoaetus coronatus* | Crowned Eagle | Kroonarend |
| 146 | *Terathopius ecaudatus* | Bateleur | Berghaan |
| 148 | *Haliaeetus vocifer* | African Fish Eagle | Visarend |
| 149 | *Buteo buteo* | Steppe Buzzard | Bruinjakkalsvoël |
| 150 | *Buteo oreophilus* | Forest Buzzard | Bosjakkalsvoël |
| 152 | *Buteo rufofuscus* | Jackal Buzzard | Rooiborsjakkalsvoël |
| 153 | *Buteo augur* | Augur Buzzard | Witborsjakkalsvoël |

| No | Scientific Name | English Name | Afrikaans Name |
|---|---|---|---|
| 158 | *Accipiter melanoleucus* | Black Sparrowhawk | Swartsperwer |
| 161 | *Micronisus gabar* | Gabar Goshawk | Witkruissperwer |
| 165 | *Circus ranivorus* | African Marsh Harrier | Afrikaanse Paddavreter |
| 169 | *Polyboroides typus* | Gymnogene | Kaalwangvalk |
| 171 | *Falco peregrinus* | Peregrine Falcon | Swerfvalk |
| 172 | *Falco biarmicus* | Lanner Falcon | Edelvalk |
| 181 | *Falco tinnunculus* | Rock Kestrel | Rooivalk |
| 188 | *Francolinus coqui* | Coqui Francolin | Swempie |
| 189 | *Francolinus sephaena* | Crested Francolin | Bospatrys |
| 190 | *Francolinus africanus* | Greywing Francolin | Bergpatrys |
| 192 | *Francolinus levaillantii* | Redwing Francolin | Rooivlerkpatrys |
| 194 | *Francolinus adspersus* | Redbilled Francolin | Rooibekfisant |
| 195 | *Francolinus capensis* | Cape Francolin | Kaapse Fisant |
| 197 | *Francolinus hartlaubi* | Hartlaub's Francolin | Klipfisant |
| 198 | *Francolinus afer* | Rednecked Francolin | Rooikeelfisant |
| 200 | *Coturnix coturnix* | Common Quail | Afrikaanse Kwartel |
| 203 | *Numida meleagris* | Helmeted Guineafowl | Gewone Tarentaal |
| 204 | *Guttera pucherani* | Crested Guineafowl | Kuifkoptarentaal |
| 207 | *Grus carunculata* | Wattled Crane | Lelkraanvoël |
| 208 | *Anthropoides paradisea* | Blue Crane | Bloukraanvoël |
| 209 | *Balearica regulorum* | Crowned Crane | Mahem |
| 213 | *Amaurornis flavirostris* | Black Crake | Swartriethaan |
| 223 | *Porphyrio porphyrio* | Purple Gallinule | Grootkoningriethaan |
| 224 | *Porphyrula alleni* | Lesser Gallinule | Kleinkoningriethaan |
| 226 | *Gallinula chloropus* | Moorhen | Waterhoender |
| 231 | *Neotis denhami* | Stanley's Bustard | Veldpou |
| 232 | *Neotis ludwigii* | Ludwig's Bustard | Ludwigse Pou |
| 233 | *Eupodotis cafra* | Whitebellied Korhaan | Witpenskorhaan |
| 236 | *Eupodotis ueppelliir* | Rüppell's Korhaan | Woestynkorhaan |
| 237 | *Eupodotis ruficrista* | Redcrested Korhaan | Boskorhaan |
| 238 | *Eupodotis melanogaster* | Blackbellied Korhaan | Langbeenkorhaan |
| 240 | *Actophilornis africanus* | African Jacana | Grootlangtoon |
| 241 | *Microparra capensis* | Lesser Jacana | Dwerglangtoon |
| 249 | *Charadrius tricollaris* | Threebanded Plover | Driebandstrandkiewiet |
| 294 | *Recurvirstra avosetta* | Avocet | Bontelsie |
| 298 | *Burhinus vermiculatus* | Water Dikkop | Waterdikkop |
| 305 | *Glareola nordmanni* | Blackwinged Pratincole | Swartvlerksprinkaanvoël |
| 334 | *Sterna balaenarum* | Damara Tern | Damarasterretjie |
| 349 | *Columba guinea* | Rock Pigeon | Kransduif |
| 351 | *Columba delegorguei* | Delegorgue's Pigeon | Withalsbosduif |
| 355 | *Streptopelia senegalensis* | Laughing Dove | Rooiborsduifie |
| 356 | *Oena capensis* | Namaqua Dove | Namakwaduifie |
| 360 | *Aplopelia larvata* | Cinnamon Dove | Kaneelduifie |
| 364 | *Poicephalus meyeri* | Meyer's Parrot | Bosveldpapegaai |
| 365 | *Poicephalus rueppellii* | Rüppell's Parrot | Bloupenspapegaai |
| 367 | *Agapornis roseicollis* | Rosyfaced Lovebird | Rooiwangparkiet |
| 370 | *Tauraco corythaix* | Knysna Lourie | Knysnaloerie |
| 371 | *Tauraco porphyreolophus* | Purplecrested Lourie | Bloukuifloerie |
| 373 | *Corythaixoides concolor* | Grey Lourie | Kwêvoël |
| 377 | *Cuculus solitarius* | Redchested Cuckoo | Piet-my-vrou |
| 387 | *Ceuthmochares aereus* | Green Coucal | Groenvleiloerie |
| 391 | *Centropus superciliosus* | Burchell's Coucal | Gewone Vleiloerie |
| 395 | *Asio capensis* | Marsh Owl | Vlei-uil |
| 405 | *Caprimulgus pectoralis* | Fierynecked Nightjar | Afrikaanse Naguil |
| 412 | *Apus barbatus* | Black Swift | Swartwindswael |
| 413 | *Apus bradfieldi* | Bradfield's Swift | Muiskleurwindswael |
| 415 | *Apus caffer* | Whiterumped Swift | Witkruiswindswael |

| No | Scientific Name | English Name | Afrikaans Name |
|---|---|---|---|
| 418 | *Apus melba* | Alpine Swift | Witpenswindswael |
| 421 | *Cypsiurus parvus* | Palm Swift | Palmwindswael |
| 422 | *Telacanthura ussheri* | Mottled Spinetail | Gevlekte Stekelstert |
| 423 | *Neafrapus boehmi* | Böhm's Spinetail | Witpensstekelstert |
| 424 | *Colius striatus* | Speckled Mousebird | Gevlekte Muisvoël |
| 427 | *Apaloderma narina* | Narina Trogon | Bosloerie |
| 428 | *Ceryle rudis* | Pied Kingfisher | Bontvisvanger |
| 429 | *Ceryle maxima* | Giant Kingfisher | Reuse Visvanger |
| 430 | *Alcedo semitorquata* | Halfcollared Kingfisher | Blouvisvanger |
| 431 | *Alcedo cristata* | Malachite Kingfisher | Kuifkopvisvanger |
| 435 | *Halcyon albiventris* | Brownhooded Kingfisher | Bruinkopvisvanger |
| 438 | *Merops apiaster* | European Bee-eater | Europese Byvreter |
| 445 | *Merops hirundineus* | Swallowtailed Bee-eater | Swaelstertbyvreter |
| 447 | *Coracias caudata* | Lilacbreasted Roller | Gewone Troupant |
| 448 | *Coracias spatulata* | Rackettailed Roller | Knopsterttroupant |
| 449 | *Coracias naevia* | Purple Roller | Groottroupant |
| 452 | *Phoeniculus purpureus* | Redbilled Woodhoopoe | Gewone Kakelaar |
| 454 | *Phoeniculus cyanomelas* | Scimitarbilled Woodhoopoe | Swartbekkakelaar |
| 455 | *Bycanistes bucinator* | Trumpeter Hornbill | Gewone Boskraai |
| 456 | *Bycanistes brevis* | Silverycheeked Hornbill | Kuifkopboskraai |
| 457 | *Tockus nasutus* | Grey Hornbill | Grysneushoringvoël |
| 458 | *Tockus erythrorhynchus* | Redbilled Hornbill | Rooibekneushoringvoël |
| 459 | *Tockus flavirostris* | Yellowbilled Hornbill | Geelbekneushoringvoël |
| 461 | *Tockus bradfieldi* | Bradfield's Hornbill | Bradfieldse Neushoringvoël |
| 462 | *Tockus monteiri* | Monteiro's Hornbill | Monteirose Neushoringvoël |
| 465 | *Lybius leucomelas* | Pied Barbet | Bonthoutkapper |
| 466 | *Stactolaema leucotis* | White-eared Barbet | Witoorhoutkapper |
| 474 | *Indicator indicator* | Greater Honeyguide | Grootheuningwyser |
| 475 | *Indicator variegatus* | Scalythroated Honeyguide | Gevlekte Heuningwyser |
| 480 | *Geocolaptes olivaceus* | Ground Woodpecker | Grondspeg |
| 484 | *Campethera notata* | Knysna Woodpecker | Knysnaspeg |
| 486 | *Dendropicos fuscescens* | Cardinal Woodpecker | Kardinaalspeg |
| 488 | *Mesopicos griseocephalus* | Olive Woodpecker | Gryskopspeg |
| 495 | *Mirafra apiata* | Clapper Lark | Hoëveldklappertjie |
| 497 | *Mirafra africanoides* | Fawncoloured Lark | Vaalbruinlewerik |
| 500 | *Mirafra curvirostris* | Longbilled Lark | Langbeklewerik |
| 512 | *Galerida magnirostris* | Thickbilled Lark | Dikbeklewerik |
| 514 | *Ammomanes grayi* | Gray's Lark | Namiblewerik |
| 529 | *Hirundo fuligula* | Rock Martin | Kransswael |
| 540 | *Coracina caesia* | Grey Cuckooshrike | Bloukatakoeroe |
| 545 | *Oriolus larvatus* | Blackheaded Oriole | Swartkopwielewaal |
| 547 | *Corvus capensis* | Black Crow | Swartkraai |
| 550 | *Corvus albicollis* | Whitenecked Raven | Withalskraai |
| 557 | *Anthoscopus minutus* | Cape Penduline Tit | Kaapse Kapokvoël |
| 558 | *Anthoscopus caroli* | Grey Penduline Tit | Gryskapokvoël |
| 560 | *Turdoides jardineii* | Arrowmarked Babbler | Pylvlekkatlagter |
| 566 | *Pycnonotus capensis* | Cape Bulbul | Kaapse Tiptol |
| 567 | *Pycnonotus nigricans* | Redeyed Bulbul | Rooioogtiptol |
| 568 | *Pycnonotus barbatus* | Blackeyed Bulbul | Swartoogtiptol |
| 572 | *Andropadus importunus* | Sombre Bulbul | Gewone Willie |
| 577 | *Turdus olivaceus* | Olive Thrush | Olyflyster |
| 579 | *Turdus gurneyi* | Orange Thrush | Oranjelyster |
| 580 | *Turdus litsitsirupa* | Groundscraper Thrush | Gevlekte Lyster |
| 581 | *Monticola rupestris* | Cape Rock Thrush | Kaapse Kliplyster |
| 582 | *Monticola explorator* | Sentinel Rock Thrush | Langtoonkliplyster |
| 583 | *Monticola brevipes* | Shorttoed Rock Thrush | Korttoonkliplyster |
| 586 | *Oenanthe monticola* | Mountain Chat | Bergwagter |

| No | Scientific Name | English Name | Afrikaans Name |
|---|---|---|---|
| 588 | *Oenanthe bifasciata* | Buffstreaked Chat | Bergklipwagter |
| 589 | *Cercomela familiaris* | Familiar Chat | Gewone Spekvreter |
| 590 | *Cercomela tractrac* | Tractrac Chat | Woestynspekvreter |
| 591 | *Cercomela sinuata* | Sicklewinged Chat | Vlaktespekvreter |
| 592 | *Cercomela schlegelii* | Karoo Chat | Karoospekvreter |
| 593 | *Thamnolaea cinnamomeiventris* | Mocking Chat | Dassievoël |
| 601 | *Cossypha caffra* | Cape Robin | Gewone Janfrederik |
| 606 | *Pogonocichla stellata* | Starred Robin | Witkoljanfrederik |
| 611 | *Chaetops frenatus* | Cape Rockjumper | Kaapse Berglyster |
| 612 | *Chaetops aurantius* | Orangebreasted Rockjumper | Oranjeborsberglyster |
| 613 | *Erythropygia leucophrys* | Whitebrowed Robin | Gestreepte Wipstert |
| 614 | *Erythropygia coryphaeus* | Karoo Robin | Slangverklikker |
| 615 | *Erythropygia paena* | Kalahari Robin | Kalahariwipstert |
| 618 | *Namibornis herero* | Herero Chat | Hererospekvreter |
| 641 | *Bradypterus victorini* | Victorin's Warbler | Rooiborsruigtesanger |
| 644 | *Seicercus ruficapillus* | Yellowthroated Warbler | Geelkeelsanger |
| 658 | *Camaroptera fasciolata* | Barred Warbler | Gebande Sanger |
| 661 | *Sphenoeacus afer* | Grassbird | Grasvoël |
| 662 | *Achaetops pycnopygius* | Rockrunner | Rotsvoël |
| 669 | *Cisticola subruficapilla* | Greybacked Cisticola | Grysrugtinktinkie |
| 670 | *Cisticola lais* | Wailing Cisticola | Huiltinktinkie |
| 681 | *Cisticola fulvicapilla* | Neddicky | Neddikkie |
| 683 | *Prinia subflava* | Tawnyflanked Prinia | Bruinsylangstertjie |
| 686 | *Prinia maculosa* | Spotted Prinia | Karoolangstertjie |
| 690 | *Muscicapa adusta* | Dusky Flycatcher | Donkervlieëvanger |
| 695 | *Melaenornis mariquensis* | Marico Flycatcher | Maricovlieëvanger |
| 700 | *Batis capensis* | Cape Batis | Kaapse Bosbontrokkie |
| 701 | *Batis molitor* | Chinspot Batis | Witliesbosbontrokkie |
| 708 | *Trochocercus cyanomelas* | Bluemantled Flycatcher | Bloukuifvlieëvanger |
| 710 | *Terpsiphone viridis* | Paradise Flycatcher | Paradysvlieëvanger |
| 712 | *Motacilla clara* | Longtailed Wagtail | Bergkwikkie |
| 713 | *Motacilla capensis* | Cape Wagtail | Gewone Kwikkie |
| 714 | *Motacilla flava* | Yellow Wagtail | Geelkwikkie |
| 716 | *Anthus novaeseelandiae* | Richard's Pipit | Gewone Koester |
| 725 | *Anthus chloris* | Yellowbreasted Pipit | Geelborskoester |
| 727 | *Macronyx capensis* | Orangethroated Longclaw | Oranjekeelkalkoentjie |
| 728 | *Macronyx croceus* | Yellowthroated Longclaw | Geelkeelkalkoentjie |
| 730 | *Macronyx ameliae* | Pinkthroated Longclaw | Rooskeelkalkoentjie |
| 732 | *Lanius collaris* | Fiscal Shrike | Fiskaallaksman |
| 736 | *Laniarius ferrugineus* | Southern Boubou | Suidelike Waterfiskaal |
| 739 | *Laniarius atrococcineus* | Crimsonbreasted Shrike | Rooiborslaksman |
| 740 | *Dryoscopus cubla* | Puffback | Sneeubal |
| 741 | *Nilaus afer* | Brubru | Bontroklaksman |
| 742 | *Tchagra tchagra* | Southern Tchagra | Grysborstjagra |
| 746 | *Telophorus zeylonus* | Bokmakierie | Bokmakierie |
| 747 | *Telophorus quadricolor* | Gorgeous Bush Shrike | Konkoit |
| 748 | *Telophorus sulfureopectus* | Orangebreasted Bush Shrike | Oranjeborsboslaksman |
| 749 | *Telophorus nigrifrons* | Blackfronted Bush Shrike | Swartoogboslaksman |
| 750 | *Telophorus olivaceus* | Olive Bush Shrike | Olyfboslaksman |
| 753 | *Prionops plumatus* | White Helmetshrike | Withelmlaksman |
| 763 | *Lamprotornis mevesii* | Longtailed Starling | Langstertglansspreeu |
| 764 | *Lamprotornis nitens* | Glossy Starling | Kleinglansspreeu |
| 769 | *Onychognathus morio* | Redwinged Starling | Rooivlerkspreeu |
| 770 | *Onychognathus nabouroup* | Palewinged Starling | Bleekvlerkspreeu |
| 773 | *Promerops cafer* | Cape Sugarbird | Kaapse Suikervoël |
| 774 | *Promerops gurneyi* | Gurney's Sugarbird | Rooiborssuikervoël |

| No | Scientific Name | English Name | Afrikaans Name |
|---|---|---|---|
| 775 | *Nectarinia famosa* | Malachite Sunbird | Jangroentjie |
| 777 | *Nectarinia violacea* | Orangebreasted Sunbird | Oranjeborssuikerbekkie |
| 779 | *Nectarinia mariquensis* | Marico Sunbird | Maricosuikerbekkie |
| 783 | *Nectarinia chalybea* | Lesser Doublecollared Sunbird | Klein-rooiborssuikerbekkie |
| 785 | *Nectarinia afra* | Greater Doublecollared Sunbird | Groot-rooiborssuikerbekkie |
| 796 | *Zosterops pallidus* | Cape White-eye | Kaapse Glasogie |
| 808 | *Ploceus bicolor* | Forest Weaver | Bosmusikant |
| 820 | *Anomalospiza imberbis* | Cuckoo Finch | Koekoekvink |
| 832 | *Euplectesprogne* | Longtailed Widow | Langstertflap |
| 850 | *Estrilda melanotis* | Swee Waxbill | Suidelike Swie |
| 860 | *Vidua macroura* | Pintailed Whydah | Koringrooibekkie |
| 872 | *Serinus canicollis* | Cape Canary | Kaapse Kanarie |
| 873 | *Serinus scotops* | Forest Canary | Gestreepte Kanarie |
| 874 | *Serinus totta* | Cape Siskin | Kaapse Pietjiekanarie |
| 875 | *Serinus symonsi* | Drakensberg Siskin | Bergpietjiekanarie |
| 880 | *Serinus leucopterus* | Protea Canary | Witvlerkkanarie |
| 885 | *Emberiza capensis* | Cape Bunting | Rooivlerkstreepkoppie |

## MAMMALS

The following is an alphabetical list of mammals referred to in the text with their English, Afrikaans and scientific names.

| **English Name** | **Afrikaans Name** | **Scientific Name** |
|---|---|---|
| Aardwolf | Aardwolf | *Proteles cristatus* |
| Antbear | Erdvark | *Orycteropus afer* |
| Baboon, chacma | Kaapse bobbejaan | *Papio ursinus* |
| Bat, Hildebrandt's horseshoe | Hildebrandt se saalneus-vlermuis | *Rhinolophus hildebrandti* |
| Bat, rufous hairy | Rooi langhaarvlermuis | *Myotis bocagei* |
| Blesbok | Blesbok | *Damaliscus dorcas phillipsi* |
| Bontebok | Bontebok | *Damaliscus dorcas dorcas* |
| Buffalo | Buffel | *Syncerus caffer* |
| Bushbaby, lesser | Nagapie | *Galago moholi* |
| Bushbuck | Bosbok | *Tragelaphus scriptus* |
| Bushpig | Bosvark | *Potamochoerus porcus* |
| Caracal | Rooikat | *Felis caracal* |
| Cat, African wild | Vaalboskat | *Felis lybica* |
| Cheetah | Jagluiperd | *Acinonyx jubatus* |
| Civet, African | Afrikaanse siwet | *Civettictis civetta* |
| Dassie, rock | Klipdas | *Procavia capensis* |
| Dassie, yellow-spotted rock | Geelkoldas | *Heterohyrax brucei* |
| Dog, wild | Wildehond | *Lycaon pictus* |
| Dormouse, spectacled | Gemsbokmuis | *Graphiurus ocularis* |
| Duiker, blue | Blouduiker | *Philantomba monticola* |
| Duiker, common | Gewone duiker | *Sylvicapra grimmia* |
| Duiker, red | Rooiduiker | *Cephalophus natalensis* |
| Eland | Eland | *Taurotragus oryx* |
| Elephant, African | Afrikaanse olifant | *Loxodonta africana* |
| Fox, Cape | Silwervos | *Vulpes chama* |
| Gemsbok | Gemsbok | *Oryx gazella* |
| Giraffe | Kameelperd | *Giraffa camelopardalis* |
| Grysbok | Grysbok | *Raphicerus melanotis* |
| Grysbok, Sharpe's | Sharp se grysbok | *Raphicerus sharpei* |
| Hartebeest, Lichtenstein's | Lichtenstein se hartbees | *Sigmoceros lichtensteinii* |
| Hartebeest, red | Rooihartbees | *Alcelaphus buselaphus* |
| Hippopotamus | Seekoei | *Hippopotamus amphibius* |
| Hyaena, brown | Strandjut | *Hyaena brunnea* |
| Hyaena, spotted | Gevlekte hiëna | *Crocuta crocuta* |
| Impala | Rooibok | *Aepyceros melampus* |
| Jackal, black-backed | Rooijakkals | *Canis mesomelas* |
| Jackal, side-striped | Witkwasjakkals | *Canis adustus* |
| Klipspringer | Klipspringer | *Oreotragus oreotragus* |
| Kudu | Koedoe | *Tragelaphus strepsiceros* |
| Lechwe, red | Rooi-lechwe | *Kobus leche* |
| Leopard | Luiperd | *Panthera pardus* |
| Lion | Leeu | *Panthera leo* |
| Mole, golden, yellow | Geel gouemol (kruipmol) | *Calcochloris obtusirostris* |
| Mongoose, small grey | Klein grysmuishond | *Galerella purverulenta* |
| Monkey, samango | Samango-aap | *Cercopithecus mitis* |
| Monkey, vervet | Blouaap | *Cercopithecus aethiops* |
| Mouse, Verreaux's | Verreaux se muis | *Praomys verreauxii* |
| Nyala | Njala | *Tragelaphus angasii* |
| Oribi | Oorbietjie | *Ourebia ourebi* |
| Otter, Cape clawless | Groototter | *Aonyx capensis* |
| Otter, spotted-necked | Klein otter | *Lutra maculicollis* |
| Pangolin | Ietermagô | *Manis temminckii* |

| English Name | Afrikaans Name | Scientific Name |
|---|---|---|
| Porcupine | Ystervark | *Hystrix africaeaustralis* |
| Rat, dassie | Dassierot | *Petromys typicus* |
| Reedbuck | Rietbok | *Redunca arundinum* |
| Reedbuck, mountain | Rooiribbok | *Redunca fulvorufula* |
| Rhebok, grey | Vaalribbok | *Pelea capreolus* |
| Rhinoceros, black (hook-lipped) | Swartrenoster | *Diceros bicornis* |
| Rhinoceros, white (square-lipped) | Witrenoster | *Ceratotherium simum* |
| Roan | Bastergemsbok | *Hippotragus equinus* |
| Sable | Swartwitpens | *Hippotragus niger* |
| Serval | Tierboskat | *Felis serval* |
| Sitatunga | Waterkoedoe | *Tragelaphus spekei* |
| Springbok | Springbok | *Antidorcas marsupialis* |
| Springhare | Springhaas | *Pedetes capensis* |
| Squirrel, ground | Waaierstertgrondeekhoring | *Xerus inauris* |
| Steenbok | Steenbok | *Raphicerus campestris* |
| Suni | Soenie | *Neotragus moschatus* |
| Tsessebe | Tsessebe | *Damaliscus lunatus* |
| Warthog | Vlakvark | *Phacochoerus aethiopicus* |
| Waterbuck | Waterbok | *Kobus ellipsiprymnus* |
| Wildebeest, black | Swartwildebees | *Connochaetes gnou* |
| Wildebeest, blue | Blouwildebees | *Connochaetes taurinus* |
| Zebra, Burchell's | Bontsebra | *Equus burchelli* |
| Zebra, Cape mountain | Kaapse bergsebra | *Equus zebra zebra* |
| Zebra, Hartmann's mountain | Hartmann se bergsebra | *Equus zebra hartmannae* |

# *Glossary of Environmental and Geological Terms and Afrikaans Words*

Listed below are explanations for environmental and geological terms and Afrikaans words you will come across in this book or in the course of your backpacking.

**Environmental Terms**

*Aquatic* — living in water
*Arboreal* — living in trees
*Browser* — an animal that feeds on the leaves and shoots of trees and shrubs
*Carnivore* — a member of the mammal order Carnivora, whose members are mainly predators and are flesh-eating, such as lions, dogs and seals, but are in some instances omnivorous, like the African civet, which is mainly vegetarian
*Carrion* — the decaying flesh of dead animals
*Diurnal* — active mainly during the day
*Ecology* — the study of the interactions and relationships between living organisms (plants and animals) and their non-living environment
*Ecosystem* — the dynamic interaction of plants, animals and units of air, water and soil
*Endemic* — a plant or animal that is restricted to a particular area
*Epiphytic* — a plant that grows on another plant or object (eg stone) without being parasitic, ie no nourishment is taken from the host
*Estuary* — a river mouth where fresh and sea water mix
*Family* — a grouping used to classify several genera of plants or animals together. Similar families are grouped together in an order
*Fauna* — all animal life
*Floodplain* — usually a grass or reed-covered fringe alongside a river or estuary which is seasonally inundated (known as *melapo* in the Okavango Delta).
*Flora* — all plant life
*Fynbos* — the richly varied fine-leaved bush vegetation of the south-western Cape which is mainly composed of Ericaceae, Proteaceae and Restionaceae (reeds and rushes)
*Genus* — the classification used for a group of closely related animals or plants. Several genera form a family, while the genus is divided into different species
*Gestation* — the time from conception to birth in animal species
*Grazer* — an animal that feeds on grass
*Gregarious* — living in groups or flocks
*Habitat* — the surroundings in which an animal or plant lives
*Herbivore* — a plant-eating animal
*Indigenous* — occurring naturally in a particular area, but not necessarily restricted to that area
*Insectivorous* — animals that are predominantly insect-eating (eg shrews), as well as plants (eg sundew [*Drosera*] living off insects
*Intra-African migrant* — birds that migrate within Africa
*Lagoon* — an area of water formed when the course of a river to the sea is blocked

*Monocotyledon* — flowering plant that has only one leaf arising from the seed, bulb or corm. It has long leaves with parallel veins

*Migrant* — animals, especially birds, that move seasonally

*Nocturnal* — active mainly by night

*Omnivorous* — eating both animals and plants

*Palaearctic migrant* — bird that migrates from the northern hemisphere, ie north Africa, Europe and Asia, to the southern hemisphere

*Perennial* — a plant living for more than two years; or a stream/river that can be expected to contain water throughout the year

*Predator* — animal that kills and feeds on other animals

*Raptor* — a bird that hunts and feeds on other animals

*Riparian* — of or on a riverbank

*Savanna* — grassland containing scattered trees, shrubs and scrub vegetation

*Species* — the most basic unit used in the classification of animals and plants. Members of the same species are identical in structure and are capable of reproducing within the group, but not outside it

*Terrestrial* — living on land

*Woodland* — vegetation type characterised by trees with a well-developed, but not completely closed canopy

### Geological Terms

*Archaean rocks* — rocks formed in the oldest era in geological history, which ended 1850 million years ago. The earliest sandstones were transformed by heat into the basement complex

*Basalt* — a fine-grained, dark grey igneous rock

*Basement* — *see* Archaean

*Conglomerate* — a sedimentary rock containing fragments of other rocks that have been cemented together by clay and finer material

*Dolerite* — a coarse-grained, light-coloured rock of volcanic origin often occurring in dykes and sills and containing quartz and feldspar

*Dyke* — a vertical or steeply inclined wall-like sheet of dolerite that is only exposed during subsequent erosion

*Fault* — a fracture along which the rocks on the one side have been displaced relative to those opposite

*Feldspar* — a white or pink crystalline mineral found in rocks

*Gabbro* — a coarse-grained crystalline igneous rock formed at great depths

*Gneiss* — white and black banded rock containing the same minerals as granite, which have undergone a metamorphosis by heat and pressure

*Granite* — a common, hard and coarse-grained igneous rock, mainly consisting of quartz and feldspar. It is exposed when the overlying rocks are worn away and its colour ranges from pink to grey, according to the colour of the feldspar

*Igneous rock* — formed from molten material, either on the surface from lava becoming volcanic rocks or underground magma forming plutonic rocks

*Inselberg* — the more resistant land surfaces which have remained, despite erosion, to form isolated mountains

*Lava* — molten material that appears on the surface during volcanic eruptions, cooling to form basalt

*Magma* — molten material that does not reach the surface of the earth during a volcanic eruption, but is sometimes exposed through erosion

*Metamorphic rocks* — igneous or sedimentary rocks that have undergone a metamorphosis because of temperature, pressure and chemical reactions

*Quartzite* — a sedimentary, metamorphic rock formed from silica and sandstone

*Sandstone* — the second most common, but most familiar sedimentary rock, forming about one-third of the sedimentary rocks exposed on the earth's surface. It consists of rounded grains of sand and usually quartz cemented together. The colour varies according to the mineral make-up

*Sedimentary rocks* — eroded material transported by either wind or water and deposited with the sediments, eventually forming firm rocks after a cementation process has taken place

*Series* — series are divided into beds because of their difference in composition and fossil content (term no longer used)

*Schist* — a metamorphic rock which is much coarser than gneiss and flakes easily

*Shale* — the most common sedimentary rock, forming nearly half of the exposed sedimentary rock. Grey or black in colour, it is arranged in distinct layers of fine silt and clay

*Sill* — magma which has been forced between layers of sedimentary rocks subterraneously. When the magma hardens, it forms a near horizontal sheet of igneous rock which is only exposed through subsequent erosion

**Afrikaans words**

The following Afrikaans words are frequently used to describe place names, land features and other natural phenomena.

*Berg* — mountain

*Bos* — bush

*Bosveld (Bushveld)* — when referring to the Lowveld of the eastern Transvaal the term is used to describe the vegetation type. The term is also used to refer to the western Transvaal region

*Drift* — a ford; usually natural but could be man-made

*Drostdy* — Dutch name for the residency of the landdrost (magistrate)

*Fontein* — fountain

*Gat* — hole

*Highveld* — the high-lying area (approx. 1 830 m above sea-level) which covers large areas of central South Africa. The vegetation consists of treeless grassland.

*Klip* — stone or rock

*Kloof* — gorge, ravine or narrow gully

*Koppie* — small hill

*Krantz* — cliff

*Mond* — river mouth

*Nek* — col, saddle between two high points

*Poort* — a narrow passage through a range of hills or a mountain

*Rant* — ridge

*Rondavel* — round African hut

*Rug* — ridge

*Sloot* — ditch or furrow

*Sneeu* — (as in Sneeuberg) — snow

*Spoor* — tracks, usually of animals but also of man; including scent, droppings and urine

*Spruit* — a stream that is usually almost dry, except after rains

*Stroom* — stream

*Tafel* — (as in Tafelberg) — table

*Veld* — open country with natural vegetation (uncultivated)

*Vlakte* — plains, flats

*Vlei* — a shallow water mass, smaller than a lake; usually marshy and in grassland

# INDEX

In view of the large number of possible entries a select index has been compiled. The same sequence is followed in the book in respect of the flora, fauna, history and geology of each area, making a comprehensive index superfluous. Entries in the index are limited to instances which have received more detailed description than a mere mention.